Praise for *The New Rules of Marketing & PR*

"This excellent look at the basics of new-millennial marketing should find use in the hands of any serious PR professional making the transition."

—*Publishers Weekly* (starred review)

"This is absolutely the *best* book on the new world of marketing and PR. David Meerman Scott is 'The teacher's teacher in the world of social media.' I get all my best stuff from him. In fact, I buy each new edition because, in the ever-changing world of online marketing, if you don't stay current, you die a fast death. This edition is so *new* that it includes tools I hadn't even heard of yet. You'll love it."

—**Michael Port**, *New York Times* bestselling author
of *Book Yourself Solid*

"Most professional marketers—and the groups in which they work—are on the edge of becoming obsolete, so they'd better learn how marketing is really going to work in the future."

—**BNET**, "The Best & Worst Business Books"

"*The New Rules of Marketing & PR* has inspired me to do what I have coached so many young artists to do, 'Find your authentic voice, become vulnerable, and then put yourself out there.' David Meerman Scott expertly and clearly lays out how to use many great new tools to help accomplish this. Since reading this book, I have been excited about truly connecting with people without the filter of all the 'old PR' hype. It has been really energizing for me to speak about things that I really care about, using my real voice."

—**Meredith Brooks**, Multi-Platinum Recording Artist,
Writer, and Producer, and Founder
of record label Kissing Booth Music

"I've relied on *The New Rules of Marketing & PR* as a core text for my New Media and Public Relations course at Boston University for the past 12 semesters. David's book is a bold, crystal-clear, and practical guide toward a new (and better) future for the profession."

—**Stephen Quigley, Boston University**

"What a wake-up call! By embracing the strategies in this book, you will totally transform your business. David Meerman Scott shows you a multitude of ways to propel your company to a thought leadership position in your market and drive sales—all without a huge budget. I am a huge fan and practitioner of his advice."

—**Jill Konrath, Author of *Snap Selling*,
Chief Sales Officer, SellingtoBigCompanies.com**

"David is a leading expert on how the digital age has dramatically changed marketing and PR. A great guide for large and small companies alike to navigate the 'new rules.'"

—**Martin Lindstrom,
New York Times Bestselling Author
of *Buyology: The Truth and Lies about Why We Buy***

"When I read the *New Rules* for the first time, it was a 'eureka' moment for me at HubSpot. David nailed the fundamental shifts going on in the buyer-seller relationship and wrote the classic text to help marketers take advantage of them."

—**Brian Halligan, HubSpot CEO
and Co-Author of *Inbound Marketing***

"The Internet is not so much about technology as it is about people. David Meerman Scott, in his remarkable *The New Rules of Marketing & PR*, goes far beyond technology and explores the ramifications of the web as it pertains to people. He sets down a body of rules that show you how to negotiate those ramifications with maximum effectiveness. And he does it with real-life case histories and an engaging style."

—**Jay Conrad Levinson, Father of Guerrilla Marketing
and Author, Guerrilla Marketing series of books**

"*The New Rules of Marketing & PR* teaches readers how to launch a thought leadership campaign by using the far-reaching, long-lasting tools of social media. It is an invaluable guide for anyone who wants to make a name for themselves, their ideas, and their organization."

—Mark Levy, Co-Author,
How to Persuade People Who Don't Want to Be Persuaded,
and Founder of Levy Innovation: A Marketing Strategy Firm

"*Revolution* may be an overused word in describing what the Internet has wrought, but revolution is exactly what David Meerman Scott embraces and propels forward in this book. He exposes the futility of the old media rules and opens to all of us an insiders' game, previously played by a few well-connected specialists. With this rule book to the online revolution, you can learn how to win minds and markets, playing by the new rules of new media."

—Don Dunnington, President,
International Association of Online Communicators (IAOC);
Director of Business Communications, K-Tron International;
and Graduate Instructor in Online Communication,
Rowan University, Glassboro, New Jersey

"The history of marketing communications—about 60 years or so—has been about pushing messages to convince prospects to take some action we need. Now marketing communications, largely because of the overwhelming power and influence of the web and other electronic communications, is about engaging in conversation with prospects and leading/persuading them to take action. David Meerman Scott shows how marketing is now about participation and connection, and no longer about strong-arm force."

—Roy Young, Chief Revenue Officer, MarketingProfs.com,
and Co-Author, *Marketing Champions:*
Practical Strategies for Improving
Marketing's Power, Influence, and Business Impact

"David Meerman Scott not only offers good descriptions of digital tools available for public relations professionals, but also explains strategy, especially the importance of thinking about PR from the public's perspectives, and provides lots of helpful examples. My students loved this book."
—**Karen Miller Russell, Associate Professor,
Grady College of Journalism and Mass Communication,
University of Georgia**

"This is a must-read book if you don't want to waste time and resources on the old methods of Internet marketing and PR. David Meerman Scott reviews the old rules for old times' sake while bridging into the new rules for Internet marketing and PR for your cause. He doesn't leave us with only theories, but offers practical and results-oriented how-tos."
—**Ron Peck, Executive Director,
Neurological Disease Foundation**

"*The New Rules of Marketing & PR* is all about breaking the rules and creating new roles in traditional functional areas. Using maverick, nontraditional approaches to access and engaging a multiplicity of audiences, communities, and thought leaders online, PR people are realizing new value, influence, and outcomes. We're now in a content-rich, Internet-driven world, and David Meerman Scott has written a valuable treatise on how marketing-minded PR professionals can leverage new media channels and forums to take their stories to market. No longer are PR practitioners limited in where and how they direct their knowledge, penmanship, and perception management skills. The Internet has multiplied and segmented a wealth of new avenues for directly reaching and activating key constituencies and stakeholders. A good book well worth the read by all marketing mavens and aging PR flacks."
—**Donovan Neale-May, Executive Director, CMO Council**

"*The New Rules of Marketing & PR* provides a concise action plan for success. Rather than focusing on a single solution, Scott shows how to use multiple online tools, all directed toward increasing your firm's visibility and word-of-mouth awareness."
—**Roger C. Parker, Author of *The Streetwise Guide
to Relationship Marketing on the Internet*
and *Design to Sell***

"Once again we are at a critical inflection point on our society's evolutionary path, with individuals wresting away power and control from institutions and traditional gatekeepers who control the flow of knowledge and maintain the silo walls. As communications professionals, there is little time to figure out what has changed, why it changed, and what we should be doing about it. If you don't start doing things differently and start right now, you may as well start looking for your next career path. In a world where disruption is commonplace and new ways of communicating and collaborating are invented every day, what does it take for a hardworking, ethical communications professional to be successful? David Meerman Scott's book, *The New Rules of Marketing & PR*, is an insightful look at how the game is changing as we play it and some of the key tactics you need to succeed in the knowledge economy."

—**Chris Heuer, Co-Founder, Social Media Club**

Also by David Meerman Scott

Real-Time Marketing & PR: How to Instantly Engage Your Market, Connect with Customers, and Create Products that Grow Your Business Now

Marketing Lessons from the Grateful Dead: What Every Business Can Learn from the Most Iconic Band in History (with Brian Halligan)

Newsjacking: How to Inject Your Ideas into a Breaking News Story and Generate Tons of Media Coverage

Marketing the Moon (with Richard Jurek)

World Wide Rave: Creating Triggers that Get Millions of People to Spread Your Ideas and Share Your Stories

Tuned In: Uncover the Extraordinary Opportunities that Lead to Business Breakthroughs (with Craig Stull and Phil Myers)

Cashing in with Content: How Innovative Marketers Use Digital Information to Turn Browsers into Buyers

Eyeball Wars: A Novel of Dot-Com Intrigue

The NEW RULES of MARKETING & PR

The NEW RULES of MARKETING & PR

HOW TO USE SOCIAL MEDIA, ONLINE VIDEO, MOBILE APPLICATIONS, BLOGS, NEWS RELEASES, & VIRAL MARKETING TO REACH BUYERS DIRECTLY

Fourth Edition

DAVID MEERMAN SCOTT

WILEY

Cover design: Mike Freeland

Published by John Wiley & Sons, Inc., Hoboken, New Jersey.
Published simultaneously in Canada.

Limit of Liability/Disclaimer of Warranty: While the publisher and author have used their
best efforts in preparing this book, they make no representations or warranties with respect to
the accuracy or completeness of the contents of this book and specifically disclaim any
implied warranties of merchantability or fitness for a particular purpose. No warranty may be
created or extended by sales representatives or written sales materials. The advice and
strategies contained herein may not be suitable for your situation. You should consult with a
professional where appropriate. Neither the publisher nor the author shall be liable for
damages arising herefrom.

For general information about our other products and services, please contact our Customer
Care Department within the United States at (800) 762–2974, outside the United States at
(317) 572–3993 or fax (317) 572–4002.

Wiley publishes in a variety of print and electronic formats and by print-on-demand. Some
material included with standard print versions of this book may not be included in e-books or
in print-on-demand. If this book refers to media such as a CD or DVD that is not included in
the version you purchased, you may download this material at http://booksupport.wiley.com.
For more information about Wiley products, visit www.wiley.com.

Library of Congress Cataloging-in-Publication Data:
Scott, David Meerman.
  The new rules of marketing & PR: how to use social media, online video, mobile
applications, blogs, news releases, and viral marketing to reach buyers directly/David
Meerman
Scott.–4th edition.
    pages cm
  Includes index.
  ISBN 978-1-118-48876-8 (pbk.); ISBN 978-1-118-71107-1 (ebk);
ISBN 978-1-118-71120-0 (ebk)
  1. Internet marketing.   2. Public relations.   I. Title.
  HF5415.1265.S393 2013
  658.8'72–dc23

Printed in the United States of America

10 9 8 7 6

For the Scott women

My mother, Carolyn J. Scott;
my wife, Yukari Watanabe Scott;
and my daughter, Allison C.R. Scott

Contents

Foreword

You're not supposed to be able to do what David Meerman Scott is about to tell you in this book. You're not supposed to be able to carry around a $250 video camera, record what employees are working on and what they think of the products they are building, and publish those videos on the Internet. But that's what I did at Microsoft, building an audience of more than 4 million unique visitors a month.

You're not supposed to be able to do what Stormhoek did. A winery in South Africa, it doubled sales in a year using the principles discussed here.

Something has changed in the past 10 years. Well, for one, we have Google now, but that's only a part of the puzzle.

What really has happened is that the word-of-mouth network has gotten more efficient—much, much more efficient.

Word of mouth has always been important to business. When I helped run a Silicon Valley camera store in the 1980s, about 80 percent of our sales came from it. "Where should I buy a camera this weekend?" you might have heard in a lunchroom back then. Today that conversation is happening online. But instead of only two people talking about your business, now thousands and sometimes millions are either participating or listening in.

What does this mean? Well, now there's a new medium to deal with. Your PR teams had better understand what drives this new medium (it's as influential as the *New York Times* or CNN now), and if you understand how to use it, you can drive buzz, new product feedback, sales, and more.

But first you'll have to learn to break the rules.

Is your marketing department saying you need to spend $80,000 to do a single video? (That's not unusual, even in today's world. I just participated in such a video for a sponsor of mine.) If so, tell that department "Thanks, but no thanks." Or even better, search Google for "Will it blend?" You'll find a Utah blender company that got 6 million downloads in less than 10 days. Oh, and 10,000 comments in the same period of time. All by spending a few hundred bucks, recording a one-minute video, and uploading that to YouTube.

Or study what I did at Microsoft with a blog and a video camera. *Economist* magazine said I put a human face on Microsoft. Imagine that. A 60,000-employee organization, and I changed its image with very little expense and hardly a committee in sight.

This advice isn't for everyone, though. Most people don't like running fast in business. They feel more comfortable if there are lots of checks and balances or committees to cover their asses. Or they don't want to destroy the morale of PR and marketing departments due to the disintermediating effects of the Internet.

After all, you can type "OneNote Blog" into Google, Bing, or Yahoo! and you'll find the OneNote team at Microsoft. You can leave a comment and tell them their product sucks and see what they do in response. Or even better, tell them how to earn your sale. Do they snap into place?

It's a new world you're about to enter, one where relationships with influentials *and* search engine optimization strategy are equally important, and one where your news will be passed around the world very quickly. You don't believe me?

Look at how the world found out I was leaving Microsoft for a Silicon Valley start-up.

I told 15 people at a videoblogging conference—not A-listers either, just everyday videobloggers. I asked them not to tell anyone until Tuesday—this was on a Saturday afternoon, and I still hadn't told my boss.

Well, of course, someone leaked that information. But it didn't pop up in the *New York Times*. It wasn't discussed on CNN. No, it was a blogger I had never even heard of who posted the info first.

Within hours, it was on hundreds of other blogs. Within two days, it was in the *Wall Street Journal*, in the *New York Times*, on the front page of the BBC website, in *BusinessWeek, Economist*, in more than 140 newspapers around the world (friends called me from Australia, Germany, Israel, and England, among other countries), and other places. Waggener Edstrom, Microsoft's PR agency, was keeping track and said that about 50 million media impressions occurred on my name in the first week.

All due to 15 conversations.

Whoa, what's up here? Well, if you have a story worth repeating, bloggers, podcasters, and videobloggers (among other influentials) will repeat your story all over the world, potentially bringing hundreds of thousands or millions of people your way. One link on a site like Digg alone could bring tens of thousands of visitors.

How did that happen?

Well, for one, lots of people knew me, knew my phone number, knew what kind of car I drove, knew my wife and son, knew my best friends, knew where I worked, and had heard me in about 700 videos that I posted at http://channel9.msdn.com on behalf of Microsoft.

They also knew where I went to college (and high school and middle school) and countless other details about me. How do you know they know all this? Well, they wrote a page on Wikipedia about me at http://en.wikipedia.org/wiki/Robert_Scoble—not a single thing on that page was written by me.

What did all that knowledge of me turn into? Credibility and authority. Translation: People knew me, knew where I was coming from, knew I was passionate and authoritative about technology, and came to trust me where they wouldn't trust most corporate authorities.

By reading this book, you'll understand how to gain the credibility you need to build your business. Enjoy!

—Robert Scoble
Co-author, *Naked Conversations*
Scobleizer.com

Introduction

As I write this, it is several months after Barack Obama was reelected president of the United States. While there are many reasons for his winning a second term, one that stands out is his campaign's use of the ideas in this book; their use led to more engagement with voters online. The Obama campaign used social networking to reach and engage voters, rather than just advertising to them online, as the Romney campaign frequently did. And people responded by showing their online support. For example, at the time of the election on November 6, 2012, the Obama for America Facebook page had 32 million "Likes," while Mitt Romney's Facebook page had about 12 million. Barack Obama's Twitter feed had nearly 22.8 million followers on Election Day, while Mitt Romney had just 1.7 million.

Social networks matter in the daily lives of voters. The *Social Media and Political Engagement* report from the Pew Research Center's Internet & American Life Project finds that 66 percent of American social media users—or 39 percent of all American adults—have used social media for civic or political activities such as showing support for a candidate, encouraging others to vote, or posting their thoughts about the election. Against that backdrop, we might well speculate that voters engaged with the Obama campaign online may have made the difference in the election.

This significance goes beyond U.S. presidential elections. For any business, nonprofit, or other organization, the old rules of marketing and public relations don't apply anymore. Television advertising, direct mail, robocalls, and other interruption-based techniques don't win elections—or sell products—like they used to.

Also in early November 2012, Hurricane Sandy barreled up the U.S. East Coast, causing billions of dollars in damage and knocking out power to tens of millions of people. Companies helped victims in the immediate aftermath by publishing helpful information. For example, Duracell used its Facebook page to alert people to the availability of mobile recharging stations set up in areas without power, so consumers could charge their mobile phones for free. Using the web to drive people to an offline initiative is an important aspect of the *New Rules*.

But while companies like Duracell succeeded in helping those in need (and generated tremendous goodwill with customers as a result), others used online media to selfishly advertise amid the crisis. American Apparel promoted a 36-hour, 20-percent-off sale to people located in states affected by Hurricane Sandy. That's right: Despite the loss of life, homes, and property, some companies still tried to use the storm as a hook to market products. This traditional advertising approach backfired tremendously, with critics taking to social networks like Twitter to voice their disgust with American Apparel and other companies seen as exploiting the suffering. Mainstream media took notice and wrote about these companies' failures too.

The web provides tremendous opportunities to reach buyers directly, and I'll show you how to harness that power. I'll also discuss the pitfalls.

There used to be only three ways to get noticed: Buy expensive advertising, beg the mainstream media to tell your story for you, or hire a huge sales staff to bug people individually about your products. Now we have a better option: publishing interesting content on the web—content that your buyers *want* to consume. The tools of the marketing and PR trade have changed. The skills that worked offline to help you buy or beg or bug your way into opportunity are the skills of interruption and coercion. Online success comes from thinking like a journalist and a thought leader.

The New Rules

At the height of the dot-com boom, I was vice president of marketing at NewsEdge Corporation, a NASDAQ-traded online news distributor with more than $70 million in annual revenue. My multimillion-dollar marketing budget included tens of thousands of dollars per month for a public relations agency, hundreds of thousands per year for print advertising and glossy brochures, and expensive participation at a dozen trade shows per year. My team put these things on our marketing to-do list, worked like hell to execute, and paid the big bucks because that's what marketing and PR people did. These efforts made us feel good because we were *doing something*, but the programs were not producing significant, measurable results because we were working based on the rules of the past.

At the same time, drawing on experience I had gained in my previous position as Asia marketing director for the online division of Knight-Ridder (then one of the largest newspaper companies in the world) my team and I quietly created content-based, thought leadership marketing and PR programs on the web. Against the advice of the PR agency professionals we had on retainer (who insisted that press releases were only for the press), we wrote and sent dozens of releases ourselves. Each time we sent a release, it appeared at online services such as Yahoo! and *resulted in sales leads*. Even though our advertising agency told us not to put the valuable information "somewhere where competitors could steal it," we created a monthly newsletter called *The Edge*, about the exploding world of digital news. We made it freely available on the homepage of our website *because it generated interest from buyers, the media, and analysts*. Way back in the 1990s, when web marketing and PR was in its infancy, my team and I ignored the old rules, drawing instead on my experience working at an online publisher, and created a marketing strategy using content to reach buyers directly on the web. The homegrown programs we created at virtually no cost consistently generated more interest from qualified buyers, the media, and analysts—and resulted in more sales—than the big-bucks programs that the "professionals" were running for us. People we never heard of were finding us through search engines. We had stumbled on a better way to reach buyers.

In 2002, after NewsEdge was sold to The Thomson Corporation, I started my own business to refine my ideas and teach others through writing, speaking at conferences, and conducting seminars for corporate groups. The objective in all this work was to help others reach buyers directly with web content. Since then, many new forms of social media have burst onto the scene, including social networks like Twitter, Facebook, Foursquare, and Pinterest, plus blogs, podcasts, video, and virtual communities. But what all the new web tools and techniques have in common is that they are the best way to communicate *directly* with your marketplace.

This book actually started as web marketing on my blog. In January 2006, I published an e-book called *The New Rules of PR*,[1] immediately generating remarkable enthusiasm (and much controversy) from marketers and businesspeople around the world. Since the e-book was published, it has been downloaded more than one million times and commented on by thousands

---

[1] www.webinknow.com/2006/01/new_complimenta.html

of readers on my blog and those of many other bloggers. To those of you who have read and shared the e-book, thank you. But this book is much more than just an expansion of that work, because I have made its subject marketing *and* PR and because I've included many different forms of online media. I've also conducted years of additional research.

This book contains much more than just my own ideas, because I blogged the book, section by section, as I wrote it. And as I have done revisions, including this fourth edition, I've continued to blog the stories that appear here. Thousands of you have followed along, and many have contributed to the writing process by offering suggestions through comments on my blog, Twitter, and by email. Thank you for contributing your ideas. And thank you for arguing with me when I got off track. Your enthusiasm has made the book much better than it would have been if I had written in isolation.

The web has changed not only the rules of marketing and PR, but also the business-book model, and *The New Rules of Marketing & PR* is an interesting example. My online content (the e-book and my blog) led me directly to a print book deal. I published early drafts of sections of the book on my blog and used the blog to test ideas for inclusion into subsequent editions. Other publishers would have freaked out if an author wanted to put parts of his book online (for free!) to solicit ideas. John Wiley & Sons encouraged it. So my thanks go to them as well.

Life with the New Rules

The New Rules of Marketing & PR has sold remarkably well since the initial release in June 2007, remaining a top title for more than six years among thousands of books about marketing and public relations. It even made the *BusinessWeek* best-seller list multiple months.

Wanna know the amazing thing? I didn't spend a single penny advertising or promoting it.

Here's what I did do: I offered advance copies of the first edition to approximately 130 important bloggers, I sent out nearly twenty news releases (you'll read later in the book about news releases as a tool to reach buyers directly), and my publisher alerted contacts in the media. That's it. Thousands of bloggers have written about the book over the years (thank you!), significantly driving its sales. And the mainstream media have found me as a result of this blogger interest. The *Wall Street Journal* called several times for interviews that landed me quotes in the paper because they read about my ideas online first. I've appeared on national and local television and radio, including MSNBC, Fox Business, and NPR. I've been interviewed on hundreds of podcasts. Magazines and newspaper reporters email me all the time to get quotes for their stories. How do they find me? Online, of course! And it doesn't cost me a single penny. I'm not telling you all this to brag about my book sales or my media appearances. I'm telling you to show you how well these ideas work.

But the coolest part of my life since the book was published isn't that I took advantage of the new rules of marketing and PR, nor that this book has been selling like hotcakes as a result. No, the coolest part of my life right now is that people contact me every day to say that the ideas in these pages have transformed their businesses and changed their lives. Really! That's the sort of language people use. They write just to thank me for putting the ideas into a book so that they could be enlightened to the new realities of marketing and PR.

Every day I get exciting feedback from people who are charged up about the new rules. Take Jody. He sent me an email to tell me the book had an unexpected effect on him and his wife. Jody explains that, to them, the really exciting and hopeful idea is that they can actually use their genuine voices online; they've left behind the hype-inflated, PR-speak their agencies had used so tediously.

Or Andrew. He left a comment on my blog: "David, your book so inspired me, I decided to start a brand-new business (launching shortly) based around the principles you espouse. You cogently expressed many of the things that I'd been grappling with myself. So your book has certainly changed one life."

Mike wrote to say that his company's software, which helps small and medium-size businesses get found by the right prospects and capture more leads, takes advantage of all the trends and techniques described in the book. He purchased a bunch of copies to share with everyone in his organization. Larry bought copies for all the members of his professional association. Richard did too. Robin, who works for a company that offers public relations services, purchased 300 copies for clients. Len, who runs a strategic marketing agency, sent copies to his clients as well. Julie, who is a senior executive at a PR firm, handed out copies to all 75 of her staff members. People approach me at conferences asking me to sign wonderfully dog-eared, coffee-stained, Post-it-noted copies of the book. Sometimes they tell me some funny secrets, too. Kathy, who works in PR, said that if everyone read it, she'd be out of a job! David told me he used what he learned to find a new job.

While all this incredible feedback is personally flattering, I am most grateful that my ideas have empowered people to find their own voices and tell their own stories online. How cool is that?

Now let me disclose a secret of my own. As I was writing the first edition of this book, I was a bit unsure of the global applicability of the new rules. Sure, I'd found a number of anecdotal stories about online marketing, blogging, and social networking outside North America. But I couldn't help but wonder at the time: Are organizations of all kinds reaching their buyers directly, with web content written in languages other than English and for cultures other than my own? I quickly learned that the answer is a resounding yes! About 25 percent of the book's English-language sales have come from outside the United States. And as I write this, the book has been or is being translated into more than 25 other languages, including Bulgarian, Finnish, Korean, Vietnamese, Serbian, and Turkish. I'm also receiving invitations from all over the world to speak about the new rules. In the past few years, I've traveled to many countries, including Bulgaria, Sweden, Saudi Arabia, India, Japan, the United Kingdom, Spain, Estonia, Latvia, Turkey, Egypt, Italy, Croatia, the Netherlands, Australia, New Zealand, Malaysia, and the Dominican Republic. So I can say with certainty that the ideas in these pages do resonate worldwide. We are indeed witnessing a global phenomenon.

What's New

This fourth edition of the book builds on the completely revised third edition with another extensive rewrite. I have checked every fact, figure, and URL. But I've also listened. In the past few years, I've met thousands of people like you, people who have shared their stories with me. I have drawn from those experiences and included in these pages many new examples of success. Including so many new stories and examples has resulted in my removing many of the originals, but I'm convinced these exciting replacements are even more valuable. And for those of you who have read earlier editions, you'll still find many fresh ideas in these pages.

I've made some more significant additions as well. The tools of marketing and public relations are constantly evolving. Consider this: When I wrote the first edition of the book, Twitter didn't even exist and Facebook was only available to students. Now Twitter is an essential tool of marketing and

Facebook is used by a remarkable 1 billion people worldwide. And those are just two examples.

The real-time web has sparked a tremendous opportunity for reaching members of the media directly—as they are writing breaking news stories. So I've added a brand new section on Newsjacking, the technique of injecting your ideas into a breaking news story to generate tons of media coverage. And in the time since I wrote the third edition of the book, marketing using images has exploded. So I've added a section on highly visual social networks like Pinterest and Instagram, as well as the use of Infographics.

Writing Like on a Blog, But in a Book

Because the lines between marketing and PR have blurred so much as to be virtually unrecognizable, the best online media choice is often not as obvious as in the old days. But I had to organize the book somehow, and I chose to create chapters for the various tools, including blogs, video, social networking, and so on. But the truth is that all these techniques intersect and complement one another.

These online media are evolving very rapidly, and by the time you read these words, I'll no doubt come across new techniques that I'll wish I could have put in the fourth edition. Still, I believe that the fundamentals are important, which is why Chapter 11 (where you'll start to develop your own online marketing and PR plan) is steeped in practical, commonsense thinking.

The book is organized into three parts. Part I is a rigorous overview of how the web has changed the rules of marketing and PR. Part II introduces and provides details about each of the various media. Part III contains detailed how-to information and an action plan to help you put the new rules to work for your organization.

While I think this sequence is the most logical way to present these ideas, there's no reason why you shouldn't flip from chapter to chapter in any order that you please. Unlike a mystery novel, you won't get lost in the story if you skip around. And I certainly don't want to waste your time. As I was writing, I found myself wishing that I could send you from one chapter to another chapter with hyperlinks, like on a blog. Alas, a printed book doesn't allow that, so instead I have included more old-fashioned references where I suggest you skip ahead or go back for review on specific topics. I have also included hundreds of URLs as footnotes, so you can choose to visit the blogs, websites, and other online media that I discuss. You'll notice that I write in a familiar and casual tone, rather than the more formal and stilted voice of many business books. That's because I'm using my "blog voice" to share the new rules with you. It's how I like to write, and believe it also makes things easier for you, the reader.

When I use the words *company* and *organization* throughout this book, I'm including all types of organizations and individuals. Feel free to mentally insert *nonprofit*, *government agency*, *political candidate*, *church*, *school*, *sports team*, *legal firm*, or other entity in place of *company* and *organization*. Similarly, when I use the word *buyers*, I also mean subscribers, voters, volunteers, applicants, and donors, because the new rules work for reaching all these groups. Are you a nonprofit organization that needs to increase donations? The new rules apply to you as much as to a corporation. Ditto for political campaigns looking for votes, schools that want to increase applicants, consultants hunting for business, and churches seeking new members.

This book will show you the new rules and how to apply them. For the people all over the world interacting on the web, the old rules of marketing and PR just don't work. Today, all kinds of organizations communicate directly with their buyers online. According to the International Telecommunications Union,[2] an agency of the United Nations, the Internet is now used by one third of the world's population. Even more remarkably, there were 5.3 billion mobile subscriptions at the end of 2010. It's projected to rise to 5.6 billion by 2013. That's enough for more than three quarters of the world's population—more people than have access to a toothbrush. So it's no surprise that, in order to reach the individuals who would be interested in their organizations, smart marketers everywhere have altered the way they think about marketing and PR.

Showcasing Successful Marketers

The most exciting aspect of the book is that, throughout these pages, I have the honor of showcasing some of the best examples of marketers building successful programs on the web. There are nearly 50 profiles throughout the book, many of them in the marketers' own words from my interviews with them. These profiles bring the concepts to life. You'll learn from people at Fortune 500 companies and at businesses with just a handful of employees.

---

[2] www.itu.int

These companies make products ranging from racing bicycles to jet helicopters and from computer software to hamburgers. Some of the organizations are well known to the public, while others are famous only in their market niche. I profile nonprofit organizations, political advocacy groups, and citizens supporting potential candidates for political office. I tell the stories of independent consultants, churches, rock bands, and lawyers, all of whom successfully use the web to reach their target audiences. I can't thank enough the people who shared their time with me, on the phone and in person. I'm sure you'll agree that they are the stars of the book. My favorite part is that many of them are people who read earlier editions and shared their success with me. How cool is that? You can read this edition and be equipped to create programs that could grow your business and lead you to achievements that might inform readers of *future* editions!

As you read the stories of successful marketers, remember that you will learn from them even if they come from a very different market, industry, or type of organization than your own. Nonprofits can learn from the experiences of corporations. Consultants will gain insight from the success of rock bands. In fact, I'm absolutely convinced that you will learn more by emulating successful ideas from outside your industry than by copying what your nearest competitor is doing. Remember, the best thing about new rules is that your competitors probably don't know about them yet.

Finally, I must give credit to the thousands of smart people who found success with the new rules before I ever put the ideas into print. They deserve the credit for pioneering the ideas I've chronicled.

Thank you for your interest in the new rules. I hope that you too will be successful in implementing these strategies and that your life will be made better as a result.

—DAVID MEERMAN SCOTT
David@DavidMeermanScott.com
www.WebInkNow.com
twitter.com/dmscott

How the Web Has Changed the Rules of Marketing and PR

1 The Old Rules of Marketing and PR Are Ineffective in an Online World

S everal times in the past few years, I have thought about buying a new car. As it is for billions of other global consumers, the web is my primary source of information when I consider a purchase. So I sat down at the computer and began poking around.

Figuring they were the natural place to begin my research, I started with some big automaker sites. That was a big mistake. I was assaulted on the home pages with a barrage of TV-style broadcast *advertising*. And most of the one-way messages focused on price. For example, at the end of 2012 at Ford,[1] the headlines screamed, "100 Hour Sales Event Year-End Celebration. Our freshest lineup now with Big Savings." Chrysler[2] announced a similar offer: "Big Finish 2012." And over at Chevrolet,[3] they were offering the Cruze model with "0% for 60 Months."

I'm not planning to buy a car in the next 100 hours, thank you. I may not even buy one within 100 days! I'm just kicking the virtual tires. All three of these sites assume that I'm ready to buy a car *right now*. But I actually just wanted to learn something. Sure, I got flash-video TV commercials, pretty pictures, and low financing offers on these sites, but little else.

I looked around for some personality on these sites and didn't find much, because the automaker websites portray their organizations as nameless, faceless corporations. In fact, the three sites I looked at are so similar that

---

[1] ford.com

[2] chrysler.com

[3] chevrolet.com

they're effectively interchangeable. At each site, I felt as if I was being marketed to with a string of messages that had been developed in a lab or via focus groups. It just didn't feel authentic. If I wanted to see TV car ads, I would have flipped on the TV. I was struck with the odd feeling that all of the big three automakers' sites were designed and built by the same Madison Avenue ad guy. These sites were advertising *to* me, not building a relationship *with* me. They were luring me in with one-way messages, not educating me about the companies' products. Guess what? When I arrive at a site, you don't need to grab my attention; you already have it!

Automakers have become addicted to the crack cocaine of marketing: big-budget TV commercials and other off-line advertising. Everywhere I turn, I see automobile ads that make me think "This has got to be really freakin' expensive." The television commercials, the "sponsored by" stuff, and other high-ticket Madison Avenue marketing might make you feel good, but is it effective?

These days, when people are thinking of buying a car (or any other product or service), they usually go to the web first. Even my 78-year-old mother does it! When people come to you online, they are not looking for TV commercials. They are looking for information to help them make a decision.

Here's the good news: I did find some terrific places on the web to learn about cars. Unfortunately, the places where I got authentic content and where I became educated and where I interacted with humans weren't part of the big three automakers' sites. Edmunds Forums[4] is a free, consumer-driven, social networking and personal pages site. It features photo albums, user groups based on make and model of car, and favorite links. The site was excellent in helping me narrow down choices. For example, in the forums, I could read more than 2,500 messages just on the Toyota FJ Cruiser. I could see pages where owners showed off their vehicles. This is where I was making my decision, *dozens of clicks removed from the big automaker sites.*

Since I first wrote about automaker sites on my blog, hundreds of people have jumped in to comment or email me with similar car-shopping experiences and frustrations with automaker websites. And while I certainly recognize that the automakers have improved their sites since I first wrote about them, the focus is still on advertising. Something is seriously broken in the automobile business if so many people tell me they are unable to find,

---

[4] edmunds.com/forums

directly on a company site, the information they need to make a purchase decision.

But it's not just automakers.

Think about your own buying habits. Do you make purchase decisions based on your independent research, via information you find with search engines like Google? Do you contact your friends and colleagues via social media like Twitter and Facebook and ask them about products and services you're interested in? If so, you are not alone. And yet many sellers fail to reach you in this process.

In the years before she headed to college, my daughter researched appropriate schools by searching online and connecting with her friends. Over the course of her high school years, she carefully narrowed her choices down to a handful of schools that were a good fit for her. When applications were due, she was all set.

Yet in the months leading up to the application deadline, she received hundreds of very expensive direct-mail packages from universities around the world. Many sent large, thick envelopes containing glossy brochures with hundreds of pages. These efforts were completely wasted, because my daughter had already made up her mind by doing her own research on the web. This huge investment in direct-mail advertising simply didn't work.

> Before the web, organizations had only two significant options for attracting attention: Buy expensive advertising or get third-party ink from the media. But the web has changed the rules. The web is not TV. Organizations that understand the New Rules of Marketing and PR develop relationships directly with consumers like you and me.

I'd like to pause here a moment for a clarification. When I talk about the new rules and compare them to the old rules, I don't mean to suggest that all organizations should immediately drop their existing marketing and PR programs and use this book's ideas exclusively. Moreover, I'm not of the belief that the only marketing worth doing is on the web. If your newspaper advertisements, Yellow Pages listings, media outreach, and other programs are working for you, that's great! Please keep going. There is room in many marketing and PR programs for traditional techniques.

That being said, there's no doubt that today people solve problems by turning to the web. Just consider your own habits as you contemplate a purchase.

Consider another form of marketing, the art of finding a new job. Several times per month, I receive email or phone calls from people who are searching for work. They usually send their CV to me and want to "network" with me to find a job. What these people are doing is advertising a product (their labor) by sending me an unsolicited email message. Like the auto companies and the universities, the typical job seeker is advertising a product. Yet the vast majority of these people are not positioning themselves to be found on the web because they don't have a personal website, they aren't blogging or creating online videos, and except for maybe a Facebook or LinkedIn profile, they aren't active in social media. They are not creating the content that will help an employer to find them when they need new staff.

If you aren't present and engaged in the places and at the times that your buyers are, then you're losing out on potential business—no matter if you're looking for a job or marketing your company's product or your organization's service. Worse, if you are trying to apply the game plan that works in your mainstream-media-based advertising and PR programs to your online efforts, you will not be successful.

So take a minute to ask yourself this simple question: *How are my existing advertising and media relations programs working?*

Advertising: A Money Pit of Wasted Resources

In the old days, traditional, nontargeted advertising via newspapers, magazines, radio, television, and direct mail was the only way to go. But these media make it very difficult to target specific buyers with individualized messages. Yes, advertising is still used for megabrands with broad reach and probably still works for some organizations and products (though not as well as before). Guys watching football on TV drink a lot of beer, so perhaps it makes sense for mass-marketer Budweiser to advertise on NFL broadcasts (but not for small microbrews that appeal to a small niche customer base). Advertising also works in many trade publications. If your company makes deck sealant, then you probably want to advertise in *Professional Deck Builder* magazine to reach your buyers (but that won't allow you to reach the do-it-yourself market). If you run a local real estate agency in a smaller community, it might make sense to do a direct mailing to all of the homeowners there (but that won't let you reach people who might be planning to move to your community from another location).

However, for millions of other organizations—for those of us who are professionals, musicians, artists, nonprofit organizations, churches, and niche product companies—traditional advertising is generally so wide and broad that it is ineffective. A great strategy for Procter & Gamble, Paramount Pictures, and the Republican U.S. presidential candidate—reaching large numbers of people with a message of broad national appeal—just doesn't work for niche products, local services, and specialized nonprofit organizations.

> The web has opened a tremendous opportunity to reach niche buyers directly with targeted information that costs a fraction of what big-budget advertising costs.

One-Way Interruption Marketing Is Yesterday's Message

A primary technique of what Seth Godin calls the TV-industrial complex[5] is interruption. Under this system, advertising agency creative people sit in hip offices dreaming up ways to interrupt people so that they pay attention to a one-way message. Think about it: You're watching your favorite TV show, so the advertiser's job is to craft a commercial to get you to pay attention, when you'd really rather be doing something else, like quickly grabbing some ice cream before the show resumes. You're reading an interesting article in a magazine, so the ads need to jolt you into reading an ad instead of the article. Or you're flying on US Airways from Boston to Philadelphia (which I have frequently done), and 20 minutes or so after takeoff, the airline deems it important to interrupt your nap with a loud advertisement announcing vacation destinations in the Caribbean. The goal in each of these examples is to get prospects to stop what they are doing and pay attention to a message.

---

[5] sethgodin.typepad.com/seths_blog/2006/01/nonlinear_media.html

Moreover, the messages in advertising are product-focused, one-way spin. Advertisers can no longer break through with dumbed-down broadcasts about their wonderful products. The average person now sees hundreds of seller-spun commercial messages per day. People just don't trust them. We turn it off in our minds, if we notice it at all.

> The web is different. Instead of one-way interruption, web marketing is about delivering useful content at just the precise moment a buyer needs it. It's about interaction, information, education, and choice.

Before the web, good advertising people were well versed in the tools and techniques of reaching broad markets with lowest-common-denominator messages via interruption techniques. Advertising was about great "creative work." Unfortunately, many companies rooted in these old ways desperately want the web to be like TV, because they understand how TV advertising works. Advertising agencies that excel in creative TV ads simply believe they can transfer their skills to the web.

They are wrong. They are following outdated rules.

The Old Rules of Marketing

- Marketing simply meant advertising (and branding).
- Advertising needed to appeal to the masses.
- Advertising relied on interrupting people to get them to pay attention to a message.
- Advertising was one-way: company to consumer.
- Advertising was exclusively about selling products.
- Advertising was based on campaigns that had a limited life.
- Creativity was deemed the most important component of advertising.
- It was more important for the ad agency to win advertising awards than for the client to win new customers.
- Advertising and PR were separate disciplines run by different people with separate goals, strategies, and measurement criteria.

> None of this is true anymore. The web has transformed the rules, and you must transform your marketing to make the most of the web-enabled marketplace of ideas.

Public Relations Used to Be Exclusively about the Media

For nearly a decade, I was a contributing editor at *EContent* magazine. I currently write for the *Huffington Post*, contribute guest articles to many other publications, and maintain a popular blog. As a result, I receive hundreds of broadcast email press releases and pitches per month from well-meaning PR people who want me to write about their products and services. Guess what? In five years, I have *never* written about a company because of a nontargeted broadcast press release or pitch that somebody sent me. Think about that: Tens of thousands of press releases and pitches. Zero stories.

Discussions I've had with journalists in other industries confirm that I'm not the only one who doesn't use unsolicited press releases. Instead, I think about a subject that I want to write about, and I check out what I can find on blogs, on Twitter, and through search engines. If I find a press release on the subject through Google News or a company's online media room, great! But I don't wait for press releases to come to me. Rather, I go looking for interesting topics, products, people, and companies. And when I do feel ready to write a story, I might try out a concept on my blog first, to see how it flies. Does anyone comment on it? Do any PR people jump in and email me?

Here's another amazing figure: In more than 10 years, only a tiny number of PR people have commented on my blog or reached out to me as a result of a blog post or a story I've written in a magazine. How difficult can it be to read the blogs and Twitter feeds of the reporters you're trying to pitch? It teaches you precisely what interests them. Then you can email them with something interesting that they are likely to write about rather than spamming them with unsolicited press releases. When I don't want to be bothered, I get hundreds of press releases a week. But when I do want feedback and conversation, I get silence.

Something's very wrong in PR land.

> Reporters and editors use the web to seek out interesting stories, people, and companies. Will they find you?

Public Relations and Third-Party Ink

Public relations was once an exclusive club. PR people used lots of jargon and followed strict rules. If you weren't part of the in crowd, PR seemed like an esoteric and mysterious job that required lots of training, sort of like being a space shuttle astronaut or court stenographer. PR people occupied their time by writing press releases targeted exclusively to reporters and editors and by schmoozing with those same reporters and editors. And then they crossed their fingers and hoped that the media would give them some ink or some airtime ("Oh, please write about me!"). The end result of their efforts—the ultimate goal of PR in the old days–was the clip, which proved they had done their job. Only the best PR people had personal relationships with the media and could pick up the phone and pitch a story to the reporter for whom they had bought lunch the month before. Prior to 1995, outside of paying big bucks for advertising or working with the media, there just weren't any significant options for a company to tell its story to the world.

> This is not true anymore. The web has changed the rules. Today, organizations are communicating directly with buyers.

Yes, the Media Are Still Important

Allow me to pause for a moment to say that the mainstream and trade media are still important components of a great public relations program. On my blog and on the speaking circuit, I've sometimes been accused of suggesting that the media are no longer relevant. That is not my position. The media are critically important for many organizations. A positive story in *Rolling Stone* propels a rock band to fame. An article in the *Wall Street Journal* brands a company as a player. A consumer product talked about on the *Today Show* gets noticed. In many niche markets and vertical industries, trade magazines and journals help decide which companies are important. However, I do believe that, while all these outlets are important aspects of a larger PR program, there are easier and more efficient ways to reach your buyers. And here's something really neat: If you do a good job of telling your story directly, the media will find out. And then they will write about you!

Public relations work has changed. PR is no longer just an esoteric discipline where companies make great efforts to communicate exclusively to a handful of reporters who then tell the company's story, generating a clip for the PR people to show their bosses. These days, great PR includes programs to reach buyers directly. The web allows direct access to information about your products, and smart companies understand and use this phenomenal resource to great advantage.

> The Internet has made public relations public again, after years of almost exclusive focus on media. Blogs, online video, news releases, and other forms of web content let organizations communicate directly with buyers.

Press Releases and the Journalistic Black Hole

In the old days, a press release was actually a release to the press, so these documents evolved as an esoteric and stylized way for companies to issue their "news" to reporters and editors. Because it was assumed that nobody saw the actual press release except a handful of reporters and editors, these documents were written with the media's existing understanding in mind.

In a typical case, a tiny audience of several dozen media people got a steady stream of product releases from a company. The reporters and editors were already well versed on the niche market, so the company supplied very little background information. Jargon was rampant. *What's the news?* journalists would think as they perused the release. *Oh, here it is—the company just announced the Super Techno Widget Plus with a New Scalable and Robust Architecture.* But while this might mean something to a trade magazine journalist, it is just plain gobbledygook to the rest of the world. Since press releases are now seen by millions of people who are searching the web for solutions to their problems, these old rules are obsolete.

The Old Rules of PR

- The only way to get ink and airtime was through the media.
- Companies communicated to journalists via press releases.
- Nobody saw the actual press release except a handful of reporters and editors.
- Companies had to have significant news before they were allowed to write a press release.
- Jargon was okay because the journalists all understood it.
- You weren't supposed to send a release unless it included quotes from third parties, such as customers, analysts, and experts.
- The only way buyers would learn about the press release's content was if the media wrote a story about it.
- The only way to measure the effectiveness of press releases was through clip books, which noted each time the media deigned to pick up a company's release.
- PR and marketing were separate disciplines run by different people with separate goals, strategies, and measurement techniques.

> None of this is true anymore. The web has transformed the rules, and you must transform your PR strategies to make the most of the web-enabled marketplace of ideas.

The vast majority of organizations don't have instant access to mainstream media for coverage of their products. People like you and me need to work hard to be noticed in the online marketplace of ideas. By understanding how the role of PR and the press release has changed, we can get our stories known in that marketplace.

There are some exceptions. Very large companies, very famous people, and governments might all still be able to get away with using the media exclusively, but even that is doubtful. These name-brand people and companies may be big enough, and their news just so compelling, that no effort is required of them. For these lucky few, the media may still be the primary mouthpiece.

- If you are J.K. Rowling and you issue a press release about a new book, the news will be picked up by the media.
- If Apple Computer CEO Tim Cook announces the company's new iPhone at a trade show, the news will be picked up by the media.
- If Brad Pitt and Angelina Jolie issue a press release about adopting another baby, the news will be picked up by the media.
- If President Obama announces his pick to fill a vacancy on the U.S. Supreme Court, the news will be picked up by the media.

> If you are smaller and less famous but have an interesting story to tell, you need to tell it yourself. Fortunately, the web is a terrific place to do so.

Learn to Ignore the Old Rules

To harness the power of the web to reach buyers directly, you must ignore the old rules. Public relations is not just about speaking through the media, although the media remain an important component. Marketing is not just about one-way broadcast advertising, although advertising can be part of an overall strategy.

I've noticed that some marketing and PR professionals have a very difficult time changing old habits. These new ideas make people uncomfortable. When I speak at conferences, people sometimes fold their arms in a defensive posture and look down at their shoes. Naturally, marketing and PR people who learned the old rules resist the new world of direct access. It means that to be successful, they need to learn new skills. And change is not easy.

But I've also noticed that many enlightened marketing executives, CEOs, entrepreneurs, nonprofit executives, and professionals jump at the chance to tell their stories directly. These people love the new way of communicating with buyers and are eager to learn. Smart marketers are bringing success to their organizations each and every day by communicating through the web.

Here's how to tell if the new rules are right for you. Consider your goals for communicating via marketing and public relations. Are you buying that Super Bowl ad to score great tickets to the game? Are you designing a creative magazine ad to win an award for your agency? Do you hope to create a book of press clips from mainstream media outlets to show to your bosses? Does your CEO want to be on TV? If the answers to these questions are yes, then the new rules (and this book) are not for you.

However, if you're like millions of smart marketers and entrepreneurs whose goal is to communicate with buyers directly, then read on. If you're working to make your organization more visible online, then read on. If you want to drive people into your company's sales process so they actually buy something (or apply or donate or join or submit their names as leads), then read on. I wrote this book especially for you.

2 The New Rules of Marketing and PR

My wife, Yukari, was checking out her Twitter stream one day and noticed that someone she follows tweeted about Hotel & Igloo Village Kakslauttanen.[1] Yukari clicked the link and learned that the resort is located in the Saariselkä fell area of Lapland in northern Finland. In winter, you can stay there in a private glass igloo, which means that from bed you can check out the stars (or, if you are lucky, the Aurora Borealis). She found this terribly exciting, so she tweeted a response from her Twitter ID @yukariwatanabe: "I want to go there!"

We discussed the hotel that evening over dinner. Why not go? Our daughter was off to university, so we had the time. The next day we booked the trip for several months later. Done deal.

Now, I know that a winter vacation above the Arctic Circle might seem like a punch line to a bad joke. Heck, the sun didn't even rise when we were there in mid-December (the "day" consists of just four hours of twilight at that time of year). But for us it seemed perfect, because we've traveled all over the world and are always looking for unusual adventures.

How did we know that we wanted to go? By the hotel's website, of course. The site lists all sorts of winter activities for guests. When I saw "Husky Sledding Safari," I was ready to pack my bags (bucket list . . .). But Yukari wanted to do one more check, so she Googled the hotel, looked at the reviews on Trip Advisor, and also read about the hotel in a *New York Times* article.

---

[1] kakslauttanen.fi/en

Everybody I know has a story like this. Somebody makes a comment via a social network site. It leads someone else to a website where the content educates and informs. And that person ends up becoming a customer of a company that he or she had never heard of moments before. We're living in a new world of marketing and PR.

If you are the seller in this transaction, it all comes down to content: What are you creating compared to what are others saying about you?

You're in control. You create the content. You bring in the business.

Our time in Lapland was amazing. We had all kinds of wonderful adventures. The dogsledding was especially fun, because I got to drive (well, more like hang on). And we never would have had this amazing experience if the Hotel & Igloo Village Kakslauttanen only marketed their property using the old rules. We never would have heard about it.

The Most Important Communication Revolution in Human History

I'd like to step way back and look at the big picture. This is not a view, to use the cliché, from 30,000 feet. It's more like the view from the moon. The new rules of marketing and public relations are part of the much bigger and important communications revolution we're currently living through—the most important communication revolution in human history.

Johannes Gutenberg's invention of printing with mechanical movable type (circa 1439) was the second most important communications breakthrough in history. It meant books could be mass-produced, rather than painstakingly copied by hand. It meant ordinary people could refer to things in books, like laws. These used to have to be committed to memory.

The printing press created the first important communications revolution by freeing people's minds from memorization and allowing them to use that extra brainpower to be creative. At the same time, this first communications revolution (which took many decades) helped large numbers of people became literate and raised living standards along the way. It brought humanity out of the medieval period and into the renaissance.

Some 556 years later, in 1995, an even more important communications revolution began. I choose 1995 because it was the year that Netscape went public on the success of Netscape Navigator, the first popular product to allow easy Internet connection and web browsing.

We're fortunate to be living in this time in history, the time of another important communications revolution. I figure we're about halfway through it. The first eighteen years or so were fast-paced, and things changed very quickly. Usage went from a few million people online to billions. But many organizations still aren't communicating in real-time on the web.

The next few decades will bring a continuation of the revolution. The pace of that change means that I need to update this book every two years. Soon, this fourth edition will be replaced by the fifth. And then the sixth. We need to be constantly learning and updating our skills to reach buyers as they're looking for the products and services we sell.

Are you one of the revolutionaries? Or do you support the old regime? Are you marketing your product or service like Hotel & Igloo Village Kakslauttanen? Or are you failing to produce content that will do well in the search engines and social networks? For your sake, I hope it's the former—or soon will be with the help of this book.

Open for Business

Gerard Vroomen will tell you that he is an engineer, not a marketer. He will tell you that the companies he cofounded, Cervélo Cycles[2] and Open Cycle (aka OPEN),[3] do not have any marketing experts. But Vroomen is wrong. Why? Because he is obsessed with the buyers of racing bikes from Cervélo and mountain bikes from OPEN. And he's obsessed with the engineering-driven products he offers them.

Cervélo Cycles, which Vroomen sold in 2011 but for which he remains a board member and advisor, is a Canadian manufacturer of racing bicycle frames. He focused Cervélo to help his customers win races—and they do. In the 2005 Tour de France, David Zabriskie rode the fastest time trial in the race's history on a Cervélo P3C at an average speed of 54.676 kph (33.954 mph). The winner of the 2008 Tour de France, Carlos Sastre, did so on a Cervélo. And at the Beijing and London Olympics, Cervélo bikes were ridden by dozens of athletes, resulting in multiple gold, silver, and bronze medals. Besides building excellent bikes, Vroomen also excels at using the web to tell cycling enthusiasts compelling stories, to educate them, to engage them in conversation, and to entertain them. Vroomen is a terrific marketer

---

[2] cervelo.com
[3] opencycle.com

because he uses web content in interesting ways and sells a bunch of bikes in the process.

"In marketing, if the point is for our company to get noticed, we can't do it the same as everybody else," Vroomen says. "A big part of that is to do something unexpected and being remarkable. For example, we were the first to blog at the Tour de France and the first to do video there."

The Cervélo site works extremely well because it includes perfect content for visitors who are ready to buy a bike and also for people who are just browsing. The content is valuable and authentic compared to the marketing messages that appear on so many other sites. "Our goal is education," Vroomen says. "We have a technical product, and we're the most engineering-driven company in the industry. Most bike companies don't employ a single engineer, and Cervélo has eight. So we want to have that engineering focus stand out with the content on the site. We don't sell on the newest paint job. So on the site, we're not spending our time creating fluff. Instead, we have a good set of content."

Ryan Patch is an amateur triathlon competitor on the Vortex Racing team—just the sort of customer Cervélo wants to reach. "On the Cervélo site, I learned that Bobby Julich rides the same bike that is available to me," Patch says. "And it's not just that they are riding, but they are doing really well. I can see how someone won the Giro de Italia on a Cervélo. That's mind-blowing, that I can get the same bike that the pros are riding. I can ride the same gear. Cervélo has as much street cred as you can have with shaved legs."

Patch says that if you're looking to buy a new bike, if you are a hard-core consumer, then there is a great deal of detailed information on the Cervélo site about the bikes' technology, construction, and specs. "What I really like about this website is how it gives off the aura of legitimacy, being based in fact, not fluff," he says.

Search engine marketing is important for Cervélo. Because of the keyword-rich cycling content available on the site, Vroomen says, Cervélo gets the same amount of search engine traffic as many sites for bike companies that are ten times larger. As a result, Cervélo has grown quickly into one of the most important bike companies in the world.

In 2011, Vroomen shifted gears and now spends the majority of his time at Open Cycle, the mountain bike company he cofounded with Andy Kessler and launched in mid-2012. By early 2013, OPEN was selling via forty retail stores in twenty countries. He took to heart what he learned at Cervélo, making every aspect of the company "open" to customers. Right from the start, OPEN focused on social engagement throughout the site, with community aspects and social networking links. Anyone can comment on anything.

The OPEN site also features a blog.[4] What's interesting is that Vroomen and Kessler had been blogging for a year as they secretly developed the technology for their new bike, but the blog posts went unpublished until launch. "We talk not only about the product but also about how we're running the company," Vroomen says. "So a part of that was publishing that blog after we launched, so people could see what we'd been doing the year leading up to us becoming visible."

Vroomen is committed to having the community of enthusiasts help them, and that's a big reason why they chose the name Open Cycle. "Every page on the site has a question and answer section at the bottom," he says. "So it's very easy, as soon as you've read something, to say, 'Hey, I don't quite understand this.' We answer all of those as soon as we can, time-zone permitting, but certainly within a day, usually sooner. People see that when they ask something, they actually get a response. But the crazy part is that consumers don't expect it. So we said, 'How about if we ask people to talk to us, and we respond?' That's the basic premise of OPEN."

The company's use of questions and answers on every page of the OPEN site, the comment feature on the OPEN blog, and social networks like Twitter (@gerardvroomen has 11,000+ followers) serves as a terrific way to market the new company. "I don't think of it as marketing," Vroomen says. "It feels simply like talking to people. And networks like Facebook, Twitter, et al. have given us some interesting ways to do that. They turn companies such as Open Cycle into the global version of the village baker of yesteryear. You know your customers and they know you, so you want to treat them well. You want to give them good quality, and they tell their neighbors. That's the opposite of what's happening at many companies today. And, of course, the flip side is that, if you don't treat them well, they'll tell the rest of the village."

All signs point to OPEN being on a trajectory to replicate the tremendous success of Cervélo—with the site, the blog, and social networking leading the way forward. And that's no coincidence. As Vroomen would tell you, the ideas you'll read about in this book work.

---

[4] opencycle.com/blogs

"This is the future for companies like us," Vroomen says. "You can be very small and occupy a niche and still sell your products all over the world. It's amazing, when we go into a new country, the amount of name recognition we have. The Internet gives you opportunities you never had before. And it's not rocket science. It's pretty easy to figure out."

The Long Tail of Marketing

The theory of the Long Tail as popularized by Chris Anderson in his book of the same name is that our culture and economy is increasingly shifting away from a focus on a relatively small number of "hits" (mainstream products and markets) at the head of the demand curve and toward a huge number of niches in the tail. As the costs of production and distribution fall, especially online, there is now less need to lump products and consumers into one-size-fits-all containers. In an era without the constraints of physical shelf space and other bottlenecks of distribution, narrowly targeted goods and services can be as economically attractive as mainstream fare.[5]

Some of today's most successful Internet businesses leverage the long tail to reach underserved customers and satisfy demand for products not found in traditional physical stores. Examples include Amazon, which makes available at the click of a mouse hundreds of thousands of books and other products not stocked in local chain stores; iTunes, a service that legally brings niche music not found in record stores to people who crave artists outside the mainstream; and Netflix, which exploited the long tail of demand for movie rentals beyond the blockbuster hits found at the local DVD rental shop. The business implications of the long tail are profound and illustrates that there's much money to be made by creating and distributing at the long end of the tail. Yes, hits are still important. But as these businesses have shown, there's a huge market beyond *The Hobbit*, U2, Adele, and Top Gear.

So, what about marketing? While Anderson's book focuses on product availability and selling models on the web, the concepts apply equally well to marketing. There's no doubt that there is a long-tail market for web content created by organizations of all kinds—corporations, nonprofits, churches, schools, individuals, rock bands—and used for reaching buyers—those who buy, donate, join, apply—directly. As consumers search the Internet for answers to their problems, as they browse blogs and chat rooms and websites

---

[5] thelongtail.com/about.html

for ideas, they are searching for what organizations like yours have to offer. Unlike in the days of the old rules of interruption marketing with a mainstream message, today's consumers are looking for just the right product or service to satisfy their unique desires at the precise moment they are online. People are looking for what you have to offer right now.

> Marketers must shift their thinking from the short head of mainstream marketing to the masses to a strategy of targeting vast numbers of underserved audiences via the web.

As marketers understand the web as a place to reach millions of micro-markets with precise messages just at the point of consumption, the way they create web content changes dramatically. Instead of a one-size-fits-all website with a mass-market message, we need to create just-right content—each aimed at a narrow target constituency. As marketing case studies, the examples of Netflix, Amazon, and iTunes are also fascinating. The techniques pioneered by the leaders of long-tail retail for reaching customers with niche interests are examples of marketing genius.

Tell Me Something I Don't Know, Please

Amazon.com has been optimized for browsing. At a broad level, there are just two ways that people interact with web content: They search and they browse. Most organizations optimize sites for searching, which helps people answer their questions but doesn't encourage them to browse. But people also want a site to tell them something they didn't think to ask. The marketers at Amazon understand that when people browse the site, they may have a general idea of what they want (in my case, perhaps a book for my daughter about surfing) but not the particular title. So if I start with a search on Amazon for the phrase "surfing for beginners," I get 99 titles in the search results. With this list as a starting point, I shift into browse mode, which is where Amazon excels. Each title has a customer ranking where I instantly see how other customers rated each book. I see reader-generated reviews, together with reviews from other media. I can see "Customers who bought this item also bought" lists and also rankings of "What do customers ultimately buy after viewing items like this?" I can check out customer tags (a way for consumers to categorize a book to purchase later or to aid other consumers) on the item, or I can tag it myself. And I can poke around the contents of the book itself. After I purchase the perfect book for my daughter (*The Girl's Guide to Surfing*), I might get an email from Amazon weeks or months later, suggesting, based on this purchase, another book that I might find useful. This is brilliant stuff.

The site is designed to work for a major and often-ignored audience: people who do their own research and consider a decision over a period of time before making a commitment. Smart marketers, like the folks at Amazon and Cervélo, unlike those at the big three automakers we saw in Chapter 1, know that the most effective web strategies anticipate needs and provide content to meet them, even before people know to ask.

Marketing on the web is not about generic banner ads designed to trick people with neon color or wacky movement. It is about understanding the keywords and phrases that our buyers are using, and creating the content that they seek.

Bricks-and-Mortar News

The new rules are just as important for public relations. In fact, I think that online content in all of its forms is causing a convergence of marketing and PR that does not really exist off-line. When your buyer is on the web browsing for something, content is content in all of its manifestations. And in an interconnected web world, content drives action.

I often hear people claim that online content such as blogs and news releases don't work as a marketing strategy for traditional bricks-and-mortar industries. But I've always disagreed. Great content brands an organization as a trusted resource and calls people to action—to buy, subscribe, apply, or donate. And great content means that interested people return again and again. As a result, the organization succeeds, achieving goals such as adding revenue, building traffic, gaining donations, or generating sales leads.

For instance, The Concrete Network[6] provides information about residential concrete products and services and helps buyers and sellers connect with each other. The company targets consumers and builders who might want to plan and build a concrete patio, pool deck, or driveway—this

---

[6] concretenetwork.com

audience makes up the business-to-consumer (B2C) component of The Concrete Network—as well as the concrete contractors who comprise the business-to-business (B2B) component. The Concrete Network's Find-A-Contractor[7] service links homeowners and builders who need a project done with contractors who specialize in 22 different services located in 221 metropolitan areas in both the United States and Canada. The company's web content, combined with a comprehensive direct-to-consumer news release strategy, drives business for The Concrete Network. Yes, ladies and gentlemen, web content sells concrete! (You can't get any more bricks-and-mortar than, well, mortar.)

"The new rules of PR are that anybody who wants to be the leader has to have news coming out," says Jim Peterson, president of The Concrete Network. The company's ongoing PR program includes two direct-to-consumer news releases per week; a series of articles on the site; free online catalogs for categories such as countertops, pool decks, patios, and driveways; and photo galleries for potential customers to check out what is available. As a result of all of the terrific content, The Concrete Network gets more than 10 times the traffic of any other site in the concrete industry, according to Peterson. He says that releases with headlines that are tied to holidays and educational releases work best. If a release is for the Fourth of July holiday, it's going to be about pool decks, patios, outdoor fireplaces, or fire pits. News releases designed specifically to sell haven't done as well. "We ran a concrete furniture release on April Fool's Day that did really well," Peterson says. The headline, "Concrete Furniture? No April Fools with Concrete Tables, Benches, Bookcases and Even Chairs," was written in news story format. Peterson is very conscious of the words and phrases he uses in news releases and crafts them to reach specific niche targets. For example, "contemporary fireplace," "fireplace mantel," and "fireplace design" are important phrases to reach people who are in the market for a fireplace. The news releases are all sent with beautiful news photos drawn from "Earth's largest collection of decorative concrete photos" on The Concrete Network. For example, Peterson can choose from dozens of photos of just concrete patios.[8]

"We know how many visitors reach us via the news releases, and it is similar to paid search engine marketing," Peterson says, but at a lower cost.

---

[7] concretenetwork.com/contractors

[8] concretenetwork.com/photo_library/patios.htm

"We're also generating links from other sites that index the news releases, and there is a media bonus, too, when we get mentioned in a story." He adds that the site averaged 550,000 visitors per month in 2005 and 850,000 in 2006. In 2009, against a backdrop of an economic crisis, a dramatically slower construction market, and 40 percent fewer searches in the concrete category, the site broke the 1 million visitors per month barrier and is still growing. Peterson expects traffic to explode as the economy starts to improve. "Direct-to-consumer news releases are a big part of the increased traffic. When you break it down, we're spending about $20,000 per year on news release distribution. . . . We see it as another component of our marketing. Some businesses won't want to spend that, but they probably won't be the leader in their marketplace."

Advice from the Company President

As president of The Concrete Network, Peterson is that rare executive who understands the power of content marketing, search engine optimization, and direct-to-consumer news releases to reach buyers directly and drive business. What is his advice to other company presidents and CEOs? "Every business has information that can contribute to the education of the marketplace. You need to ask yourself, 'How can I get that information out there?' You have to have a bit longer view and have a sense of how your business will be better down the line. For example, we created an entire series of buyer guides, because we knew that they would be valuable to the market. You need to think about how a series of 100 news releases over two years will benefit your business and then commit to it, understanding that nothing is an overnight thing."

Peterson also suggests getting help from an expert to get started with a program. "Don't sit there and leave this [as] just a part of your list of good intentions," he says. "Businesses will live or die on original content. If you are creating truly useful content for customers, you're going to be seen in a great light and with a great spirit—you're setting the table for new business. But the vast majority of businesses don't seem to care. At The Concrete Network, we're on a mission. Get down to the essence of what your product solves and write good stories about that and publish them online."

You've got to love it. If content sells concrete, content can sell what you have to offer, too!

The Long Tail of PR

In PR, it's not about clip books. It's about reaching our buyers.

I was vice president of marketing and PR for two publicly traded companies, and I've done it the old way. It doesn't work anymore. But the new rules do work—really well.

Instead of spending tens of thousands of dollars per month on a media relations program that tries to convince a handful of reporters at select magazines, newspapers, and TV stations to cover us, we should be targeting the plugged-in bloggers, online news sites, micropublications, public speakers, analysts, and consultants who reach the targeted audiences who are looking for what we have to offer. Better yet, we no longer even need to wait for someone with a media voice to write about us at all. With social media, we communicate directly with our audience, bypassing the media filter completely. We have the power to create our own media brand in the niche of our own choosing. It's about being found on Google and Yahoo! and information sites and RSS (Really Simple Syndication) feeds. Instead of writing press releases only when we have big news—releases that reach only a handful of journalists—we should be writing releases that highlight our expert ideas and stories, and we should be distributing them so that our buyers can find them on the news search engines and vertical content sites.

To succeed in long-tail marketing and PR, we need to adopt different criteria for success. In the book world, everyone used to say, "If I can only get on *Oprah*, I'll be a success." Sure, I would have liked to be on *The Oprah Winfrey Show*, too. But instead of focusing countless (and probably fruitless) hours on a potential blockbuster of a TV appearance, wouldn't it be a better strategy to have lots of people reviewing your book in smaller publications that reach the specific audiences who buy books like yours? Oprah was a long shot, but right now bloggers would love to hear from you. Oprah ignored 100 books a day, but bloggers run to their mailbox to see what interesting things might be in there (trust me, I know from experience). Sure, it would be great to have our businesses profiled in *Fortune* or *BusinessWeek*. But instead of putting all of our public relations efforts into that one potential PR blockbuster (a mention in the major business press), wouldn't it be better to get dozens of the most influential bloggers and analysts to tell our story directly to the niche markets that are looking for what we have to offer?

The New Rules of Marketing and PR

If you've been nodding your head excitedly while reading about what some of these companies are up to, then the new rules are for you. In the next chapter, I offer interesting case studies of companies that have been successful with the new rules. In each case example, I've interviewed a particular person from that organization so we can learn directly from them. Following are chapters on specific areas of online content (such as blogging, online video, and news releases) and then more detailed how-to chapters. But before we move on, let me explicitly state the New Rules of Marketing and PR that we'll discuss throughout the rest of the book:

- Marketing is more than just advertising.
- PR is for more than just a mainstream media audience.
- You are what you publish.
- People want authenticity, not spin.
- People want participation, not propaganda.
- Instead of causing one-way interruption, marketing is about delivering content at just the precise moment your audience needs it.
- Marketers must shift their thinking from mainstream marketing to the masses to a strategy of reaching vast numbers of underserved audiences via the web.
- PR is not about your boss seeing your company on TV. It's about your buyers seeing your company on the web.
- Marketing is not about your agency winning awards. It's about your organization winning business.
- The Internet has made public relations public again, after years of almost exclusive focus on media.
- Companies must drive people into the purchasing process with great online content.
- Blogs, online video, e-books, news releases, and other forms of online content let organizations communicate directly with buyers in a form they appreciate.
- Social networks like Twitter, Facebook, and LinkedIn allow people all over the world to share content and connect with the people and companies they do business with.
- On the web, the lines between marketing and PR have blurred.

The Convergence of Marketing and PR on the Web

As I originally wrote this list and edited it down, I was struck by how important one particular concept was to any successful online strategy to reach buyers directly: This concept is the convergence of marketing and PR. In an off-line world, marketing and PR are separate departments with different people and different skill sets, but this is not the case on the web. What's the difference between what Amazon, iTunes, and Netflix are doing to reach customers via online marketing and what The Concrete Network does with direct-to-consumer news releases? There's not much difference. How is the news that Cervélo Cycles creates itself and posts on the site different from a story on *Bicycling* magazine's website? It isn't. And when a buyer is researching your product category by using a search engine, does it really matter if the first exposure is a hit on your website, a news release your organization sent, a magazine article, or a post on your blog? I'd argue that it doesn't matter. Whereas I presented two separate lists for The Old Rules of Marketing and The Old Rules of PR, now there is just one set of rules: The New Rules of Marketing and PR. Great content in all forms helps buyers see that you and your organization get it. Content drives action.

3 Reaching Your Buyers Directly

The frustration of relying exclusively on the media and expensive advertising to deliver your organization's messages is long gone. Yes, mainstream media is still important, but today smart marketers craft compelling information and tell the world directly via the web. The tremendous expense of relying on advertising to convince buyers to pay attention to your organization, ideas, products, and services is yesterday's headache.

Chip McDermott founded ZeroTrash[1] as a nonprofit organization to rid the streets and beaches of Laguna Beach, California, of trash. Population and tourism had exploded, and the city had not kept up in providing sufficient infrastructure for public trash and recycling. McDermott used the web to rally the community with a grassroots movement.

"The spark of the idea in 2007 was that trash was becoming commonplace on the streets and the sidewalks of Laguna Beach," McDermott says. "We started to tackle the problem with a Facebook[2] fan page for ZeroTrash Laguna and quickly built it to hundreds of members."

People use the ZeroTrash Facebook page to organize events and to connect local storeowners with residents. Facebook was instrumental in launching the ZeroTrash First Saturday movement, where storeowners and volunteers walk the city and pick up trash on the first Saturday of each month. The storeowners love it because people support local stores and keep

---

[1] zerotrash.org
[2] facebook.com/ZeroTrash

the shopping areas clean. In turn, McDermott has tapped storeowners as sponsors who fund the purchase of supplies and tools like trash pickers, T-shirts, trash bags, and gloves.

McDermott also uses Twitter (@ZeroTrash) to get the word out. The social media sites serve to keep people updated about what ZeroTrash is up to. For example, on a recent First Saturday, the Laguna Beach community helped to remove another 590 pounds of trash and 375 pounds of recyclables from the streets; McDermott used the social media sites to report these totals to interested people.

After the initial success in Laguna, ZeroTrash now also serves Newport Beach and Dana Point. To date, the ZeroTrash organization has removed over 60,000 pounds of trash. He has high hopes for the organization, including ambitions to spread the movement beyond California. "We want people to take individual ownership of each new local ZeroTrash community," he says. "How can they get people with a passion to take control and start in their own communities? The obvious answer is to use social media to influence people."

There's no doubt that getting the word out about an idea, a product, or a service is much simpler when you can rely on social media sites like blogs, Facebook, and Twitter. The web allows any organization—including non-profits like ZeroTrash, as well as companies large and small, candidates for public office, government agencies, schools, artists, and even job seekers—to reach buyers directly. This power is clear to nearly everyone these days, but many executives and entrepreneurs still struggle to find the right mix of traditional advertising and direct communication with buyers.

The Right Marketing in a Wired World

Century 21 Real Estate LLC[3] is the franchisor of the world's largest residential real estate sales organization, an industry giant with approximately 8,000 offices in 45 countries. The company had been spending on television advertising for years but, in a significant strategy change, pulled its national television advertising and invested those resources into online marketing.

Wow! I've seen Century 21 TV ads for years. We're talking millions of dollars shifting from TV to the web. This is a big deal.

---

[3] century21.com

"We are moving our advertising investments to the mediums that have the greatest relevance to our target buyers and sellers, and to where the return on our investment is most significant," says Bev Thorne, chief marketing officer at Century 21. "We found that our online investments provided a return that was substantively higher than our more traditional TV media investments."

Thorne and her team learned that people who are in the market to buy or sell a home rely heavily on the web and that the closer they get to a real estate transaction, the more they use online resources. "We are beginning to embrace LinkedIn, Facebook, Twitter, Active Rain, and others," Thorne says. "YouTube is already a central component of our activities, and we seek to utilize it even more."

Many companies spending large amounts of money on television advertising (and other off-line marketing such as direct mail, magazine and newspaper advertising, and Yellow Pages listings) are afraid to make even partial moves away from their comfort zones and into online marketing and social media. But the evidence describing how people actually research products overwhelmingly suggests that companies must tell their stories and spread their ideas online, at the precise moment that potential buyers are searching for answers.

It's an exciting time to be a marketer, no matter what business you're in. We have been liberated from relying exclusively on buying access through advertising or convincing mainstream media to talk us up. Now we can publish information on the web that people are eager to pay attention to.

Let the World Know about Your Expertise

All people and organizations possess the power to elevate themselves on the web to a position of importance. In the new e-marketplace of ideas, organizations highlight their expertise in online media that focus on buyers' needs. The web allows organizations to deliver the right information to buyers, right at the point when they are most receptive to the information. The tools at our disposal as marketers are web-based media to deliver our own thoughtful and informative content via websites, blogs, e-books, white papers, images, photos, audio content, video, and even things like product placement, games, and virtual reality. We also have the ability to interact and participate in conversations that other people begin on social media sites like Twitter, blogs, chat rooms, and forums. What links all of these techniques together is that organizations of all types behave like *publishers*, creating content that people are eager to consume. Organizations gain credibility and loyalty with buyers through content, and smart marketers now think and act like publishers in order to create and deliver content targeted directly at their audience.

The Lodge at Chaa Creek,[4] an eco-resort on a 265-acre rainforest reserve in Western Belize, is a publisher of valuable content about rainforest wildlife, nearby destinations such as ancient Mayan cities, and the Central American country in which it is located. This content marketing effort helps the Lodge at Chaa Creek achieve high search-engine rankings for many important phrases associated with travel to Belize. This work generates a remarkable 80 percent of new business for the Lodge. Their story is among the best I know for learning how content drives business.

As anyone who has built a website knows, there is much more to think about than just the content. Design, color, navigation, and appropriate technology are all important aspects of a good site. Unfortunately, these other concerns often dominate. Why is that? I think it's easier to focus on a site's design or technology than on its content.

The global hotel chains fall into this trap: big-budget design and poor content. If you visit the sites of any of the majors (Hilton, Starwood, Marriott, etc.), you'll notice they all look the same. The content is all created by corporate headquarters, so individual property pages rarely contain original content about the location of each hotel. The result is that most hotel sites are just big brochures that pull product features like room types and food offerings from a global database.

The Lodge at Chaa Creek's website couldn't be more different. The team behind it includes co-owner Lucy Fleming, who oversees marketing; Australia-based writer and former newspaper editor Mark Langan, who creates most of the written content; and on-site marketer Larry Waight, who focuses on social media and search engine optimization. Waight researches what people are searching on—terms like "Belize honeymoon" and "Belize all-inclusive vacation"—and then works with Fleming and Langan to craft content for the Lodge at Chaa Creek's site, as well as their Belize Travel Blog.[5] Their goal is

---

[4] chaacreek.com
[5] chaacreek.com/belize-travel-blog/

to offer content that is valuable for those researching a Belize vacation, content that will be ranked highly in the search engines.

Can you see what's happening here? Somebody goes to Google and wants to learn about bird watching in Belize. And because the content on the Chaa Creek site and blog includes stories about the birds of Belize, this searcher ends up on the site or blog. For people searching for information on planning a wedding trip to Belize, Chaa Creek publishes content such as "Ten reasons why Belize makes for Honeymoon Bliss"[6] on their Belize Travel Blog.

Please notice that this kind of information is not about the lodge itself. Instead, the Chaa Creek publishing program focuses on delivering information to people planning a trip to Belize. Then, when they are ready to book a place to stay, they're likely to consider The Lodge at Chaa Creek, the place where they learned about travel to the country.

My favorite examples of this technique are the team's articles about the Mayan sites located in the vicinity of the Lodge, such as the Xunantunich Maya Temples. Anyone using a search engine to find information on "Xunantunich Maya Temples" will see the article on the Chaa Creek site at the top of the search results. Clicking through, they learn that the temples are located near the village of San Jose Succotz and that the lower temple is famous for its stucco frieze (a band of sculpture along the facade). Let me remind you that this is a hotel website. The team even created content about the Tikal Mayan site, located about two hours from Chaa Creek in Guatemala, a whole different country!

All this content drives people from the search engines to the hotel site. Many of them will then choose to stay at The Lodge at Chaa Creek. Indeed, some 80 percent of new bookings to the Lodge come directly from this content marketing effort. This reduces the Lodge's reliance on the old-fashioned techniques of their competitors, which get a large percentage of their bookings from online travel sites (for which they must pay a commission) or advertising in travel magazines (which is very expensive). And it all starts by providing would-be travelers with the information they're looking for when they begin researching a trip.

---

[6] chaacreek.com/belize-travel-blog/2011/02/ten-reasons-why-belize-makes-for-honeymoon-bliss

Develop Information Your Buyers Want to Consume

Companies with large budgets can't wait to spend the big bucks on slick TV advertisements. It's like commissioning artwork. TV ads make marketing people at larger companies feel good. But broadcast advertisements dating from the time of the TV-industrial complex don't work so well anymore. When we had three networks and no cable, it was different. In the time-shifted, multichannel, web-centric world of the long tail, YouTube, DVRs, and blogs, spending big bucks on TV ads is like commissioning a portrait back in the nineteenth century: It might make you feel good, but does it bring in any money?

Instead of deploying huge budgets for dumbed-down TV commercials that purport to speak to the masses and therefore appeal to nobody, we need to think about the information that our niche audiences want to hear. Why not build content specifically for these niche audiences and tell them an online story that is created especially for them? Once marketers and PR people tune their brains to think about niches, they begin to see opportunities for being more effective at delivering their organization's message.

Buyer Personas: The Basics

Smart marketers understand buyers, and many build formal "buyer personas" for their target demographics. (I discuss buyer personas in detail in Chapter 11.) It can be daunting for many of us to consider who, exactly, is visiting our site. But if we break the buyers into distinct groups and then catalog everything we know about each one, we make it easier to create content targeted to each important demographic. For example, a college website usually has the goal of keeping alumni happy so that they donate money to their alma mater on a regular basis. A college might have two buyer personas for alumni: young (those who graduated within the past 10 or 15 years) and older alumni. Universities also have a goal of recruiting students by driving them into the application process. The effective college site might have a buyer persona for the high school student who is considering college. But since the parents of the prospective student have very different information needs, the site designers might build another buyer persona for parents. A college also has to keep its existing customers (current students) happy. In sum, that means a well-executed college site might target five distinct buyer personas, with the goal of getting alumni to donate money, high school students to complete the application process, and parents to make certain their kids complete it. The goals for the current student aspects of the site might be making certain they come back for another year, plus answering routine questions so that staff time is not wasted.

By truly understanding the needs and the mind-sets of the five buyer personas, the college will be able to create appropriate content. Once you understand the audience very well, then (and only then) you should set out to satisfy their informational needs by focusing on your buyers' problems and creating and delivering content accordingly. As mentioned earlier, website content too often simply describes what an organization or a product does from an egotistical perspective. While information about your organization and products is certainly valuable on the inner pages of your site, what visitors really want is content that first describes the issues and problems they face and then provides details on how to solve those problems. Once you've built an online relationship, you can begin to offer potential solutions that have been defined for each audience. After you've identified target audiences and articulated their problems, content is your tool to show off your expertise. Well-organized web content will lead your visitors through the sales cycle all the way to the point when they are ready to buy from or otherwise commit to your organization.

Understanding buyers and building an effective content strategy to reach them is critical for success. And providing clear links from the content to the place where action occurs is critical. Consider Mike Pedersen, who is widely acknowledged as one of the leading golf fitness-training experts in the United States, having taught thousands of golfers the fitness approach to playing a consistently great game of golf. Pedersen runs an online business providing products to help golfers improve their game by getting in better shape. Pedersen's site[7] is chock-full of content created specifically for a narrow target market (buyer persona) and he uses Twitter (@golftrainer with 11,000+ followers) and Facebook to connect with his customers and share the content on his site. "I write for the 60-year-old golfer who has rapidly declining physical capabilities," says Pedersen. "I like to call it targeted content. When I write an article, I'm targeting a very specific element of golf for my readers. The article might be targeted to a small

---

[7] mikepedersengolf.com

aspect of the golf swing, for example, and the guys I write for know how it can help them."

Pedersen offers hundreds of free articles and tips on his site and blog, such as "Golf-Specific Warm-Ups" and "Golf Muscles Need to Be Strong and Flexible to Produce More Power in Your Golf Swing." "Most golfers don't prepare their bodies before they play golf, and they aren't able to play a good game," he says. "I write to be easy to understand and offer exercises that help people to prepare quickly and efficiently." Each article includes multiple photos of Pedersen illustrating how the exercises should be performed.

Pedersen relies on search engines to drive much of his traffic, and his site is number one on search engines for important phrases like "golf training." He also works with partners and affiliates, and he has been the featured fitness expert for *Golf* magazine's website, generating even more traffic for his own site. Pedersen says that the key to everything about his business is targeting his buyers directly with content specifically for them. His focus on his buyer persona of the older man who loves golf but is physically able to do less in his declining years is relentless. "I rely on getting into the consumers' mind and feeling their pain and their frustration," he says. "It is easy to write what I think, but much more difficult to write about what my buyers are thinking. With these guys, my target market, if they don't do anything now, they physically can't play the game that they love in future years. But I'm a 40-year-old, really fit, healthy guy. If I just wrote for myself, I'd be shooting myself in the foot because I'm not the target market."

Pedersen makes his money by selling products such as his Golf Fitness Training System for $150 (the system includes DVDs, books, and manuals) and membership in his online Golf Training Program. He also offers single-topic DVDs and exercise supplies such as weighted golf clubs. At the bottom of each article on the site, there is a clear path and a call to action. "I'm diligent about links from every page both to something free and to the products page," he says. For example, a recent offer read, "Do you want to learn how your body is keeping you from a near perfect golf swing? Get my Free Golf Fitness eBook and find out!"

When people register on the site for a free offer, they are added to Pedersen's 50,000-person email list to get alerts on significant new content added to the site and blog, as well as special offers. The majority of email messages he sends are alerts about new content and contain no sales pitch at all. "I know that if I provide valuable content, then I'll get more sales," Pedersen says.

Think Like a Publisher

The new publishing model on the web is not about hype and spin and messages. It is about delivering content when and where it is needed and, in the process, branding you or your organization as a leader. When you understand your audience, those people who will become your buyers (or those who will join, donate, subscribe, apply, volunteer, or vote), you can craft an editorial and content strategy just for them. What works is a focus on your buyers and their problems. What fails is an egocentric display of your products and services.

To implement a successful strategy, think like a publisher. Marketers at the organizations successfully using the new rules recognize that they are now purveyors of information, and they manage content as a valuable asset with the same care that a publishing company does. One of the most important things that publishers do is start with a content strategy and *then* focus on the mechanics and design of delivering that content. Publishers carefully identify and define target audiences and consider what content is required to meet their needs. Publishers consider all of the following questions: Who are my readers? How do I reach them? What are their motivations? What are the problems I can help them solve? How can I entertain them and inform them at the same time? What content will compel them to purchase what I have to offer?

Staying Connected with Members and the Community

As the demographics of America have changed over the past several decades, many mainline church organizations have struggled to attract and maintain members. Like any business or nonprofit, the churches that succeed are those whose leaders understand the problems buyers (here: churchgoers) face and use the power of publishing valuable information to reach them directly. Trinity Cathedral[8] in Cleveland is a place where ancient church practice has blended with new patterns of social interaction to build a vibrant community both online and off-line. Trinity Cathedral is a historic landmark and home to a vibrant, inclusive congregation in the heart of a city struggling to revitalize after decades of decline in manufacturing jobs. The Very Rev. Tracey Lind, dean of Trinity Cathedral, leads the effort.

---

[8] trinitycleveland.org

"The official way you count attendance or membership in the Episcopal Church is to count average Sunday attendance," Lind says. "For a long time, I and a group of my colleagues have been saying that's not an accurate measure of the work we're doing. In fact, our vitality would be better measured by average weekly touch." To touch people regularly outside of Sunday services, Lind publishes an email newsletter, her own blog,[9] audio podcasts, a Facebook page, and a Twitter feed. "Reality is that most people don't go to church every week anymore," she says. "That's just a reality of life. My attitude is that you can fight it, or you can be a part of it."

Lind's publishing efforts help create a virtual community within the congregation. Trinity Cathedral employs a full-time communications person and also relies on Rebecca Wilson and Jim Naughton of Canticle Communications (a firm that serves mainly church organizations) to help with web design and content publishing efforts. "We do everything as if we are running a web business to try to attract people to us," Lind says. "The reality is I'm not going to get everybody to church every week. If you can't get to church on Sunday, you can listen to the service on a podcast or you can read it on my blog. If you're teaching our kids or you're singing in the choir or doing something else at that hour, you can listen to it on podcast. What we find is we're reaching huge communities of people [with] our podcasting. People are listening to us all over the globe. I get emails from folks in Australia or Germany, thanking me for a sermon that I preached and wanting to engage."

Music is a particularly important aspect of Trinity Cathedral's podcasting efforts. "If you go to England, one of the things that people do is go to the great cathedrals to attend choral Evensong to listen to the men's and boy's choirs sing," Lind says. "Well, we do that at Trinity every week, and we think there's nobody in the country podcasting choral Evensong. So we started podcasting that, which is a way of making us unique. People listen to really extraordinary choral music every week, and they count on the podcast."

Marketers at companies whose buyers include a segment of older people frequently assume that they are not online and that they won't engage with a web publishing effort. I've always pushed back on this notion. So does Lind, who has demographic data to show how misguided those conventional ideas can be. "We find that in our 1,000-member congregation, all but about ten adults are on the Internet," she says. "Only ten adults are not using the web, and that includes our elders. Most of our elders are actively social

---

[9] traceylind.com

networking and on the Internet. When we suspended our print newspaper, I got just one complaint."

Trinity Cathedral attracts a very diverse group of people in the Cleveland area, and the web-publishing efforts aid in building the community of people who become members. "Our market is clear," Lind says. "We're trying to attract progressive people of faith who are concerned about the city and who want to be a part of an intentionally inclusive, diverse, engaged congregation. We're trying to attract change agents. We're intentional about trying to attract the 20s and 30s, but there's also great value in the world of the empty-nesters, and also in the third half of life: boomers, those reinventing aging. I think of one of our audiences as those who listen to NPR—thoughtful, but not necessarily highly educated. We attract a lot of really thoughtful working-class folks that you wouldn't otherwise think would be coming. We're racially diverse. We are always interested in families that are wanting something other than the bland suburbs for their kids—so a lot of alternative families, blended families, adopted families, LGBT families, single moms, single dads." Lind considers each of these markets as she creates information to publish on the web.

Developing and maintaining the publishing program at Trinity Cathedral is a major effort for an organization tight on resources. But reaching buyers through the blog, podcasting, social networking, and the email newsletter is essential, given the changing ways people relate to their churches. Just like so many leaders of for-profit businesses, Lind has had to convince stakeholders of the importance of online marketing. "When I got to Trinity, there was one computer in the place, and it was barely used. That was in 2000. Part of the dilemma is the amount of money that has to go into communications, which is an enormous paradigm shift for churches. Frankly, my communications director is as valuable as a priest. That is a shift that is sometimes hard to explain to people." But it's one that will be essential for traditional churches to understand if they are to survive and thrive in the age of the social networks.

Know the Goals and Let Content Drive Action

On the speaking circuit and via my blog, I am often asked to critique marketing programs, websites, and blogs. My typical responses—"What's the goal?" and "What problems do you solve for your buyers?"—often throw people off. It is amazing that so many marketers don't have established goals for their marketing programs and for websites and blogs in particular. And they often cannot articulate who their buyers are and what problems they solve for them.

An effective web marketing and PR strategy that delivers compelling content to buyers gets them to take action. (You will learn more about developing your own marketing and PR strategy in Chapter 11.)

Companies that understand the new rules of marketing and PR have a clearly defined *business* goal—to sell products, to generate contributions, or to get people to vote or join. These successful organizations aren't focused on the wrong goals, things like press clips and advertising awards. At successful organizations, news releases, blogs, websites, video, and other content draw visitors into the sales-consideration cycle and then funnel them toward the place where action occurs. The goal is not hidden, and it is easy for buyers to find the way to take the next step. When content effectively drives action, the next step of the sales process—an e-commerce company's Products button, the B2B corporation's White Paper Download form, or a nonprofit's Donate link—are easy to find.

Working from the perspective of the company's desire for revenue growth and customer retention (the goals), rather than focusing on made-up metrics for things like leads and website traffic, yields surprising changes in the typical marketing plan and in the organization of web content. Website traffic doesn't matter if your goal is revenue (however, the traffic may *lead to* the goal). Similarly, being ranked number one on Google for a phrase isn't important (although, if your buyers care about that phrase, it can lead to the goal).

Ultimately, when marketers focus on the same goals as the rest of the organization, we develop marketing programs that really deliver action and begin to contribute to the bottom line and command respect. Rather than meeting rolled eyes and snide comments about marketing as simply the T-shirt department, we're seen as part of a strategic unit that contributes to reaching the organization's goals.

Content and Thought Leadership

For many companies and individuals, reaching customers with web content has a powerful, less obvious effect. Content brands an organization as a thought leader. Indeed, many organizations create content especially to position them as thought leaders in their market. Instead of just directly selling something, a great site, blog, or video series tells the world that you are smart, that you understand the market very well, and that you might be a person or organization that would be valuable to do business with. Web content directly contributes to an organization's online reputation by showing thought leadership in the marketplace of ideas. See Chapter 12 for more on thought leadership.

In the following chapters that make up Part II of the book, I introduce blogs, news releases, podcasting, online video, viral marketing, and social media. Then in Part III, I present a guide to creating your marketing and PR plan (Chapter 11), followed by detailed chapters with how-to information on each technique. Content turns browsers into buyers. It doesn't matter whether you're selling premium wine cabinets or a new music CD, or advocating to stop sonar harm to whales, web content sells any product or service and advocates any philosophy or image.

II

Web-Based Communications to Reach Buyers Directly

4 Social Media and Your Targeted Audience

As millions of people use the web for conducting detailed research on products and services, getting involved in political campaigns, joining music and film fan clubs, reviewing products, and discussing hobbies and passions, they congregate in all kinds of online places. The technologies and tools, which many people now refer to collectively as *social media*, all include ways for users to express their opinions online:

- **Social networking** sites like Facebook, Twitter, and LinkedIn help people cultivate a community of friends and share information.
- **Blogs**, personal websites written by somebody who is passionate about a topic, provide a means to share that passion with the world and to foster an active community of readers who provide comments on the author's posts.
- **Video and photo sharing** sites like YouTube, Vimeo, Flickr, and Instagram greatly simplify the process of sharing and commenting on photos and videos.
- **Chat rooms and message boards** serve as online meeting places where people meet and discuss topics of interest, with the main feature being that anyone can start a discussion thread.
- **Listservs**, similar to chat rooms, send messages out by email to a collection of registered members.
- **Wikis** are websites that anybody can edit and update.

- **Social bookmarking** sites like Digg and StumbleUpon allow users to suggest content to others and vote on what is interesting.
- **Mobile applications** with GPS-generated location services like Foursquare add the component of identifying exactly where each user is in the world.

What Is Social Media, Anyway?

Since social media is such an important concept (and is so often misunderstood), I'll define it:

> Social media provide the way people share ideas, content, thoughts, and relationships online. Social media differ from so-called mainstream media in that anyone can create, comment on, and add to social media content. Social media can take the form of text, audio, video, images, and communities.

The best way to think about social media is not in terms of the different technologies and tools but, rather, how those technologies and tools allow you to communicate directly with your buyers in places they are congregating right now.

Just as a point of clarification, note that there are two terms that sound similar here: social media and social networking. *Social media* is the superset and is how we refer to the various media that people use to communicate online in a social way. Social media include blogs, wikis, video and photo sharing, and much more. A subset of social media is *social networking*, a term I use to refer to how people interact on sites like Facebook, Twitter, LinkedIn, and similar sites. Social networking occurs when people create a personal profile and interact to become part of a community of friends and like-minded people and to share information. You'll notice throughout the book that I use both terms. This chapter is about the larger concept of social media, while in Chapter 16 we dive into detail about social networking.

I'm fond of thinking of the web as a city—it helps make sense of each aspect of online life and how we create and interact. Corporate sites are the storefronts on Main Street peddling wares. Craigslist is like the bulletin board at the entrance of the corner store; eBay, a garage sale; Amazon, a superstore replete with patrons anxious to give you their two cents. Mainstream media sites like the *New York Times* online are the newspapers of the city. Chat rooms and forums are the pubs and saloons of the online world. You've even got the proverbial wrong-side-of-the-tracks spots: the web's adult-entertainment and spam underbelly.

Social Media Is a Cocktail Party

If you follow my metaphor of the web as a city, then think of social media and the ways that people interact on blogs, forums, and social networking sites as the bars, private clubs, and cocktail parties of the city. To extend the (increasingly tortured) analogy even further, Twitter can be compared to the interlude when the girls go to the ladies' room and talk about the guys, and the guys are discussing the girls while they wait.

Viewing the web as a sprawling city where social media are the places people congregate to have fun helps us make sense of how marketers can best use the tools of social media. How do you act in a cocktail party situation?

- Do you go into a large gathering filled with a few acquaintances and tons of people you do not know and shout, "BUY MY PRODUCT!"?
- Do you go into a cocktail party and ask every single person you meet for a business card before you agree to speak with them?
- Do you listen more than you speak?
- Are you helpful, providing valuable information to people with no expectation of getting something tangible in return?
- Do you try to meet every single person, or do you have a few great conversations?
- Or do you avoid the social interaction of cocktail parties altogether because you are uncomfortable in such situations?

I find these questions are helpful to people who are new to social media. This analogy is also a good one to discuss with social media cynics and those who cannot see the value of this important form of communication.

The web-as-a-city approach is especially important when dealing with people who have been steeped in the traditions of advertising-based marketing, those skilled at interrupting people to talk up products and using coercion techniques to make a sale. Sure, you can go to a cocktail party and treat everyone as a sales lead while blabbing on about what your company does. But that approach is unlikely to make you popular.

Guess what? The popular people on the cocktail circuit make friends. People like to do business with people they like. And they are eager to introduce their friends to each other. The same trends hold true in social media. So go ahead and join the party. But think of it as just that—a fun place where you give more than you get. Of course, you can also do business there, but the kind you do at a cocktail party and not at the general store. What you get in return for your valuable interactions are lasting friendships, many of which lead to business opportunities.

This chapter is an introduction to the concepts of social media. In subsequent chapters, I go into much greater detail about blogs (Chapters 5 and 17), video (Chapters 6 and 19), and social networking (Chapter 16).

Facebook Group Drives 15,000 People to Singapore Tattoo Show

I speak at dozens of conferences a year all over the world. Since organizers usually book me many months in advance, I gain a great deal of insight into how they promote the events. It tends to be the same old methods: Send an email and a postal direct mail to everyone who attended last year, buy some mailing lists, and send some more promotions. Most shows build good websites, and most have decent search engine optimization. But that's usually it.

What if you're charged with promoting a brand-new show? Because there are no previous attendees to draw from, the work is much more difficult. Or is it? When a show is new, the old rules of promotion don't apply. You can do something new and untested.

The First Annual Singapore Tattoo Show,[1] held in January 2009, was endorsed and supported by the Singapore Tourism Board and included Chris Garver of *Miami Ink* as the show's ambassador. The goal of the show's first year was to get 5,000 visitors to one place where more than 120 artists from around the globe, representing all the various traditional and modern tattoo styles, ticked away with their machines. All sorts of fun and funky exhibitors

---

[1] tattoo.com.sg

were there, and emcee and official DJ Shawn Lee kept awesome sounds pumping throughout the hall.

Andrew Peters, Asia Pacific regional director of Pacific West Communications, is the brains behind the social media promotions leading up to the Singapore Tattoo Show, working on both traditional and social media publicity. "The show was launched via social media, including Facebook, my blog, and other social networking platforms because of my belief in how social media could make a far-reaching impact," Peters says. "This ultimately becomes a collective of voices that cannot be ignored, and it becomes contagious as others want to be a part of the collective."

Peters used Facebook as a way for people to connect well before the physical event. He established a Facebook group called Tattoo Artistry[2] three months prior to the show. The group grew very quickly, securing a place as the center of tattoo artistry for the region. In a sense, the physical show started with a virtual group. Note that Peters's brilliant choice of the Facebook group name (Tattoo Artistry) was not the name of the event (The Singapore Tattoo Show). That way, the group could build momentum independently of the show and live on beyond the first year.

The passion of the Tattoo Artistry Facebook group members meant they would help promote the group to their friends, so the online community eventually included many people eager to attend the live event. Instead of relying on expensive advertising, Peters built a community of passionate fans who built anticipation and buzz for the event. "Quite simply, I was amazed at the result," he says. "One morning I checked into Facebook to see if a few people had joined the Tattoo Artistry group. Not only had people joined, they had added photos, were leaving messages, and chatting to each other. The group had come to life."

The Tattoo Artistry Facebook group quickly reached 3,000 members and was an important reason that more than 15,000 people attended the first Singapore Tattoo Show—that's three times the expected number of attendees.

The Tattoo Artistry Facebook group became Asia's largest social network for the tattoo industry, tattoo enthusiasts, and fans. The group continues to grow as an online destination to connect with about additional Singapore Tattoo Shows, which are now held annually. "Engaging community involvement is not so easily achieved in more traditional marketing methods,"

---

[2] facebook.com/group.php?gid=32140274011

Peters says. "Social media like Facebook offer immediacy, freedom to be who you are, the opportunity to meet others who are similar, and to have a place to fit in. Event organizers must see beyond their immediate need to put 'bums on seats' for the next event and instead engage people to build support and loyalty over many years."

The New Rules of Job Search

Company lost its funding. Outsourced. Caught in a merger. Downsized. Fired. It seems like every day I learn of another person who is in the job market. Usually that's because when they need a job, all of a sudden people jump into networking mode, and I hear from them after years of silence. Hey, I'm okay with that; it's always good to hear from old friends. And I've been fired three times, so I certainly know what it's like to be in the job market.

Since looking for a job is all about marketing a product (you), I wanted to include a section in the book for those of you who are currently in the job market, those soon to graduate from college or university, or otherwise looking for a career opportunity.

If you're like the vast majority of job seekers, you'd do what everyone knows is the way to find a job: You prepare a resume, obsessing over every entry to make sure it paints your background in the best possible light. You also begin a networking campaign, emailing and phoning your contacts and using networking tools like LinkedIn, hoping that someone in your extended network knows of a suitable job opportunity.

While many people find jobs the traditional way, social media allow a new way to interact and meet potential employers. The old rules of job searchers required advertising a product (you) with direct mail (your resume that you send to potential employers). The old rules of job searches required you to interrupt people (friends and colleagues) to tell them that you were on the market and to ask them to help you.

As people engage with each other on social media sites, there are plenty of opportunities to network. Just like a physical cocktail party, if you are unemployed and looking for work, the people you meet may be in a position to introduce you to that perfect employer. The opposite is also true: Smart employers look to social networking sites to find the sort of plugged-in people that would fit in at their company or in a certain job. In fact, on the day that I wrote this, a friend asked me to tweet a job opportunity. Had you been watching my Twitter feed that day, perhaps you'd have a new job now.

So you want to find a new job via social media? You have to stop thinking like an advertiser of a product and start thinking like a publisher of information. Create information that people want. Create an online presence that people are eager to consume. Establish a virtual front door that people will happily link to—one that employers will find. The new rules of finding a job require you to share your knowledge and expertise with a world that is looking for what you have to offer.

How to Find a New Job via Social Media

David Murray (@DaveMurr) says that after being laid off, he immediately did the traditional things, updating his resume and calling a bunch of contacts. But he eventually realized that he would also have to change gears and pay attention to blogs, social networks, and online communities. Murray already had a Twitter account, so he reached out to his Twitter followers and publicly announced that he was looking for work.

"I guess you could say I used a new tool for old-school networking," Murray says. "The response was overwhelming, and I received several leads and opportunities that were far more fruitful than my previous attempts."

Murray then hit on a creative way to use Twitter Search[3] in his job hunt. "I came across a comment from Chris Brogan [@ChrisBrogan] on how he used Twitter Search to keep track of his tens of thousands of followers using RSS feeds," Murray says. "So I simply began entering keywords in Twitter Search like 'Hiring Social Media,' 'Social Media Jobs,' 'Online Community Manager,' 'Blogging Jobs,' and so on. I then pulled the RSS feeds of these keyword conversations and made it a habit to check these first thing in the morning every day."

Bingo. Murray came across lots of conversations related to his keywords, and if something sounded like a good fit for him, he took the liberty of introducing himself via Twitter. "Many times, the jobs had not been officially posted," Murray says.

How cool is it that on Twitter you can express interest in a job opportunity that hasn't even been announced yet? It's like getting inside information!

---

[3] search.twitter.com

Hired. It didn't take long at all for Murray to land the ideal job. Of course, his example is of someone who had already established himself in his career; he was looking for a new job because of a layoff. But what about new (or soon-to-be) university graduates searching for an entry-level position?

When Lindsey Kirchoff was a graduating senior at Tufts University near Boston, Massachusetts, she started a terrific blog called *How to Market to Me.*[4] In her blog, Kirchoff offers her opinions on how to market to millennials like herself. "The blog is my opinion," she says. "It's about the advertisements that 'get' me as a collegiate and twenty-something consumer. The companies that understand my values, participate in my humor and reach me when/where I'm most likely to need them. It's also about companies that don't do any of those things and how they can better reach me (and people like me) in the future.'"

She used her comments on other peoples' blogs, Twitter feed (@LindseyKirchoff), and other social networking tools to share her ideas about how companies should market to people like her—a focus that also served to showcase her understanding of marketing.

At the time, Kirchoff was on the hunt for a job upon graduation, hopefully at a mid-to-large marketing firm with a strong entry-level program. Soon Kirchoff's active social networking led to discussions both online and in person with marketers at HubSpot, a Boston-based marketing software company. Partly based on her solid understanding of social media as demonstrated by her blog and use of Twitter, Kirchoff was hired full-time at HubSpot on the Content Creation & Blogging team and started working soon after graduation.

What Kirchoff and Murray both did was to show potential employers that they were available and ready to contribute. They put their enthusiasm and expertise out there to make themselves stand out from the other candidates, who would simply send a paper application or CV.

Some people might argue that this technique only works to find jobs related to social media and marketing (like Murray and Kirchoff did). While it's true that social-media-savvy people are often the first to use these techniques, I'm convinced that they'd work for many other kinds of job seekers. These days, Twitter is used very widely, and tweets like "I'm looking for an accountant to join my London office" appear frequently. You should be monitoring what people are saying in your field. Plus, if you're an

---

[4] howtomarkettome.com

accountant, salesperson, or production manager looking for work, then you're really going to stand out from the crowd of 1,000 resumes if you use social media to find a job.

As long as we're discussing social media and job searches, here's an important consideration: *What comes up when you Google your name with the name of your most recent employer?* Potential employers do that all the time. And you can influence what they see! Remember, on the web, you are what you publish.

Insignificant Backwaters or Valuable Places to Connect?

At specialty sites of all kinds, like-minded hobbyists, professionals, fans, and supporters meet and discuss the intricate nuances of subjects that interest them. Interactive forums were once seen as insignificant backwaters by PR and marketing people—not worth the time to even monitor, let alone participate in. I've heard many marketers dismiss online forums with disdain, saying things like "Why should I worry about a bunch of geeks obsessively typing away in the dead of night?" However, as many marketers have learned, ignoring forums can be hazardous to your brand, while participating as a member allows you to reap rewards.

In a post on his blog titled "Sony, Rootkits and Digital Rights Management [DRM] Gone Too Far,"[5] Mark Russinovich presented his detailed analysis on characteristics of the software used on Sony BMG[6] music CDs to manage permissions for the purchased music. Russinovich argued that shortcomings in the software design create security issues that might be exploited by malicious software such as worms or viruses. He also showed that both the way the software is installed and its lack of an uninstaller utility were troublesome.

"The entire experience was frustrating and irritating," Russinovich wrote on his blog. "Not only had Sony put software on my system that uses techniques commonly used by malware [malicious software] to mask its presence, the software is poorly written and provides no means for uninstall. Worse, most users that stumble across the cloaked files with an RKR scan

---

[5] blogs.technet.com/markrussinovich/archive/2005/10/31/Sony-rootkits-and-digital-rights-management-gone-too-far.aspx

[6] sonymusic.com

will cripple their computer if they attempt the obvious step of deleting the cloaked files. While I believe in the media industry's right to use copy protection mechanisms to prevent illegal copying, I don't think that we've found the right balance of fair use and copy protection, yet. This is a clear case of Sony taking DRM too far."

The reaction to Russinovich's post was immediate and dramatic. In the next several days, hundreds of comments, many harshly critical of Sony BMG Music, were posted on his blog. "Thank you very much for bringing to light what Sony is doing. I have purchased many thousands of dollars of their products over the years. Next year's purchases will be zero," said User101. "I SAY BOYCOTT THE BASTARDS!!" said Jack3617. "If you plan on boycotting, let the offending company know. They need to know that they are losing customers and WHY. Perhaps others companies will get the message as well," said Kolby. "Great article by Mark and scandalous behavior by Sony," said Petter Lindgren.

Hundreds of other bloggers jumped in with their own take on the issue, and chat rooms and forums such as Slashdot[7] were abuzz. Many people expressed frustration that the music industry disapproves of music piracy and sues music downloaders, yet it treats its customers poorly (which reflected negatively on the entire industry, not just Sony BMG). Soon, reporters from online news sites such as ZDNet and InformationWeek wrote their own analyses, and the issue became international news.

So where was Sony BMG during the online hullabaloo? Not on the blogs. Not on the message boards. Nobody from Sony BMG participated in the online discussions. Nobody spoke with online media. Sony BMG was dark (not participating in the communities at all), which added to the frustrations of those who were concerned about the issues. Finally, five days later, Sony BMG's global digital business president Thomas Hesse went on NPR's *Morning Edition* to defend the company. The choice of radio as a forum to react to a storm of protest on the web was a poor one. Had Hesse immediately commented on Russinovich's blog or agreed to speak with a technology reporter for an online publication, he could have gotten his take on the issue onto the screens of concerned people early in the crisis, helping to diffuse their anger. But instead of understanding customer concerns, Hesse downplayed the issue on *Morning Edition*, saying he objected to terms such as *malware, spyware,* and *rootkit.* "Most people, I think, don't even

---

[7] it.slashdot.org

know what a rootkit is, so why should they care about it?" he said in the interview.

Online debate intensified. Sony BMG reacted with the announcement of an exchange program. "To Our Valued Customers," the announcement read. "You may be aware of the recent attention given to the XCP content protection software included on some SONY BMG CDs. This software was provided to us by a third-party vendor, First4Internet. Discussion has centered on security concerns raised about the use of CDs containing this software. We share the concerns of consumers regarding these discs, and we are instituting a mail-in program that will allow consumers to exchange any CD with XCP software for the same CD without copy protection and receive MP3 files of the same title. . . ."

Unfortunately for Sony BMG, the exchange program didn't end the issue. Texas Attorney General Greg Abbott sued Sony BMG under the state's 2005 spyware law. California and New York followed with class-action lawsuits. Soon after, law student Mark Lyon started a blog[8] to track Sony BMG XCP rootkit lawsuits. "I trusted Sony BMG when they asked to install a 'small program' on my computer," Lyon wrote on his blog. "Instead, they infected my computer with poorly written code, which even if it wasn't designed for a malicious purpose (like reporting my activities—something they expressly promised they were not going to do), opened me up to a number of computer viruses and security problems. This site exists to help others who have been harmed by Sony BMG and their XCP Content Protection." As of this writing, Sony has settled with 40 states, and Lyon has continued to cover all the action on his Sony Suit blog.

We will never know what would have happened if someone from Sony BMG had quickly jumped into the blogstorm, apologized, stated Sony's plan of action, and offered the exchange program immediately. Yes, I'm sure it would still have been a crisis situation for the music publisher, but I'm also certain that the negative effects would have been substantially reduced.

What's important for all organizations to take away from this incident is that it is critical to respond quickly to situations as they unfold on the web. Reacting quickly and honestly in the same forums where the discussions are taking place is essential. You may not be able to completely turn a negative situation around, but you will instantly be seen as a real person who gives a name and a personality to a large, seemingly uncaring organization. Just by

---

[8] sonysuit.com

participating, you will contribute to making the situation right. The web's power of linking should ensure that participants who see your posts on one forum or blog will link to them from other forums and blogs, so you don't have to worry about contributing to multiple places. What's important is first getting out there; after that, remember that authenticity and honesty are always paramount.

Your Best Customers Participate in Online Forums—So Should You

On the web, customers, stakeholders, and the media can immediately see what's on people's minds. There's never been so good an opportunity to monitor what's being said about you and your products than the one we have now. The Internet is like a massive focus group with uninhibited customers offering up their thoughts for free!

Tapping this resource is simple: You've got to monitor what's being said. And when an organization is the subject of heated discussions, particularly negative ones, it just feels weird if a representative of that organization doesn't jump in with a response. If the company is dark, not saying a thing online, participants start wondering, "What are they hiding?" Just having a presence on the blogs, forums, and chat rooms that your customers frequent shows that you care about the people who spend money with your organization. It is best not to wait for a crisis. You should participate as appropriate all the time. How can you afford not to become closer to your most vocal constituents?

Let's look at another example, but one with a much different outcome. It happened when Nikon introduced a new "prosumer" digital camera, the D200 model, which appeals to very advanced amateur photographers and professionals alike. Nikon launched the new model globally through specialty distributors and high-end camera stores frequented by these target buyers. But Nikon also offered the D200 outside the normal distribution channels by selling the model in big box stores such as Circuit City and Best Buy. The camera was a hot commodity when launched just prior to the holidays, and supply was constrained when it first hit the stores.

"The places where camera guys like me normally get Nikon gear were caught out because of a lack of supply," says Alan Scott, an experienced photographer and long-time Nikon customer. "People who preordered the

D200 or who were waiting for camera retailer sites to go live with an announcement of availability were gnashing their teeth wanting to get the camera."

Like many other photographers, Scott frequents popular online digital photography forums, including Nikonians: The Nikon User Community and DPR: Digital Photography Review. "The forums were active with lots of people complaining that they couldn't get the camera from their normal long-term suppliers but that the big box stores had them," Scott says. "Then a thread was started on Nikonians[9] and later picked up on DPR[10] that discussed how popular New York City photography supplier B&H Photo-Video, a trusted source with a knowledgeable staff that many professionals and high-end hobbyists go to, had taken orders but then were canceling them."

The first post, from ceo1939, said, "I ordered a D200 from B&H this afternoon about 4:30 Mountain Time. The charge was made against my credit card. An hour later I got an email that said they had a technical problem and the camera was actually not in stock, but they would hold my order and charge for it when they actually get in stock. I tried canceling the charge, and got an email back on how to handle a disputed charge. I will see what happens when I call them in the morning."

Many camera enthusiasts and customers of B&H were monitoring the thread at this point. "Within a few hours, several dozen posts appeared on the thread, and the tone had become critical of B&H, with people complaining that the company was purposely screwing them," Scott says. "Forum participants said that email notifications from B&H did not work and people who called in were getting cameras in front of those who had signed up for an alert system."

The B&H situation sounds a bit like the Sony BMG incident, doesn't it? In both cases, avid participants in specialty online forums sounded off about a company, its products, and its business practices. Both sets of threads occurred in little-known nooks of the web, far outside mainstream media channels and other typical places that PR people monitor for what's being said about their company and its products. But the B&H case is very different because a B&H employee was an active participant on the boards.

---

[9] nikonians.org

[10] forums.dpreview.com/forums

"Unfortunately as everyone who frequents this site knows, Nikon USA has been remarkably reluctant (diplomatic, eh?) to put this camera in retailers' hands," wrote Henry Posner of B&H Photo-Video, Inc. on the DPR thread. "The result in this particular case is that had we left the order open, we'd still be sitting on your money and would have been unable to fulfill the D200 order and it's reasonable to presume you'd be chafing to get your camera, which we'd have been (and are) unable to supply due to circumstances beyond our control. . . . We regret and apologize for having vexed you."

Unlike in the Sony BMG example, people at B&H had been monitoring the messages and were prepared to participate. "So in steps Henry Posner, who is with B&H," Scott says. "He came into the forum and said, basically, 'you're right, we screwed you,' but then explained what happened, apologized, and said that B&H will make it right. By acknowledging the issue, one guy with one post changed the whole tone of the thread and the reputation of B&H. After that, the posts changed to become incredibly positive."

Indeed, they were. "Henry's participation in various web forums is something I respect greatly," wrote BJNicholls on one thread. "I can't think of someone of power with any other business who engages in public discussion of store issues and products."

"I also admire his forthrightness," added N80. "He admits there have been some mistakes and that the situation has been hard to handle. However, he firmly denies the charges of lying and deceitfulness that have been flying around. And I absolutely believe him."

What happened at B&H was not a coincidence or a one-time situation. The message boards and online forums are a critical component of the company's marketing and communications strategy.

"I spend a great deal of time poking around in the forums," says Henry Posner, director of corporate communications for B&H Photo-Video Inc. "Being a part of the forums is really important and is actually in my job description. Because my background is in professional photography, as a person who has actually used the equipment we sell I have legitimacy in the forums." Before joining B&H in the mid-1990s, Posner worked for a company that provided photography services for colleges and high schools; he covered events such as basketball and football games.

Posner monitors about a dozen message boards and forums on a daily basis. "I try to find things about photography equipment or technique where I can make a meaningful contribution," he says. "We want to make certain that my credibility is maintained—that's the most important thing—so I don't go in and say something like 'that's right' just to get my name and the B&H name into a conversation. But if I see that there is a discussion that I can add value to, about equipment or a technique that I am familiar with, I will jump in."

B&H has a mail-order catalog, an e-commerce website, and a 35,000-square-foot retail store in Manhattan. "Our customer is anyone from the amateur up to the professional photographer working in Beirut who is running around with cameras bouncing on his hips while looking for a Wi-Fi connection to send images back to the bureau," he says. "I contribute to the forums when it is appropriate, but if anyone ever asks about where to buy something being discussed, I immediately take the conversation offline via email. I don't want to promote my company directly. The other conversations I look for are when people are talking about B&H itself. I often hold back and let others speak for me. Other people will often say positive things about B&H because I am so active in the forums. So if someone does jump in about B&H, I will thank them, and then I will address the issue directly."

Don't you wish your customers had been as understanding as the photography enthusiasts on these forums the last time your company screwed up? Well, as Henry Posner shows, if you actively participate in the online communities that your customers frequent, you will earn their sympathy and patience when things go wrong.

Your Space in the Forums

The last two examples were of companies that had discussions started about them on online forums. But how should a marketer interact? "Participation in forums is a must," says Robert Pearlman, editor of collectSPACE: The Source for Space History & Artifacts.[11] Pearlman started collectSPACE in 1999 because there wasn't a single site to serve collectors of space memorabilia and to preserve space history. "Before the Internet, there were space memorabilia collectors, but they were in pockets of communities in Germany and Japan, in Houston, and near the Kennedy Space Center in Florida," he says. "But there was no way for them to communicate with each other. The biggest impact is that collectSPACE has educated the market. We've brought the various pockets of collectors into one place."

---

[11] collectspace.com

The collectSPACE community has grown into a network of collectors around the world who share their knowledge of the pieces that they own. The site counts 100,000 registered users (about 5,000 actively post on the site) and reaches about 4.5 million readers monthly through syndication of its news articles and the approximately 375,000 unique readers who visit the site each month. Interestingly, collectSPACE also includes many people who worked in the early space program; they participate in the forums and talk about the history of the artifacts that they had a hand in building. Pearlman says many astronauts read the forums because they are able to get a sense of the market for the memorabilia that they may have amassed over the years and to find out what fellow astronauts are up to on the lectures and appearances front. Astronauts also use the forums to monitor the history of the space program and protect their legacy.

"In other areas of collecting, collectors and museums have been at odds," says Pearlman. "Museums looked at collectors as hoarders storing stuff in the basement, while their own mission was more altruistic: sharing with the public. And collectors looked at museums and said that they did a good job with major items like spacesuits and spacecraft but did a lousy job with literally the nuts and bolts except put them away in the archive. What collectSPACE does is allow museums to read what their 'competition' is doing and interact with collectors and ask their advice. Collectors have helped to plan exhibits and loaned items to the museums, and at the same time, museums were able to sell surplus items to collectors."

Pearlman sees a huge benefit to participating in the collectSPACE forums for dealers, manufacturers, and auction houses that specialize in space items. "By participating in the forums, dealers and manufacturers now know what collectors are interested in," he says. "Products can be developed based on what the current trends are in the market. Auction houses and dealers have been able to preview items to the market before a sale to gauge interest. In the case of unique items, you get instant feedback through a mini-market study."

As moderator of the collectSPACE forums, Pearlman has personally followed hundreds of thousands of posts and seen the good and the bad from space memorabilia dealers. "If there is a post that is not flattering to a business, someone from that business needs to have been monitoring the posts and respond as required," he says. "In discussion forums where people have a common bond, people feel that the forum is theirs. We see people who have 1,000 or even 5,000 posts, and they treat that as a badge of honor. People who represent businesses need to let the collectors know that you care enough about them to go to [their] turf instead of expecting them to come to yours."

As Pearlman advises and as the Sony BMG and B&H Photo-Video examples show, marketers must actively participate in the communities that matter for their markets. But you can't just stand on the virtual sidelines and post only when you have something for sale or comment about your products or services. The most successful companies come in and provide ideas and advice on a wide variety of subjects and topics in their field. They are full and active participants in the community. Then, when people complain or want specific product advice from a company, they trust the community member more. Active participation can pay off exponentially for companies who are treated as members of the community.

Wikis, Listservs, and Your Audience

Close cousins to the forums like Nikonians and collectSPACE include group email lists (often called listservs) and wikis. Just like forums, a listserv is a way that groups of like-minded people stay connected to one another. Typically, any member can post to the list, but instead of requiring people to go to a central place to read messages, a listserv sends messages out to the members of the group via email.

Lisa Solomon, Esq.[12] provides legal research and writing services to other attorneys on an outsourced basis. Solomon has been extremely involved in participating in listservs such as the Solosez[13] discussion list for solo attorneys, which is run by the American Bar Association. "The listserv has been important in the way that I develop my law practice. I am an active participant and try to always add value to the subjects that are being discussed. In my listserv signature is my web address. That is the place that I send people to show them what I do. I have writing samples on the site, and that's how they can check out what I do at their convenience. The participation has been great for meeting contacts and building business."

Wikis are websites that permit users to update, delete, or edit the content on the site. The most famous wiki is Wikipedia,[14] the free encyclopedia that anyone can edit, which has more than 23 million articles in some

---

[12] questionoflaw.net

[13] americanbar.org/groups/gpsolo/resources/solosez.html

[14] wikipedia.org

275 languages, all contributed by people like you and me. If you haven't done so already, you should hightail it over to Wikipedia and conduct searches on your organization name, important brand names, your CEO, and other notable executives and board members. The fact is that Wikipedia entries loom large in search engine rankings, and Wikipedia is in the top 10 most visited sites on the web.

When you find an entry about your company or brand, you should check it for accuracy. It's fair game to correct any inaccuracies (such as the number of employees in your company). But don't try to manipulate the entry. The Wikipedia community is quick to react when articles are edited to present a certain point of view. It is not uncommon to see an entry updated several times per day, and with larger organizations, the updates can be much more frequent. In fact, one of the pillars of the community is "All Wikipedia articles must be written from a neutral point of view, representing views fairly and without bias." So if your organization was party to a lawsuit that makes you look bad in some way and it's in Wikipedia, don't try to remove the reference.

Sometimes, it might be best to create a new article on Wikipedia. For some organizations, authoring something on a particular niche where you have expertise may have tremendous value. Make sure that you aren't promoting your company and its products or services, though; it needs to be an article of value to people researching the topic you know well. As a starting point, you might notice that there are articles in the area where you are knowledgeable and that those articles link to an empty Wikipedia page. Blue (or purple, if you have already visited them) links represent pages that do exist. Red links point to pages that don't yet have any content. If you see a bunch of red links indicating that an author expects new content to be added, and you have knowledge and expertise in that area, maybe it's time for you to create a page to fulfill a need. For example, a technology company might provide details on patents it holds that relate to products that already have Wikipedia entries.

Creating Your Own Wiki

It's entirely possible that for your organization's area of expertise, no appropriate forum, Listserv, or wiki has been established. Just like Robert Pearlman of collectSPACE, you may find an unfulfilled need in your marketplace to organize people and ideas into a single resource. A wiki could be just what the doctor ordered—and you can start it, gaining tremendous value for your organization as a result.

Consider Alacra, a company that creates online technology and services for financial institutions and professional service firms to find, package, and present business information. In the crowded field of professional information services, Alacra, a company of about 60 people, competes with much bigger players such as Thomson Reuters (60,000 employees) and Reed Elsevier (30,000 employees). An important part of Alacra's marketing and communications strategy has been its early forays into corporate blogs and corporate wikis.

Alacra and its CEO, Steve Goldstein, host AlacraWiki,[15] an open and collaborative resource for producers and consumers of business information. AlacraWiki brings together in-depth profiles of information sources, companies, and important people in the industry (and much more). The front page, which populates via RSS feeds, is filled with information and industry news from the premier analysts and trade publications. "We had amassed a tremendous amount of valuable information on publishers and databases through our content licensing efforts," Goldstein says. "We thought it would be useful to make this information available on the web, and a wiki was clearly the best format."

Goldstein was surprised that at the time AlacraWiki was launched, there was no directory of business information in the market. "We included reference data for the industry in a wiki form as a service to industry," he says. The wiki is a collaborative effort where anybody can create and update listings. To start the project, Goldstein hired a summer MBA student intern, who built the infrastructure and initial listings in just eight weeks. Although many people have contributed, some don't update their personal or company profiles. "It's strange that people don't go in and change it, because it's so easy," he says.

As someone who has created both a blog and a wiki, how would Goldstein compare the skill sets to create them? "To be successful at blogging, you need to have something to say," Goldstein says. "You need to have some communications skills to be successful. Over on the wiki side, you need to be an expert in something to get it populated to begin with, and then you need the resources to keep it up."

---

[15] alacrawiki.com

Social Networking Drives
Adagio Teas' Success

As social networks become more important for organizations of all kinds, the challenge becomes how to integrate them effectively. Adagio Teas,[16] a family-owned gourmet tea company founded in 1999, has used social networking to become the most popular online destination for tea enthusiasts. Social sharing and crowdsourced product creation aren't "bolted on" strategies at Adagio Teas. Unlike at most companies, social networking is a critical component for driving business.

I learned about Adagio Teas from my daughter, Allison. She's a loyal customer and eagerly shared with me how the company works. As of this writing, Adagio Teas sells a remarkable 24,242 blends of tea. The vast majority of blends are created by their customers either for their own enjoyment (think private blends) or as one that is sold to others on the site. Creating blends via crowdsourcing is a brilliant strategy for driving social interaction, because people are eager to share their creations on networks like Facebook, Twitter, and Tumblr.

"The idea of customer-created blends came from growing up in a Russian background," says Ilya Kreymerman, chief technology officer and member of the family that founded and runs Adagio Teas. "Tea was always something that was in the house, and when my mom and dad had company over, they would always drink this blend of tea that my mom made herself. So the idea of having people create these unique blends was second nature to us. We found a way that people can not only make it but also share with friends, the same way that my mom would share it when people came over. The idea is not just making it for yourself but making it for yourself *and* for a large community."

Avid tea connoisseurs can search the database for a perfect blend, or as with Amazon's bestseller list, browse teas based on popularity and customer reviews. That's another important social aspect: Like popular authors on Amazon, those who create delicious blends build a following with Adagio customers, driving sales with their ratings and reviews. If you like a blend, you can see what other blends that creator has made. Repeat customers can create a profile to keep track of teas they enjoy most, and they can also add teas they want to try.

---

[16] adagio.com

For example, the fourth-ranked ranked tea as I write this, Sherlock, is a blend by Cara McGee: "All at once exotic and mysterious and perhaps a little bit insane, with a lingering hint of smoke. Inspired by BBC's *Sherlock*, which I am in no way affiliated with. This is created purely for my own enjoyment. Ingredients: lapsang souchong, assam melody, oriental spice."

McGee uploaded a video where she talks about the blend. There are also customer reviews (187 as I write this) and social sharing tools that include Facebook (with 502 "likes"), Twitter, Tumblr, and Pinterest. The Sherlock blend is part of a theme that Adagio calls Fandom Signature Blends, which also include such teas as Avatar, Big Lebowski, Doctor Who, Harry Potter, and many more blends based on popular movies, TV shows, and books.

"A lot of what drives people to buy the tea is not really the tea itself, it's this story around the tea," Kreymerman says. "You take a pot of tea and infuse it with a character or TV show or video game and suddenly people have an attachment. You're piggybacking on their love for a specific character. Instead of it just being a cup a tea, it's now got all of this background and emotion baked in." And people are naturally eager to talk on Facebook, Twitter, and other social networks about tea that has a connection to the books, movies, and TV shows they love.

Another social aspect kicks in when customers add friends to their profile. If you log in to Adagio with a Gmail account, you can instantly find out which one of your contacts also has an Adagio Teas profile. Or if you're reading a review and like someone's taste in tea, you can friend that person.

With all the sharing going on with customers at Adagio, it's no surprise that the company itself is active on social networks. They have an excellent Tumblr blog[17] ("The official blog from the people behind Adagio"), and they are active on Twitter (@AdagioTeas, 15,000+ followers), on Facebook (30,000+ likes), and other social sites.

"People historically have spent a lot of money to advertise products," Kreymerman says. "But we never use traditional marketing, advertising, things like that because it's incredibly expensive. You're kind of shooting in the dark. I think the more interesting thing is to provide customers with value by putting the money towards a really interesting site or really interesting idea or making their experience better instead of just kind of directing them towards your store. We listen to the audience, and a lot of our good ideas come from listening to what people are talking about on Twitter

---

[17] adagioteas.tumblr.com

and Tumblr. And once in a while, we hear the same question coming up over and over again and realize that we have to address it."

And they really are active, using social networks to communicate with customers. The mistake made by so many other companies is just using social media like Twitter as a one-way broadcast advertising channel. For example, recently @AdagioTeas tweeted: "We are developing a wish list feature & would love feedback. Would you use it as a bookmark for yourself, or as a list to help guide others?" A follow-up tweet thanked customers for their suggestions, announced the launch of the wish list, and prompted further discussion.

People love this kind of interaction and happily talk up organizations that provide it. For example, @jamieworley tweeted: "It's so cool that @Adagio-Teas sends me twitter DMs to let me know where my tea shipment is!" And it is cool. I wish some of the companies I frequently do business with used Twitter DMs to communicate.

Over the Thanksgiving holiday, Allison made her own blend because she wanted to have interesting Christmas and holiday gifts for family and friends. The "Create a Blend" widget is really easy to use. Many people love mixing teas, and Adagio has made it fun and easy to mix different flavors to create a unique and tasty blend: You name your creation and choose the types of teas and the percentages of each. You then have an opportunity to create a custom label, either simple text or something much more elaborate.

Here social networking pops up yet again because you can upload a Facebook photo to be part of your custom label. Instead, Allison made a hand drawing for her label, which she scanned and saved as a JPEG and then imported into Adobe Photoshop. There she added text before uploading the image to the Adagio Teas app. Her scottea dog blend is "Just a cute jumpy Christmas blend of assam melody, hazelnut, and peppermint."

Another fun social aspect of Adagio Tea is that the creator of a custom tea earns points whenever a customer buys their blend. Points can be used to get discounted or free tea. This encourages social sharing by people who create blends—when their new blends are ready to be sold, many people will tweet about them, or post an image of the label with a link on Facebook, or make a Tumblr post talking about the blend. After all, it's in their best interest to do so.

By building social networking features into all aspects of the customer experience, Adagio teas drives business success. As customers talk about teas on social networks, fan their favorite blends, or even create their own to share with their friends, new people learn about the company. It sure beats traditional advertising to get the word out.

Social media sites are places where people congregate to discuss things that are important to them. Where are people discussing your industry and the products and services you offer? If that place already exists, you should monitor it and participate as appropriate. If it doesn't yet exist, consider starting a place for colleagues and customers to meet and revel in information that is important to your market. Now let's turn to blogs, another form of social media.

5 Blogs: Tapping Millions of Evangelists to Tell Your Story

Blogging is my front door. Since 2004, my blog[1] has been where I post my ideas, both big and small. There's no doubt that my blog is the most important marketing and PR tool I have as a marketing and PR speaker, writer, and advisor to companies. Even after seven years and close to a thousand blog posts, I'm always surprised at how effectively this tool helps me accomplish my goals.

My blog allows me to push ideas into the marketplace as I think of them, generating instant feedback. Sure, many blog posts just sit there with little feedback, few comments, and no results. But I learn from these failures, too; when my audience doesn't get excited about something, it's probably either a dumb idea or poorly explained. On the other hand, some posts have had truly phenomenal results, quite literally changing my business in the process. I'll admit that my ravings about the importance of my blog may sound over the top. But the truth is that blogging really has changed my life.

The first time I shared my ideas about the new rules of PR, in a post on my blog that included a link to an e-book I had written, the reaction was dramatic and swift. In the first week, thousands of people viewed the post. To date, more than a million people have seen the ideas, hundreds of bloggers have linked to them, and thousands of people have commented on them, on my blog and others'. That one blog post—and the resulting refinement of my ideas after receiving so much feedback, both positive and negative—created the opportunity to write the book you are now

---

[1] www.webinknow.com

reading. As I was writing the first edition of the book during much of 2006, the second edition in 2009, the third, in 2011 and this edition in 2013, I continually posted parts of it, which generated even more critical feedback—thousands of comments—that made the book much better.

Thanks to the power of search engines, my blog is also the most vital and effective way for people to find me. Every word of every post is indexed by Google, Bing, Yahoo!, and the other search engines, so when people look for information on the topics I write about, they find me. Journalists find me through my blog and quote me in newspaper and magazine articles *without my having to pitch them*. Conference organizers book me to speak at events as a result of reading my ideas on my blog. I've met many new virtual friends and created a powerful network of colleagues.

As I write and talk to these corporate audiences and other professionals about the power of blogging, many people want to know about the return on investment (ROI) of blogging. In particular, executives want to know, in dollars and cents, what the results will be. The bad news is that this information is difficult to quantify with any degree of certainty. For my small business, I determine ROI by asking people who contact me for the first time, "How did you learn about me?" That approach will be difficult for larger organizations with integrated marketing programs including blogs. The good news is that blogging most certainly generates returns for anyone who creates an interesting blog and posts regularly to it. So what about me? My blog has gotten my ideas out to tons of people who had never heard of me before. It has helped me get booked for important speaking gigs around the world. I've determined that about 25 percent of the new speaking business I've brought in during the past eight years has been either through the blog directly or from purchasers who cited the blog as important to their decision to hire me. Consider this: If I didn't have a blog, you literally wouldn't be reading these words, because I couldn't have been writing this book without it.

Will writing a blog change your life, too? I can't guarantee that. Blogging is not for everyone. But if you're like countless others, your blog will reap tremendous rewards, both for you personally and for your organization. Yes, the rewards may be financial. But your blog will most certainly serve you as a valuable creative outlet, perhaps a more important reward for you and your business.

The rest of this chapter describes more about blogs and blogging. You will meet other successful bloggers who have added value to their organizations and benefited themselves by blogging. I'll describe the basics of getting started with blogs, including what you should do first—monitor the blogosphere and comment on other people's blogs—before even beginning to write your own. The nitty-gritty stuff of starting a blog, what to write about, the technology you will need, and other details are found in Chapter 17.

Blogs, Blogging, and Bloggers

Weblogs (blogs) are a popular way to create content because the technology is such an easy and efficient way to get personal (or organizational) viewpoints out into the market. With easy-to-use blog software, anyone can create a professional-looking blog in just minutes. Most marketing and PR people monitor what's being said about their company, products, and executives on this important medium. A significant number of people are also blogging for marketing purposes, some with amazing success.

I have found writing this chapter to be a challenge because there is great variance in people's knowledge of blogs and blogging. I sometimes ask the audiences I present to, via a show of hands, "How many people read blogs?" I'm continually surprised that only about half read blogs. That's a ridiculously low percentage. There's never been an easier way to find out what the marketplace is thinking about you, your company, and your products! When I ask how many people are writing their own blogs, the number is usually less than 10 percent. While even the people who are currently reading and writing blogs have varying expertise in the blogosphere, there are significant misconceptions about blogs and blogging among those who don't read them at all. So with apologies in advance to readers who already understand them, I'd like to start with some basics.

A blog is just a website. But it's a special kind of site that is created and maintained by a person who is passionate about a subject and wants to tell the world about his or her area of expertise. A blog is almost always written by one person who has fire in the belly and wants to communicate with the world. There are also group blogs (written by several people) and even corporate blogs produced by a department or entire company (without individual personalities at all), but these are less common. The most popular form by far is the individual blog.

A blog is written using software that puts the most recent update, or post, at the top of the site (reverse chronological order). Posts are tagged to appear in selected information categories on the blog and often include identifiers about the content of the post to make it easy for people to find what they want on the blog and via search engines. Software for creating a blog functions essentially as an easy-to-use, personal *content management system* that allows bloggers to become authors without any HTML experience. If you can use Microsoft Word or buy a product online from Amazon, you have enough technical skills to blog! In fact, I often suggest that small companies and individual entrepreneurs create a blog rather than a standard website because a blog is easier to create for someone who lacks technical skills. As the lines between what is a blog and what isn't blur, today there are thousands of smaller companies, consultants, and professionals who have a blog but no regular website.

Many blogs allow readers to leave comments. But bloggers often reserve the right to remove inappropriate comments (spam or profanity, for example). Most bloggers tolerate negative comments on their blogs and don't remove them. I actually like some controversy on my blog because it can spark debate. Opinions that are different from mine on my blog are just fine! This might take some getting used to, especially for a traditional PR department that likes to control messaging. However, I strongly believe that comments from readers offering different viewpoints from the original post are actually a good thing on a blog, because they add credibility to your viewpoint by showing two sides of an issue and by highlighting that your readership is passionate enough to want to contribute to a debate on *your blog*. How cool is that?

A Blog (or Not a Blog)

Before we look at some examples, I'd like to comment for just a moment on the term *blog*. A blog is just a website written by someone who is passionate about a subject and wants to share that passion with the world. And as we've discussed here, it's also a terrific marketing tool.

However, the term sometimes carries negative connotations among people who have heard of blogs but do not make an effort to read them regularly. These folks assume that blogs are frivolous and without value. As I mentioned, when I ask people if they read blogs, the show of hands tells me that half the audience does. I am certain that this number is wrong. Many more of them, I'm convinced, do read blogs but don't realize what kind of content they are reading when they land on one. They usually find their way there via a Google search or a link suggested by a friend, colleague, or family member, but since they didn't seek out blog content intentionally, it doesn't occur to them that that's what they've found.

What's more, too many people are still hung up with outdated, artificial demarcations between "mainstream media" and "blogs," arguing that one is more legitimate. This leads to flawed marketing and PR strategic decisions.

This is especially true of many (but not all) public relations agencies whose reps do their clients a disservice by focusing on one form of media over another.

That's nonsense. The distinctions have nearly disappeared, and smart individuals and firms have already eliminated this prejudice.

Whenever this subject pops up, I'm prompted to ask a series of questions that I hope illustrate the changes afoot:

- What is a blog?
- What is an online news site, like *Huffington Post*?
- What do we call it when a print newspaper like the *New York Times* or a television network like the BBC publishes an online news site?
- What do we call it when readers can post comments on an online story from a magazine?
- What do we call it when a reporter for the BBC maintains a blog?

Guess what? It's all just media, real-time media in this case.

The *Huffington Post* is technically a blog. It is written on the Blogger platform, so there is no significant difference between when I write an article for the *Huffington Post* or when I write a post on my personal blog, *Web Ink Now* (no difference but the size of the audience, that is).

The *Huffington Post* is a blog. But it's one of the most important news sites on the web, with an Alexa ranking as I write this of 77. That ranking places the blog in the top 100 most popular of all sites of any kind in the world.

The *Huffington Post* is a blog. But it won the Pulitzer Prize in the category of national reporting for senior military correspondent David Wood's 10-part series about wounded veterans, "Beyond the Battlefield."

The BBC is mainstream media, but readers can comment on stories. Thousands do, just like on *Huffington Post*.

The New Yorker is a magazine, but people can share links to stories within the magazine's website, using widgets for Facebook, Twitter, LinkedIn, Pinterest, Google+, and Tumblr.

The difference between mainstream media and the blogosphere has blurred, and this blurring has important implications for your business. When your buyers search Google or another search engine for information related to your business, they don't really care if the top results come from a "news site" like the BBC, a "blog" like the *Huffington Post*, or your own blog or content-rich website. So you need to eliminate the bias.

When buyers ask a question on social media, they are happy when someone sends a valuable link to information on the web. They don't scrutinize what's recommended to them and dismiss the blog content and only read newspaper and magazine articles. They're happy for an article that educates and entertains, wherever it comes from.

The best marketing and PR strategies must include creating your own content, including text, video, and images. It should also include strategies for getting noticed by important voices, so they write about you. And getting noticed comes back to the content you create.

Content is content, no matter what it is called. If you are creating valuable information to market your business, don't let someone's anxiety with the term *blog* hold you back.

If you find in your company that you're encountering resistance to starting one, perhaps you shouldn't call it a blog at all. Instead, you could speak with your managers about starting a regularly updated information site or creating ongoing content for your buyers in order to help drive sales. I'd say this renaming could even apply to the links from your main site to your blog. Rather than a link on your home page to "Our Blog," you could link to the name of the blog (without using the actual word) or to "Our Industry Commentary."

Content is content, no matter what it is called. If you are creating valuable information to market your business, don't let the term *blog* hold you back.

Understanding Blogs in the World of the Web

Blogs are independent, web-based journals containing opinions about anything and everything. *However, blogs are often misperceived by people who don't read them.* Journalists as well as public relations and marketing professionals are quick to dismiss the importance of blogs because they often insist on comparing blogs to magazines and newspapers, with which they are comfortable. But the blogger's usual focus of promoting a single point of view is dramatically different from the journalist's goal of providing a balanced perspective. In my experience, blogs are deemed bad or wrong only by people who do not read them regularly. In journalism school and on their first beat assignments when they begin their careers, aspiring reporters and editors are taught that stories are developed through research and interviews with knowledgeable sources. Journalists are told that they can't express their own opinions directly but instead need to find experts and data to support their views. The journalist's craft demands fairness and balance.

Blogs are very different. Blogging provides experts and wannabes with an easy way to make their voices heard in the web-based marketplace of ideas. Companies that ignore independent product reviews and blog discussions about service quality are living dangerously. Organizations that don't have their own authentic and human blog voices are increasingly seen as suspect by many people who pay attention to what's being said on blogs. But as millions of independent voices shout and whisper all over the Internet, certain mainstream media and PR people still maintain rigid defensive postures, dismissing the diverse opinions emerging from the web's main streets and roads less traveled.

Many people prefer to box blogs into their existing worldview rather than understand blogs' and bloggers' unique roles on the web. Often people who don't understand these roles simply react with a cry of "Not real journalism!" But bloggers never claimed to be real journalists; unfortunately, many people continue to think of the web as a sprawling online newspaper, and this mentality justifies their need to (negatively) compare blogging to what journalists and PR people do. But the metaphor of the web as a newspaper is inaccurate on many levels, particularly when you are trying to understand blogs. It is better to think of the web as a huge city teeming with individuals, and blogs as the sounds of independent voices, just like those of the street-corner soapbox preacher or that friend of yours who always recommends the best books.

Consider the now well-known September 2004 example of how blogs exerted tremendous influence on an issue but were dismissed by people who didn't understand bloggers' role in information dissemination. The controversy, dubbed the memogate or Rathergate case, involved documents critical of President George W. Bush's service in the U.S. National Guard. In a *60 Minutes Wednesday* broadcast aired by CBS on September 8, 2004, the documents were presented as authentic but had not been properly authenticated by CBS. The situation unfolded just hours later on the Free Republic news forum site, where Buckhead posted a message and said the memos Dan Rather used as the basis of his story appeared typographically impossible.[2] Buckhead's post was followed the next morning by entries to blogs including Little Green Footballs[3] and PowerLine[4] that raised questions about the documents' authenticity. For days, Rather dug in while CBS dismissed the bloggers as a bunch of geeks in pajamas typing away in the dead of night. Ignoring bloggers cost Rather his job. Had he taken the bloggers seriously and immediately investigated the documents, perhaps he, too, would have very quickly concluded that they were fake. In that case, an explanation and apology might have resulted in the affair blowing over. But dismissing bloggers and their opinions was clearly a mistake. That was years ago. Although bloggers have become more influential since then, there is still a great deal of similarly dismissive behavior going on inside media companies and corporate PR departments.

Okay, so bloggers aren't journalists. Many people in traditional media companies and corporate communications positions trip up because they misunderstand bloggers' actual role in information dissemination. Consider it from the web-as-a-city perspective: The woman next to you at the bar may not be a journalist, but she sure knows something, and you can choose to believe her or not.

Should you believe everything you read on blogs? Hell, no! That's akin to believing everything you hear on the street or in a bar. Thinking of the web as a city, rather than a newspaper, and of bloggers as individual citizen voices provides implications for all net citizens. Consider the source (don't trust strangers), and find out if the information comes from the government, a newspaper, a big corporation, someone with an agenda, or some banker's ex-wife who is just dying to give you $20 million.

Blogs and bloggers are now important and valuable sources of information, not unlike your next-door neighbor. Take them with a grain of salt, but ignore them at your peril. Just remember that nobody ever said your neighbor was the same as a newspaper. The challenge for marketers and PR people is to make sense of the voices out there (and to incorporate their ideas into our own). Organizations have the power to become

---

[2] freerepublic.com/focus/f-news/1210662/posts?page=47#47

[3] littlegreenfootballs.com/weblog/?entry=12526

[4] powerlineblog.com

tremendously rich and successful by harnessing the millions of conversations found in web city.

The Four Uses of Blogs for Marketing and PR

As you get started with blogs and blogging, you should think about four different ways to use them:

1. To easily monitor what millions of people are saying about you, the market you sell into, your organization, and its products.
2. To participate in those conversations by commenting on other people's blogs.
3. To work with bloggers who write about your industry, company, or products.
4. To begin to shape those conversations by creating and writing your own blog.

There are good reasons for jumping into the blog world using these four steps. First, by monitoring what people are saying about the marketplace you sell into as well as your company and products, you get a sense of the important bloggers, their online voices, and blog etiquette. It is quite important to understand the unwritten rules of blogging, and the best way to do that is to read blogs. Next, you can begin to leave comments on the blogs that are important for your industry or marketplace. That starts you on the way to being known to other bloggers and allows you to present your point of view before you create your own blog. Many organizations cultivate powerful relationships with the bloggers who write about their industry. You should work with bloggers so they know as much as possible about what you do. Finally, when you feel comfortable with blogs and bloggers, you can take the plunge by creating your own blog.

In my experience, corporate PR departments' concerns about blogs always focus on issues of actually writing them. But if you've monitored blogs and know that there are, say, a dozen influential bloggers writing about your market and that those blogs have thousands of loyal readers, you can show a PR person the importance of simply monitoring blogs. Some of the more popular blogs have readerships that are larger than that of the daily newspaper of a major city. PR people care about the readership of the

Boston Globe, right? Then they should care about a blog that has a similar number of readers. If you become known within your organization as an expert in monitoring blogs, it is a much smaller leap to gaining permission to create your own.

Monitor Blogs—Your Organization's Reputation Depends on It

"Organizations use blogs to measure what's going on with their stakeholders and to understand corporate reputation," says Glenn Fannick, a text-mining and media measurement expert at Dow Jones. "Reputation management is important, and media measurement is a key part of what PR people do. Companies are already measuring what's going on in the media; now they need to also measure what's going on with blogs."

Text-mining technologies extract content from millions of blogs so you can read what people are saying; in a more sophisticated use, they also allow for measurement of trends. "You can count massive numbers of blogs and look for words and phrases and see what's being said as a whole," Fannick says. "You really need to rely on technology because of the massive volumes of blogs and blog posts out there. There is an unprecedented amount of unsolicited comments and market intelligence available on blogs. It is a unique way to tap into the mind of the marketplace. It is an interesting and fertile ground."

As a starting point, all marketing and PR people need to go to blog search engines and run a query on their organization's name, the names of their products and services, and other important words and phrases such as executives' names. Technorati[5] is an excellent blog search engine. It allows you to instantly see if any of the more than *100 million* blogs that it tracks have any information you need to know. Google Blog Search is another popular blog search engine. I can't imagine an organization that wouldn't find value in knowing what's being said about them or their products or the industry or market they sell into on blogs.

More sophisticated marketers then start to analyze trends. Is your product getting more or fewer blog mentions than your nearest competitor's product? Are the blog posts about your company positive or negative

---

[5] technorati.com

in tone? How does that compare with the ratios from six months ago? "It's naive to think that what your stakeholders think is not important," Fannick says. "Opinions are offered on blogs, and understanding the sum of those opinions is very important. You can't just make decisions on what you think your products do; you need to make decisions on the perceptions of what people are actually doing with your products. Seeing the blogosphere as a source of market intelligence is now vital for companies."

So become an expert in what's being said about your organization on blogs. There's never been a better time for marketers to get a true feel for what's going on in the real world. Bloggers provide instantaneous and unsolicited comments on your products, and this free information is just waiting for you to tap into it.

Comment on Blogs to Get Your Viewpoint Out There

Once you've got a sense of who is out there blogging about your company, its products, and the industry and marketplace you work in, it's time to think about posting comments. Most blogs have a feature that allows anyone to comment on individual posts. Leaving comments on someone's blog is one of the best ways to participate in a conversation. You have the opportunity to offer your viewpoint, adding to the ongoing discussion. However, it takes an understanding of blogs and blogging etiquette to pull it off without sounding like a corporate shill. The key is to focus on what the blog post says and comment on that. As appropriate, you can point to your blog (if you have one) or your website as your contact information, but make sure that in addition to contact information you provide some content of relevant value.

One of the currencies of social media is that when you participate, people find out who you are. When you leave a comment on someone else's blog post, you can link to your profile on the web. All the blogging tools have a place where you can leave a virtual calling card, your own web URL where people who read your comment (especially the blogger) can find out who you are and perhaps contact you.

If you have a blog, then you're all set—just include your blog URL in that comment field. However, most people don't have a blog. What the heck do you do then?

I've seen many solutions, most very limiting:

- Leave no URL (in which case nobody can find you).
- Leave a LinkedIn or Facebook profile URL (this has limitations, because people must ask to be your friend to see your full profile).
- Leave a company home page (this shows your affiliation, but nothing about you personally).

I've found an alternative solution that works very well. Create a public Google profile[6] (or your Google Plus URL if you are on G+) for yourself and then use that as the URL that you point people to when you leave a comment on a blog, or join a social networking site like Twitter. You can include a photo, a bio, and contact details. It's really cool—and it's free.

I chose to make my Google profile[7] simple because I want people to visit my site or my blog. You can make yours much more detailed if you wish (see the examples on the sign-up page). Once you've got a public profile, use it as your calling card all over the web. Here's just one example: Link to your Google profile from your Amazon review page so the authors of the books you review can see who you are.

Work with the Bloggers Who Talk about You

On U.S. Election Day 2012, the Pew Internet & American Life Project found that 22 percent of registered voters let others know how they voted on a social networking site. Social media platforms have also become a notable venue for people trying to convince their friends to vote. For example, 30 percent of registered voters were encouraged by family or friends via posts on social media to vote for Democrat Barack Obama or Republican Mitt Romney. And, 20 percent of registered voters encouraged others to vote by posting on a social networking site such as Facebook or Twitter. The large numbers of socially active voters are always looking to share content from their candidate of choice, which is why blog posts from the candidates are so valuable.

---

[6] profiles.google.com/me

[7] google.com/profiles/davidmeermanscott

In the case of Barack Obama, his campaign had put a focus on content creation and social media way back before he even declared himself a candidate the first time around. By Election Day 2008, an amazing 25 percent of Obama supporters were already directly linked to him through social media, including blogs, Facebook, Twitter, and other social sites, according to the *Nation*. Putting aside politics and just considering the election from a marketing standpoint, I am absolutely convinced that Obama won the 2008 election, and was reelected in 2012, because he was the candidate who most strongly and authentically embraced social media.

Kevin Flynn, who worked on the Obama campaign's New Media Blogging Team, was part of a Chicago-based core group of online campaigners. "I was part of the blogging team, and in the midst of the new media brain trust," he says. "I ended up working on the social media efforts for 15 states. Each state had their own blog, which had localized content, and I built contacts with people in each state who sent me stories, photos, and other information for the blogs. People were excited to have someone in the organization who wanted to help, so they all fed me great content. Once they saw their photos on the national campaign pages, they got even more excited."

During the campaign, Flynn was responsible for editing and creating posts for a collection of state blogs that included Alaska, Arizona, Georgia, Hawaii, Kansas, and Texas. "The Obama candidacy was exciting for his supporters and those of us working in the campaign," Flynn says. "The technology is easy. If you provide people with the technology tools and there is excitement, then people will make it successful."

The Obama campaign marketed itself in many more ways than just through social media. But the use of television, direct mail, door-to-door outreach, and rallies have been used for decades and are subject to limitations. "There is no way to talk back with traditional marketing like radio and TV," Flynn says. "With blogging, it creates a conversation and the campaign gets feedback. If there is interest in a topic, then the campaign can change quickly. People can get involved because it is two-way instead of just one direction. You can grow when there is a dialogue."

Prior to working on the Obama campaign, Flynn had worked in the Chicago financial markets, so he has an ideal perspective to offer advice to corporations on blogging and social media. "Don't be afraid of change," he says. "Don't be afraid to hear things that are uncomfortable, because only by hearing things will you be able to adjust and grow. In this rapidly changing world, you need to listen; otherwise you won't be able to survive."

The staff and volunteers from the Obama campaign worked very closely with the bloggers who cover politics and provided them with valuable information that helped them to write better posts. While some enlightened organizations do focus on influencing important bloggers by reaching out to them, most have a policy of ignoring bloggers, even as they spend a great deal of effort attempting to cultivate relationships with members of the mainstream media. This is a mistake. Bloggers are important voices. Just ask the Obama campaign—bloggers helped elect a president of the United States.

The Obama campaign example shows that making a concerted effort to integrate other bloggers' content into your own works very well. Although this example is from politics, similar strategies for engaging and influencing other bloggers can work for almost any organization. Another organization that's boldly working with bloggers is the New York Islanders professional ice hockey team. The team created what they call the Islanders Blog Box, a program that provides bloggers with press credentials for games. The program was among the first of its kind for a major professional sports team. Each season, about a dozen bloggers are chosen to receive credentials, and the team links to their blogs from its site.[8]

Bloggers Love Interesting Experiences

Many organizations have had success setting up blogger days, where influential people in their industry get the chance to spend all or part of a day with the company. In fact, any citizen journalist should be invited to attend, including those who have a video series or podcast show. On blogger days, guests are given information about new product releases, treated to lunch with employees, and perhaps given an opportunity to meet with the CEO or other executives.

For example, Christopher Barger, the director of global social media at General Motors, organized an opportunity for bloggers and other influential people to test-drive the not-yet-released Chevy Volt electric car at the South by Southwest conference. This event resulted in hundreds of blog posts and thousands of tweets.

Or consider the U.S. Marine Corps' Marine Week, held at various locations throughout the year. I attended one in Boston where bloggers and members of the media were given an opportunity to take a 20-minute

---

[8] islanders.nhl.com/club/page.htm?id=43149

flight in a V-22 Osprey tilt-rotor aircraft. The flight originated at Hanscom Air Force Base in Bedford, Massachusetts, went out into suburban Boston, flew over downtown, and returned. Unlike on commercial aircraft, we were encouraged to use our wireless mobile devices throughout the flight. It was very satisfying to live tweet while flying. I and many other participants blogged about the flight, generating awareness for the Marines.

If you don't have a hot toy to give people rides in, you can still organize a dinner for bloggers to meet with executives at your company. Or perhaps you can invite a small group of them to a special webinar for the exclusive announcement of a new product offering. These outreach programs are critical to providing bloggers with the information and sense of connection that will help them tell your story for you.

How to Reach Bloggers around the World

Global technology PR agency Text 100 examined the communications preferences of bloggers across the globe. Their web-based survey was designed to clarify bloggers' relationships with PR people and corporations. Some of the findings in the survey of 449 bloggers from 21 countries are worth noting as you contemplate how you will engage with bloggers. The good news is that more than 90 percent of the bloggers surveyed welcome contact from representatives of companies in the area that they write about. However, the way that you approach those bloggers is important.

"Bloggers are united in their desire for distinctive content, particularly around new product developments and reviews, feedback on content posted on their blog, and interviews with key people," says Jeremy Woolf, global social media lead for Text 100. "Photographs are the most frequently used form of supplied content, followed by charts and graphs, and video."

However, Woolf says the study reveals that the bad habits of the PR profession don't work in trying to pitch bloggers. "PR professionals are failing to read the blogs and truly understand their target bloggers' communities," he says. "They seem to expect bloggers to post corporate material, demonstrating a lack of understanding of the medium and the very reason why bloggers blog."

There's no doubt that the vast majority of bloggers welcome contact from organizations. But to be successful, company representatives need to treat bloggers as individuals and to provide them with valuable information that complements the work they're already doing on their blogs. Don't just blindly send them corporate press releases, which are ineffective at best and may even diminish your organization's reputation with the people you're trying to reach out to.

Do You Allow Employees to Send Email? How about Letting Them Blog?

Chapter 17 presents everything you'll need to know to start your own blog. If you already know that you are ready, feel free to jump ahead to learn about how to decide what to blog about, what software you'll need, how to find your voice, and other important aspects. If you're still considering a blog for yourself or your organization, you might be hesitant because of fears that blogging isn't right for your organization.

As I work with companies to help develop a blog strategy, I see much consternation within organizations about the issue of allowing people to blog (or not) and allowing them to post comments on other people's blogs (or not). It's been fascinating to both observe and participate in the debate about blogs in the enterprise. Just like the hand-wringing over personal computers entering the workplace in the 1980s, and also echoing the web and email debates of the 1990s, company executives seem to be getting their collective knickers in a twist about blogs these days. Remember when executives believed email might expose a corporation to its secrets being revealed to the outside world? Do you remember when only so-called important employees were given email addresses? How about when people worried about employees freely using the public Internet and all of its (*gasp!*) unverified information?

It's the same debate all over again today with blogs and other social media. On one side of the corporate fence, the legal eagles are worried about secrets being revealed by their employees while creating content or commenting on blogs. And on the other, there's the feeling that much of the information being created today is not to be trusted. Corporate nannies want to make certain that their naive charges don't get into trouble in the big scary world of information.

Well, we're talking about people here. Employees do silly things. They send inappropriate email (and blog posts), and they believe some of the things on TV news. This debate should be centered on people, not technology. As the examples of previous technology waves should show us, attempting to block the technology isn't the answer.

So my recommendation to organizations is simple. I'd suggest implementing corporate policies saying such things as employees can't sexually harass anyone, that they can't reveal secrets, that they can't use inside information to trade stock or influence prices, and that they shouldn't talk ill of the competition *in any way or via any media*. The guidelines should include email, delivering a speech, writing a blog, commenting on blogs (and online forums and chat rooms), and other forms of communication. Rather than focus on putting guidelines on blogs and other social media like Facebook and Twitter (the technology), it is better to focus on guiding the way people behave. However, as always, check with your own legal advisors if you have concerns.

Some organizations take a creative approach to blogging by saying that all blogs are personal and the opinions expressed are of the blogger, not the organization. That seems like a good attitude to me. What I disagree with is putting in place draconian command-and-control measures saying either that employees cannot blog (or submit comments) or that they must pass all blog posts through the corporate communications people before posting. Freely published blogs are an important part of business and should be encouraged by forward-thinking organizations.

Not Another Junky Blog

Tania Venn is director of PR at 1–800-GOT-JUNK?, the largest full-service professional junk removal company in the world. She oversees a team that creates content with a focus on reaching customers who may not think that they need a junk removal service. "Once they hear about what junk removal could do for them and how it could impact their lives, they become interested in our service," she says.

Venn and her colleagues work to identify the kind of information that would be valuable for buyers as they create content for the 1–800-GOT-JUNK? Blog, Not Another Junky Blog.[9] They then use their Facebook page and Twitter feed (@1800GOTJUNK) to let their followers know about new posts.

---

[9] blog.1800gotjunk.com

"We think about what's relevant," she says. "That could be tips and suggestions for people on getting their space back. It could be about de-cluttering. We also focus on environmental sustainability: what happens to the stuff we haul away and creative ways to reuse junk."

They also create timely content (I'll talk more about this technique in Chapter 23 about Newsjacking). "When the holidays are coming up, we'll post about making space to have your in-laws over and making room for new things you might get as gifts," Venn says. "And with New Year's, everyone has resolutions. We know that the top 10 New Year's resolutions include 'getting organized' and 'simplifying.' We also look at what's trending. For example, there is a trend called 'trashion,' where people make fashion out of trash, so we'll write about that."

Because it is written for buyers, Not Another Junky Blog focuses on people's real junk problems, rather than egocentric advertising messages. "We know there's an emotional component to getting rid of the stuff that you have," Venn says. "Our customers have an emotional release and an amazing magical feeling of 'that crap is not there anymore' when their junk is taken away. They don't realize until it's gone how good it feels. We hear it time and time and time again from our customers. So we build that into our blog because it's what customers are looking for." The 1–800-GOT-JUNK? business is a franchise model, so the content they create also appeals to franchisees who learn about clever ways to market in their local area.

When you focus on buyers' problems as you create content, you'll often write about something that doesn't relate to what your organization actually does. This is true for 1–800-GOT-JUNK?

"We might talk about how to set up your own garage sale," Venn says. "That wouldn't get us business necessarily, but we've got the experience and we can share that with people. We know that readers may not be able to afford our service right now, but some day they will be able to. They'll have learned something from us that can help them out: something that can help them get rid of some of their junk, but they can do it themselves."

Venn knows that the content published in Not Another Junky Blog and shared on Facebook and Twitter is working because she uses analytics to measure success. "I look at how many people view our blog on a daily basis and a weekly basis," she says. Venn also pays attention to any content that becomes particularly popular with readers. "We've learned that we need to create content in order to be recognized on the web. It's a way of engaging with customers. It's a great way to get information directly to whom you want to reach rather than going through the media."

The Power of Blogs

It is remarkable what a smart individual with passion can do with a blog. People have blogged their way to dream jobs (and book deals) through the ideas they express. Rock bands have built loyal followings and gained record contracts. Political candidates have broken out of the pack. And companies have competed effectively, even against much larger, better-funded players.

"You are what you publish," says Steve Goldstein, CEO of Alacra, whom we met in Chapter 4, discussing AlacraWiki. "It is better to have a reputation than no reputation. Certainly AlacraBlog[10] is valuable for us as a way to get our name out there."

Goldstein was an early CEO blogger, launching AlacraBlog in March 2004. "We didn't know what would happen, but we wanted to try it," he says. "The competitors are really big. By blogging I am able to put a face on [our] company."

Goldstein uses his blog platform as a way to communicate with his clients, prospects, and partners. He uses the blog to tell his constituents things quickly and informally. "I can highlight interesting aspects of the company, like employees and partners, that wouldn't go into a more formal press release," he says. "Internally the blog is important, too. We have a London office, so I use the blog to communicate to employees there."

It's fascinating that there are so few bloggers in the publishing industry, perhaps because publishers are cautious about giving content away for free, or maybe because large publishers feel threatened by blogs. But by starting a blog early and keeping the information flowing, Goldstein has positioned Alacra ahead of many information companies hundreds of times the size of Alacra. "Many publishers are still unsure about blogging, and very few are doing it," Goldstein says.

Get Started Today

There's no doubt that every organization should be monitoring blogs to find out what people are saying about them. I find it fascinating that most of the

---

[10] alacrablog.com

time when I mention a company or product on my blog, I do not get any sort of response from that organization. However, maybe 30 percent of the time, I'll get a comment on my blog from someone at that company or a personal email. These are the 30 percent of companies that monitor the blogosphere and react to what's being said. You should be doing this, too, if you're not already.

It's also clear to me that in most industries and product categories, early bloggers develop a reputation as being innovative. There are still opportunities for first-mover advantage in many blog categories. Once you're comfortable with reading and commenting on blogs, get out there and start your own! Chapter 17 contains all the information you'll need to get going.

6 Audio and Video Drive Action

A udio and video on the web are not new. Clips have been available on websites since the early days. But until recently, neither audio nor video was used much online because the content was difficult to locate and impossible to browse, and there was no easy way to get regular updates. And since much audio and video content was lengthy—as much as an hour or more—and people had no idea what was in these files without actually watching or listening to them, not many did.

The migration of audio and video from online backwaters to the forefront with valuable content happened because of sites like YouTube, Vimeo, and iTunes, with easy ways for people to view and listen. In addition, high-speed Internet connections became the norm, and the technology to create and upload audio and video became simple enough that anybody can do it (including you).

Create Goodwill with Customers

Videos use emotion to tell stories in ways that most other forms of marketing cannot. That's a technique that Tim Washer, senior manager of social media at Cisco Systems, uses all the time. The videos Tim creates are used to market to Cisco's service provider customers—large telecommunications companies like AT&T, Verizon, and Telstra. He uses both humor and drama in a series called "The Network Effect: Telecom's Socioeconomic Impact," which markets the Cisco business in a subtle way.

"One way to create goodwill with service providers is to help their customers understand what service providers do . . . to make our customers heroes to their customers," Washer says.

A five-minute "mini-documentary" in the video series titled *Developing Commerce in Africa: Phone Company In A Box*[1] has nearly 150,000 views on YouTube. To look at how telecom infrastructure works elsewhere in the developing world, Washer went to Costa Rica and conducted interviews, which he edited into a story. "We spoke to people who were service providers there and some folks in the government. So it has a global feel to it," he says.

The video shows how telecom companies in developing countries, such as Telifonica in Guatemala, work within local infrastructure. "We're very careful to make sure we had a visually interesting story to create awareness of the telecom network. One of the challenges that service providers have right now is that they're providing the network for all these apps to be downloaded on your smart phone and for all this content to be purchased over the cable network. But service providers get very little attention from consumers."

As true thought leadership content, the video never mentions Cisco products or features Cisco employees. "That's what I think really separates it from most marketing," Washer says. "We were careful not to include anybody from our company in the video. If you put someone from the company in there, particularly marketers and execs, they're so trained to fit our speaking points in the interview. The objective was to make sure this is an interesting story that will connect with people. When you're creating entertainment, you want the viewer to get lost in the story and just forget that they're being marketed to."

While there are no Cisco products or employees in the videos, Cisco generates tremendous value: The videos are hosted on the Cisco YouTube channel, promoted on Cisco websites and social networks, and sent to customers by Cisco salespeople.

And excellent videos are frequently shared by others. Such was the case with Cisco's *Developing Commerce in Africa: Phone Company In A Box*. A *New York Times* reporter found the video and talked about it. The video launch on the Cisco Service Provider blog helped them win "best corporate blog" from *BtoB Magazine*. And the president of ShortsTV liked the video and broadcast

---

[1] youtube.com/watch?v=WHaQY2MlHV8

it on his TV network. These results certainly helped Cisco create positive buzz from their service provider customer base.

Many organizations create video to showcase their expertise and provide valuable information to buyers in an easy-to-understand medium. The interview format is very popular because it's so easy to interview guests and post the resulting video. Other common forms of online video include humor-based approaches (frequently used to try to garner many views and go viral), product overviews, and executive speeches. An added benefit of producing video for your organization is that the media, bloggers, and others in a position to talk you up tend to like to watch video to get story ideas. See Chapter 19 for more information on video and details about how to create your own.

What University Should I Attend?

Many marketers are reluctant to focus on video because they don't see how a video on YouTube or on their company website will lead to a sale. As I was writing this section of the book, I received an email from a student who attends the University of Pennsylvania. She explained that she chose to apply to the University of Pennsylvania because she saw a Penn video on YouTube[2] as she was researching universities and she fell in love with the school without even having a chance to visit. In the video, singer and five-time Grammy Award winner John Legend explains why he has a deep affection for the University of Pennsylvania, his alma mater.

This story is certainly not unique. People are looking for the products and services that you offer right now. They go to Google and the other search engines, and they ask their friends for advice. Frequently, what they find is a video. Will you be in it?

Many organizations encourage their customers or fans to produce videos for them. These customer-generated video efforts often take the form of contests and can be highly successful, especially for a product or service that has a visual impact. For example, Nalgene bottles are virtually indestructible. If you go to YouTube, you'll find hundreds of videos where people try to break them in creative ways, such as running them over with a lawnmower, throwing them out of buildings, and freezing water in them and then hitting them with a hammer. For the makers of the Nalgene

---

[2] youtube.com/watch?v=gNUiBIlMk1s

bottle, this is a valuable phenomenon, since the company does not have any part in the videos.

The Best Job in the World

I'm often asked: "How do I market a commodity product?" People seem to think that if their product is similar to others, then the new rules of marketing do not apply to them and the only way to sell is a function of lowest price or best distribution. If you've read this far in the book, you ought to be able to predict my answer: Create interesting information, and people will find it, share your ideas, and tell your stories. Yes, even if you market a commodity.

Sandy beaches in warm and sunny locations are a commodity product. This may come as a complete shock to people in tourism marketing, but it's true. The traditional approach of showing white beach sand with footprints near lovely blue water and a bikini or two just doesn't cut it because that's what everybody does. How can you stand out?

Tourism Queensland[3] created a fantastic video contest called The Best Job in the World.[4] The winner was chosen as Caretaker of the Islands of the Great Barrier Reef. The position had a few minor tasks, but the main thing was to use social media to talk up the islands. The job of blogging and posting videos paid 150,000 Australian dollars for a six-month gig. The contest required each applicant to post a one-minute video explaining why he or she should be chosen as caretaker of Hamilton Island on the Great Barrier Reef. More than 30,000 people applied, and the videos were seen by millions. In addition, thousands of bloggers and media outlets (magazines, radio, television, and newspapers) wrote and broadcast about The Best Job in the World, producing even more buzz about not only the contest but also the location as a tourist destination.

Tourism Queensland created a huge phenomenon. When the contest was in full swing, I took a poll of the groups I visit as speaker. By a show of hands, I asked if they had heard of The Best Job in the World. In Washington, DC, 20 percent of the room had (the lowest percentage). In Tartu, Estonia, a whopping 60 percent had (the highest). The average, over several thousand people in six countries, was more than 30 percent. Amazing! Imagine if

---

[3] queenslandholidays.com.au
[4] youtube.com/user/islandreefjob

30 percent of the world had heard of your product through videos people had created for you.

How did Queensland, Australia, get so much attention? I've been to Queensland and the Great Barrier Reef twice. Yes, it is beautiful. But so are many other sandy, beachy, sparkly, bikini-friendly places I've been: Koh Samui, Santorini, Barbados, Puerto Vallarta, and on and on. The answer is simple: Tourism Queensland found a way to get people to share their ideas and tell their stories.

The Best Job in the World was conceived and created by the Brisbane, Australia–based advertising agency, CumminsNitro. Tourism Queensland also worked with Quinn & Co.,[5] a New York public relations firm that handled media relations. I spoke to John Frazier and Melissa Braverman, part of the Quinn & Co. team who worked on the Best Job in the World, to help understand this amazing success.

John Frazier says that the job announcement broke in Australia, and by breakfast time in London, the Associated Press was interviewing Tourism Queensland's UK director for a broadcast package that turned up later that day on the morning shows in the United States. Within two days, there were thousands of media pickups. Tourism Queensland set a goal to get 400,000 new visitors to their website over the course of the one-year campaign. They blew past that in about 30 hours and had a million hits on the second day.

"We learned that if you hit the sweet spot of the right story at the right time, it will travel like a tsunami all the way around the globe," says Melissa Braverman. "Traditional media (a Reuters exclusive) broke the story, which immediately went viral because it was a chance to have the coolest job in the world at a time when everyone else was getting laid off."

Because so many people saw the announcement about the job opening on both mainstream media and blogs, video applications for the job started to come in at a rapid clip. And because people were hearing about it all over the world, applicants represented many countries. Of course, all that attention also sparked interest and awareness of Queensland, Australia, as a tourist destination.

"You can't reheat a soufflé," says Frazier. "There were quickly a number of copycat campaigns that didn't quite take off in as big a way. My best advice is to try to develop an idea that resonates authentically in the lives of real

---

[5] quinnandco.com

people and then find a way to mount it across as many platforms (such as traditional media, YouTube, Twitter, Facebook) as possible."

Ben Southall from the United Kingdom was selected as the ideal candidate and won the job. But the real winner was Tourism Queensland. Frazier estimates there were 1,100 television placements of the story. The video contest for The Best Job in the World was a huge success in drawing attention to the islands of Australia's Great Barrier Reef. At one point, the official Island Reef Job website was getting 4,000 hits per *second*. According to Peter Lawlor, Queensland's state tourism minister, preliminary results from a tourism campaign promoting Tropical North Queensland to U.S. tourists drew a 34 percent increase in flight bookings to Cairns, gateway to the area. "The campaign's aim was to increase international visitation to Cairns and the Great Barrier Reef and to raise awareness of the region's unique experiences and attractions. The results so far are outstanding, especially considering current economic difficulties."

Have Fun with Your Videos

Is there anything more tediously boring than the air safety video on commercial airliners? Well, It doesn't have to be that way. Video is a great format to use humor, especially when you take on a normally boring topic that the members of your buyer personas all know about. That's what Air New Zealand did with a safety video produced with the New Zealand All Blacks rugby team for use on the airline's Boeing 737 aircraft. The video, Air New Zealand—Crazy about Rugby—Safety Video was released on YouTube and quickly generated nearly a million views. That's right: a million views for an airline safety video. So how did they do it?

In the video, the players, coaches, and commentators of the New Zealand All Blacks rugby team serve as actors, along with Air New Zealand staff. The plane is full of fans in crazy getups. There are even credits at the end. I watched it a bunch of times because I kept missing bits and pieces of the hilarious but often subtle humor. Air New Zealand also posted a companion behind-the-scenes video showing how they created the piece.

The timing of the video's release was significant. The All Blacks had just beaten the South Africa Springboks, 29 to 22. In the riveting final five minutes, they scored two tries to claim the Tri Nations crown. So the entire country was thinking about rugby!

Sometimes when I talk about using humor, people who work in serious firms like business-to-business companies, nonprofits, and government agencies insist that they can't use humor. In particular, I'd like to challenge the assumption that business-to-business (B2B) marketing must be dreadfully boring.

I think this attitude came about because B2B marketers hear the word *business* (twice) and think "I am marketing to a business." This results in an overly serious tone. After all, marketing to, say, technology companies is different from consumer marketing, right?

Wrong.

The B2B marketers seem to forget that what all marketers need to do is communicate to *people*. People want to do business with people, and the B2B companies that understand that develop a following.

National Instruments is a B2B supplier of measurement and automation equipment used by engineers and scientists. The tried-and-true marketing strategy of companies like National Instruments is to focus on feeds-and-speeds, technical data sheets, specs, and so on. We're talking about the engineering community, right?

Yes, but while National Instruments does provide product specs, they also realize that their buyers are human beings. "We've always had the motto, both internally and externally, that it's okay to have fun," says John M. Graff, VP of marketing and customer operations at National Instruments. That fun-loving attitude has produced many ways to communicate with the technical audience that buys NI products.

For example, I'm a fan of a video blog produced by Todd Sierer, an engineer at National Instruments. It's called *An Engineering Mind*, and it is highly effective. In one episode, he talks about the meaning of the word *Marketecture* in a humorous way. It's the sort of thing that an engineer would get a kick out of. Thus, it does exactly what good marketing should do—reach buyers.

"We first debuted these videos two years ago at our annual user conference held in Austin, Texas, where over 3,000 engineers and scientists gather to see and discuss latest technologies for measurement and automation," Graff says. "In addition to the usual technical product demonstrations, we also try to have some fun, including inviting an engineer from the Spike TV show *Deadliest Warriors* to the stage. We've found that our audience greatly appreciates this approach to communication, since they get plenty of examples of the drab, speeds-and-feeds technical fire hose. We believe it's greatly enhanced our reputation."

Are you a B2B marketer? Are you treating your buyers like human beings? Are you having some fun? Really, it's okay to have some fun. I dare you.

Audio Content Delivery through Podcasting

Moving now to the audio-only side of the spectrum, note that the transformation from static audio downloads to radio station-like podcasts, which are much more valuable to listeners (and also more valuable as marketing vehicles for organizations), occurred because of two developments. The first was the ability to add audio feeds and notifications to RSS. This enables listeners who subscribe to an audio feed to download new updates soon after they are released. When audio content was liberated from the need for one large download and went instead to being offered as a series of continuous audio clips, the concept of shows took off. Hosts modeled their shows on radio, producing content on specific subjects catering to distinct audiences. But the podcasting business model is very different from broadcast radio. Radio spectrums can support only a finite number of stations, and radio signals have limited geographic range. To support the technical infrastructure of radio, broadcasters need large audiences and lots of advertising to pay the bills (or donors, in the case of public radio). Contrast that with Internet audio podcasting, which is essentially free (except for minimal hosting fees and some cheap equipment). A podcast show reaches a potentially worldwide audience, allowing anyone to create shows and listen to them.

The second major development was the availability of those podcast feeds through iTunes. Now people can simply subscribe to a feed (usually at no cost), and then every time they plug their mobile device into their computer, the new shows from the feeds they subscribe to automatically download. People who commute and listen in the car or on the train, or those who work out while listening, suddenly have access to regularly updated shows from the myriad niches that they specifically choose. With podcasting, people instantly liberate themselves from the tyranny of mainstream, hit-driven broadcast radio and can listen to shows based on their specific interests.

Perhaps we should back up for just a moment. The term *podcasting* confuses some people. A podcast is simply audio content connected to an RSS feed. The medium does not specially require iPods, although that's how the word was derived. You can listen to a podcast on any MP3 player or directly from your computer—no iPod required.

Now marketers have a tool to efficiently create and deliver audio content to people who want to listen. Marketers can easily develop a show that targets their buyer personas and can thus regularly deliver updated content that is welcome and useful to the audience. By appealing to a niche market and delivering audio that people have chosen to hear, an organization is seen as a thought leader and is first choice for listeners looking to make a purchase.

Putting Marketing Back in Musicians' Control

Music is a classic example of a long-tail business. Before the web came along, bands that didn't have a major label behind them couldn't hope to get national or global attention. The best they could do was establish a local audience in a city or region, or perhaps with a definable market such as northeastern U.S. college students. Enter podcasting. Now any band or DJ with some simple and easy-to-use equipment can set up as a radio station and get instant global distribution via iTunes and other distribution services.

George L. Smyth hosts the Eclectic Mix podcast,[6] where he challenges listeners to open their minds to new and diverse music and at the same time promotes bands he likes. The banner of his site even has a definition of *eclectic* to make sure people understand his approach: choosing what appears to be the best from diverse sources, systems, or styles.

"On each show, I select an artist and spotlight their music," Smyth says. "I play literally anything from classical to punk. My interest in music goes back to my college days, when I would copy records to tape and trade with my friends. I had lost track of music for a while, but recently I've found that there's really great music out there, and I can share it with many more people than with the tapes."

Smyth is evangelical in his description of how podcasting has changed the face of music. "Podcasting of music has been a real success with the under-25 crowd," he says. "Podcasting has allowed people to hear the music of groups that are good but perhaps don't have a big label behind them. In the past there

---

[6] eclecticmix.com

was no choice, but now there is a choice. Many artists will tell you that they just want people to hear the music. If you do listen, maybe you'll like it and want to spend money on tickets and perhaps a download of music from iTunes. Many bands don't make much money from CDs, so they really want people to go to the shows, which is where the big money is for the smaller bands."

Smyth is careful of copyrights and permissions in his podcasts and uses only podsafe music (music that the artist has cleared and has said it is permissible to podcast). The more famous bands typically don't allow podcasting (or to be more precise, their record labels don't). But many indie acts embrace podcasting and people like Smyth who promote their music via podcasts. "Uncle Seth is an example of a group that has made it easy for podcasters like me to work with them," Smyth says. "Uncle Seth is an indie band, but they cross genres, and I like to play them."

"Podcasters are a different breed; they're like you and me," says Jay Moonah, a Toronto-based musician and songwriter whose many music projects include Uncle Seth. "TV and commercial radio and MTV-type people work and talk from on high. Podcasting is different. It's neat that we've made fans out of some of these podcasters, such as George Smyth of Eclectic Mix. It's fun when they play our music, and then if I email them, it is great to start a conversation." Moonah says that indie bands like Uncle Seth that took the lead with podcasting have benefited greatly through wider distribution, which generates new fans.

Editorial note to music fans: Uncle Seth's single, an upbeat cover of Joni Mitchell's classic song, "Both Sides, Now" (available at iTunes), is a killer.

"Podcasting has become a real part of the social networking thing," Moonah says. "From a technical aspect, you could do podcasting a long time ago. But for us, the social aspect is really neat; bands and other organizations combine the music and the community and mix them together. For example, there is a community of Canadian Jam bands[7] where we've met a lot of friends. Like other online communities, it has a real-world community associated with it."

As Moonah has honed his expertise with podcasting and musician websites, he's developed a side business working with bands, labels, and other musicians on podcasting strategy. "Especially in Canada, it's difficult making a living as a musician," he says. "My thing of combining the businesses into a big circle of music and consulting and podcasting really works well for me.

---

[7] jambands.ca

"I like people to understand that podcasting has so many uses," Moonah continues. "It is a legitimate thing, not a toy for kids. So the advice I have for managers and label people is to not jump into your own podcast until you listen to other podcasts. Find podcasts that you like and you think might play you, and submit your music to them to get going. Then think about what you want to do if you want to make your own podcast. The people who make it work are those who understand it. As a band, you can compete with radio via podcasts because you can get onto several podcasts, and then people will hear you several times, just like a radio rotation."

Podcasting: More Than Just Music

Smyth's and Moonah's advice about podcasting is important for organizations, not just musicians, that want to reach buyers directly. For content that is best delivered via audio or for buyers who prefer to listen to content, podcasting is obviously essential. For example, many politicians and churches podcast so that supporters can keep up with speeches and sermons when they can't hear them live. You'll learn more about podcasting, including tips for setting up your own podcast, in Chapter 19.

As a component of a larger content-marketing strategy, podcasting is also an increasingly important part of the marketing mix. For example, customer service departments increasingly deliver how-to podcast series to keep users of their products informed. Companies that market to people who are on the road often (such as traveling salespeople) and have downtime in cars or on airplanes have had success reaching people with entertaining podcasts. For many organizations, podcasting for marketing purposes is not an either-or decision. Instead, podcasting coexists with blogging, a great website, e-books, and other online marketing tools and programs in a cohesive marketing strategy.

Grammar Girl Podcast

Mignon Fogarty, creator of the Grammar Girl podcast and founder of the Quick and Dirty Tips podcast network, has been podcasting since 2006. Grammar Girl[8] provides short, friendly tips to improve writing. Covering the grammar rules and word choice guidelines that can confound even the

---

[8] grammar.quickanddirtytips.com

best writers, Grammar Girl makes complex grammar questions simple. I should know. I never know when I should use *whom*, so I avoid it altogether. However, this is exactly the sort of grammar problem the podcast solves.

"I get an overwhelming amount of feedback from my audience," Fogarty says. "I had to hire a part-time assistant to help field my messages because they were taking all my time. I get a lot of grammar questions, which I try to answer; a lot of 'I love you' messages; and a lot of people disagreeing with my recommendations. Grammar can get pretty contentious, and people absolutely love it (in a gotcha kind of way) when I make a mistake or typo."

Creating a podcast show is a great way to get your information into the market. Instead of hyping your products and services, an informational show brands you as someone worthy of doing business with. In Fogarty's case, her sound ideas lead people to want to purchase her book, *Grammar Girl's Quick and Dirty Tips for Better Writing*. The free podcast drives her book sales.

"The fan interaction is definitely different from off-line marketing," Fogarty says. "I feel weird even calling the people fans because they feel more like friends with the constant messages that go back and forth. (Someone on Facebook recently said I am 'the most helpful person he doesn't know.') The immediacy of the feedback is also different from off-line marketing. I hear within 24 hours (usually faster) if something I'm doing is working or not. If I post a link or a contest on Twitter, I can usually tell within five minutes whether it's getting traction or not."

When Fogarty was ready to release her book, the podcast and her participation in other social networking sites like Twitter and Facebook allowed her to launch the book to her existing fan base. "When I went out on my book tour, the crowds were much bigger than expected, and I believe it is at least in part because of all the groundwork I laid on social networks for over a year before the book came out," she says. "During the first three or four stops on my book tour, bookstores ran out of books. In Atlanta, they ran out of books before I even arrived. A lot of the people who came out were people I had connected with on Twitter or Facebook, and I had posted messages about where I was going to be to both of those services multiple times."

The Grammar Girl podcasts have now been downloaded more than *20 million* times, and Fogarty has dispensed grammar tips on *Oprah* and appeared on the pages of the *New York Times*, the *Wall Street Journal*, and *USA Today*. *Grammar Girl's Quick and Dirty Tips for Better Writing* is a *New York Times* bestseller. "Having an established network of people is really valuable when you're launching something new," Fogarty says.

Podcasting and online video are great ways to connect with an audience and develop a following who will be eager to buy your products. Chapter 19 provides details on how to start a video or podcast series of your own.

7 The New Rules of News Releases

G uess what? Press releases have never been exclusively for the press.

My first job in the mid-1980s was on a Wall Street trading desk. Every day, I would come to work and watch the Dow Jones Telerate and Reuters screens as they displayed specialized financial data, economic information, and stock prices. The screens also displayed newsfeeds, and within these newsfeeds were press releases. For decades, financial market professionals have had access to company press releases distributed through BusinessWire, PR Newswire, and other electronic press release distribution services. And they weren't just for publicly traded corporations; any company's release would appear in trading rooms within seconds.

I distinctly remember traders intently watching the newswires for any signs of market-moving events. Often the headline of a press release would cause frenzy: "Did you see? IBM is acquiring a software company!" "It's on the wire; Boeing just got a 20-plane order from Singapore Airlines!" For years, markets often moved and stock prices rose and fell based on the raw press release content issued directly by companies, *not* on the news stories written minutes or hours later by reporters from newswire outlets like Reuters and Dow Jones (and later Bloomberg).

Press releases have also been available to professionals working within corporations, government agencies, and law firms, all of which have had access to raw press releases through services like those from NewsEdge, Dow Jones, and LexisNexis. These services have been delivering press releases to all kinds of professionals for competitive intelligence, research, discovery, and other purposes for decades.

Of course, since about 1995, the wide availability of the web has meant that press releases have been available for free to anyone with an Internet connection and web browser.

> Millions of people read press releases directly, unfiltered by the media. You need to be speaking directly to them!

As I tell this story to PR pros, I hear cries of "Hang on! We disagree! The role of public relations and the purpose of the press release as a tool are about communicating with the *media*." For an example of this thinking, look to Steve Rubel, one of the most influential PR bloggers in the world. He responded to my ideas about press releases by writing a post on his blog, titled "Direct to Consumer Press Releases Suck."

Let's take a look at the objections of traditional PR folks. According to the Public Relations Society of America (PRSA),[1] "Public relations is the professional discipline that ethically fosters mutually beneficial relationships among social entities." In 1988, the governing body of the PRSA—its Assembly—formally adopted a definition of public relations that has become the most accepted and widely used: "Public relations helps an organization and its publics adapt mutually to each other." Nowhere does this description mention the media. PR is about reaching your audience.

I think many PR professionals have a fear of the unknown. They don't understand how to communicate directly with consumers and want to live in the past, when there was no choice but to use the media as a mouthpiece. I also think there's a widely held view about the purity of the press release as a tool for the press. PR professionals don't want to know that hundreds of millions of people have the power to read their releases directly. It's easier to imagine a closed audience of a dozen reporters. But this argument is based on fear, not the facts; there is no good reason why organizations shouldn't communicate directly with their audiences, without a media filter, via releases.

---

[1] prsa.org

Obviously, the first word of the term *press release* throws off some people, particularly PR professionals. On my blog and on other sites, a semantic debate played out. The consensus of the dozens of professional communicators who weighed in was to call releases aimed at consumers *news releases*. This sounds good to me, so from this point on, I'll refer to direct-to-consumer releases as *news releases*.

News Releases in a Web World

The media have been disintermediated. The web has changed the rules. Buyers read your news releases directly, and you need to be speaking their language. Today, savvy marketing and PR professionals use news releases to reach buyers directly. As I mentioned in Chapter 1, this is not to suggest that media relations are no longer important; mainstream media and the trade press must be part of an overall communications strategy. In some markets, mainstream media and the trade press remain *critically* important, and of course, the media still derive some content from news releases. But your primary audience is no longer just a handful of journalists. Your audience is millions of people with Internet connections and access to search engines and RSS readers. Here, then, are the rules of this new direct-to-consumer medium.

The New Rules of News Releases

- Don't just send news releases when big news is happening; find good reasons to send them all the time.
- Instead of targeting a handful of journalists, create news releases that appeal directly to your buyers.
- Write releases that are replete with the keyword-rich language used by your buyers.
- Include offers that compel consumers to respond to your release in some way.
- Place links in releases to deliver potential customers to landing pages on your website.
- Link to related content on your site such as videos, blog posts, or e-books.
- Optimize news release delivery for searching and browsing.

- Add social media tags for Technorati, Digg, StumbleUpon, and Delicious so that your release can be found.
- Point people to your news releases from your social sites like Twitter, Facebook, and LinkedIn.
- Drive people into the sales process with news releases.

You need to fundamentally change the way you use news releases. If you follow these specific strategies for leveraging this once-lowly medium by turning it into one of the most important direct marketing tools at your disposal, you will drive buyers straight to your company's products and services at precisely the time that they are ready to buy.

If They Find You, They Will Come

Several years ago, I was preparing a keynote speech called "Shorten Your Sales Cycle: Marketing Programs That Deliver More Revenue Faster" for the Software Marketing Perspectives Conference & Expo. To be honest, I was kind of procrastinating. Facing a blank PowerPoint file, I decided to hit Google in search of inspiration.

I entered the phrase "accelerate sales cycle" to see if there was anything interesting I could use in my presentation. The highest-ranked listings for this phrase were from WebEx, a company that provides online collaboration services. What was most interesting to me was that the links pointed to *news releases* on the WebEx site. That's right; at the top of the Google search results was a news release about a new WebEx product, and right there in the first sentence of the news release was the phrase I was looking for: "accelerate sales cycle."

> **WebEx Launches WebEx Sales Center: Leader Expands**
> **Suite of Real-Time Collaborative Applications**
> *Enhance Team Selling Process, Engage Prospects*
> *throughout Sales Cycle, and Enable Managers*
> *to Monitor and Measure Web Sales Operations*
>
> *SAN JOSE, Calif.*—WebEx Communications, Inc. (NASDAQ: WEBX), the leading provider of on-demand collaborative applications, today launched WebEx Sales Center, a new service that helps companies accelerate sales cycles, increase win rates, and close more deals by leveraging online sales calls. . . .

Then I went over to Google News[2] and checked out the same phrase. Sure enough, WebEx also had the number-one listing on Google's news search with a very recent news release: *Application Integration Industry Leader Optimizes Marketing and Sales Processes with WebEx Application Suite*. The news release, about a WebEx customer, had been sent through PR Newswire[3] and had a direct web link to the WebEx site to provide additional information. WebEx also provided links in some news releases directly to free trial offers of their services. How cool is that?

"That is exactly our strategy," says Colin Smith, director of public relations for WebEx. "Google and news keywords have really transformed the news release as a distribution vehicle. Our thinking is that, especially for companies that have an end-user appeal, news releases are a great channel."

It's certainly no accident that I found WebEx; I was searching on a phrase that Smith had optimized for search. His research had shown that buyers of the communications services that WebEx provides search on the phrase "accelerate sales cycle" (and also many others). So when I searched on that phrase, WebEx was at the top of the listings.

As a result, WebEx provided me with an excellent (and real) example of a company that had optimized the content of news releases to include relevant terms such as the one I was looking for. And WebEx has greatly benefited from their efforts. In addition to the consumers they already reach online, they've added to their audience by getting the information to someone who tells other people about it (me!). I've used this example in speeches before well over 10,000 marketing and web content professionals and executive audiences, and it was also downloaded more than a million times as part of my *New Rules of PR* e-book. And now you're reading it here, too.

"People are saying that press releases are dead," Smith says. "But that's not true for direct-to-consumer news releases." As Smith has developed his news release strategy to reach buyers directly, he has had to refine his writing and PR skills for this evolving, but very much alive, medium. "I learned the very structured *AP Style Guide* way to write releases," he says. "But that's changed as keywords and phrases have suddenly become important and the scale and reach of the Internet have opened up end users as a channel."

Smith doesn't let keywords dominate how he writes, but he tries to be very aware of keywords and phrases and to insert key phrases, especially, into

---

[2] news.google.com

[3] prnewswire.com

releases whenever he can. "We don't think that a single keyword works, but phrases are great," he says. "If people are doing a specific search, or one with company names that are in our release, then the goal is that they will find our news release."

Driving Buyers into the Sales Process

Smith is careful to include product information in the end-user-focused news releases he crafts for WebEx. "We try to think about what's important to people," he says. "We put free trial offers in the releases that are about the product." About 80 percent of the releases that WebEx puts out are product or customer related. "WebEx is a great mix of real end-user stories," he says. "People get why you need web meetings, so it is easy to tell the story using news releases."

Because the web meeting story is compelling even for those who don't know the product category, Smith also looks for ways to create a viral marketing buzz. For example, he pays attention to major events in the news where WebEx online collaboration would be useful.[4] "We donated free service for limited use during the time that Boston traffic was snarled as a result of the Big Dig tunnel closures. We did the same thing for the New York City transit strike." Smith knows that people are likely to consider WebEx services during this kind of unusual situation. Offering the service for free often creates loyal future users.

Direct-to-consumer news releases are an important component of the marketing mix at WebEx. "We do track metrics, and we can see how many people are going from the release to the free trial," Smith says. The numbers are significant. But with such success, there's also a danger. "We don't want to abuse the news release channel," Smith says, explaining that the company also has a media-relations strategy, of which news releases are a part. "We want the news releases to be interesting for journalists but also to provide consumers with things to do, such as get the free trial."

WebEx is successful in using news releases to appeal to both the journalists who write (and speak) about WebEx products and services, and also the consumers who are searching for what WebEx has to offer. WebEx and thousands of other organizations like it prove that a direct-to-consumer

---

[4] webexone.com/go/bigdig

news release strategy can coexist within an organization that cares about media relations.

Since an earlier edition of this book was released, WebEx was acquired by Cisco Systems, Inc., a major networking and communications technology company.

Reach Your Buyers Directly

Under the old rules, the only way to get published was to have your news release picked up by the media.

We've come a long way. The web has turned all kinds of companies, nonprofits, political campaigns, individuals, and even churches and rock bands into just-in-time and just-right publishers. As publishers, these organizations create news releases that deliver useful information directly onto the screens of their buyers—no press involved!

8 Going Viral: The Web Helps Audiences Catch the Fever

As I write this, the number of YouTube views of Korean pop star Psy's video "Gangnam Style" has reached well over 1 billion.[1] That makes it the most-watched video of all time. The catchy song, wacky horse dance, and interesting scene locations combined to make it a hit all over the world. When I ask in my talks if participants have seen the video, more than half always have, and it doesn't matter what country I'm in. I've asked people in Belize, Egypt, Bulgaria, the UK, and India about "Gangnam Style." As soon as I do, smiles emerge.

Even parodies of Psy's video have achieved huge view counts. There are hundreds of them: character-based parodies by Sponge Bob (2.2 million views) and the Oregon Duck (6.6 million); location-based parodies like "London Style" (5 million views) and "Minnesota Style" (1 million); and organization-based parodies like "Bay Area Wedding Music" (2 million), MIT University (5 million), and "Inbound Style"[2] from the folks at HubSpot (nearly a quarter million views—and if you add to the total you'll catch a cameo from yours truly).

For marketers, one of the coolest things about the web is that when an idea takes off, it can propel a brand or company to fame and fortune for free. Whatever you call it—viral, buzz, or word-of-mouse marketing—having other people tell your story drives action. Many viral phenomena start

---

[1] youtube.com/watch?v=9bZkp7q19f0
[2] http://blog.hubspot.com/blog/tabid/6307/bid/33599/HubSpot-Releases-Gangnam-Style-Parody-Inbound-Style-MUSIC-VIDEO.aspx

innocently: Somebody creates a funny video clip, a cartoon, or a story to amuse friends. Then one person sends it to another, and that person sends it to yet another, and on and on. The creator might have expected to reach at most a few dozen friends, but the result is something more—way more. One of the first examples I remember was the dancing baby from the mid-1990s. It was grainy and low-tech, but it was cool, and it spread like crazy. Instead of reaching a few hundred friends and colleagues, dancing baby struck a nerve and reached millions.

Minty-Fresh Explosive Marketing

Amazingly, if you toss a Mentos candy into a bottle of Diet Coke, you get a marketing explosion. More tangibly, the mint-cola reaction triggers a geyser that sprays 10 feet or more. This phenomenon was popularized in video experiments produced by Fritz Grobe and Stephen Voltz[3] on their eepybird site. After their initial success, Grobe and Voltz made a video of an extreme experiment to answer the following question: "What happens when you combine 200 liters of Diet Coke and over 500 Mentos mints?" Web audiences were mesmerized by the result—it's insane—and caused a classic viral phenomenon. In only three weeks, 4 million people viewed the video. Hundreds of bloggers wrote about it. Then mainstream media jumped in, with Grobe and Voltz appearing on *Late Night with David Letterman* and *The Today Show*.

Imagine the excitement in Mentos marketing offices when the videos took off online—millions of Mentos exposures at no cost (more on this later). The price tag to get results like that from traditional marketing might have totaled tens, if not hundreds, of millions of dollars.

The challenge for marketers is to harness the amazing power of viral. There are people who will tell you that it is possible to create a viral campaign, and there are even agencies that specialize in the area. But when organizations set out to go viral, the vast majority of campaigns fail. Worse, some companies set up fake viral campaigns where people who are employed by the company are in some way compensated to write about a product. The web is hyperefficient at collective investigative reporting and smoking out trickery, so these campaigns rarely succeed and may even cause great harm to reputations. Often a corporate approach is some gimmicky game or

---

[3] http://eepybird.com

contest that just feels forced and advertisement-like. It is virtually impossible to create a web-marketing program that is guaranteed to go viral. A huge amount of luck and timing are necessary. A sort of homemade feel seems to work, while slick and polished usually doesn't. For example, the Numa Numa Dance that was so popular several years ago was about as homemade as you can get—just a guy with a web camera on his computer—and it helped to popularize the song and sell a bunch of downloads.

Of course, it's not just crazy dancing that goes viral. The formula is a combination of some great (and free) web content (a video, a blog entry, or an e-book) that is groundbreaking or amazing or hilarious or involves a celebrity, plus a network of people to light the fire, and all with links that make it very easy to share. While many organizations plan viral marketing campaigns to spread the word about their products or services, don't forget that something may go viral that you didn't start (like Mentos and Diet Coke), and it may show you or your products in either a positive or negative light. You need to be monitoring the web for your organization and brand names so you are alerted quickly regarding what people are talking about. And if a positive viral explosion that you didn't initiate begins, don't just hang on for the ride—push it along!

Monitoring the Blogosphere for Viral Eruptions

Every day, on blogs, podcasts, video, and Twitter, people promote and pan products. Consumers tell good and bad tales in which products and services play a starring role. Sadly, most companies are clueless about what's going on with the social web. At a minimum, marketing professionals need to know immediately when their brand names or executives are mentioned (refer back to the discussion about monitoring blogs in Chapter 5). Beyond mention-counting, analysis is important. What are the significant trends in words and phrases currently popular, as they relate to your organization, product, and industry? On the day that the Diet Coke and Mentos experiments went viral, there was a tenfold spike in the number of blog posts mentioning Mentos. If you follow the word *Mentos*, you'd want to know what was going on, so you could either respond to the crisis or leverage the positive development. At the least, you should learn the reason for the spike and alert company managers; when the *Wall Street Journal* calls for comment, "Huh?" is not the savviest response.

Over at Alexa,[4] a service that measures the reach and popularity of websites, the comparisons between the viral eepybird site created by Grobe and Voltz to showcase their videos and the official Mentos site[5] are remarkable. Marketers use Alexa to figure out what sites are hot and use that information to make their own sites better. The three-month average website ranking among all sites on the web after the release of the video was 282,677 for the official Mentos site, while eepybird was 8,877.

"The whole Mentos geyser phenomenon seems to bubble up every few years," says Pete Healy, vice president of marketing for Perfetti Van Melle USA, makers of Mentos. "But this was the first time it came around that there was an infrastructure where people could post videos online. We contacted the two guys at eepybird and said that we really liked the way the Mentos brand was represented. We had recently conducted a meeting about our brand personality, and we decided that if our brand was a person, it would be like Adam Sandler—quirky, tongue-in-cheek, and fun. Because the eepybird video had those qualities, we were delighted."

Healy recognized that he had an opportunity and worked to push the viral excitement forward. First, he linked to the video from the official Mentos site. Then he offered Grobe and Voltz the company's support. "When they appeared on *Late Night with David Letterman* and *The Today Show*, we were there with our 'Mentos ride,' a classic convertible with Mentos branding, giving away samples on the street to add support." Soon after, Healy decided that there might be others who would want to create their own video, so the company launched a Mentos geyser video contest. The top prize was 1,000 iTunes downloads and a year's supply of Mentos, 320 rolls, and according to Healy, more than 100 videos were submitted and posted to the site, which was viewed nearly a million times. (Incidentally, note the wisdom of choosing iTunes downloads as a prize; the folks at Mentos reasonably suspected that the kinds of media-savvy people who would submit entry videos are likely to be more interested in free music downloads than in traditional prizes like shopping sprees or free trips. This contributes to the authentic feel of Mentos's attempts to further spread this viral phenomenon.)

"The power to influence what a brand means to others is something that poses a dilemma, but also an opportunity, for the owners of a brand," says

---

[4] alexa.com

[5] us.mentos.com

Healy. "It has always been true that what a brand means is determined by a consumer, the end user. Now there is a feedback loop that didn't exist before. The Internet is like the town plaza or the town square. For any company that is marketing a brand, the first thing is to be genuine in communicating what the brand is about, the personality of the brand. If we had pretended that the Mentos brand is more than it is, then we would have gotten shot down."

Interestingly, while Healy supported and helped drive the viral aspects of the videos, marketers at Coca-Cola tried to distance the Diet Coke brand from the phenomenon. "When the Mentos and Diet Coke video became big, Coca-Cola took a few shots from the market, because they felt that the eepybird site didn't fit the Diet Coke brand. They took hits from bloggers," Healy says. "As long as we keep in mind that we are just a candy manufacturer, creators of a small pleasure, we can work with interesting things that might happen to our brands on the web."

Healy did an excellent job of pushing the Mentos and Diet Coke buzz without getting in the way by being too much of a corporate nanny. Too often, corporate communications people at large companies distance themselves from what's going on in the real world of blogs, YouTube, Twitter, and chat rooms. But it's even worse when they try to control the messages in ways that the marketplace sees as inauthentic.

Creating a World Wide Rave

When I finished writing the first edition of this book, I became obsessed with the phenomenon of people spreading ideas and sharing stories. How amazing is it that something you create has the potential to keep spreading from one person to the next and, in the process, expose your ideas to people you don't even know? I was so fascinated with this idea that I wrote a book about it, *World Wide Rave: Creating Triggers That Get Millions of People to Spread Your Ideas and Share Your Stories*. That book was released in March 2009, between the first and second editions of this book. I'm adding a short section here to provide you with the basic ideas of *World Wide Rave*, in the hope that you might create your own. If you want to read the *World Wide Rave* in its entirety, I've made it totally free as a PDF (no registration required) and free on Kindle, iPad, Nook, and Kobo e-book readers. Just go to WorldWideRave.com to download your copy.

A World Wide Rave is when people around the world are talking about you, your company, and your products—whether you're located in San

Francisco, Dubai, or Reykjavók. It's when global communities eagerly link to your stuff on the web. It's when online buzz drives buyers to your virtual doorstep. And it's when tons of fans visit your website and your blog because they genuinely want to be there.

> You can trigger a World Wide Rave, too—just create something valuable that people want to share, and make it easy for them to do so.

The World Wide Rave is one of the most exciting and powerful ways to reach your audience. Anyone with thoughtful ideas to share—and clever ways to create interest in them—can become famous and find success on the web. The challenge for marketers is to harness the amazing power of the World Wide Rave. The process is actually quite simple; anyone can do it, including you. However, if you're already an experienced marketer, you need to know that achieving success requires a far different approach than what you're likely to be doing now. Many of the easy techniques for triggering a World Wide Rave are the exact opposite of what you've learned on the job or have been taught in school. Similarly, if you're a CEO, business owner, or entrepreneur, you should know that these ideas are likely precisely what your agency partners and marketing staff tell you not to do.

Let's look at the important components for generating a World Wide Rave of your own. As you read the next few paragraphs, consider how completely different these ideas are from what you're doing today.

Rules of the Rave

It's obvious as hell that for thousands or even millions of people to share your ideas and stories on the web, you must make something worth sharing. But how do you do that? Here are the essential components. This list is so important, and each item such a strong predictor of success, that I call them your *Rules of the Rave*.

- **Nobody cares about your products (except you).** Yes, you read that right. What people do care about are themselves and ways to solve their problems. People also like to be entertained and to share in something remarkable. To have people talk about you and your ideas, you must resist the urge to hype your products and services. Create something interesting that will be talked about online. But don't worry—because when you're famous on the web, people will line up to learn more and to buy what you offer!

- **No coercion required.** For decades, organizations of all kinds have spent buckets of money on advertising designed to coerce people into buying products. *Free shipping! This week only, 20 percent off! New and improved! Faster than the other guys!* This product-centric advertising is not how you get people talking about you. When you've got something *worth sharing*, people will share it—no coercion required.

- **Lose control.** Here's a component that scares most people silly. You've got to lose control of your messages, you need to make your valuable online content totally free (and freely sharable), and you must understand that a World Wide Rave is not about generating sales leads. Yes, you can measure success, but not through business school ROI calculators.

- **Put down roots.** When I was a kid, my grandmother said, "If you want to receive a letter, you need to send a letter to someone first." Then when I was in college, my buddies said, "If you want to meet girls, you have to go where the girls are." The same thing is true in the virtual world of the web. If you want your ideas to spread, you need to be involved in the online communities of people who actively share.

- **Create triggers that encourage people to share.** When a product or service solves someone's problem or is very valuable, interesting, funny, or just plain outrageous, it's ready to be shared. To elevate your online content to the status of a World Wide Rave, you need a trigger to get people talking.

- **Point the world to your (virtual) doorstep.** If you follow the Rules of the Rave as I've described them, people will talk about you. And when they do, they'll generate all sorts of online buzz that will be indexed by the search engines, all relating to what your organization is up to. Forget about data-driven search engine technologies. The better approach to drive people to your stuff via the search engines is to create a World Wide Rave. As a result, your organization's websites will quickly rise to prominence in the rankings on Google, Bing, Yahoo!, and the other search engines.

That's it. Simple, right?

Sure, generating a World Wide Rave is as simple as can be. You should be thinking of how you can create an initiative that will get people to spread your ideas and share your stories. That's why I made *World Wide Rave* free, so people will talk about my work. When people are talking about you, then you're reaching many more people than you would otherwise. Let's take a look at an example.

Film Producer Creates a World Wide Rave by Making Soundtrack Free for Download

As I say many times in these pages, a great way to generate interest in products and services is to make select content available for free online. There's no doubt that free content sells. So it was with great interest that I had an opportunity to connect with Ryan Gielen, executive producer of *The Graduates*,[6] to learn about his strategy of making the soundtrack of his film available for free download. *The Graduates* is an award-winning comedy about four friends who head to the beach without a care in the world. Prior to release, the film had been developing a loyal following among the 18- to 34-year-old demographic following a dozen sold-out festival and sneak preview screenings. It had been advertised solely by word-of-mouth and a free soundtrack download.

The film features the music of some incredible indie bands (The New Rags, Plushgun, Sonia Montez, The Mad Tea Party, Our Daughter's Wedding, and The Smittens) that are popular with the buyer personas who might see the movie. So the idea of making the entire soundtrack available for free[7] is a brilliant strategy.

Of course, the bands also benefit because new listeners are exposed to their music and, if they like it, may decide to buy an album or see them live. "We're a very indie film, with very indie bands on our soundtrack," Gielen says. "Both the bands and the film need as much promotional help as possible, because we're competing with studio films, major marketing budgets, stars. We don't compete exclusively with low-budget films. We compete with everyone. So what do we have to offer our potential audience to set us apart? A great film and a great soundtrack isn't enough—we need people to know about it."

---

[6] thegraduatesmovie.com
[7] thegraduatesmovie.com/music

He also sells the music for those without the code, making the free download seem more valuable. These codes are given away at film festivals, at places where the members of the film's buyer personas congregate, at the various bands' live shows, and more. "We felt it made sense to give away the soundtrack to build loyalty, show off the product, and compensate for a zero-dollar marketing budget, all in one fell swoop," he says.

I wondered about the musicians whose music was given away. Did any of them resist? "My producers and I all loved this idea, and when we carefully explained it to the musicians, they came along. I think it helped that everyone was aware of how hard the producers and I are working to promote the film and the individual bands on the soundtrack."

Interestingly, Gielen does not see this model catching on with major films. "Movie studios will probably be very slow to adopt this model, possibly because they load soundtracks with famous music that is too expensive to give away," he says. "Music licensing is an enormous headache for indie filmmakers. We all agreed early on that we would go out and find great bands that hadn't been discovered because that would help us license the music, and they would be excited by the exposure. I expect that if we had pitched this to established, signed bands, we would've been laughed out of the room. The media landscape is so broad that we literally had 9,000 bands submit music, something like 100,000 songs to choose from. If our little film takes off, people all over the country will discover the new music. The worst-case scenario for even an established band is that we just crafted a $100,000 music video for them. The Rolling Stones should laugh us out of the room, but this is a good opportunity for many, many bands." The strategy has worked well for Gielen. "The free soundtrack has been a real success," he says. "The totally free music promo opened us up to many more people."

So what can you give away to create a World Wide Rave of your own?

Using Creative Commons to Facilitate Mashups and Spread Your Ideas

I'm a huge fan of Creative Commons,[8] a nonprofit organization that makes it easy for people to both share and build on the digital creations of others. With a Creative Commons attribution for photos, blog posts, e-books, and

---

[8] creativecommons.org

other information published on the web, originators of works assert legal copyright ownership but also grant others free licenses to incorporate these works into new ones. That way, others can share, remix, use commercially, or otherwise mash up the content without asking explicit permission (a mashup is when somebody takes your work and expands on it in some way while giving you attribution).

This strategy of giving up control of your content to facilitate its sharing is dramatically different from the typical legal department mandated approach of slapping draconian "do not copy" restrictions onto all web content. But when you allow mashups, you never know what interesting things might emerge. People have created mashups from my work. I've picked out some original ones to share with you:

- A publisher in Bulgaria translated my free e-book *The New Rules of PR* into Bulgarian and created a Bulgarian-language Facebook page to promote the work.
- A company in Japan, News2U, created a Japanese-language version of my free marketing strategy template, which I'll be discussing in Chapter 11.
- Kathy Drewien and others took another one of my e-books, *The New Rules of Viral Marketing*, and turned it into a free online slide show on SlideShare that has more than 1,800 views. These are views of the e-book I might not have generated otherwise.
- Pushan Banerjee from Hyderabad, India, created a presentation based on some of my ideas and gave me credit.

As you consider how to get others to spread your ideas, make sure you make it easy for those ideas to be shared.

Viral Buzz for Fun and Profit

It can be difficult to purposely create viral marketing buzz. But I do believe it's possible—otherwise I wouldn't have written an entire book about World Wide Raves! The way to create viral programs is a lot like the way venture capitalists invest in start-up companies and studios create films. A typical venture capitalist has a formula that states that most ventures will fail, a few might do okay, and 1 out of 20 or so will take off and become a large enterprise that will pay back investors many times the initial investment. Record companies and movie studios follow the same principles, expecting that most of the projects they green-light will have meager sales but that the one hit will more than pay back the cost of a bunch of flops. The problem is that nobody knows with certainty which movie or venture-backed company in the portfolio will succeed, so it requires a numbers game of investing in many prospects. The same goes for viral efforts. Create a bunch of different things, see what hits, and then nurture the winners along.

The Virgin Mary Grilled Cheese Sandwich and Jerry Garcia's Toilet

Consider GoldenPalace.com, the Internet casino that has cornered the market on eccentric eBay purchases for viral promotional purposes.[9] The online casino is the proud owner of dozens of offbeat knickknacks such as Pete Rose's corked baseball bat, William Shatner's kidney stone, Jerry Garcia's toilet, and the famous Virgin Mary grilled cheese sandwich. The marketers at GoldenPalace.com also grab unusual advertising space sold on eBay, such oddities as a woman's cleavage, the opportunity to tattoo a logo on someone's forehead, and billboard space on the back of a person's wheelchair. Some of this stuff, all purchased on eBay, generates significant viral marketing buzz for GoldenPalace.com. For example, when Shatner's kidney stone was nabbed, it seemed like every TV station, newspaper, and online outlet reported on the sale: "Shatner Passes Kidney Stone to GoldenPalace.com," the headline ran. "Ha, ha, ha," the reporters and bloggers went, dismissing the money spent as foolish. But each story referenced GoldenPalace.com! At a mere $25,000, this foray into a place where no man has gone before was the viral marketing and advertising bargain of the century. And kudos, too, to Shatner, who got his name plastered all over the place (and donated the cash to Habitat for Humanity).

The professional eBay bidders at GoldenPalace.com know that not every one of the hundreds of quirky purchases they make will be a hit with bloggers and the media. But they can count on some of them, maybe 1 out of 20, hitting the mark in just the right way.

---

[9] goldenpalaceevents.com/auctions

Clip This Coupon for $1 Million
Off Fort Myers, Florida, Home

When there is a glut of luxury homes on the market, what can a homeowner do to make his property stand out? Get people talking about it, of course! Homeowner Rich Ricciani decided to offer potential buyers a coupon good for $1 million off the price of his $7 million Fort Myers, Florida, home. He created a site for the coupon and placed it in newspapers in lieu of a typical real estate advertisement. This creative approach sure beat simply reducing the price of the home on the real estate Multiple Listing Service database.

Ricciani worked with Lani Belisle of VIP Realtors to list the home and book the advertising space for the coupon, which initially ran in the Sunday edition of the *Fort Myers News-Press*. Then it was time for Tina Haisman Public Relations to get the word out. Haisman used PRWeb to send a well-written, search-engine-optimized press release complete with photos, an embedded YouTube video, and links to the coupon and the home's website. "I also used PR MatchPoint to compile a list of real estate writers in the south and northeastern U.S., and I personally targeted the big news outlets such as CNN, FOX, NBC, and more," Haisman says.

In southwest Florida, the story appeared on the front pages of both the *Fort Myers News-Press* and the *Naples Daily News*, and it aired on WINK-TV and local radio stations. "*Florida Weekly* named the Million Dollar Coupon the best marketing stunt of the year!" Haisman says. "Within four days of its release, the Million Dollar Coupon story went viral on real estate blogs nationwide, creating a worldwide buzz."

As a result, it aired on television stations in major cities around the country, and the homeowner even did a live interview on Neal Cavuto's *Your World* show on FOX News. Major papers, including the *Los Angeles Times*, covered it, and the idea also appeared in the *Huffington Post*. The team then ran the coupon in the Sunday *New York Times*, the *Wall Street Journal*, and the *Boston Globe*. I love the selection of the *Globe*, chosen because Fort Myers, Florida, is the home of the Boston Red Sox spring training facility—an excellent example of buyer persona profiling. Bloggers talked about it, and many people were buzzing about it on Twitter.

Some may call this strategy a gimmick. Nonsense. When people are talking about you, your product stands out in a crowded market. And guess what? This kind of marketing is fun! If you're a realtor, it sure beats pounding wooden signs into front yards.

When You Have Explosive News, Make It Go Viral

Although I've said that I think it is difficult to dream up campaigns that will definitely go viral and become a World Wide Rave, there are times that an organization possesses news that is so important to the target market they serve that they just know the news has significant viral potential. The hiring of a famous CEO away from another company, a merger or acquisition announcement, or a huge celebrity endorsement deal might be just the thing that lights up the blogs in your marketplace. If that's the case, it is important to get that news out in order to create the maximum effect. (Of course, there is the opposite example—bad news—which also goes viral, and which you would prefer to contain or minimize. But in this chapter, let's just focus on the kind of good news that you want to get out to as wide an audience as possible.) If you want to push news along to maximum effect, it's critical to have a plan and a detailed timeline of whom you will tell the news to and when.

When Outsell, Inc.,[10] a research and advisory firm for the information industry, had just completed but not yet released a report titled "Click Fraud Reaches $1.3 Billion, Dictates End of 'Don't Ask, Don't Tell' Era," which was the first to quantify, in real dollars and advertiser sentiment, the click-fraud problems that plague advertisers on search engines, they knew they were sitting on big news. The Outsell report, based on a study of 407 advertisers responsible for about $1 billion in ad spending, told the explosive story of a problem threatening the core business model of search engines like Google. The analysts at Outsell revealed the scope of the problem of fraudulent clicks on web advertisements that appear as part of search results, clicks that companies doing the advertising were paying for. Outsell analysts knew they had a story with viral potential.

"At first we hinted at the report in our client newsletter," says Chuck Richard, vice president and lead analyst at Outsell and the author of the report. "We always make certain that the paying clients get access to reports before they hit the media. But internally and with our PR firm, Warner Communications,[11] we thought it was going to be big." Outsell had a logistical problem in that the report was to be released to clients over the

---

[10] outsellinc.com

[11] warnerpr.com

U.S. Independence Day holiday weekend. The PR firm sent a media advisory, headlined "Outsell, Inc. Pegs Click Fraud as $1.3 Billion Problem That Threatens Business Models of Google, Others; Study Shows 27% of Advertisers Slowing or Stopping Pay-Per-Click Ads Due to Fraudulent Billings," to selected media. The advisory offered an early look at the report to approved media under an embargo period—stories could not appear until Wednesday, July 5, at the earliest. Verne Kopytoff of the *San Francisco Chronicle* spent the holiday weekend researching the problem identified by Outsell, interviewing Richard, and reaching out for comment from spokespeople at the search engines. His story, "Click Fraud a Huge Problem: Study Finds Practice Widespread; Many Cut Back Online Ads," was the first to break.

"The viral aspect came from bloggers and built over the course of a week or so," Richard says. Within just five days, more than 100 bloggers had picked up the story, including heavy hitters such as John Batelle's *Searchblog*, Jeff Jarvis's *BuzzMachine*, *ClickZ News Blog*, Danny Sullivan at *Search Engine Watch*, and paidContent.org. After the story broke, Richard was busy doing interview after interview for mainstream media, resulting in a wave of nearly 100 stories in just the first week. Outlets including NPR, MSNBC, *Barron's*, the *Financial Times*, *AdAge*, *eWeek*, the *Boston Globe*, the *Los Angeles Times*, ABC News, ZDNet, *BusinessWeek Online*, and TheStreet.com all ran stories online, in print, and via broadcast media.

In the following weeks, Richard, now seen in the market as an expert in click fraud, received many press requests based on an existing Arkansas click-fraud class-action settlement that Google was proposing. Within a week, Google announced it would start providing statistics on the fraudulent clicks it intercepted, one of the key changes called for in the Outsell study; many media referenced this development in follow-up stories. Richard believes that the online buzz has prompted the paid search business to finally accept that it can't escape having its own click-fraud tracking, auditing, and certification processes. "This is great news for users, publishers, and advertisers," Richard says.

"For a small company to have access to this kind of reach of journalists and bloggers is remarkable," Richard says. "It couldn't have happened this way even a few years ago. The exposure has made a fundamental difference in [people's] awareness of the firm. Many of our clients have contacted us to say 'congratulations,' that they were happy to see us be more visible. And I've gotten on the prime source lists of many reporters who cover the space, and they proactively call me for comment on stories now." Indeed, *BusinessWeek* wrote a cover story, "Click Fraud: The Dark Side of Online Advertising," and quoted the Outsell report.

But Richard is also aware of how a significant news item or report can influence a company or even an entire industry. "It's given us a reminder of our responsibility," he says. "If something like this can affect a company's share price or performance or investor inquiries on earnings calls, we need to be confident on our opinions."

The Outsell example clearly illustrates that a piece of news, properly delivered to the market, can go viral. But with careful nurturing over the news cycle and an awareness of traditional news media's and bloggers' roles in promoting ideas, the story can reach much larger audiences and help a smart organization to reach its goals.

Viral marketing—creating a World Wide Rave by having others tell your story for you—is one of the most exciting and powerful ways to reach your audiences. It's not easy to harness the power, but with careful preparation when you are sitting on news and with clever ideas for what has the potential to create interest, any organization has the power to become famous on the web.

The Content-Rich Website

I f you've read from the beginning of the book, at this point you might be tempted to think that each of the media that innovative marketers use to reach buyers—blogs, podcasts, news releases, and all the rest—is a stand-alone communications vehicle. And while each certainly could be a self-contained unit (your blog does not need to link to your corporate site), most organizations integrate their online marketing efforts to help tell a unified story to buyers. Each medium is interrelated with all the others. Podcasts work with blogs. A news release program works with an effective website and online media room. Twitter feeds point people to other company information. Multiple websites for different divisions or countries come together on a corporate site. No matter how you choose to deploy web content to reach your buyers, the place that brings everything together in a unified place is a content-rich website.

As anyone who has built a website knows, there is much more to think about than just the content. Design, color, navigation, and appropriate technology are all important aspects of a good website. Unfortunately, in many organizations these other concerns dominate. Why is that? I think it's *easier* to focus on a site's design or technology than on its content. Also, there are fewer resources to help website creators with the content aspects of their sites—hey, that's one of the reasons I wrote this book!

Often the only person allowed to work on the website is your organization's *webmaster*. At many companies, webmasters—the kings of technology—focus all their attention on cool software plug-ins; on HTML, XML, and all sorts of other 'MLs; and on nitty-gritty stuff like server technology and Internet service providers. But with a webmaster in charge, what happens to the content? In other organizations, webmasters are pushed aside by graphic designers and advertising people who focus exclusively on creating websites that look pretty. At these organizations, well-meaning advertising agencies obsess over hip designs or hot technology such as Flash. I've seen many examples where site owners become so concerned about technology and design that they totally forget that great *content* is the most important aspect of any website.

Thus, the best websites focus primarily on content to pull together their various buyers, markets, media, and products in one comprehensive place where content is not only king but president and pope as well. A great website is an intersection of every other online initiative, including podcasts, blogs, news releases, and other online media. In a cohesive and interesting way, the content-rich website organizes the online personality of your organization to delight, entertain, and—most important—inform each of your buyers.

Political Advocacy on the Web

The Natural Resources Defense Council (NRDC) is the nation's most effective environmental action organization. According to its website,[1] the organization uses law, science, and the support of 1.3 million members and online activists to protect the planet's wildlife and wild places and to ensure a safe and healthy environment for all living things. What makes the organization interesting is the vast amount of web content available on its site, the various media that its marketers deploy, and the tools it provides to online activists and political bloggers to spread the group's message. The professionals at NRDC, which was named by *Worth* magazine as one of America's 100 best charities, know that more than 1 million members are the best storytelling asset available. By developing a terrific website to enlist people to donate their online voices, NRDC expands the team and its message-delivery capabilities considerably.

The site includes environmental news, resources, and information on topics such as clean air and energy; clean drinking water and oceans; wildlife and fish; and parks, forests, and wetlands. In addition, it offers online

---

[1] nrdc.org

publications, links to laws and treaties, and a glossary of environmental terms. The NRDC delivers the organization's message via audio, video, and text and also encourages others to support the cause through giving their time and money and through reusing online content.

Throughout the site, widgets (small applications found on websites and blogs) and links are available for bloggers to use in helping spread the message. Prominent widgets include social bookmarking tools to add tags to StumbleUpon, Delicious, and Digg (to make it easier for people who use those sites to find information from NRDC). The site also offers independent bloggers and website owners virtual badges (graphical images that look like banner ads) that they add to their blog or site and then link back to NRDC to show support. For example, people who wish to help find solutions to both global warming and dependency on oil might put a biofuels badge[2] on their blog or website; the badge links to NRDC content about biofuels. The badges available include small ones that look like the RSS links found on many blogs and larger ones similar to banner ads. The NRDC has also created Squidoo lenses such as "Understanding Global Warming (from the experts at NRDC),"[3] and it encourages its constituents to do the same. (A Squidoo lens is a web page built by someone with expertise on a topic—for more about Squidoo, see Chapter 16.)

"I came to NRDC from NPR initially, doing media relations," says Daniel Hinerfeld, associate director of communications for NRDC. "But because I'm in the L.A. office and we have entertainment industry contacts, I've started creating multimedia content for the site. We have a video called *Lethal Sounds*,[4] narrated by Pierce Brosnan, that was my first big taste of multimedia." The video, which has been a hit on the festival circuit, details evidence linking sonar to a series of whale strandings in recent years. To encourage people to take action, the landing page for the video has multiple widgets and tools. From this page, viewers can easily send messages to elected officials, donate money, and send online postcards to friends. Links to additional content, such as an NRDC press release titled "Navy Sued over Harm to Whales from Mid-Frequency Sonar" and a detailed report titled "Sounding the Depths II," are just a click away. All this well-organized content, complete with easy ways to link to related information and to share

---

[2] nrdc.org/badges/biofuels.asp
[3] squidoo.com/globalwarmingprimer
[4] nrdc.org/wildlife/marine/sonar.asp

content on blogs and with friends, is pulled together on the site and contributes greatly to the NRDC leadership position. And online content experts at NRDC are constantly looking for new ways to deliver their important messages.

"We created a podcast channel with broadcast-quality, journalistic-style packages," Hinerfeld says. "Our communications strategy is not just to reach the media, but to also reach the constituents directly." Hinerfeld draws extensively from his experience at NPR when he produces shows for the NRDC podcasts. "I always try hard to include points of view that are at odds with our own," he says. "I think it makes it more interesting, and it reinforces our own position. For example, when we conduct interviews with our own staff, we challenge people with difficult questions, not just softballs, much like a journalist would. Going this route makes it authentic. People don't want PR, they want something that's real."

Hinerfeld says that multimedia is very exciting because it gives NRDC an opportunity to reach younger constituencies. "I've come across people who are huge consumers of podcasts, and many listen to them during long commutes," he says. "We use this sort of content to bond with people in a different, less wonky way. We also profile our younger staff members, which is a way to personalize the institution." Many staff members have social networking profiles and use them to spread the word as well.

Within the news media that cover environmental issues on Capitol Hill, NRDC is very well known. But the site content, the audio and video, and the site components that are offered to bloggers to spread the message (and cause it to go viral) make the organization much more approachable, especially to online activists and the younger Facebook generation. The NRDC staffers are active participants in the market and on the sites and blogs their constituents read. All these efforts make their content authentic, because it is contextually appropriate for the audiences the group needs to reach.

Content: The Focus of Successful Websites

The NRDC site is an excellent example of a website that is designed to reach buyers. For the NRDC, the buyers are the more than 1 million members, advocates, and activists who use the site to work to protect the planet's wildlife and wild places and to promote a healthy environment.

Unfortunately, the vast majority of sites are built with the wrong focus. Yes, appearance and navigation are important: Appropriate colors, logos, fonts, and design make a site appealing. The right technologies, such as content-management systems, make sites easier to update. But what really matters is the *content*, how that content is organized, and how it drives action from buyers.

To move content to its rightful place in driving a successful marketing and PR strategy, content must be the single most important component. That focus can be tough for many people, both when their agencies push for hip and stylish design and when their IT departments obsess about the architecture. It is your role to think like a publisher and begin any new site or site redesign by starting with the content strategy.

Reaching a Global Marketplace

In recent years, I've delivered presentations in many countries, including New Zealand, Malaysia, India, Turkey, and the Dominican Republic. As I traveled to my keynote speeches in each of the Baltic countries (Latvia, Lithuania, and Estonia), I was struck by how plugged in to the web their residents are. For example, among Estonia's population of just under 1.3 million people are 993,785 Internet users as of June 2012, representing 78.0 percent of the population, according to the ITU, the U.N. agency for information and communication technologies. My high-speed connections in this part of the world were much faster than in most parts of the United States.

The incredibly successful marketers I met in each of these small countries impressed me greatly with their outward thinking. When you live in a country like Latvia, your home market is tiny, requiring you to sell your products and services internationally. It also requires that you think deeply about your buyers in the global marketplace.

Consider LessLoss Audio Devices,[5] a company based in Kaunas, Lithuania. LessLoss creates amazing (and fabulously expensive) high-end audio products and has become famous among rabid audiophiles worldwide for power cords, filters, cables, and other equipment. LessLoss sells all over the world, and its site has a deliberately global focus. The e-commerce and SEO platform is managed by Globaltus,[6] also a Lithuanian company.

---

[5] lessloss.com

[6] globaltus.com

The LessLoss site includes amazingly detailed information about the audio devices, together with terrific photos. For example, there's an essay on "The Concept of Noise," which details why a sound-preserving technique known as power filtering is important. After all, when you sell power cables that can cost a thousand U.S. dollars, they had better be good. (And it's probably a good idea to explain *why* they're so good.)

"It is amazing how people from such a small country can reach customers worldwide and prove to be well respected," says Tomas Paplauskas, CEO of Globaltus. "The power of the Internet gives the opportunity to reach huge markets. Just imagine how few of these amazing power cords you could sell in Lithuania. There are no more local businesses—all businesses are global."

I think there is an important lesson here. We can all learn from the successful companies in these small countries, companies that have learned to create content-rich websites to reach a global audience. And we can all reproduce their success. The marketplace is the outside world, not just your home city, state, or country.

Putting It All Together with Content

As you're reading through this discussion of unifying your online marketing and PR efforts on your website, you might be thinking, "That's easy for a smaller organization or one that has only one product line, but I work for a large company with many brands." Yes, it is more difficult to coordinate wide varieties of content when you have to juggle multiple brands, geographic variation, languages, and other considerations common to large companies. But with a large, widely dispersed organization, putting it all together on a corporate site might be even more important because showing a unified personality reaps benefits.

"The key is the collaboration between the different business units, the corporate offices, and the departments," says Sarah F. Garnsey, head of marketing and web communications at Textron Inc.[7] "At Textron, each business has its own independently operated website, which makes coordination difficult because each is a well-defined brand that may be more familiar to people than our corporate brand."

Textron Inc, a global company with yearly revenues of $14 billion and more than 37,000 employees in 33 countries, is recognized for strong brands

---

[7] textron.com

such as Bell Helicopter, Cessna Aircraft, and E-Z-GO (golf carts). The company has several dozen websites, typically for the individual brands, such as Bell Helicopter.[8] "Through search logs we learned that many people were searching for product and business information on the corporate [Textron] site," Garnsey says. "That was a wakeup call for us, because we had thought that people were going to the business sites for this information. So we've built out the corporate site with more content about each of the businesses." On a visit to the site, I was able to watch a video featuring the CEO of Cessna Aircraft,[9] check out a lot of great photos of the products, and read feature stories about employees such as John Delamarter, who's the program manager of Lycoming's Thunderbolt Engine and who discussed his pride and pleasure in his work. Textron has a well-organized online media room, and because the company's stock is traded on the New York Stock Exchange, there is also an investor relations section on the site.

"We work with the businesses to showcase interesting things, and we try to have fresh content on the site and update it with new weekly stories," Garnsey says. "But the content is only as good as the management of the content and the processes. With a large site, rigor of process is required that many companies might underestimate. It takes coordination and management. For example, I can't make the content in the recruiting section of the site compelling unless I get the complete cooperation of the human resources department. People had grown to believe that you just throw the content at a webmaster and it all just works. But it doesn't—the days of the guy with the server under the desk are over."

Garnsey has a set of processes and procedures to make certain that the Textron site meets the needs of buyers and that everything on it works well, and she has a small team that works with her to coordinate with the people who manage division and product company websites. "We have a content management process to make sure everything is fresh, has been reviewed, and is passed by legal," she says. "But a primary component is that we make sure that the voice of the customer is captured and built into all of our electronic communications. We work on how to draw users into the content and use the site to form a relationship with them. Even if they don't purchase something from us right away, maybe they will become interested in the company stock or in something from one of the brands like Cessna." To

---

[8] www.bellhelicopter.textron.com

[9] cessna.com

make sure the site follows best practice, Garnsey brings people into a lab for annual usability tests and research. "We also do an audit of all of our dot-com sites every year to make sure that all sites comply with the standards," she says. "And each year we hold a web summit of all the Textron people working on web initiatives from all over the company. We try to foster a community of people who otherwise would have no reason to speak with each other because the individual businesses don't have a lot in common."

Great Websites: More Art Than Science

The more I research websites—and I've checked out thousands over the past several years—the more I realize that the best ones unite many important factors in a way that is difficult to describe. They just feel right—as if the creator of the site cares a great deal and wants that passion to shine through. Like a sprinkling of fairy dust, the effect is important but indescribable. However, I'm convinced that the key is to understand buyers (or those who may donate, subscribe, join, or vote) and build content especially for them.

Consider Sasha Vujacic:[10] the official website of "The Machine," a professional athlete fan page for the basketball star now playing for Anadolu Efes of the Turkish Basketball League. Sasha was a member of the Slovenian junior national team and was drafted by the Los Angeles Lakers in the 2004 NBA draft. He played for the Lakers through 2010 and won two NBA championships with the team before moving to the New Jersey Nets in the 2010 to 2011 season and Anadolu Efes starting in 2011. The Sasha site is beautifully designed and contains a huge amount of information about the player, including videos, photos, and much more. And get this: There's content in multiple languages (English, Italian, Slovenian, and even Chinese and Japanese) because Sasha has fans from all over the world. His multi-language content appeals to different buyer personas.

There is an RSS feed of "regularly updated insider information and stories that you may publish on your website automatically as Sasha publishes them." The best part of the site is that it gives off the vibe that Sasha is approachable. There are many casual photos of him, and there's a tool where fans can ask him questions and even create their own T-shirt design and send it to him. If Sasha likes the design, he posts it on his official online store. Sasha is active on Twitter as well (@SashaVujacic).

---

[10] sashavujacic18.com

Vladimir Cuk and his firm Attention Interactive built the site for Sasha. But more important, Cuk and his firm developed a terrific strategy for Sasha to interact with his fans and the media. "The site is a hit with fans and officials alike," Cuk says. Sasha and his management team are amazed at how the site looks and at the level of interaction and response from the fan community, according to Cuk. Other players have noticed as well and are intrigued about the possibilities of engaging more intimately with the public via the web and social media, Cuk also notes.

When Cuk was pitching Sasha's people for the business while Sasha was playing for the Lakers, he was up against the traditional public relations firms that frequently work with other NBA players. Sasha and his manager asked very intelligent questions during the meetings and came away ready to try what (to date) is a nontraditional promotion strategy for a pro basketball player. Most players use the media exclusively to deliver messages and are removed from interacting directly with fans. Not Sasha.

Effective sites like Sasha's draw on the passion of the people who build them and reflect the personality of someone dedicated to helping others. As you develop content to further your organizational goals, remember that a successful approach is often more art than science. The content you offer must have distinctive qualities, and your personality needs to show. A well-executed website, like a high-quality television program or film, is a combination of content and delivery. But on the web, many organizations spend much more time and money on the design and delivery aspects than on the content itself. Don't fall into that trap. Perfecting that critical mix of content, design, and technology is where the art comes in. Adding personality and authenticity and reaching particular buyer personas make the challenge even more daunting. Just remember, there is no absolute right or wrong way to create a website; each organization has an individual and important story to tell.

10 Marketing and PR in Real Time

I n July 1969 the world came together to watch a grainy black and white image on television of Neil Armstrong and Buzz Aldrin taking mankind's first steps on the moon. But those who watched the Apollo 11 mission were confined to their living rooms.

On October 14, 2012, the online world came together to witness Felix Baumgartner break multiple aerospace records in his Red Bull Stratos mission. And we shared it with each other in real-time. Baumgartner traveled higher in a balloon than anyone—more than 127,800 feet—and from that height he made the highest skydive, breaking a previous record that had stood for more than 50 years. While in free fall, he traveled Mach 1.24—833.9 miles per hour—making him the first human to travel faster than the speed of sound without being inside a craft.

It was riveting to witness, a real-time spectacle live on the web in HD that we could share via social networks. Event organizers said more than 130 digital outlets carried the live feed live. Another record was broken when it was reported that more than 8 million people watched a live stream on YouTube of the record-breaking attempt.

I learned about the impending jump on, where else, Twitter. When I started to watch, the balloon was at about 40,000 feet, so I tweeted to my followers and posted on Facebook. Millions of others did the same. It was great to watch the live YouTube video stream and also keep an eye on the twitter stream at the same time. I texted my daughter when the jump was about to happen and she texted back that she was already watching.

My wife Yukari Watanabe Scott was tweeting live with many of her friends in Japan.

The online global community came together for an hour to witness history and I don't recall anything like it. Everyone was positively giddy. For an hour we came together over one breathtaking event. The real-time component was magnified because the team had attempted the jump several other times. That day's attempt was delayed for a few hours. So nobody knew if and when it might happen. Unlike a prescheduled sporting event that everyone knows will air at a precise time, there was no preparing for Baumgartner's jump. Suddenly it was on and instantly we were compelled to watch. We told each other via social networks. Tens of millions of us alerted each other. That the jump happened on a Sunday (it was mid-afternoon U.S. Eastern time) made it easy for many people to watch live from their homes.

The jump was audacious. It was incredibly visual. It was unfolding in real time. And we could watch it together while commenting on social networks. It was one of those "I'll always remember where I was" moments. After Baumgartner landed, Red Bull posted a picture to Facebook of him kneeling on the ground. It generated nearly 216,000 likes, 10,000 comments, and more than 29,000 shares in less than 40 minutes according to the *Washington Post*. At the time, half of worldwide trending topics on Twitter had something to do with the jump.

That day we saw some incredible records broken. And we saw the future of how we will witness real-time events. But more than that, I was struck, again, at the power of instant communications. That marketers can tap instant communications is still quite new, but an incredibly powerful tool to grow your business.

Real-Time Marketing and PR

When Paris Hilton was arrested with her boyfriend—he charged with misdemeanor DUI, she with felony drug possession—the story was all over the news.

In today's real-time world, anyone can share their thoughts with the world as news is unfolding. Hilton did so in a tweet to the millions of fans who follow her: "These rumors going around are so ridiculous, untrue and cruel. I'm not going to even pay attention to them, because I know the truth."

Marketing and public relations have gone real-time as well. If you pay attention to what's happening in your marketplace and react instantly, you can insert yourself into stories as they unfold, generating market attention not possible if you wait even a day to react.

What I absolutely love about the Paris Hilton story is that, soon after her arrest, Wynn Resorts Ltd. spokeswoman Jennifer Dunne told the Associated Press that Hilton is barred from the company's Wynn Las Vegas and Encore hotels.

What Dunne did was absolutely brilliant! Now the media had another news hook. That the party girl got banned was now a story in its own right. And a huge one. I'd guess that this was one of the biggest PR bonanzas that Wynn has ever received. And because Hilton is a hotel heiress, the story took on yet another delicious angle.

As this situation was unfolding, I ran a quick Google news search for both "Paris Hilton" and "Wynn" (looking for stories that mentioned both), which returned a remarkable 5,286 items from news outlets around the globe. In stories about Paris Hilton's arrest, the media also consistently mentioned Wynn Resorts!

In a world where speed and agility are now essential to success, most organizations still operate slowly and deliberately, cementing each step months in advance and responding to new developments through careful but time-consuming processes. Most companies could not have responded quickly to an opportunity in the way that Wynn Resorts did because they are operating under the old rules of controlled engagement planned well in advance. But the Internet has fundamentally changed the pace of business, compressing time and rewarding speed.

The idea of real time—of creating marketing or public relations initiatives *right now*, while the moment is ripe—delivers tremendous competitive advantage. You've got to operate quickly to succeed in this world. These ideas are the subject of my 2012 book, *Real-Time Marketing & PR: How to Instantly Engage Your Market, Connect with Customers, and Create Products That Grow Your Business Now*. This chapter highlights some of the tactics that you can use to instantly engage your buyers when they are eager to hear from you. If you've read *Real-Time Marketing & PR*, you might want to read on anyway because the stories here are not in that book.

Real time means news breaks over minutes, not days. It's when people watch what's happening on social networks such as Twitter, Facebook, and YouTube and cleverly insert themselves into stories. Real-time urgency is also important in customer service, where organizations fix issues instantly rather than taking the typical days or weeks to respond to a complaint. Real time means companies develop (or refine) products or services instantly, based on feedback from customers or events in the marketplace. In all aspects of business, anyone who sees an opportunity and becomes the first to act on it gains tremendous advantage.

My first job was on a Wall Street trading desk in the 1980s. I witnessed real-time technology transforming financial trading into a game where instant information informs split-second decisions worth millions of dollars.

Traders desperately search their real-time newsfeeds and analysis tools for an angle, any angle. Who's the president meeting with today? Is there any disruption in the energy markets, perhaps because of unrest in the Middle East? What's happening in Japan? Germany? The United Kingdom? As they pore through data and news, the traders are poised, ready to commit huge sums of money when the moment is right.

It has taken decades, but the impact of the real-time revolution is now being felt in all industries, including marketing and public relations.

We can react instantly to what's happening in the news, just like a bond trader. We can engage members of the media on their timetables, precisely when they are writing stories. But we've got to develop a business culture that encourages speed over sloth. The MBA-style approach of working from spreadsheets that predict what to do months into the future is no help when news is breaking in your industry right now.

> In the emerging real-time business environment, size is no longer a decisive advantage. Speed and agility win the moment.

As financial market players know, advantage comes from reacting to market opportunities first. The same thing is true for all companies. If you're first to engage the market, people notice, and your offering gains valuable attention. If you react early and connect with customers as their concerns arise, they see you as thoughtful and caring. And the mainstream media are always looking to cover the latest trend or fast-moving company, so you're likely to get much more coverage if you operate in real time.

Develop Your Real-Time Mind-Set

When I speak with people about the ideas of real-time marketing and public relations, they understand that our access to today's communications tools means we can communicate immediately. Twitter allows instant dialogue with buyers. Blog posts help you get your ideas into the marketplace right now. And monitoring tools like Google Alerts and TweetDeck provide up-to-the-second knowledge of what people are saying about you, your company, and its products. However, while people do generally *understand* the situation, many have difficulty adopting the personal and corporate mind-set and habits required for success. Too many individuals, and the organizations they work for, take the cautious and careful approach: always wait and see, always check with the experts before acting on an opportunity. Unfortunately, this typical behavior will lose you the advantage.

As an example of one organization that has developed the mind-set required for success, consider the GolinHarris approach of what they call "The Bridge"[1]—a network of real-time storytelling centers—staffed in the Americas, Europe, and Asia Pacific. This Wall Street trading room approach is exactly what I've constantly talked about and I'm excited to see it being implemented, so I connected with Jim Dowd, Executive Director, National Media for GolinHarris International, a communications firm and part of the Interpublic Group, to learn more. "We use The Bridge as a listening outpost, but we are doing it a little differently because we have the mainstream media folks and the digital folks working side by side," Dowd says. "So we are not just looking at social media, which is obviously the flavor of the day. Digital and mainstream are literally sitting next to each other and they are coming up with ideas and are pitching media together and that is where we have seen just terrific traction."

For example, on the day that Michelle Obama announced a new food pyramid called MyPlate, the GolinHarris team watched the press conference live on CNN looking for ways to get their clients into the emerging memes. "We are watching all the activity online and took an idea to Hartz to create a food pyramid for dogs," Dowd says. The client loved the idea and reacted quickly and the team generated some attention as a result.

With most clients working at a glacially slow pace, requiring lengthy legal and PR client-side reviews, I wondered how GolinHarris is able to get speedy

---

[1] golinharris.com/#!/approach/the-bridge

signoffs on ideas generated from The Bridge. "Yeah, approval is always tricky, particularly with legal departments," Dowd says. GolinHarris works with clients to develop topics ahead of time in anticipation of potential stories so that they can work quickly. "With clients like McDonalds we have general topics that we predict, like if something comes up about the Happy Meal. McDonalds have preapproved that we can have certain conversations about Happy Meals with language we can go out with."

The Bridge is set up just like a 24-hour Wall Street trading desk with three regions—Asia, Europe, and North America—passing the work around the globe. "We are truly doing it globally," Dowd says, "We are 24/7 so we will scour the landscape the first few hours of the day here in New York, then we will pass all of our results and insights onto Chicago and Chicago to LA. And you know, the whole notion of offices and cubes may go away. It's exciting to be able to walk in The Bridge and literally see what is going on."

When you have a real-time mind-set and the tools of a facility like The Bridge, then newsjacking becomes second nature. (Newsjacking is inserting your ideas into a breaking news story by writing a real-time blog post or shooting a video to interest reporters and generate coverage. It is the subject of my 2011 book by that name. I discuss newsjacking in detail in Chapter 23). "Our client AutoTrader.com challenged us to make them the leader in all of the post-Super Bowl auto commercial coverage," Dowd says. AutoTrader.com did not advertise during the Super Bowl but wanted to generate a bunch of attention anyway—a classic newsjacking strategy.

AutoTrader's analysts worked with GolinHarris to create data on consumers' real-time search patterns during the Super Bowl. They used data from the AutoTrader.com site and correlated that to the times auto commercials aired looking for lift (how much of a boost in search activity each vehicle got in the hour after its ad appeared). They provided the resulting data to the media who used it in stories like "Acura NSX Won Big with Super Bowl Spot, Survey Says," which appeared on the *Wall Street Journal* site.

"There are lot of clients who love the notion of the bridge and real-time marketing and what we are doing but aren't jumping on it out of fear—fear of the unknown, fear of the new," Dowd says. "A lot of our clients are still quite old school and traditional."

There's nothing like success to break down the fear barrier. Dowd cites Dow Chemical as a noteworthy GolinHarris real-time success. The company is very careful with stories related to such topics as chemistry or chemical engineering or stem research, but that doesn't mean they can't engage in real time.

"We were in The Bridge tracking that President Obama was going to give the Teacher of the Year Award and we were watching live on CNN," he says. "And it was a chemistry teacher who won that award so we immediately got approval from Dow Chemical to go ahead and offer up public congratulations to the teacher and that resulted in some nice coverage. Even with the trickier clients there are always topics that will work."

The real-time mind-set recognizes the importance of *speed*. It is an attitude to business (and to life) that emphasizes *moving quickly* when the time is right.

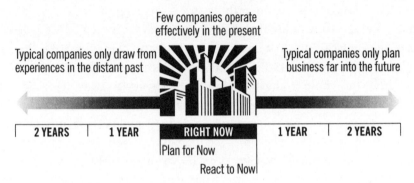

Don't get me wrong. I'm not saying you should focus only on the now and not plan for the future. Developing a real-time mind-set should not feel like an either-or proposition; you can and should do both.

Real-Time Blog Post Drives $1 Million in New Business

Imagine that you're among the first to know that a huge company is about to acquire one of your competitors. What would you do right now?

Not tomorrow. Now!

How about writing a blog post about it in real time?

That's what Eloqua CEO Joe Payne did when he learned that Oracle, a software giant, was to acquire the assets of marketing automation company and Eloqua competitor Market2Lead. A colleague mentioned the acquisition, and as soon as Payne confirmed the news on the Oracle website, he started working on his blog post.

The Oracle announcement,[2] which was located in a difficult-to-find part of the company's website, contained only a terse one-paragraph

---

[2] oracle.com/market2lead/index.html

announcement: *Oracle has acquired the intellectual property assets of Market2Lead, a provider of demand generation and marketing automation software. Market2Lead's technology helps companies improve demand generation to increase sales and marketing effectiveness. Oracle plans to integrate Market2Lead's technology into Oracle CRM applications. The financial details of the transaction were not disclosed.*

Payne realized that there was a tremendous opportunity *right now* to write a blog post. He figured that if *he* hadn't known about the acquisition, then others probably didn't know either. "The announcement was buried on the Oracle website," he says. "No one else had found it yet." Payne had a unique opportunity to define what the deal meant to the market.

In his post "Oracle Joins the Party,"[3] Payne wrote, in part: *I expect Oracle's entry to make a major difference in the attention paid to this sector. It's going to open marketers' eyes, and, as a result, expand the market. This is exactly the type of movement this industry needs. You see, the potential market for lead management systems is less than 10 percent penetrated.*

Payne chose to write a high-level blog post that talks about what the acquisition meant to the market for this kind of software. "We needed to give people information they could sink their teeth into," he says. "And it was picked up very quickly by the media because of what I wrote. News organizations immediately wrote their own stories and blog posts, and they quoted my post as if they had done an interview with me."

Can you see what Payne did? Oracle announces an acquisition but provides almost no details. The media is hungry for something to say and someone to quote. Bingo, a Google search pops up Payne's post, and now reporters, analysts, and bloggers have an authority to cite in their stories.

As a result of this real-time market commentary, Eloqua became an important part of the resulting stories published in outlets that included *BusinessWeek, InfoWorld, Customer Experience Matrix, PC World,* and *Customer Think.*

But Payne and the Eloqua team didn't stop there. The next step in this real-time outreach was to alert existing and potential Market2Lead clients to Payne's blog post. "Eloqua salespeople who had lost a deal to Market2Lead immediately sent emails to each customer, linking to the blog post," he says. "In many cases, we broke the news to those clients that their marketing

---

[3] blog.eloqua.com/oracle-joins-the-party

automation company had been acquired. We outlined what the change would likely mean to them. That gave us credibility with the clients and hurt Oracle and Market2Lead, because they were not the first to describe to their buyers what the deal meant."

The Eloqua sales team then offered a money-back guarantee to any Market2Lead customer who wanted to switch to Eloqua. "We wanted to take away the friction of moving," Payne says. "The tone of the offer was designed to be helpful and informative, to let people know 'We're here, and we would love to have your business.'" And the guarantee meant that if the customer was unhappy with the switch, Eloqua would give them their money back.

Eloqua salespeople began hearing back right away. "Market2Lead clients responded by email and said things like 'We didn't know this, thank you very much' and 'Hey, we should talk.'" Soon these Market2Lead clients were engaged in discussions about moving their business over to Eloqua.

Payne says that within two weeks, Eloqua closed a deal with software company Red Hat that was worth more than $500,000 over two years. They also closed with TRUSTe, a major Internet privacy services company. The half dozen new Eloqua customers gained from this real-time communications effort combined to generate just under $1 million in business—all business directly related to Payne's real-time blog post. "There are other intangible benefits you can't put a price on as a real-time marketer," he says. "We got tremendous credibility in our industry for being a trusted source of news and information. People like that we are straight shooters."

Because Payne's post and the resulting media stories are all indexed by Google and the other search engines, people looking for information about the transaction even months later still found Eloqua in the thick of the discussion. If you're an analyst combing the marketing automation industry, or if you are evaluating marketing automation platforms, Eloqua moves to the head of the pack.

I'm constantly amazed at what a real-time blog post can do. In this case, it generated a million dollars' worth of new business! When everyone else is pitching the media using traditional methods, why not frame the discussion happening right now with your own well-placed commentary on the news?

There's an interesting footnote to this real-time story. In early 2013 Oracle acquired Eloqua in a transaction worth $871 million.

The Time Is Now

As you develop your own real-time mind-set, be on the lookout for ways to engage your marketplace when the time is right. There are many ways to communicate instantly, and the tools and strategies will be different for each situation. Let's take a look at some of the ways you can engage in real time.

Create Advertising Based on Real-Time Events

In a world of boring advertising campaigns, real-time marketing and PR gets noticed. During the London Summer Olympics of 2012 during coverage broadcast on NBC, AT&T ran several near real-time ads involving swimming that astonished me. The ads showed a young person watching the actual footage of a world record swim from the day before on a mobile phone. You see the NBC clip of the world record finish and hear the actual commentary. Then you realize the young person is a swimmer and he or she is writing the new world record time with the word "goal" on a whiteboard at home.

One AT&T ad was Ryan Lochte's world record 400-meter Individual Medley where he beat Michael Phelps.

A few nights later the AT&T ad was even better because Rebecca Soni broke the 200-meter breaststroke world record the day before in the semi-finals. The near real-time ad ran the next day immediately after the finals, which she won beating her own world record. These commercials were interesting because they related directly to the Olympic event results from the previous day and therefore generated more interest among viewers than the standard TV spot.

Respond to Citizens Right Away

While I was in Kolkata (Calcutta), India, several people told me about the remarkable use of Facebook by the Kolkata Traffic Police. Amazingly, as I write this, more than 30,000 people "like" the Kolkata Traffic Police Facebook page.[4]

In a world where many are skeptical about social media and real-time communications (dismissing tools like Facebook as "for kids"), the Kolkata

---

[4] facebook.com/pages/Kolkata-Traffic-Police/129115403803409

Traffic Police serves citizens in the way they prefer—via social media and in real time.

The Kolkata Traffic Police Facebook page includes traffic status updates, such as "Traffic along R B Connector & P C Connector are heavy due to water logging" together with detailed reports posted as photos. This one had 119 "likes" and 46 comments such as: "immensely helpful..:) Thanks a ton KTP" and "This is very proactive. Thank you, Kolkata Traffic Police!" Can you believe that people are fans of the police and are thanking them in public?

In real time, citizens can use the page to lodge complaints and the police will follow up. Many such complaints are about the widespread problem of taxi drivers' refusal of certain fares. With Facebook, a complaint is lodged (people upload photo and video evidence to Facebook) and the police follow up with the result of the inquiry. For example:

> @Akhil Malik. As per your Facebook complaint regarding taxi refusal vide memo No F/B-58 dated- 11.01.13, this is to inform you that the driver of the cabs (WB04D8217 & WB04D5996) have been prosecuted. . . . You may be asked to appear before Ld. Court, if required. Thanks & regards.

This serves as a transparent way for the police to show in real-time the work they are doing and also publically calls out the offender if caught. And over time, as taxi drivers figure out what's going on, the problems should diminish.

Like!

I just love this real-time use of social media. So do the citizens of Kolkata. The effort serves as positive PR for the police. Heck, if a police force can use Facebook for real-time communications at work, why are so many organizations still fearful and say "no"?

Create a Real-Time Product

Uber is an iPhone app (it is also available on Android) that you use to book private driver service, typically in a Lincoln Town Car, in cities including San Francisco, New York, Boston, Paris, and London.

For a passenger, the real-time aspect comes in as you use the app to see if available cars are nearby. Then you tap a button to request a ride and immediately see how long it will take for your driver to reach you (all done in real-time with geolocation). You get a message with your driver's name, mobile number, and car license plate number. And in just a few minutes your ride appears.

The beauty of Uber was in full glory for me when I arrived at San Francisco airport for the 2012 Dreamforce event. As 50,000 other people were also arriving for Dreamforce during those few days the taxi line was one hour long (I asked the people at the head of the line). So I popped up Uber and five minutes later I was seated in a comfortable black Lincoln Town Car being whisked in style to my hotel. Brilliant. The real-time aspects of the app for a passenger are amazing.

The app is just as slick for drivers. If they are free, they get a beep on their phone and can instantly see that a passenger is waiting for a ride. They can choose to accept or decline the ride. If they accept, the passenger's name and mobile number are made available and the passenger's exact location displayed. When the ride starts, the driver hits the start button and then again at the destination, he terminates the ride on the app. Because the passenger's credit card number is charged and the credit made to the driver's Uber account, no cash changes hands and it is very quick. Both passenger and driver can rate one another on a 5-star scale much like eBay. Easy!

Like many businesses before it, the market for private car services is being transformed by real-time mobile technology. Just like books (with instant Kindle downloads) and many other industries, real-time technology is disintermediating traditional businesses.

Donate Your Product to Those in Need

It has been estimated that more than a billion people worldwide witnessed part of the live broadcast of the dramatic rescue of the 33 Chilean miners in October 2010. Recall that they had been trapped in the darkness of the underground mine for many weeks.

Thus, many of those billion people also saw the Oakley sunglasses the miners were wearing as they emerged into daylight. That's because Oakley donated the sunglasses, which provided the miners' sensitive eyes with protection from ultraviolet light

No matter how you choose to measure it, the benefit of such a marketing coup is enormous. According to research done for CNBC by Front Row Analytics, just the worldwide television impact alone generated $41 million in equivalent advertising for Oakley.

To succeed with a real-time product donation like Oakley, you need to be aware of what's happening in your market category and be prepared to spring into action at a moment's notice.

Tweet Thoughts to Your Market When They Are Watching

As HBO was replaying his 1997 movie *Private Parts*, radio personality Howard Stern popped onto Twitter and offered a real-time running commentary on the movie. It wasn't planned or announced. You had to be there. He tweeted about 100 times with fun insider observations.

Lucky fans who were (1) watching the movie on HBO, (2) simultaneously monitoring Twitter, and (3) following Stern were in the real-time loop.

Many had their questions answered live, as in this reply from @HowardStern: "Giamatti was brilliant. made it all so easy. RT @burtmania How was it working with Giamatti before he was such a well-known actor?"

The buzz generated by Stern prompted many fans to tweet their friends and encourage them to tune in and see what he had to say about the movie.

While very few people have an audience as large as Howard Stern's, we all have opportunities to use Twitter to comment in real time as something is happening in our marketplace. Perhaps you can offer running commentary on a speech at an industry event. Or maybe, like Stern, you can live-tweet comments about a television show as it is broadcast. I'm imagining a clothing designer commenting on the fashion at the Academy Awards or a golf coach offering real-time commentary on an important tournament.

Comment on Regulatory Change in Your Industry

Officials from the U.S. Federal Communications Commission (FCC) were holed up in meetings to discuss the issue of bill shock, the surprise a consumer experiences when receiving a mobile phone bill with much higher charges than expected. While the meeting was taking place, Jeff Barak of Amdocs, a company that provides customer care, billing, and order management systems for telecommunications carriers and Internet services providers, posted: "No need to be (bill) shocked" on the company blog.[5] Barak argued that it's actually in the mobile phone service providers' interest

---

[5] blogs.amdocs.com/voices/2010/10/14/no-need-to-be-bill-shocked

to work with customers to avoid bill shock, because preserving customer loyalty is so important in a highly competitive market.

This clever tactic works because people interested in the potential legislation that might emerge from a meeting of government officials are eagerly looking at the news for any real-time updates. So when a company like Amdocs comments, the information gets picked up by those people's real-time Google Alerts.

Amdocs was rewarded soon after, when Penton Media publication *Connected Planet* devoted an entire blog post to the Amdocs position in a piece called "Not Being Shocked by Bill Shock." Reaching an important industry journalist in real time gets you noticed. Plus, the relationship that's built lasts much longer than just that moment. After the meetings were completed, the FCC published its proposal for new rules requiring companies to notify customers when they are about to exceed plan limits and incur extra charges. Anyone researching the proposal could come upon the Amdocs piece as well.

As we saw in both the Eloqua and Amdocs examples, your blog is a great place to add your take on a story as it is breaking. But don't just write the post and walk away. Alert people to the information by tweeting about it, posting it in your company's online media room, or sending a link to the journalists who might be interested.

Use a News Release to React to Another Company's Announcement

While busy at an industry conference, Richard Harrison, president of email marketing technology company SMTP.com, learned that Amazon.com had just made an announcement that they were entering the email delivery market. Harrison decided to put out an immediate press release with the headline "SMTP, Inc. Welcomes Amazon to the Email Delivery Market."[6]

He received a call from a reporter at online industry trade publication *ClickZ* right away, and soon a story appeared featuring his take on the announcement: "Will Amazon's Commodity E-Mail Service Harm ESPs?"

Harrison's take on the experience? "Its all about momentum," he says. "It's hard to create momentum on your own as the small guy, but if someone

---

[6] marketwire.com/press-release/smtp-inc-welcomes-amazon-to-the-email-delivery-market-1385573.htm

else creates it, the sooner you can ride it, the more you can benefit. Like momentum stocks, you don't know how far they will go, but the sooner you buy, the more you make."

These are just a few examples to get you thinking about the power of real-time communications. As I've studied the phenomenon of instant engagement, I've noticed that speed is typically an advantage that the smaller, nimbler outfits have over the larger ones. If you're an upstart in a competitive industry, real-time marketing and public relations allow you to compete and win. They even permit one person with a computer or mobile phone to start a movement to help thousands of people in time of need, making a huge difference in the world.

Crowdsourced Support

I followed with interest the terrible flooding situation in and around Brisbane in Queensland, Australia, in 2011. And I also followed the remarkable story of Baked Relief, a crowdsourced support group that emerged to help those affected.

Baked Relief is a movement of thousands of people who bake and cook. They provided home-prepared food to people directly affected by the floods, as well as to volunteers, emergency workers, and the military. The Baked Relief movement was started by Danielle Crismani. "I was just watching the stuff on the news," she says. "I thought, 'Oh gosh, all these people are sandbagging. I wonder what I could do. I can't go and sandbag, but I wasn't going to sit around.'" So she tweeted to tell her followers that she was about to take cupcakes to the volunteer sandbaggers working near her home.

The next day, she used the #bakedrelief hashtag on Twitter and was surprised that many others started to use it as well, building on her idea of helping those affected by offering their own support to the volunteers and emergency workers. A real-time movement began, which Crismani then poured all of her energy into. "I got onto Twitter and said, 'Hey, if you're stuck at home and you can't go to work, how about you bake for the SES [State Emergency Service] and take some stuff down to the people that are sandbagging?' Then I got on Facebook and did the same thing," she says.

Several days later, #bakedrelief was so popular that it was the second highest trending hashtag (the second most popular topic discussed at the time on Twitter in Australia) with #qldfloods (the hashtag used for general information about the floods) in the number one spot.

Things happened quickly, and it soon became apparent that matching thousands of people who were willing to help with those who needed it was too difficult to manage on Twitter alone. "There were a lot of people who wanted to get more involved," Crismani says. "We needed a base to be able to record lots of information every day. So instead of people constantly contacting us through Twitter asking, 'Where do I take my three batches of biscuits?' we needed somewhere to link to and say, 'For this morning, this is where the food needs to go. Come back at midday, and we'll update the blog and this is where the food will need to go then.'"

Once the need was identified, a bakedrelief.org site was developed extremely quickly using a WordPress platform. "Kay, one of the women who worked very closely with us, just did the site up. She called me and said, 'I've got a surprise for you. Have a look in your inbox.' When I got to my inbox, there was the link to the bakedrelief.org. She said it took her like 45 minutes to do it up. We made a few changes over time and added a few things, but we needed something simple." I love that the site was made so quickly. Most people, when considering a new website, imagine months of work, but this took just 45 minutes. The site provides details for those willing to volunteer and those in need. It also accepts cash donations from people (like me) who are far away from the devastation and cannot donate food.

Crismani launched an .ORG site to communicate quickly in this time of crisis. When important news affecting your organization breaks fast, sometimes the best way to connect with customers and the media is to quickly build a new website in real time. An .ORG domain name is an excellent option in this case because it has an inherent reputation of trust, integrity, and credibility.

The key with bakedrelief.org was to get the new site up very quickly, right at the time when people were eager to locate credible information on the breaking issue.

Many people blogged and tweeted to spread the word, and soon Australia's national mainstream media picked up on the movement. Even people outside the area jumped in to help, with some driving for hours to deliver food. One group, Funky Pies, drove up from Sydney (about 1,000 km, a 12-hour drive) to deliver their pies to volunteers, people working at Queensland Police and an evacuation center.

During this period of time, Crismani was working 20 hours per day on Baked Relief. "I was going to sleep for four hours or so and then waking up and doing it all over again every day," she says. "I hadn't properly eaten with a knife and fork for two weeks."

The Australian government got involved in the movement when Deputy Prime Minister and Federal Treasurer Wayne Swan started talking up Baked Relief. "There was bakedrelief.org on the home page of his website," Crismani says. "You'd click on it, and it'd give you all the information. And whenever you'd call his office, they would answer the phone with 'Hi, you've reached the office of Treasurer Wayne Swan. If you're phoning about Baked Relief . . . .' We had a big laugh. He called me up, and he said, 'How do you like the treasurer working for you?' That was funny."

Soon after, Anna Bligh, the premier of Queensland, used Twitter (her Twitter ID is @theqldpremier) to set up a meeting with Crismani to discuss community recovery and assistance for families of those affected. "The premier wanted me to meet with her team to tell them my ideas," Crismani says. "That meeting happened with the head of the Department of Communities and the premier's director-general, and the concerns of the residents of the Lockyer Valley and in the Cyclone areas of Far North Queensland were expressed by me during that meeting. All coordinated via Twitter!"

One person with an Internet connection and a Twitter feed started a movement by communicating in real time. Her efforts helped thousands and was recognized at the national level in Australia. That's power that you have, too. "You can motivate other people; your reach is far broader than you think," Crismani says. "I think it is pretty amazing, and I'm really proud of what's happened. It has taught me the power of social media. I will not be so blasé about it all now!"

This story is a great example of the power of real-time crowdsourcing using social media. No traditional advertising, media relations, or marketing techniques were used. The entire effort was crowdsourced in real time.

Crowdsourcing involves taking a task usually performed by one or a few people and distributing it among a crowd of people—outsourcing it to a crowd—via online social networks and in real time. There are many ways that organizations are tapping the crowd to perform tasks more quickly or cheaply than by using traditional techniques. During live broadcasts, programs like *American Idol* and *Britain's Got Talent* get audiences to evaluate performers by calling a special phone number or texting their votes. The best example of an enormous crowdsourced project is Wikipedia, the free online encyclopedia that anybody can add to or edit.

Or consider the revolution in Egypt that toppled the Mubarak regime in 2011 after 30 years in power. The protest movement was crowdsourced using a Facebook page called "Kullena Khaled Said"—initially administered anonymously by Wael Ghonim, a Dubai-based Egyptian citizen—to organize people and direct them to the places where demonstrations were to take place. "Kullena Khaled Said" eventually grew to 2.6 million "likes," and posts on the page during the early 2011 protests routinely had a million views and thousands of comments. Ghonim's fascinating 2012 memoir *Revolution 2.0: The Power of the People Is Greater Than the People in Power: A Memoir* is well worth checking out if you're interested in learning more about the role of Facebook in the Egyptian revolution. Ghonim, who at the time was employed by Google, was eventually arrested and spent more than a week in prison. His book reads like a spy novel as he describes the ways he hid his identity and had people help him with the page even when he was unable to.

Just think—if crowdsourcing is powerful enough to bring together tens of thousands of people to help during a natural disaster or even force a government out of power, it has tremendous potential for any business. In mine, public speaking, I used the technique to create a new speaker video. At the MarketingSherpa Email Summit, a dozen people with handheld video cameras filmed me speaking, and I used those crowdsourced shots to make a video to share with meeting planners.[7]

Real-time marketing and public relations deliver a decisive competitive advantage to those organizations that engage quickly. It doesn't matter what business you're in; these ideas can work for you, too.

Now let's spend some time on the specifics of how you can implement the new rules for your own organization. Part III of this book starts with a discussion of how you build a comprehensive marketing and PR plan to reach your buyers directly with web content. Once armed with your plan, continue to the chapters that follow, which will give you advice for developing thought leadership content and writing for your buyers. Finally, I provide detailed information on how to implement a news release program, build an online media room, create your own blog and podcast, and work with social networking sites. Because I'm convinced of the value of hearing from innovative marketers who have had success with these ideas, I continue to sprinkle case studies throughout the remaining chapters to give you some examples of how others have implemented these ideas and to help you get your own creative juices flowing.

---

[7] vimeo.com/dmscott/real-time-trailer

Action Plan for Harnessing the Power of the New Rules

11

You Are What You Publish: Building Your Marketing and PR Plan

Does your company sell great products? Or if you don't work in a traditional company, does your organization (church, nonprofit, consulting company, school) offer great services? Well, get over it! Marketing is not *only* about your products! The most important thing to remember as you develop a marketing and PR plan is to put your products and services to the side for just a little while and focus your complete attention on the *buyers* of your products (or those who will donate, subscribe, join, or apply). Devoting attention to buyers and away from products is difficult for many people, but it always pays off in the form of bringing you closer to achieving your goals.

Think Starbucks for a moment. Is the product great? Yeah, I guess the three-dollar cup of coffee I get from Starbucks tastes pretty good. And most marketers, if given the opportunity to market Starbucks, would focus on the coffee itself—the product. But is that really what people are buying at Starbucks, or does Starbucks help solve other buyer problems? Maybe Starbucks is really selling a place to hang out for a while. Or for that matter, isn't Starbucks a convenient place for people to meet? (I use Starbucks several times a month as a place to connect with people or conduct interviews.) Or do people use Starbucks for the free wireless Internet connections? Maybe Starbucks saves 10 minutes in your day because you don't have to grind beans, pour water into a coffee maker, wait, and clean up later. For some of us, Starbucks just represents a little splurge because, well, we're worth it. I'd argue that Starbucks does all those things. Starbucks appeals to many different buyer personas, and it sells lots of things besides just coffee. If you were marketing Starbucks, it would be your job to segment buyers and appeal to them based on their needs, not just talk about your product.

The approach of thinking about buyers and the problems our organizations solve for them can be difficult for many marketers, since we've constantly been told how important a great product or service is to the marketing mix. In fact, standard marketing education still talks about the four *P*s of marketing—product, place, price, and promotion—as being the most important things. That's nonsense. To succeed on the web under the new rules of marketing and PR, you need to consider your organizational goals and then focus on your buyers *first*. Only when you understand buyers should you begin to create compelling web content to reach them. Yes, marketers often argue with me on this. But I strongly believe that the product or service you sell is secondary when you market your organization on the web.

So I will ask you to put aside your products and services as you begin the task for this chapter: building a marketing and PR plan that follows the new rules. While the most important thing to focus on during this process is buyers, we will do that in the context of your organizational goals. Trust me—this will be like no marketing and PR plan you've created before.

What Are Your Organization's Goals?

Marketing and PR people have a collective difficulty getting our departmental goals in sync with the rest of the company. And our management teams go along with this dysfunction. Think about the goals that most marketers have. They usually take the form of an epic to-do list: "Let's see; we should do a few trade shows, buy Yellow Pages ads, maybe create a new logo, get press clips, produce some T-shirts, increase website traffic, and, oh yeah, generate some leads for the salespeople." Well, guess what? Those aren't the goals of your company! I've never seen leads or clips or T-shirts on a balance sheet. With typical marketing department goals, we constantly focus on the flare-up du jour and thus always focus on the wrong thing. This also gives the marketing profession a bad rap in many companies as a bunch of flaky slackers. No wonder marketing is called the branding police in some organizations and is often the place where failed salespeople end up.

Many marketers and PR people also focus on the wrong measures of success. With websites, people often tell me things like "We want to have

10,000 unique visitors per month to our site." And PR measurement is often similarly irrelevant: "We want 10 mentions in the trade press and three national magazine hits each month." Unless your site makes money through advertising so that raw traffic adds revenue, traffic is the wrong measure. And simple press clips just don't matter. What matters is leading your site's visitors and your constituent audiences to where they help you reach your real goals, such as building revenue, soliciting donations, and gaining new members.

This lack of clear goals and real measurement reminds me of seven-year-olds playing soccer. If you've ever seen little children on the soccer field, you know that they operate as one huge organism packed together, chasing the ball around the field. On the sidelines are helpful coaches yelling, "Pass!" or "Go to the goal!" Yet as the coaches and parents know, this effort is futile: No matter what the coach says or how many times the kids practice, they still focus on the wrong thing—the ball—instead of the goal.

That's exactly what we marketers and PR people do. We fill our lists with balls and lose sight of the goal. But do you know what's even worse? Our coaches (the management teams at our companies) actually encourage us to focus on balls (like sales leads or press clips or website traffic statistics) instead of real organizational goals such as revenue. The VPs and CEOs of companies happily provide incentives based on leads for the marketing department and on clips for the PR team. And the agencies we contract with—advertising and PR agencies—also focus on the wrong measures.

What we need to do is align marketing and PR objectives with those of the organization. For most corporations, the most important goal is profitable revenue growth. In newer companies and those built around emerging technologies, this usually means generating new customers, but in mature businesses, the management team may need to be more focused on keeping the customers that they already have. Of course, nonprofits have the goal of raising money; politicians, to get out the vote; rock bands, to get people to buy CDs, iTunes downloads, and tickets to live shows; and universities, to get student applications and alumni donations.

So your first step is to get with the leaders of your organization—your management team or your associates in your church or nonprofit or your spouse if you run a small business—and determine your business goals. If you run a nonprofit, school, church, or political campaign, consider your goals for donations, applications, new members, or votes. Write them down in detail. The important things you write down might be "grow revenue in

Europe by 20 percent," "increase new member sign-ups to 100 per month in the fourth quarter," "generate a million dollars in web donations next quarter," or "generate five paid speaking engagements in the upcoming year."

Now that you have the marketing and PR plan focused on the right goals (i.e., those of your organization), the next step is to learn as much as you can about your buyers and to segment them into groups so you can reach them through your web publishing efforts.

Buyer Personas and Your Organization

Successful online marketing and PR efforts work because they start by identifying one or more buyer personas to target, so you need to make buyer personas a part of your planning process. A buyer persona (which we touched on back in Chapter 3) is essentially a representative of a type of buyer that you have identified as having a specific interest in your organization or product or having a market problem that your product or service solves. Building buyer personas is the first step and probably the single most important thing that you will do in creating your marketing and PR plan. Consider the U.S. presidential elections of 2004. Marketers for the two major candidates segmented buyers (voters) into dozens of distinct buyer personas. Some of the names of the buyer personas (sometimes called *microtargets* in the political world) became well known as the media began to write about them, while many other persona labels remained internal to the candidates. Some of the better-known buyer personas of the 2004 presidential election were NASCAR Dads (rural working-class males, many of whom are NASCAR fans) and Security Moms (mothers who were worried about terrorism and concerned about security). In 2008, vice presidential candidate and former Alaska governor Sarah Palin targeted Mama Grizzlies (independent-minded conservative women) and in the 2012 election cycle, Walmart Moms, a key swing voter (female voters with children 18 or younger at home who have shopped at Walmart at least once in the last month) was targeted by both candidates. By segmenting millions of voters into distinct buyer personas, candidates built marketing campaigns and PR programs that appealed specifically to each. Contrast this approach with a one-size-fits-all campaign that targets everybody but appeals to nobody.

Another example I quite like for illustrating the point of buyer personas is the market for tricycles. The user of the most common tricycle is a preschool child. Yet a preschooler doesn't buy the tricycle. The most common buyer personas for children's tricycles are parents and grandparents. So what problem does the tricycle solve? Well, for parents, it might be that the child has been asking for one and the purchase quiets the child down. Parents also know that the child is growing quickly and will want a two-wheeler with training wheels soon enough, so a basic trike is typically enough in their eyes. However, grandparents buy tricycles to solve the problem of providing an extravagant gift, so they often buy the expensive models to show their love to the child and his or her parents. When you think about tricycles from the perspective of buyer personas, you can see how the marketing might be different for parents and grandparents.

You, too, need to segment buyer personas so you can then develop marketing programs to reach each one. Let's revisit the college example from Chapter 3 and expand on it. Remember that we identified five different buyer personas for a college website: young alumni (those who graduated within the past 10 or 15 years), older alumni, the high school student who is considering college, the parents of the prospective student, and existing customers (current students). That means a well-executed college site might target five distinct buyer personas.

A college might have the marketing and PR goal of generating 500 additional applications for admission from qualified students for the next academic year. Let's also pretend that the college hopes to raise $5 million in donations from alumni who have never contributed in the past. That's great! These are real goals that marketers can build programs around.

The Buyer Persona Profile

After identifying their goals, the marketing people at the college should build a buyer persona profile, essentially a kind of biography, for each group they'll target to achieve those goals. The college might create one buyer persona for prospective students (targeting high school students looking for schools) and another for parents of high school students (who are part of the decision process and often pay the bills). If the school targets a specific type of applicant, say, student athletes, they might build a specific buyer persona profile for the high school student who participates in varsity sports. To effectively target the alumni for donations, the school might decide to build a buyer persona for younger alumni, perhaps those who have graduated in the past 10 years.

For each buyer persona profile, we want to know as much as we can about this group of people. What are their goals and aspirations? What are their problems? What media do they rely on for answers to problems? How can we reach them? We want to know, in detail, the things that are important for each buyer persona. What words and phrases do the buyers use? What sorts of images and multimedia appeal to each? Are short and snappy sentences better than long, verbose ones? I encourage you to write these things down based on your understanding of each buyer persona. You should also read the publications and websites that your buyers read to gain an understanding of the way they think. For example, college marketing people should read the *U.S. News & World Report* issue that ranks America's best colleges as well as the guidebooks that prospective students read, such as *Countdown to College: 21 To-Do Lists for High School: Step-by-Step Strategies for 9th, 10th, 11th, and 12th Graders* and *The Ultimate College Acceptance System: Everything You Need to Know to Get into the Right College for You.* Reading what your buyer personas read will get you thinking like them. By doing some basic research on your buyers, you can learn a great deal, and your marketing will be much more effective.

The best way to learn about buyers and develop buyer persona profiles is to interview people. I have no doubt that representatives of the 2012 presidential candidates interviewed many Walmart Moms to build profiles for this and many other buyer personas they identified. Similarly, the marketing person at our hypothetical college must interview people who fit the personas the school identified. The college marketing people might learn a great deal if they turned the traditional in-person college admissions interview around by asking prospective students questions such as the following: When did you first start researching schools? Who influenced your research? How did you learn about this school? How many schools are you applying to? What websites do you read or subscribe to? Once you know this firsthand information, you should subscribe to, read, and listen to the media that influence your target buyer. When you read what your buyers read, pay attention to the exact words and phrases that are used. If students frequent Facebook or other social network sites, so should you, and you should pay attention to the lingo students use. By triangulating the information gathered directly from several dozen prospective students plus information from the media that these students pay attention to, you easily build a buyer persona for a high school student ready to apply to a college like yours.

"A buyer persona profile is a short biography of the typical customer, not just a job description but a person description," says Adele Revella,[1] who has been using buyer personas to market technology products for more than 20 years. "The buyer persona profile gives you a chance to truly empathize with target buyers, to step out of your role as someone who wants to promote a product and see, through your buyers' eyes, the circumstances that drive their decision process. The buyer persona profile includes information on the typical buyer's background, daily activities, and current solutions for their problems. The more experience you have in your market, the more obvious the personas become."

This may sound a bit wacky, but I think you should go so far as to name your persona the way that the campaigns did with Walmart Moms. You might even cut out a representative photo from a magazine to help you visualize him or her. This should be an *internal name only* that helps you and your colleagues to develop sympathy with and a deep understanding of the real people to whom you market. Rather than a nameless, faceless prospect, your buyer persona will come to life.

For example, a buyer persona for a male high school student who is a varsity athlete and whom you want to target might be named Sam the Athlete, and his persona might read something like this: "Sam the Athlete began thinking about colleges and the upcoming application process way back when he was a freshman in high school. His coach and parents recognized his athletic talent and suggested that it will help him get into a good college or even secure a scholarship. Sam knows that he's good, but not good enough to play on a Division 1 school. Sam first started poking around on college websites as a freshman and enjoyed checking out the athletic pages for the colleges in his home state and some nearby ones. He even attended some of these colleges' games when he could. Sam has good grades, but he is not at the top of his class because his sports commitments mean he can't study as much as his peers. He has close friends and likes to hang out with them on weekends, but he is not heavily into the party scene and avoids alcohol and drugs. Sam frequents Facebook, has his own Facebook page, and has a group of online friends that he frequently Instant Messages with. He is hip to online nuance, language, and etiquette. Sam also reads *Sports Illustrated*. Now that he is a junior, he knows it is time to get serious about college applications, and he doesn't really know where to start. But to learn, he's now paying more attention to the applications pages than the athletic pages on college websites."

---

[1] buyerpersona.com

Okay, so you're nodding your head and agreeing with this buyer persona profiling thing. "But," you ask, "how many buyer personas do I need?" You might want to think about your buyer personas based on what factors differentiate them. How can you slice the demographics? For example, some organizations will have a different profile for buyers in the United States versus Europe. Or maybe your company sells to buyers in the automobile industry and in the government sector, and those buyers are different. The important thing is that you will use this buyer persona information to create specific marketing and PR programs to reach each buyer persona, and therefore you need to have the segmentation in fine enough detail that when they encounter your web content, your buyers will say, "Yes, that's me. This organization understands me and my problems and will therefore have products that fit my needs."

Marketers and PR pros are often amazed at the transformation of their materials and programs as a result of buyer persona profiling. "When you really know how your buyers think and what matters to them, you eliminate the agony of guessing about what to say or where and how to communicate with buyers," says Revella. "Marketers tell me that they don't have time to build buyer personas, but these same people are wasting countless hours in meetings debating about whether the message is right. And of course, they're wasting budgets building programs and tools that don't resonate with anyone. It's just so much easier and more effective to listen before you talk."

Reaching Senior Executives

Many people ask me about reaching senior executives via the web. That executives do not use the web as much as other people is a commonly held belief, one that I've never bought. Frequently, business-to-business marketers use this misperception as an excuse for why they don't have to focus on building buyer personas and marketing materials for senior executives. Based on anecdotal information from meeting with many of them, I have always argued that executives are online in a big way. However, I've never had any solid data to support my hunch until now.

Forbes Insights, in association with Google, released a study called *The Rise of the Digital C-Suite: How Executives Locate and Filter Business Information.*[2] The findings clearly show that executives consider the web to be

---

[2] forbes.com/forbesinsights/digital_csuite/index.html

their most valuable resource for gathering business information, outstripping at-work contacts, personal networks, trade publications, and so on. In a follow-up study, *Video in the C-Suite: Executives Embrace the Non-Text Web*, Forbes Insights found that 75 percent of executives surveyed said they watch work-related videos at least weekly, and 65 percent have visited a vendor's website after watching a video. The social element of online video is strong in the executive suite. More than half of senior executives share videos with colleagues at least weekly and receive work-related videos as often.

"The common perception is that top executives at the largest companies do not use the Internet, but the reality is just the opposite," says Stuart Feil, editorial director of Forbes Insights. "These findings show that C-level executives are more involved online than their counterparts, and younger generations of executives—those whose work careers have coincided with the growth of the PC and the Internet—are bringing profound organizational change to these companies."

The Importance of Buyer Personas in Web Marketing

One of the simplest ways to build an effective website or to create great marketing programs using online content is to target the specific buyer personas that you have created. Yet most websites are big brochures that do not offer specific information for different buyers. Think about it—the typical website is one size fits all, with the content organized by the company's products or services, not by categories corresponding to buyer personas and their associated problems.

The same thing is true about other online marketing programs. Without a focus on the buyer, the typical press release and media relations program are built on what the organization wants to say rather than what the buyer wants to hear. There is a huge difference. Companies that are successful with direct-to-consumer news release strategies write for their buyers. The blogs that are best at reaching an organizational goal are not about companies or products but rather customers and their problems.

Now that you've set quantifiable organizational goals and identified the buyer personas that you want to reach, your job as you develop your marketing and PR plan is to identify the best ways to reach buyers and develop compelling information that you will use in your web marketing programs. If you've conducted interviews with buyers and developed a buyer persona profile, then you know the buyer problems that your product or service solves, and you know the media that buyers turn to for answers. Do they go first to a search engine? If so, what words and phrases do they enter? Which blogs, chat rooms, forums, and online news sites do they read? Are they open to audio or video? You need to answer these questions before you continue.

In Your Buyers' Own Words

Throughout the book, I often refer to the importance of understanding the words and phrases that buyers use. An effective web marketing plan requires an understanding of the ways your buyers speak and the real words and phrases they use. This is important not only for building a positive online relationship with your buyers but also for planning effective search engine marketing strategies. After all, if you are not using the phrases your buyers search on, how can you possibly reach them?

Let's take a look at the importance of the actual words buyers use, by way of an example. Several years ago, I worked with Shareholder.com to create a web content strategy to reach buyers of the company's new Whistleblower Hotline product and move those buyers into and through the sales cycle. The Shareholder.com product was developed as an outsourced solution for public companies to comply with rule 301 (the so-called Whistleblower Hotline provision) of the U.S. Sarbanes-Oxley legislation that passed in 2002 in the wake of corporate scandals such as Enron. Most important, we interviewed buyers (such as chief financial officers within publicly traded companies) who were required to comply with the legislation. We also read the publications that our buyers read (such as *CFO, Directors Monthly*, and the *AACA Docket* of the American Corporate Counsel Association), we actually downloaded and read the massive Sarbanes-Oxley legislation document itself, and we studied the agendas of the many conferences and events that our buyers attended that discussed the importance of Sarbanes-Oxley compliance.

As a result of the buyer persona research, we learned the phrases that buyers used when discussing the Sarbanes-Oxley Whistleblower Hotline rule, and so the content that we created for the Shareholder.com website[3] included such important phrases as "SEC mandates," "complete audit trail,"

---

[3] shareholder.com/home/Solutions/Whistleblower.cfm

"Sarbanes-Oxley rule 301," "confidential and anonymous submission," and "safe and secure employee reporting." An important component of the website we created (based on our buyer persona research) was thought-leadership-based content, including a webinar called "Whistleblower Hotlines: More Than a Mandate" that featured guest speakers Harvey Pitt (former chairman of the U.S. Securities and Exchange Commission) and Lynn Brewer (author of *House of Cards: Confessions of an Enron Executive*). Because this webinar discusses issues of importance to *buyers* (not only Shareholder.com products), and the guest speakers are thought leaders that buyers are interested in learning from, 600 people eagerly watched the presentation live.

"The webinar was very important because when we launched the product we were starting from a position with no market share within this product niche," says Bradley H. Smith, director of marketing/communications at Shareholder.com. "Other companies had already entered the market before us. The webinar gave us search engine terms like 'Harvey Pitt' and 'Enron' and offered a celebrity draw. Search engine placement was important because it created our brand as a leader in Whistleblower Hotline technologies even though we were new to this market. Besides prospective clients, the media found us, which resulted in important press including prominent placement in a *Wall Street Journal* article called 'Making It Easier to Complain.'"

Shareholder.com then took the service to the Canadian market, where the legislation was called "Ontario Securities Commission and the Audit Committees Rule of the Canadian Securities Administrators Guidelines Multilateral Instrument 52–110" (quite a mouthful). Smith and his colleagues interviewed buyers in Canada and did some buyer persona research to determine if there were any differences in the words and phrases used in Canada. There were! Unlike the other U.S. companies attempting to enter the Canadian market for hotline solutions by just using their U.S. marketing materials, Shareholder.com created a separate set of web content for Canadian buyers. Used in the pages for these buyers were specific phrases that were used by Canadian buyers (but not buyers in the United States), such as "governance hotline," "conducting a forensic accounting investigation," and the exact name of the Canadian legislation.

Because the marketers at Shareholder.com had done extensive buyer persona research and had created web content with the words and phrases used by buyers, the Shareholder.com pages were visited frequently and linked to often, and they became highly ranked by the search engines. In fact, at the time of this writing, Shareholder.com is number one out of 258,000 hits on Google for the phrase "whistleblower hotline."

As a result of traffic driven from the search engines and great web content for both U.S. and Canadian buyers (such as webinars), the product launch was a success. "In the four months immediately after the webcast, we signed 75 clients," Smith says. "Furthermore, the webcast archive of the event continued to work for us throughout the year, advancing our brand presence, generating sales leads, and contributing to the strongest Shareholder.com stand-alone product launch ever."

After I wrote the original version of this story, the Nasdaq Stock Market, Inc. acquired Shareholder.com.

Figuring out the phrases for your market requires that you buckle down and do some research. Although interviewing buyers about their market problems and listening to the words and phrases they use is best, you can also learn a great deal by reading the publications they read. Check out any blogs in your buyers' marketplace (if you haven't already), and study the agendas and topic descriptions for the conferences and seminars that your buyers frequent. When you have a list of the phrases that are important to your buyers, use those phrases not only to appeal to them specifically but also to make your pages appear in the search engine results when your buyers search for what you have to offer.

What Do You Want Your Buyers to Believe?

Now that you have identified organizational goals, built a set of one or more buyer personas, and researched the words and phrases your buyers use to talk about and search for your product or service, you should think about what you want each of your buyer personas to *believe* about your organization. What are the actual words and phrases that you will use for each buyer persona? Think back again to the 2004 U.S. presidential election. Once they had identified buyer personas such as NASCAR Dads and Security Moms, the campaigns had to create a set of messages, websites, TV ads, direct mail campaigns, and talking points that the candidates would use in speeches to these groups. For example, George W. Bush appealed to Security Moms with speeches and advertising that claimed that families would be safer from the threats of terrorism with his "stay the course" approach if he were reelected rather than if John Kerry were elected.

In the 2008 election, Barack Obama focused on his buyer personas and identified as crucially important the concept of change. Everywhere you saw the Obama campaign, you saw nods to this theme: on the podium where the candidate was speaking, on T-shirts and buttons, on posters, and of course, on the web. The Obama campaign shrewdly understood that when primary voters pulled the lever to vote for Obama, they were buying into the idea of the need for change. They were choosing an idea, not just a man. The Obama campaign clearly understood, and articulated, what they wanted their buyer personas to believe that the candidate would bring.

You must do the same thing with your buyer personas. What do you want each group to believe about your organization? What messages will you use to reach them on the web? Remember, the best information is not just about your product. What is each buyer persona really buying from you? Is it great customer service? The safe choice? Luxury? For example, Volvo doesn't just sell a car; it sells *safety*.

And don't forget that different buyer personas buy different things from your organization. Think about Gatorade for a moment. For competitive athletes, Gatorade has been the drink of choice for decades. I found some interesting messages on the Gatorade website,[4] including "If you want to *win*, you've got to replace what you *lose*" and "For some athletes, significant dehydration can occur within the initial 30 minutes of exercise." These are interesting messages, because they target the buyer persona of the competitive athlete and focus on how Gatorade can help those athletes win.

Now I'm not an expert on Gatorade's buyer personas, but it seems to me that they could further refine their buyer personas based on the sports athletes play or on whether they are professionals or amateurs. If tennis players see themselves as very different from football players, then Gatorade may need to create buyer persona profiles and messages to target both sports separately. Or maybe women athletes make up a different buyer persona for Gatorade than men.

---

[4] gatorade.com

But there's another buyer persona that I have never seen Gatorade address. I remember back to my early 20s, when I lived in an apartment in New York City and was single and making the rounds in the party circuit and late-night club scene. To be honest, I was partying a little too hard some weeknights, skulking home in the wee hours. I then had to make it down to my Wall Street job by 8 A.M. I discovered that drinking a large bottle of Gatorade on the walk to the subway stop helped make me feel a lot better. Now I don't *actually* expect Gatorade to develop messages for young professionals in New York who drink too much, but that buyer persona certainly has different problems from those that Gatorade solves for athletes. Imagine advertising for this buyer persona: "Last night's third martini still in your system? Rehydration is not just for athletes. Gatorade."

I told this Gatorade story to a group of people at a seminar I ran for marketing executives, and a woman told the group that her mother always served Gatorade to her when she had a cold or the flu. How interesting—another buyer persona for Gatorade—mothers who are caring for sick children and who want to make sure they are properly hydrated.

The point is that different buyer personas have different problems for your organization to solve. And there's no doubt that your online marketing and PR programs will do better if you develop information specifically for each buyer persona, instead of simply relying on a generic site that uses one set of broad messages for everyone.

Developing Content to Reach Buyers

You must now think like a publisher. You should develop an editorial plan to reach your buyers with focused content in the media they prefer. Your first action might be to create a content-rich website with pages organized by buyer persona. This does not mean you need to redesign the entire existing website, nor does it necessitate a change in the site architecture. You can start by just creating some new individual pages, each with specialized content customized for a particular buyer persona, creating appropriate links to these pages, and leaving the rest of the site alone. For example, our hypothetical college might create content for each of the buyer personas they identified. Sam the Athlete (the high school student who is a varsity athlete and a candidate for admission) should have specific content written for him that describes what it is like to be a student athlete at the college and also gives tips for the admission process. The college could include profiles of current student athletes or even a blog by one of the coaches. In addition, appropriate links on the home page and the admissions pages should be created for Sam. An appropriate home page link such as "high school athletes start here" or "special information for student athletes" would attract Sam's attention.

At the same time, the college should develop pages for parents of high school students who are considering applying for admission. The parents have very different problems from those of the students, and the site content designed for parents would deal with things like financial aid and safety on campus.

As you keep your publisher's hat on, consider what other media your organization can publish on the web to reach the buyers you have identified. A technology company might want to consider a white paper detailing solutions to a known buyer problem. Perhaps you have enough information to create an e-book on a subject that would be of interest to one or more of your buyer personas. You may want to develop a series of a dozen direct-to-consumer news releases focusing on a series of issues that you know your buyer is interested in. Or it might be time to start a blog, a podcast, or online video channel to reach your buyers.

Consider creating an editorial plan for each buyer persona. You might do this in the form of a calendar for the upcoming year that includes website content, an e-book or white paper, a blog, and some news releases. Notice as you build an editorial plan and an editorial calendar for the next year that you're now focused on creating the compelling content that your buyers are interested in. Unlike the way you might have done it in the past (and the way your competitors are marketing today), you are not just creating a big brochure about your organization. You're writing for your buyers, not your own ego.

Bozeman, Montana–based RightNow Technologies, a provider of customer relationship management software and now a part of Oracle, rebuilt its company website around buyer personas. "The RightNow persona development exercise was broader than just for creating website content but was designed for all marketing content," says Steve Bell, product marketing manager for RightNow. "The goal of the website project was to turn RightNow.com into a website that sells. We created the new website with conversion paths (entry points into the buying process) for each persona, and more overall conversion points than the original site."

To help the web development team at RightNow build appropriate information for the site, detailed buyer personas were created for four different personas:

1. **Atul**—Director of Information Technology (a technical evaluator for a company that's considering RightNow Technologies' products).
2. **Chuck**—Customer Services Director (an operational prospect for RightNow Technologies—someone who manages a team that would use the product to do their jobs).
3. **Olivia**—Senior Vice President (a RightNow Technologies strategic prospect—the top executive in the department that will use the product to do their jobs).
4. **Trinh**—Financial Analyst (a RightNow Technologies information seeker who wants to know more about the company itself).

Bell and his team developed details about these buyer personas. The best way to do this is to interview representatives of each group. As an example, some details about Chuck's goals include:

- Chuck wants to improve his team's efficiency, due to his inability to fund new hires to keep up with demand.
- Chuck wants to decrease his staff's call and email volume, so they can spend more time with customers who really need help instead of routinely answering the same questions.
- Chuck needs to find a solution that doesn't involve complicated IT and can be implemented quickly.
- Chuck wants to improve customer satisfaction, but he assumes that will happen if he can reduce his team's call and email volume.

It's worth clarifying that the detailed information about your buyer personas is for your internal information and shouldn't be posted on the site. However, what you learn helps you create valuable information to be posted on the public site. For example, on the RightNow home page, there is a list of questions on the left-side navigation. The pages that these links point to are specifically built around buyer personas and address problems that these personas face.

- *I need to transform my call center.*
- *I need to capture customer feedback.*
- *I need to add live chat.*

"Chuck's content is built around his specific needs ('I need to . . .'), which are illustrated on the home page and take him down a specific conversion path," Bell says. "Olivia, who is more senior, is more focused on strategy and is more brand-conscious, so a big part of the banner areas on the home page are dedicated to her, such as 'Weathering the Storm.' The CEO blog and the customer experience strategies are also targeted at Olivia. There was a brand new technology section dedicated to Atul."

According to Bell, the results have exceeded expectations. RightNow has seen significant improvement in important web measurements of the new site compared with the previous one: a fourfold increase in overall conversions, a fivefold increase in live demo request conversions, and an increase in Flash demo conversions by a factor of more than three.

As the RightNow Technologies example shows, there are clear benefits to marketing based on detailed understanding of buyer personas. In particular, when you stop talking about you and your products and services and instead use the web to educate and inform important types of buyers, you will be more successful.

Marketing Strategy Planning Template

Over the past several years, as I've connected with people from around the world who have read earlier editions of this book, I've heard from some readers that they've struggled with getting started. Most of the implementation challenges that people describe involve the shift from focusing on products and services to the more effective approach of focusing on buyer personas and information that helps solve buyers' problems. A secondary challenge people share is the shift in emphasis from off-line marketing techniques and programs (such as direct mail, trade shows, and advertising) to reaching buyers on the web.

Taking a suggestion from Toby Jenkins and Adam Franklin of Australian web strategy firm Bluewire Media, I've devised an aid to tackling these challenges: a simple marketing and PR strategy-planning template. Jenkins and Franklin had been working on a similar template when we first got connected, so we decided to collaborate. You can download a full-color and more user-friendly version on my website.[5]

---

[5] davidmeermanscott.com/documents/Marketing_Strategy_Template.pdf

Marketing & PR Strategy: Planning Template

WHO	**BUYER PERSONA**	
	Description Who is this person? What problems does this buyer have?	
WHAT	**Problems you solve for this buyer** Why are they buying from you?	
	Actions you'd like them to take Download, buy, connect, etc.	
WHY	**How are you remarkable?** What value do you bring?	
	Proof Credibility indicators, media/analysts, testimonials, etc.	
WHERE	**Where are they?** Google, blogs, Facebook, Twitter, etc.	
HOW	**Your company personality** What kind of company are you?	
	Creative/Design Look and feel	
	Tone of voice Language you'd use	
	Keyword phrases What buyers type into search engines	
	Marketing tactics & Content strategy Blog, Twitter, YouTube, email newsletter, Google Ads, e-books, webinars, podcasts, etc.	

	WHEN Things to do today	Things to do next week
	1.	1.
	2.	2.
	3.	3.

Marketing & PR Strategy: Publishing Information for Your Buyers

CONTENT CREATION

- blogs
- Facebook profile
- Twitter feed
- e-books
- webinars
- articles
- galleries
- media
- directories
- testimonials
- speaker bios
- guest blog posts
- expert articles for industry sites
- mobile content
- blog directories
- news releases
- podcasts
- _____
- _____

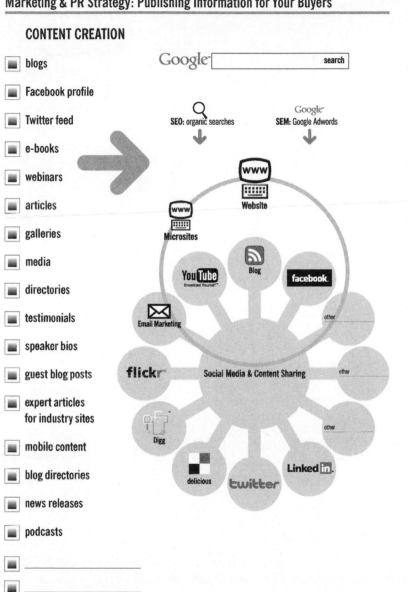

Marketing & PR Strategy: Driving Action

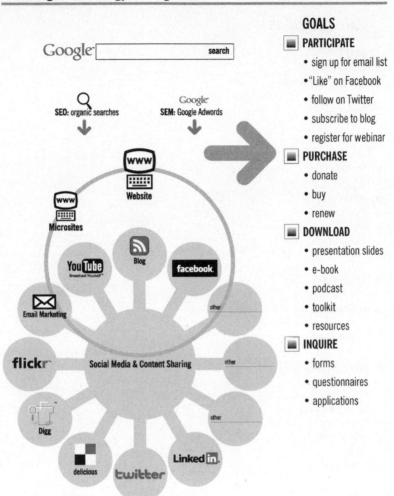

I created the template to help people implement strategies for reaching buyers directly. I believe it's essential to shift out of the marketer's comfort zone of preaching about products and services. For example, if you were to say to me, "I want to start a blog," I would point you to the template and have you start asking the following questions:

- Who are you trying to reach with the blog?
- Is a blog the best tool? Or might another form of content be better?

- What problems can you help solve for your buyers?
- What value do you bring as creator of this content?
- What search terms are people entering to find you? (This will help you name the blog itself and to title individual posts.)
- What sort of person are you, and what is your company's personality? (This is helpful for creating the design.)
- What do you want people to do—buy, donate, subscribe? (Helpful to create appropriate links to additional content.)

The marketing and PR strategy planning template is built on the same principle I use throughout this book: that understanding buyers and publishing information on the web especially for them drives action. This approach becomes clear on the second and third pages of the strategy template. The second page points out that when you publish valuable information (videos, blogs, Twitter feeds, e-books, and so on), you are creating the sorts of links that search engine algorithms love. Thus, your content surfaces when buyers are looking for help solving their problems! The third page reminds you that the information people find will drive them to action and help you achieve your goals. Moreover, you can monitor your own effectiveness: You can measure how many people follow you on Twitter, sign up for your email newsletter, or download a white paper. You can also measure how your marketing strategies are helping your organization reach its most important goals, such as new sales and revenue growth.

The New Rules of Measurement

Readers of my blog and those who have seen my talks know that I am very critical of the old ROI (return on investment) approach to measuring marketing and public relations success, an approach still popular today. In my days as vice president of marketing and PR for a NASDAQ-traded business-to-business technology company more than a decade ago, we measured success in two ways. Our marketing programs were measured via sales leads: the number of people who registered to download a white paper or who tossed a business card into a fishbowl at the trade show. In other words, the only thing that mattered in our approach to marketing was how many people raised their hands by submitting personal information to us. Similarly, our public relations programs were measured via a PR clip book, a collection of all the clippings of magazine and newspaper articles written about the company. The book represented a month's worth of clippings and was usually bound for us by our PR agency. We'd then calculate the advertising equivalency value of those press clips, that is, how much we would have to have paid to purchase a similar amount of ad space in that publication. These were the measures my bosses used to gauge my success. And I'm told by tons of marketing and PR people that sales leads and clip books are still the primary metric used today.

Asking Your Buyer for a Date

To illustrate how the old form of measurement based on sales leads is flawed, I like to appeal to a dating analogy. Imagine that a man went up to someone he found attractive at a bar and the first thing out of his mouth was "Give me your phone number."

Imagine that a woman saw someone she found interesting at the local coffee emporium and started off the conversation with "How much money do you make?"

If you're a famous celebrity or amazingly hot, this approach might work. However, mere mortals are not likely to get too far in the dating world by acting like this.

Yet this is exactly the way that many companies behave. They apply to the web the old rules they learned for off-line marketing. They require the disclosure of personal information before sending an interested party a white paper. They design inane "contact us" forms to fill out before it's possible to speak with a human. How does that make *you* feel? So the next time you have to design a marketing strategy, think about how you would approach it if you were trying to date the buyer.

Measuring the Power of Free

While the dating discussion helps us understand what's at stake for *marketing* measurement, what about for *public relations?* How do we measure the effectiveness of PR?

A reader named Lee put it bluntly: "Wow you really don't like us poor old PR people do you? So—how do you replace the clip books, which you are so scathing of and our bosses and client still demand? Can you help me understand how to explain to a client exactly what they have paid for on a monthly basis? They want to see results."

Here is a longer version of what I answered back to Lee:

The problem I have with clip book measurement is that it does not reflect the realities of what we can do today to reach our audiences via the web. A clip book implies that all we care about is ink from mainstream media. Measuring success by focusing only on the number of times the mainstream media write or broadcast about you misses the point.

If a blogger is spreading your ideas, that's great.

If a thousand people watch your YouTube video, that's awesome.

If a hundred people email a link to your information out to their networks, tweet about you, or post about you on their Facebook pages, that's amazing.

If 100 people join your LinkedIn group, go ahead and shout "Woo Hoo!"

If you come up on the first page of Google results for an important phrase, break out the champagne!

You're reaching people, which was the point of seeking media attention in the first place, right?

So the problem is that most PR people only measure traditional media like magazines, newspapers, radio, and TV, and this practice doesn't capture the value of sharing. There's nothing wrong with a clip book, but it's not enough.

What You Should Measure

These days, the web gives everyone—not only B2B companies like the one I worked for but also consumer brands, consultants, nonprofits, schools, and many others—a tremendous opportunity to reach people and engage them in new and different ways. Now we can earn attention by creating and publishing online for free something interesting and valuable: a YouTube video, a blog, a research report, photos, a Twitter stream, an e-book, a Facebook page.

But how *should* we measure the success of this new kind of marketing? The answer is that we need new metrics.

Take another look at the last page of the marketing and PR strategy planning template. Under Goals is a list of many things that you can measure and observe, such as how many people participate in your social networking sites, how many people are reading and downloading your work, and how many are making inquiries about or buying your products and services.

Here are seven things you can measure:

1. How many people are eager to participate in your online efforts? (You can measure how many people *like* you on Facebook, subscribe to your blog, follow you on Twitter, sign up for your email newsletter, or register for a webinar.)
2. How many people are downloading your stuff? (You can measure how many people are downloading your e-books, presentation slides, videos, podcasts, and other content.)
3. How often are bloggers writing about you and your ideas?
4. (And what are those bloggers saying?)
5. Where are you appearing in search results for important phrases?
6. How many people are engaging with you and choosing to speak to you about your offerings? (You can measure how many people are responding to contact forms and making requests for information.)
7. How are sales looking? Is the company reaching its goals? (Ultimately, the most important form of measurement within management teams is revenue and profit.)

For much more on measurement, check out Jim Sterne's *Social Media Metrics: How to Measure and Optimize Your Marketing Investment*. This book is part of my own New Rules of Social Media book series.

Registration or Not? Data from an e-Book Offer

My research into the differences in download frequency for content such as e-books when they are made completely free versus when they require registration suggests that you will generate between 10 and 50 times more downloads when you do not require registration. That's right, based on data from companies that have tested offers with and without registration, it's a good guess that if you're getting 100 downloads per month with registration, you might get as many as 5,000 downloads per month without registration.

Think about your own behavior for a moment. When you're interested in a free white paper, do you eagerly give up your email address to get the paper? Or are you reluctant, even refusing? Now if the paper were completely free, how would you feel? And what's even more interesting, ask yourself if you'd be willing to share a link to the white paper with your followers on Twitter or via email to your friends and colleagues if there were no registration? You'd be much more willing to share, right? Because you have nothing to lose. But if there were a registration requirement, would you share the link? The vast majority of people tell me they wouldn't, because they fear that their contacts might get put on a sales list and then receive unwanted emails and phone calls. This is exactly why free e-books with no registration have so many more inbound links and much higher search engine rankings.

I'm always interested in metrics that help inform this debate. John Mancini, president of the nonprofit AIIM, agreed to share his experience. AIIM represents the users and suppliers of document, content, and record-management technologies and publishes content on this subject as part of its marketing program.

Mancini released the organization's first e-book, *8 Reasons You Need a Strategy for Managing Information—Before It's Too Late*,[6] as a totally free download, with no registration required. In just the first month, the e-book was downloaded 5,138 times. AIIM also created a presentation version of the book and posted it, also with no registration requirement, on SlideShare. This version had 3,353 downloads. That makes for a total of 8,491 downloads that month.

"Making the e-book available for free and totally without registration was a new approach for us," Mancini says. "These results for unfettered access are particularly impressive when considered against a couple of more traditional examples, i.e., content requiring a registration on our website."

As a case in point, Mancini compares the e-book to one of his organization's most popular pieces of content, AIIM Industry Watch research papers. "We require registration for these papers because they are also used as a lead generation program for the sponsors," he says. "During roughly the same period as the e-book, there were [only] 513 actual downloads. I am convinced that open access is best for content like my e-books."

Although it's impossible to know for sure, since we're comparing two different pieces of content, AIIM's data suggest that there is a significant advantage in not requiring registration. Specifically, unlocking content at AIIM seems to have meant more than a 16-fold increase in the number of downloads. Mancini is convinced that the more forward-looking of AIIM's sponsors will start to realize that the future lies in creating as much visibility

---

[6] aiim.org/Research-and-Publications

as possible for their content—rather than viewing this marketing problem solely through the prism of name acquisition and lead generation.

Still not convinced about the power of free? When asked about this debate in my live presentations, I also offer a third option, which is a hybrid. I suggest the first offer be totally free, such as a totally free e-book with no registration requirement. Then, within the e-book, I suggest including a secondary offer that requires a registration that you can use to capture leads. This secondary offer might be access to a webinar or similar premium content. This way, you can spread your ideas yet still collect contact information.

Educating Your Salespeople about the New Sales Cycle

Okay, I hope I've managed to convince you of the benefit of measuring the total exposure to your ideas (e-book downloads, blog post views, and so on) rather than the number of people willing to hand over their private information. If so, you'll need to make sure that the others in your organization, especially the salespeople, understand this new approach.

Back in the mid-1990s, there was little love lost between marketing and sales. At many companies, the relationship was downright adversarial. The tension often extended all the way up to senior management. It stemmed from the sales process involving a handoff. Marketing generated leads and then handed them over to sales. Then the sales team owned them until close.

Like a marriage gone bad, the dialogue circa 1994 was an endless tape loop:

Sales said, "Get us some good leads! These leads stink! Our people can't sell."

Marketing responded, "You've got good leads! Your people just stink at closing!"

I've been in the middle of these discussions at several companies. They are so 20 years ago.

We're in a world now where sales and marketing can cooperate throughout the entire sales process. As this entire book discusses and I hope you realize now, buyers are evaluating your offerings throughout the marketing and sales process based on what they see and do on your site and in social networks. This approach of creating amazing content and publishing it on the web serves as a parallel way of communicating about your company, which works in sync with what buyers eventually hear from a salesperson.

Savvy marketing and sales professionals understand that sales and marketing *must* work together to move buyers through the entire cycle. This is especially important in complex sales with long decision-making cycles and multiple buyers that must be influenced. The good news is that web content can drive people through, and even shorten, these complex sales cycles.

Imagine a buyer interested in a new motorcycle. The buyer takes a look at a dealer's website and sees all kinds of excellent information, including videos, a blog, and more. The content is free, with no registration. All of this educational information serves to drive the buyer into the showroom to meet in person with a sales representative. The key here is that the marketing content on the web works in parallel with the salesperson. It's not like in the old days, when marketing's job was to get people to the showroom and all the product education comes from the salesperson. Today, the best companies integrate marketing and sales, educating the buyer throughout the process.

Smart marketers need to educate salespeople so the latter understand that we're all in this together. We are no longer in a world where marketing hands off to sales. Marketing needs to create content for each step in the process. And salespeople, if they are active in social media, can drive people into the beginning of the sales process just like marketers can.

As a marketer, the most important thing you can do is make sure sales and the management team understand this point that leads are no longer the primary metric. Explain that registration requirements just don't work in an environment where Google delivers the best content. Free content is what drives action today. And the most successful companies are those where salespeople and marketers work together to move people through the sales process.

Now let's close this chapter with a look at an organization that tossed aside its concern with old forms of measurement and achieved the ultimate form of success.

Obama for America

I want you to stop, take a deep breath, and let me close this chapter on building your marketing and PR plan by making a few observations about why Barack Obama was elected to be the 44th president of the United States.

Even though this example is from 2004, it is still the most important new marketing case study in the world, because it opened people's eyes to the power of online content. Of course, this is a book about the new rules of marketing and PR, not a book about presidential politics. These are not political observations but, rather, thoughts about the amazing success Obama and his campaign team had in embracing voters using the new rules of marketing and PR. If you are an American citizen, it doesn't matter who you (or I) supported or voted for during the 2008 U.S. presidential election. *Everyone* (those who work in companies large and small, non-profits, independent consultants, job seekers, musicians, well, everyone) can learn from Obama's victory. I certainly have. After all, who would have predicted in 2006 that a young, skinny, half-black man with a strange name—Barack Hussein Obama—and funny ears, who had served less than one term in the U.S. Senate, could be elected to the most powerful position in the world, despite facing more than 20 other candidates, many of them better known and better funded? There is no doubt in my mind that Obama was elected because his campaign used the ideas that I describe in this book. Mind you, I'm not saying his aides had copies of it on the campaign bus. But I am saying that the campaign observed and acted on the very same online opportunities that we've been discussing in this book, and they did it better than just about anyone else.

> Barack Obama is the most successful new marketer in history. Study his campaign so that you can adapt the ideas for your business.

"Voters in 2008 were not just passive followers of the political process," says Aaron Smith, research specialist at the Pew Internet & American Life Project and author of the project's report, *The Internet's Role in Campaign 2008.*[7] "They used a wide range of digital tools and technologies to get involved in the race, to harness their creativity in support of their chosen candidate, and to join forces with others who shared their same political goals."

---

[7] pewinternet.org/Press-Releases/2009/The-Internets-Role-in-Campaign-2008.aspx

Smith's findings indicate widespread use of the web to research candidates and support campaigns. The 2008 election was the first in which more than half the voting-age population used the Internet for political purposes. Some 55 percent of all adults—and 74 percent of all Internet users—said they went online for news and information about the election or to communicate with others about the race. The research found that social media platforms such as blogs, social networking sites, and video-sharing sites played a key role in 2008, as voters went online to share their views with others and try to mobilize them to their cause.

As you read these remarkable statistics from Smith's report, please be aware that the numbers are probably very similar as they relate to your own business. In fact, it's likely even more pronounced because there are more people active online today than there were in 2008. It is clear that the web and social media are now a mainstream way for people to do research. Are people finding you, your company, and its products and services the way they found Barack Obama?

- 45 percent of wired Americans watched videos online related to politics or the election. Young adults led the way in their online video consumption, as nearly half of all 18- to 29-year-olds watched online political videos during the 2008 election cycle.
- 33 percent of Internet users shared digital political content with others—whether by forwarding political writing or multimedia content over email or by sharing information with others through other online mechanisms.
- 52 percent of those with a social networking profile used their social network site for political purposes.

While I was not personally active in the political campaigns of the 2008 U.S. presidential election, I did spend a great deal of time studying the marketing aspects of the candidates. Again, these are not political observations; rather, they are my thoughts on why Obama won the election, presented as tips so you can apply them to your own business:

Focus on buyer personas. As we learned in Chapter 5 from Kevin Flynn, who worked on the Obama social media team, the campaign targeted buyer personas (voters) on a state-by-state basis. There was specific focus on getting out each and every one of the Obama base of supporters to vote, as well as a strong focus on undecided voters.

Don't underestimate the importance of social media and the new rules of marketing and PR. The other campaigns seemed to be using the playbooks of past campaigns, the old rules of marketing and PR. Hillary Clinton was relying on what worked to elect Bill Clinton. John McCain was relying on what worked to elect George W. Bush. The Obama campaign realized that for him to become president, he had to deliver information online primarily, not as an afterthought. The number of people the campaign reached on the web is staggering: According to the *Nation*, 13 million people signed up for the Obama campaign email list, more than 5 million friended Obama on Facebook, 2 million joined MyBO (an online organizing site where people could sign up to support the campaign as a volunteer), and more than 1 million people subscribed to campaign text messages on mobile phones.

Embrace citizen journalists. My friend Steve Garfield,[8] author of the book *Get Seen: Online Video Secrets to Building Your Business*, is a well-known video blogger. He's got tens of thousands of followers. During the primaries, Garfield attended several rallies held by various candidates. When he asked to go to the media section at a Hillary Clinton rally in Boston, he was turned away (because he was "not a real journalist") and had to cover it from the back of the crowd. However, Obama's campaign immediately brought him up to the media section, where he was placed with print reporters from the major dailies and TV crews from the networks. The Obama campaign understood that citizen journalists (bloggers, podcasters, video bloggers) have immense power.

Clearly and simply articulate what you want people to believe. From the beginning, Obama was about change. The word *change* was everywhere in his campaign, so much so that the entire world knew what Obama stood for. I asked a group of 300 people in Riyadh, Saudi Arabia, what was the one word they thought of when I said "Barack Obama," and all in the room said, "Change." Quick: What did the following candidates stand for? John McCain, John Edwards, Hillary Clinton, Mitt Romney, or any others. Hard to say, isn't it?

Remember that people don't care about products and services; instead, they care about themselves and about solving their problems. The Obama campaign understood that his job was to solve the problems facing voters. He also knew that voters were buying into solutions, not just an individual. Did you notice in speeches how often Obama referred to his audience

---

[8] stevegarfield.com

compared with how often he referred to himself? For example, in his inaugural address,[9] new President Obama used what I call inclusive language (such as *our, we,* and *us*) a total of 142 times in 20 minutes, while he used what I call internal language (*me, I,* and *my*) just three times. (Yes, I counted.) The other candidates talked about *themselves* a hell of a lot more than Obama did.

Don't obsess over the competition. Obama rarely talked about his competition. Once in a while, he would, but mainly he talked about the problems facing voters. McCain talked a lot about Obama. Interestingly, Clinton and McCain both tried to associate themselves with the *change* word (the competition's word), but both failed because people already associated it with Obama.

Put your fans first. Obama used many techniques to craft an inclusive campaign and alert fans about developments first. For example, I found out on Obama's Twitter feed that Joe Biden was to be Obama's running mate. It was stunning to me that Obama told his fans *before* mainstream media. (Of course, smart reporters were following his Twitter feed and learned at the same time as Obama supporters.)

Don't interrupt your buyers. Do you like getting phone calls from telemarketers at dinnertime? McCain supporters seemed to think so, since they unleashed a barrage of so-called robocalls, which seem to have backfired.

Negativity doesn't sell. Obama's theme of hope and the idea that life can be better with change was uplifting to many people. The campaigns based on fear didn't work.

Get your customers to talk about you. Obama tapped more than 3 million donors who together provided $640 million to the campaign. The majority contributed small amounts online. Once people donate money, they have a vested interest in the candidate and tend to talk about them on social networking sites and in person. So to get the word out, lots of small donors are better than a few fat cats.

Take time for your family. (Yes, this really is a marketing observation, because it has to do with positioning and what a candidate stands for.) Obama frequently took time to be with his wife and daughters when he could have done another rally somewhere. He took several days at the end of the race to spend time with his ailing grandmother. While he was pulled

---

[9] youtube.com/watch?v=VjnygQ02aW4

away from work, I think people respected his devotion to family, and they saw something they liked in this attitude.

Marketers can learn a great deal from political campaigns (just like, once upon a time, the campaigns learned from us). I encourage you to take a look at these lessons from the Obama campaign and apply them to your business. As you are developing your own marketing and PR plan using the new rules, think back to the inspirational marketing and PR unleashed by Obama's team during the U.S. presidential election of 2008.

Stick to Your Plan

If you've read this far, thank you. If you've developed a marketing and PR plan that uses the new rules of marketing and PR and you're ready to execute, great! The next 14 chapters will give you more specific advice about implementing your plan.

But now I must warn you: Many people who adhere to the old rules will fight you on this strategy. If you are a marketing professional who wants to reach your buyers directly, you are likely to encounter resistance from corporate communications people. PR folks will get resistance from their agencies. They'll say the old rules are still in play. They'll say you have to focus on the four Ps. They'll say you need to talk only about your products. They'll say that using the media is the only way to tell your story and that you can use press releases only to reach journalists, not your buyers directly. They'll say that bloggers are geeks in pajamas who don't matter.

They are wrong.

As the dozens of successful marketers profiled in this book say, the old rules are old news. Millions of people are online right now looking for answers to their problems. Will they find your organization? And if so, what will they find?

Remember, on the web, you are what you publish.

12 Online Thought Leadership to Brand Your Organization as a Trusted Resource

If you've read this book starting from the beginning, I hope I've been able to convince you that web content sells. (If you've skipped ahead to this chapter, welcome!) An effective online content strategy, artfully executed, drives action. Organizations that use online content well have a clearly defined goal—to sell products, generate leads, secure contributions, or get people to join—and deploy a content strategy that directly contributes to reaching that goal. People often ask me: "How do you recommend that I create an effective _____?" (fill in the blank with *blog, video, white paper, e-book, email newsletter, webinar,* and so on). While the technologies for each form of online content are a little different, the one common aspect is that through all of these media, your organization can exercise thought leadership rather than simple advertising and product promotion; a well-crafted white paper, e-book, or webinar contributes to an organization's positive reputation by setting it apart in the marketplace of ideas. This form of content brands a company, a consultant, or a nonprofit as an expert and as a trusted resource.

Developing Thought Leadership Content

What is thought leadership, and how do you do it?

The first thing you need to do is put away your company hat for a moment and—you guessed it—think like one of your buyer personas. The content that you create will be a solution to those people's problems and *will not mention your company or products at all!* Imagine for a moment that you are a marketer at an automobile tire manufacturer. Rather than just peddling your tires, you might write an e-book or shoot a video about how to drive safely in the snow and then promote it on your site and offer it free to other companies (such as automobile clubs and driver's education schools) to put on their sites. Or imagine that you run a local catering company and you have a blog or a website. You might have a set of web pages or videos available on your site. The topics could include "Plan the Perfect Wedding Reception" and "What You Need to Know for the Ideal Dinner Party for Twelve." A caterer with a video series like this educates visitors about their problems (planning a wedding or a dinner party) but does *not* sell the catering services directly. Instead, the idea here is that people who learn through the caterer's information are more likely to hire that caterer when the time comes.

Mark Howell, a consultant for Lifetogether,[1] is a pastor who works with Christian organizations and uses a thought leadership blog to get his message out. "My primary targets are people who are working in churches or Christian organizations that are trying to figure out better ways to do things," he says. "So I keep my content to things that seem secular but have broad application to churches. For example, I did a post called 'Required Reading: Five Books Every Leader Needs' where I tie broader business trends and marketing strategies to churches."

What makes Howell's blog work is that he's not just promoting his consulting services but instead is providing powerful information with a clear focus, for readers who just might hire him at some point. "My personal bias, and what I write about, is that for a lot of leaders in churches, the personal passion for what they are doing could be enhanced if they just got a taste for what more secular writers, such as Tom Peters, Guy Kawasaki, and Peter Drucker, are saying," Howell says. "There are so many ideas out there, and if I could just give people a sense of what some of these thinkers are saying, then my hope is that they can see that there is application for church leadership."

Forms of Thought Leadership Content

Here are some of the common forms of thought leadership content (of course, there may be others in your niche market). We've seen many of these

---

[1] strategycentral.org

media in earlier chapters, but let's focus now on how they can help your company establish itself as a thought leader.

White Papers

"White papers typically [argue] a specific position or solution to a problem," according to Michael A. Stelzner,[2] author of *Writing White Papers*. "Although white papers take their roots in governmental policy, they have become a common tool used to introduce technology innovations and products. A typical search engine query on 'white paper' will return millions of results, with many focused on technology-related issues. White papers are powerful marketing tools used to help key decision makers and influencers justify implementing solutions." The best white papers are *not product brochures*. A good white paper is written for a business audience, defines a problem, and offers a solution, but it does not pitch a particular product or company. White papers are usually free and often have a registration requirement (so the authors can collect the names and contact information of people who download it). Many companies syndicate white papers to business websites through services such as TechTarget[3] and Knowledge Storm.[4]

E-Books

Marketers are using e-books more and more as a fun and thoughtful way to get useful information to buyers. As I have mentioned, the book you are reading right now started as an e-book called *The New Rules of PR*, released in January 2006. For the purposes of marketing using web content, I define an e-book as a PDF-formatted document that solves a problem for one of your buyer personas. E-books come with a bit of intrigue—they're like a hip younger sibling to the nerdy white paper. I recommend that e-books be presented in a landscape format, rather than the white paper's portrait format because it will fit perfectly onto a computer screen. Well-executed e-books have lots of white space, interesting graphics and images, and copy that is typically written in a lighter style than the denser white paper. In my view,

---

[2] writingwhitepapers.com
[3] techtarget.com
[4] knowledgestorm.com

e-books (as marketing tools) should always be free, and I strongly suggest that there be no registration requirement. To get a sense of these elements, check out my free e-book *Real Time: How Marketing & PR at Speed Drives Measurable Success.*[5] E-books are used by all kinds of organizations. Here are a few e-book titles to get your creative juices flowing: *On the Journey to Prompting Loyalty with Prepaid Customers: 5 Strategies That Drive Customers Loyalty with Prepaid Service Offerings* by Rafi Kretchmer of Amdocs Inc., *Create a Safety Buzz! How Can I Change My Own Behaviors and the Behaviors of Those around Me to Create a True Safety First Culture?* by Dr. James (Skip) Ward, *100 Job Search Tips from FORTUNE 500 Recruiters* by EMC Corporation, and *Healthy Mouth, Healthy Sex! How Your Oral Health Affects Your Sex Life* by Dr. Helaine Smith.

Email Newsletters

Email newsletters have been around as long as email but still have tremendous value as a way to deliver thought leadership content in small, regular doses. However, the vast majority of email newsletters that I see serve mostly as another advertising venue for a company's products and services. You know the type I'm talking about: Each month you get some lame product pitch and a 10-percent-off coupon. Consider using a different type of email newsletter, one that focuses not on your company's products and services, but simply on solving buyers' problems once per month. Let's consider the hypothetical tire manufacturer or caterer that we discussed. Imagine the tire manufacturer doing a monthly newsletter about safe driving or the caterer writing one on party planning. I recommend putting an edition of your email newsletter on your site so people who are not yet subscribers are able to find the information. This will also be valuable content to drive people to your site from the search engines.

Webinars

Webinars are online seminars that may include audio, video, or graphics (typically in the form of PowerPoint slides) and are often used by companies as a primer about a specific problem that the company's services can solve. However, the best webinars are true thought leadership—like the traditional

---

[5] davidmeermanscott.com/documents/Real_Time.pdf

seminars from which they get their name. Often, webinars feature guests who do not work for the company sponsoring the webinar. For example, I participated as a guest speaker on a webinar series called Inbound Marketing University,[6] sponsored by HubSpot. Inbound Marketing University featured 10 sessions, each with a different speaker. Nearly 4,000 people attended at least one of the sessions the first time they were offered. "Inbound Marketing University developed a tight-knit community of marketers who view Hub-Spot as a trusted resource and leader in inbound marketing," says Mike Volpe, vice president of marketing at HubSpot. "Having received so much valuable information and tools for free, many were quite interested in learning more about HubSpot and our paid software for their own companies or clients." Inbound Marketing University was so successful that it is now repeated regularly for new students.

Wikis

Wikis as thought leadership content are started by organizations that want to be seen as important players in distinct marketplaces. "You can use wikis to reach the people you want to reach and help them to organize content," says Ramit Sethi, co-founder and vice president of marketing for Pbworks,[7] a company that provides wiki software tools. "So if you're in a company, you can use a wiki to allow your users to add their own frequently asked questions, and other people can supply answers, which helps everyone. People love being a part of the community, and they really like that a wiki gives them a way to discuss their interests." Sethi says that the personality and culture of an organization play an important role in the decision to start a company-sponsored wiki. "Companies that are a little bit fearless about letting people write their opinions make the best candidates for a wiki," he says. "But the most important thing is that you need to build something that is worth talking about, and you need to make it really easy. People don't want to install all kinds of software; they just want to get typing." (If you're interested in wikis, you might want to reread the section in Chapter 4 where Steve Goldstein shared his experience creating a wiki for Alacra.)

---

[6] inboundmarketing.com/university

[7] pbworks.com

Research and Survey Reports

Research and survey reports are used by many companies. By publishing results for free, organizations offer valuable content and get a chance to show off the kind of work they do. This can be an effective approach as long as your research or survey is legitimate and its statistically significant results are interesting to your buyers. (You will read about a survey report created by Steve Johnson of Pragmatic Marketing later in this chapter.)

Photos, Images, Graphs, Charts, and Infographics

Don't underestimate the value of an image to tell a story. If your product has visual appeal (sporting goods and real estate come to mind), you can create interesting content based on images. If your expertise lends itself to how-to instruction (example: "Learn How to Surf"), photos can be particularly useful. Expertise that can be depicted as a chart (example: "Real Estate Values in Fairfield County 1976–2013") also stands to be especially useful to your buyers. In fact, any visual representation of information (sometimes called *infographics*) is a potentially valuable form of thought leadership content. I talk much more about the use of images in Chapter 18.

Blogs

As we've seen already, a blog is a personal website written by someone who is passionate about a subject and wants the world to know about it. The benefits rub off on the company that the blogger works for. Writing a blog is the easiest and simplest way to get your thought leadership ideas out and into the market. See Chapter 17 for information on how to start your blog.

Audio and Video

Podcasts (ongoing series of audio downloads available by subscription) are very popular as thought leadership content in some markets. Some people prefer just audio, and if your buyers do, then a podcast of your own might be the thing for you. Video content, vodcasts, video blogs, and vlogs (lots of names, one medium) are regularly updated videos that offer a powerful opportunity to demonstrate your thought leadership, since most people are familiar with the video medium and are used to the idea of watching a video or television program to learn something. An easy and fun way to create audio and video content is to host an interview show with guests who have something interesting to say. The intelligence of the guests rubs off on you as you interview them. Consider interviewing customers, analysts who cover your marketplace, and authors of books in your field. See Chapter 19 for information on audio and video.

How to Create Thoughtful Content

While each technique for getting your thought leadership content into the marketplace of ideas is different, they share some common considerations:

- Do not write about your company and your products. Thought leadership content is designed to solve buyer problems or answer questions and to show that you and your organization are smart and worth doing business with. This type of marketing and PR technique is *not* a brochure or sales pitch. Thought leadership is *not* advertising.
- Define your organizational goals first (see Chapter 11). Do you want to drive revenue? Get people to donate money to your organization? Encourage people to buy something?
- Based on your goals, decide whether you want to provide the content free and without any registration (you will get many more people to use the content, but you won't know who they are) or you want to include some kind of registration mechanism (*much* lower response rates, but you build a contact list).
- Think like a publisher by understanding your audience. Consider what market problems your buyer personas are faced with and develop topics that appeal to them.
- Write for your audience. Use examples and stories. Make it interesting.
- Choose a great title that grabs attention. Use subtitles to describe what the content will deliver. The best titles and subtitles include keywords and phrases that your buyers are searching on using search engines.
- Promote the effort like crazy. Offer the content on your site with easy-to-find links. Add a link to employees' email signatures, and get partners to offer links as well.
- To drive the viral marketing effects that we looked at in Chapter 8, alert appropriate reporters, bloggers, and analysts that the content is available and send them a download link.

Measure the results, and improve based on what you learn.

Thought Leadership in Highly Regulated Industries

On the global speaking circuit, I frequently get pushback from audience members who work in highly regulated industries. They claim that laws like HIPAA (a provision that addresses the security and privacy of health data) and regulations like those from the U.S. Securities and Exchange Commission and the U.S. Food and Drug Administration (and equivalent agencies in other countries) forbid them from creating valuable content on the web or engaging in social media.

Nonsense!

This is just a fear-based excuse perpetuated by lawyers in the pharmaceutical, healthcare, and financial services industries who want to avoid risk at all cost. The fear is particularly shortsighted when considering the data on how people make decisions related to their health. I delivered a talk at the 2012 National Healthcare Marketing Summit and had an opportunity to meet many marketers who are happily reaching their audiences with valuable information. They're living in reality, not according to their fears.

According to data presented at that conference by Tim McGuire from Greenville Hospital System, Bill Moschella of eVariant, and Anne Theis of Salem Health, 80 percent of Internet users look up health information online. More than three out of four people use the web to make healthcare decisions! Yet 64 percent of hospital marketing departments devote less than 25 percent of their marketing budget to interactive content. Even more telling is how hospital marketers spend their time: 83 percent of hospitals devote less than 30 percent of staff time to interactive media. This is ridiculous.

The fearful lawyers say no to the 80 percent of customers and potential customers who use the web to research health. This fear means that hospital marketers are busy making brochures and TV ads instead of creating thoughtful web content. If you work in a highly regulated industry, can your organization afford such a disconnect?

For an example of someone who ignores what people assume to be legal restrictions and instead creates thoughtful content, consider Chris Boyer, director of digital communications and marketing for Inova Health System,[8] Northern Virginia's leading not-for-profit healthcare provider. Inova serves more than 1 million patients each year.

---

[8] inova.org

The company publishes content to reach specific buyer personas. For example, their "Life with Cancer"[9] site contains valuable information for patients and their families. In a world where others are fearful of creating content, Inova publishes videos like "Phil Gilbert's Story—Relief After Hip Replacement."[10]

In the last two years, Boyer has transformed the Inova organization to focus more on creating relevant content. "We take a lot of time understanding who our viewers are and actually write different types of content for different types of users," Boyer says. "Patients are using our patient and visitor information, so they're looking for specifics about how to make their stay easier, and we write with them in mind. Other people view our services and all the different clinical stuff that we provide at Inova. They could either be referring physicians who want to research what we're doing here or consumers who are actually shopping for healthcare. We want to provide them content that's appropriate for them. It is written so that they don't have to read through pages and pages of clinical content to get to the crux of what they're looking for."

Boyer manages the digital marketing and communications team, including a handful of editors and web graphics professionals as well as several part-timers. A full-time social media manager on the team focuses on social media channels, although there's a lot of content interaction and cross-publication efforts; the lines between social media and the website are blurring tremendously at Inova, as at so many other organizations.

"The two main editors for our website are actually former journalists," Boyer says. "So they have experience in terms of writing. Of course, they started in traditional media, but in the last few years they migrated over to focus exclusively on online journalism and communications."

I wanted to know how Boyer has dealt with the whole "fear" thing. Why has he been successful in hiring journalists and creating content when so many other management teams and legal departments refuse.

Boyer says the main concern of Inova's managers was that a shift to content marketing would mean a shift away from what they thought were the key differentiators of Inova Health System. Previously, their efforts had focused on attracting the best physicians. "It took a long time for us to educate that the existing content is not being lost. We're just providing it to

---

[9] lifewithcancer.org

[10] youtube.com/watch?v=0wbvwkM00tE

each audience in the appropriate places. There will be pages for consumers *and* pages for physicians who are looking to refer or be employed here. It took a while for them to be comfortable with that."

The size of Boyer's team means there are significant resources devoted to the Inova thought leadership effort. Boyer measures effectiveness in three areas:

1. New patients—How many people become patients who first connected online either through content on the website or social networks such as Facebook and Twitter?
2. Savings—How much money can be saved by using online tools? For example, the existing Inova nursing communications is a printed newsletter that goes out to all nursing staff and costs $80,000 per year to produce. So converting to a blog meant eliminating that expense and increasing readership.
3. Long-term patient engagement—How many patients (or potential patients) get involved in wellness programs? For example, Inova offers email content focused on how to have a healthy heart, how to eat well, and so on. He measures the number of people who stay healthy because of the information they consume and how that affects things like readmittance rates.

Boyer has taken a gradual approach in implementing these changes.

"Realize that you don't have to transform your entire organization all at once," he says. "I found a lot of success in focusing on areas where there were some obvious opportunities and used social communications in those areas. Try something and see how it's working. You're gaining valuable expertise and understanding how to use the tools. In most organizations, once you introduce social communications to your portfolio, very quickly you'll start to see how it will augment, if not replace, some of the current ways that you're communicating."

As Boyer shows, content marketing and thought leadership can survive and thrive in highly regulated industries.

Leveraging Thought Leaders Outside of Your Organization

Some organizations recruit external thought leaders that buyers trust, which is an effective technique for showing your buyers that you are plugged in and work with recognized experts. You might have a thought leader from your industry guest blog for you, author a white paper, participate on a webinar, or speak to your clients at a live event. For example, Cincom Systems, Inc., a software industry pioneer, publishes the *Cincom Expert Access*[11] e-zine that is read by more than 200,000 people in 61 countries. *Cincom Expert Access* delivers information from several dozen business leaders, authors, and analysts such as Al Reis, author of *The Fall of Advertising and the Rise of PR*; Dan Heath, author of *Made to Stick*; and Guy Kawasaki, author of *Reality Check*. I am also a member of Cincom's Ask the Expert network. *Cincom Expert Access* provides concise, objective information from personalities that Cincom's clients trust, sometimes in an irreverent, humorous manner, to help readers do their jobs better.

How Much Money Does Your Buyer Make?

"People often ask me, 'Steve, how much should we be paying our product managers?'" says Steve Johnson, an instructor at Pragmatic Marketing, the premier product marketing firm for technology companies. "I used to just throw out a number that sounded about right. But I realized that my estimated salary figure was based on old data, back from the days when I hired product managers." Because Pragmatic Marketing conducts training for product managers, the company is seen as the expert on all things related to that job function. This situation created a terrific opportunity for some thought leadership. "We realized that we didn't really know current benchmarks, so we decided to find out." After all, customer compensation is often a key demographic for understanding your buyer persona.

Johnson composed a survey to gather data from the thousands of people in the Pragmatic Marketing database. "We said, 'If you tell us your salary and other information about your job via the anonymous survey, we will tell you everyone's salary in the form of benchmarks,'" he says. The results were an instant hit with the Pragmatic Marketing buyer persona—product managers. "Our email newsletter goes out to thousands and thousands of people. In October we say 'Heads up, next month we're doing the salary survey.' Then in November we announce that the survey is live and invite people to take it.

---

[11] internetviz-newsletters.com/cincom

We get hundreds of responses in just a few days, aggregate the data, and publish the results on the web.[12] In 2010, for example, we learned that the average U.S. product management compensation is $96,580 in salary and that 77 percent of product managers get an annual bonus that averages $12,960. But we also learned other information, such as that product managers send and receive almost 100 emails a day and spend roughly two days a week in internal meetings—15 meetings per week. But 55 percent are going to 15 meetings or more each week, and 35 percent attend 20 or more meetings."

Johnson sees tremendous benefits in survey-based thought leadership. "First of all, the data is really useful," he says. "Now I command the authority to say something like '93 percent of Product Managers have completed college and 43 percent have completed a master's program.' But more importantly, the buyers we are trying to reach to sell training services to, product managers, recognize us as the thought leaders in product management because we have up-to-date information on what's really going on with technology product managers. And the data that sits on our website is fantastic for search engine marketing because anyone looking for information about product managers in technology businesses will find us."

Johnson says that product managers and product marketing managers often complain about having all the responsibility without the authority. "We've learned that authority isn't just given; it's earned . . . by having market data."

This is a new world for marketers and corporate communicators. The web offers an easy way for your ideas to spread to a potential audience of millions of people, instantly. Web content in the form of true thought leadership holds the potential to influence many thousands of your buyers in ways that traditional marketing and PR simply cannot.

To embrace the power of the web and the blogosphere requires a different kind of thinking on the part of marketers. We need to learn to give up our command-and-control mentality. It isn't about "the message." It's about being insightful. The New Rules of Marketing and PR tell us to stop advertising and instead get our ideas out there by understanding buyers and telling them stories that connect with their problems. The new rules are to participate in the discussions going on, not just try to shout your message over everyone else. Done well, web content that delivers authentic thought leadership also brands an organization as one to do business with.

---

[12] pragmaticmarketing.com/publications/survey

13

How to Create for Your Buyers

Your buyers (and the media that cover your company) want to know what specific problems your product solves, and they want proof that it works—in plain language. Your marketing and PR is meant to be the beginning of a relationship with buyers and to drive action (such as generating sales leads), which requires a focus on buyer problems. Your buyers want to hear this in *their* own words. Every time you write— yes, even in news releases—you have an opportunity to communicate. At each stage of the sales process, well-written materials will help your buyers understand how you, specifically, will help them.

Whenever you set out to write something (or shoot a video or develop other content), you should be creating specifically for one or more of the buyer personas that you developed as part of your marketing and PR plan (see Chapter 11). You should avoid jargon-laden phrases that are overused in your industry, unless this is the language the persona actually uses. In the technology business, words like *groundbreaking, industry-standard*, and *cutting-edge* are what I call gobbledygook. The worst gobbledygook offenders seem to be business-to-business technology companies. For some reason, marketing people at technology companies have a particularly tough time explaining how products solve customer problems. Because these writers don't understand how their products solve customer problems, or are too lazy to write for buyers, they cover by explaining myriad nuances of how the product works and pepper this blather with industry jargon that sounds vaguely impressive. What ends up in marketing materials and news releases is a bunch of talk about "industry-leading" solutions that purport to help companies "streamline business process," "achieve business objectives," or "conserve organizational resources." *Huh?*

An Analysis of Gobbledygook

Many of the thousands of websites I've analyzed over the years and the hundreds of news releases and PR pitches I receive each month are laden with meaningless gobbledygook words and phrases. As I'm reading a news release, I'll pause and say to myself, "Oh, jeez, not another flexible, scalable, groundbreaking, industry-standard, cutting-edge product from a market-leading, well-positioned company! I think I'm gonna puke!" Like teenagers overusing catchphrases, these writers use the same words and phrases again and again—so much so that the gobbledygook grates against all our nerves. Well, duh. Like, companies just totally don't communicate very well, you know?

I wanted to see exactly how many of these words are being used, so I created an analysis for doing so. I first analyzed gobbledygook in 2006 and published the findings on my blog and as an e-book called *The Gobbledygook Manifesto.*[1] In 2006, the most overused words and phrases included *next generation, robust, world class, cutting edge, mission critical, market leading, industry standard, groundbreaking,* and *best of breed.*

I then conducted an extensive, revised analysis in early 2009. For this new round, I first needed to select overused words and phrases, so I turned to the following sources:

- The overused words and phrases from the 2006 analysis, which I got by polling select PR people and journalists.
- Suggestions from readers, who posted comments about the original analysis on my blog.
- Seth Godin's *Encyclopedia of Business Clichés.*
- *This Paperclip Is a Solution,* a survey given to general business and trade publication editors by Dave Schmidt, VP of public relations services at Smith-Winchester, Inc.
- The book *Death Sentences: How Cliches, Weasel Words and Management-Speak Are Strangling Public Language,* by Don Watson.

---

[1] davidmeermanscott.com/documents/3703Gobbledygook.pdf

Then I turned to the Dow Jones Enterprise Media Group for help. The folks at Dow Jones used text-mining tools in their Dow Jones Insight product to analyze news releases sent in the English language during 2008. The data we gathered came from all 711,123 press releases distributed through Business Wire, Marketwire, GlobeNewswire, and PR Newswire. Dow Jones Insight identified the number of uses of the 325 gobbledygook phrases in each release.

The results were staggering. The winner for the most overused word or phrase in 2008 was *innovate* which was used in 51,390 press releases, followed closely by *unique, leading provider, new and improved, world class,* and *cost effective.* Each of these terms was used more than 10,000 times in press releases during 2008. The problem is that these words are so overused that they have become meaningless. If anything, these terms makes the reader feel as if the company is just releasing dozens of copycat me-too statements.

Poor Writing: How Did We Get Here?

When I see words like *flexible, scalable, groundbreaking, industry standard,* or *cutting-edge*, my eyes glaze over. What, I ask myself, is this supposed to mean? Just saying your product is "industry standard" means nothing unless some aspect of that standardization is important to your buyers. In the next sentence, I want to know what you mean by industry standard, and I also want you to tell me why that standard matters and give me some proof that what you say is indeed true.

People often say to me, "Everyone in my industry writes this way. Why?" Here's how the usual dysfunctional process works and why these phrases are so overused: Marketers don't understand buyers, the problems buyers face, or how their product helps solve these problems. That's where the gobbledygook happens. First, the marketing person bugs the product managers and others in the organization to provide a set of the product's features. Then the marketing person reverse-engineers the language that they think the buyer wants to hear based *not on buyer input* but on what the product does. A favorite trick these ineffective marketers use is to take the language that the product manager provides, go into Microsoft Word's find-and-replace mode, substitute the word *solution* for *product*, and then slather the whole thing with superlative-laden, jargon-sprinkled hype. By just decreeing, through an electronic word substitution, that "our product" is "your solution," these companies effectively deprive themselves of the opportunity to *convince* people that this is the case.

Another major drawback of the generic gobbledygook approach is that it doesn't make your company stand out from the crowd. Here's a test: Take the language that the marketers at your company dreamed up and substitute the name of a competitor and the competitor's product for your own. Does it still make sense to you? Marketing language that can be substituted for another company's isn't effective in explaining to a buyer why *your* company is the right choice.

I'll admit that these gobbledygook phrases are mainly used by technology companies operating in the business-to-business space. If you are writing for a company that sells different kinds of products (shoes, perhaps), then you would probably not be tempted to use many of these phrases. The same thing is true for nonprofits, churches, rock bands, and other organizations—you're also unlikely to use these sorts of phrases. But the lessons are the same. Avoid the insular jargon of your company and your industry. Instead, write for your buyers.

"Hold on," you might say. "The technology industry may be dysfunctional, but I don't write that way." The fact is that there is equivalent nonsense going on in all industries. Here's an example from the world of nonprofits:

> The sustainability group has convened a task force to study the cause of energy inefficiency and to develop a plan to encourage local businesses to apply renewable-energy and energy-efficient technologies which will go a long way toward encouraging community buy-in to potential behavioral changes.

What the heck is that? Or consider this example from the first paragraph of a well-known company's corporate overview page. Can you guess the company?

> Since its founding in 1923, [Company X] and its affiliated companies have remained faithful to their commitment to produce unparalleled entertainment experiences based on the rich legacy of quality creative content and exceptional storytelling. [Company X], together with its subsidiaries and affiliates, is a leading diversified international family

entertainment and media enterprise with four business segments: media networks, parks and resorts, studio entertainment, and consumer products.

Effective Writing for Marketing and PR

Your marketing and PR is meant to be the beginning of a relationship with buyers (and journalists). As the marketing and PR planning process in Chapter 11 showed, this begins when you work at understanding your target audience and figure out how they should be sliced into distinct buying segments or buyer personas. Once this exercise is complete, identify the situations each target audience may find themselves in. What are their problems? Business issues? Needs? Only then are you ready to communicate your expertise to the market. Here's the rule: When you write, start with your buyers, not with your product.

Consider the entertainment company language. The marketing and PR folks at Disney (did you guess it was Disney's corporate overview page I quoted from?) should be thinking about what customers want from an entertainment company, rather than just thinking up fancy words for what they think they already provide. Why not start by defining the problem? "Many television and cinema fans today are frustrated with the state of the American entertainment industry. They believe today's films and shows are too derivative and that entertainment companies don't respect their viewers' intelligence." Next, successful marketers will use real-world language to convince their customers that they can solve their problem. Be careful to avoid corporate jargon, but you don't want to sound like you're trying too hard, either—that always comes across as phony. Talk to your audience as you might talk to a relative you don't see too often—be friendly and familiar but also respectful: "Like our audience, we care about and enjoy movies and TV shows—that's why we're in this business in the first place. As such, we pledge to always. . . ." Now I have no connection with Disney and don't know about the Disney business. But I have purchased a lot of Disney products: movies, TV shows, videos, and visits to theme parks. It might seem strange to people at Disney to actually write something like I suggest. It might feel strange for the PR and marketing people at Disney to use a phrase like "movies and TV shows" rather than "quality creative content," but it's absolutely essential to establishing a relationship with customers.

The Power of Writing Feedback (from Your Blog)

I want to pause for a moment to share a story about the power of communications and feedback on the web. When I published the results of this original study on my blog[2] in a post titled "The Gobbledygook Manifesto" (I also sent a news release the next day), there were zero hits on Google for the exact phrase "gobbledygook manifesto." I purposely invented a phrase that I could establish on the web. Within just three weeks, as a result of several dozen bloggers writing about "The Gobbledygook Manifesto" and more than 100 comments on my blog and others, the exact phrase "gobble-dygook manifesto" yielded more than 500 hits on Google: zero to 500 in just three weeks. Better yet, readers of my blog and others suggested other overused gobbledygook words and phrases, such as *best practices, proactive, synergy, starting a dialogue, thinking outside of the box, revolutionary, situational fluency*, and *paradigm shift*.

Dave Schmidt, VP for Public Relations Services at Smith-Winchester, Inc., contacted me to share the results of a survey he conducted of general business and trade publication editors. Schmidt asked the editors about the overused words and phrases he's seen and wanted to find out how many editors agreed that each of the phrases was overused in news releases and company-authored articles. He received responses from 80 editors:

- *Leading* (used as an adjective, as in ". . . a leading producer of . . .")—94 percent of editors feel is overused. Since everyone wants to be the leading something, there are no longer any true leaders.
- *"We're excited about . . ."* (as used in a quote from management)—76 percent of editors feel is overused. Companies also say, "We're pleased . . ." and "We're thrilled . . ." Can you picture an editor running a CEO quote like one of these? You need to quote your spokespeople with words that you would like to see in print.
- *Solutions*—68 percent of editors feel is overused. The word *solutions* has been ruined by overuse in news releases to the point that it is best avoided, even by solutions providers.
- *". . . a wide range of . . ."*—64 percent of editors feel is overused. This has become the lazy person's way of avoiding precise writing.

---

[2] www.webinknow.com/2006/10/the_gobbledygoo.html

- *Unparalleled*—62 percent of editors feel is overused.
- *Unsurpassed*—53 percent of editors feel is overused.

Thank you to the many people who contacted me with suggestions of overused gobbledygook. I just think it is so cool that you can create something on the web, use it to get thoughtful information into the market quickly and efficiently, and then have people offer suggestions to make the original writing even better.

Most of this chapter has been about what not to do. We read a lot of the gobbledygook that so many people use when they create content for their buyers. But there are many organizations with terrific content! I'd like to showcase one and describe how they take a journalistic approach to content creation.

Brand Journalism at Boeing

When The Boeing Company[3] revamped their website and built a completely new approach to their writing for the web, they shifted dramatically from a dull, technology- and product-focused, gobbledygook-laden site to one focused on interesting stories. The new Boeing site does an excellent job at putting a human (and canine) face on the company.

One of the featured stories I enjoyed is "Rocky Earns His Rest,"[4] about a Belgian Malinois who served for 56 "dog years" as a Boeing explosive-detection dog. "Rocky's story is unusual, and we never would have used him on the site before," says Todd Blecher, communications director at Boeing. "Now we show there are real people who work in the company. And we are willing to talk about them—even if they are a dog."

Blecher heads up an editorial team at Boeing, gathering story ideas from all over the company.

"Freezin' in Florida," describes testing the 787 Dreamliner in the largest refrigerated hangar in the world. The hangar simulates temperatures as low as –65 degrees Fahrenheit or as high as 165 degrees Fahrenheit. "Rather than have a standard news release that describes testing, we take you inside the hanger to actually show what people have to do to freeze the airplane," Blecher says. "No airplane comes together without the people who work on it. Now we're talking about our technology from the perspective of the people."

---

[3] boeing.com
[4] boeing.com/Features/2010/05/feat_rocky_retires_05_10_10.html

The team also creates videos, such as "Boeing 747-8F Performs Ultimate Rejected Take-off,"[5] in which a fully-loaded 747-8 Freighter with worn-out brakes attempts an aborted takeoff on a California runway. The rejected takeoff, or maximum brake energy test, is one of the most dramatic for a new airplane. The video has 680,000 views as of this writing. The video is great brand journalism because it is not a product pitch. Rather, it is branded content that people want to consume and that shows Boeing in a good light. "We publish content that supports business objectives and fosters positive opinions about Boeing," Blecher says. "We're not (directly) selling planes. We're selling Boeing."

Interestingly, many Boeing communicators were former reporters. Blecher himself was a former real-time wire service journalist at Bloomberg News (one of his duties is to manage the @Boeing Twitter feed). When stories are posted on the Boeing site, they include the byline of the person who wrote it. "It provides the same sort of accountability mentality that bylines provide in the regular journalism world," Blecher says. "I know there are some brands that want to be completely brand agnostic, so you don't really know who's behind it. I don't subscribe to that theory. Since most of our creators had been journalists, it was something that was totally natural to them."

Effective brand journalism is about telling stories. "Find yourself some journalists who can work on your staff," Blecher says. "I don't think it's something you can totally outsource. I know some organizations try to hire people to do that. I think that it is going to be counterproductive. Successful brand journalism, at least to us, requires a level of access to our people that only comes from having the journalists who are on staff talking to our subject-matter experts all the time, relating to them, building a relationship, so you get the very best kind of story."

Your online and off-line marketing content is meant to drive action, which requires a focus on buyer problems. Your buyers want this in their own words, and then they want proof. Every time you write, you have an opportunity to communicate and to *convince*. At each stage of the sales process, well-written materials combined with effective marketing programs will lead your buyers to understand how your company can help them. Good marketing is rare indeed, but a focus on doing it right will most certainly pay off with increased sales, higher retention rates, and more ink and airtime from journalists.

---

[5] boeing.com/Features/2011/05/bca_747-8_RTO_05_04_11.html

How Web Content Influences the Buying Process

Today when people want to buy something, the web is almost always the first stop on their shopping trip. In any market category, potential customers head online to do initial research. The moment of truth is when they reach your site: Will you draw them into your sales process or let them click away?

When buyers use search engines to reach your site, link to it through another site, find it via social networking, or respond to a marketing campaign, you have an opportunity to deliver targeted information at the precise moment when they are looking for what you have to offer. Yet marketers often fail to realize the potential of their websites, which must hook buyers in from the start and hang on to them until the sale is complete. Individuals don't go to the web looking for advertising; they are on a quest for content. By providing information when they need it, you can begin a long and profitable relationship with them. Editors and publishers obsess over readership, and so should you.

In this chapter, we're going to build on some of the ideas and concepts that I've already introduced in the book. In Chapter 3, we talked about reaching buyers directly with your organization's online content, and Chapter 11 was when we put together a detailed plan to identify buyer personas and target each one with an individualized approach. Remember, great web content is about your buyers, not about you. Now I'll provide some ideas for how you can make a website that takes buyers through their consideration process and moves them toward the point where they are ready to buy (or donate, join, subscribe), which, of course, is the goal of all web content.

While it is important for your website to have an attractive design and for all of the technical aspects (HTML and so on) to work properly, these aspects are beyond the scope of this book. There are many excellent texts on how to write HTML, XML, ASP, JavaScript, and other web languages. And there are also great resources for getting the design aspects right—things like colors, fonts, logo placement, and whatnot. While these elements are critical to an overall site, I want to focus on how *content drives action* on websites, because the content aspect is often overlooked.

To best leverage the power of content, you first need to help your site's visitors find what they need on your site. When someone visits a site for the first time, the site communicates messages to the buyer: Does this organization care about me? Does it focus on the problems I face? Or does the site only include information describing what the company has to offer from its own narrow perspective? You need to start with a site navigation that is designed and organized with your buyers in mind. Don't simply mimic the way your company or group is organized (e.g., by product, geography, or governmental structure), because the way your audience uses websites rarely coincides with your company's internal priorities. Organizing based on your needs leaves site visitors confused about how to find what *they* really need.

You should learn as much as possible about the buying process, focusing on issues such as how people find your site or the length of a typical purchase cycle. Consider what happens off-line in parallel with online interactions so that the processes complement each other. For example, if you have an e-commerce site and a printed catalog, coordinate the content so that both efforts support and reinforce the buying process (i.e., include URLs for your online buying guide in the catalog and use the same product descriptions so people don't get confused). In the B2B world, trade shows should work with Internet initiatives (by collecting email addresses at the booth, for example, and then sending a follow-up email with a show-specific landing page at your site). Understanding the buying process in detail, both online and off-line, allows you to create web content that influences the buying decision.

Segmenting Your Buyers

The online relationship begins the second a potential customer hits your home page. The first thing he needs to see is a reflection of himself. That's why you must organize your site with content for each of your distinct buyer personas. How do your potential customers self-select? Is it based on their job function, on geography, or on the industry they work in? It's important to create a set of appropriate links based on a clear understanding of your buyers so that you can quickly move them from your home page to pages built specifically for them.

For example, the New York Public Library (NYPL),[1] an institution that has 52.9 million items in its collections housed at 87 locations and overseen by 3,100 staff members, has a website that must serve many varied visitors. The NYPL site appeals to a very diverse set of buyer personas (people who use the libraries' services both online and off-line) who download materials directly from the site. Here are just a few of the buyer personas that the NYPL site serves:

- Academic researchers from around the globe who need access to the NYPL digital information collections.
- People who live in the Bronx and speak Spanish as a first language. (The library offers introductory classes, conducted in Spanish at the NYPL's Bronx location, on how to use a computer.)
- Tourists to New York City who want to take a tour of the beautiful main library building on Fifth Avenue.
- Film studios, TV producers, and photographers who use the famous NYPL setting. (*Breakfast at Tiffany's*, *Ghostbusters*, and *Spider-Man* are just a few of the movies that have been partially filmed there.)
- Individuals, foundations, and corporations that support the library with donations.

The NYPL site includes detailed content throughout to reach each of these buyer personas (as well as others). The front page of the NYPL website is broken into several main sections, including "Research" (information on what is in the library's catalogs for people who need a particular book), "Locations" (branch information for those who live in New York City), "Classes and Events," and "Support the Library" (membership and giving information for people who want to donate money or time to the NYPL). Each landing page has additional information to make browsing this huge website easy.

---

[1] nypl.org

One way many organizations approach navigation is to link to landing pages based on the problems your product or service solves. Start by identifying the situations in which each target audience may find itself. If you are in the supply chain management business, you might have a drop-down menu on the home page with links that say, "I need to get product to customers faster" or "I want to move products internationally." Each path leads to landing pages built for buyer segments, with content targeted to their problems. Once the prospects reach those pages, you have the opportunity to communicate your expertise in solving these problems—building some empathy in the process—and to move customers further along the buying cycle.

Elements of a Buyer-Centric Website

As you build a site that focuses on your buyers and their purchasing process, here are a few other things to consider:

Think About Your Buyers' Preferred Media and Learning Styles

I had a great conversation with Ted Demopoulos[2] about blogging versus podcasting, people's learning styles, and the choices of what content to put on a site. He brought up an interesting point: It's not an either-or decision. "It's worth having your message in different formats," he says. "I love to read. And I often listen to informative audio while driving, biking, or mowing the lawn. But I do not like video. It's not like reading; it progresses at its own rate. I can't watch faster or skim easily, like with text, and it demands total attention, unlike with audio." Of course, other people are the opposite of Demopoulos. They don't like to read but love video content. We all have different learning styles and media preferences. So on your site, you should have appropriate content designed for your buyers. This does not mean that you need to have every single format, but you should think about augmenting text with photos and maybe some video content. "Not only do people like different formats, but psychologists have shown that people learn better with different media," Demopoulos adds. "Marketers should have messages in as many formats as practical. Even though the messages

---

[2] demop.com

are the same, they will appeal to different groups of people. For example, some will want an e-book, but you can take the same content and turn it into a tele-seminar."

Develop a Site Personality

It is important to create a distinct, consistent, and memorable site, and an important component of that goal is the tone or voice of the content. As visitors interact with the content on your site, they should develop a clear picture of your organization. Is the personality fun and playful? Or is it solid and conservative? For example, on the Google home page, when people search they can click "I'm Feeling Lucky," which is a fun and playful way to get you directly to the top listing in the search results. That one little phrase, "I'm Feeling Lucky," says a lot about Google. And there's much more. For example, in the collection of more than 100 languages that Google supports, from Afrikaans to Zulu, there is also Google in the language of Elmer Fudd,[3] with everything translated into what Elmer Fudd would say, such as "I'm Feewing Wucky." Google also has a fun tradition of modifying its home page logo to mark special events. Called Google's Doodles, these whimsically altered logos that vary around the world celebrate everything from Australia Day to Cezanne's birthday. This is cool, but it wouldn't work for a more conservative company—it would just seem strange and out of place. Contrast that with Accenture's homepage.[4] At the time of this writing, just under the Accenture logo was the phrase "High Performance. Delivered." There are photos with messages such as "We have advised clients on more than 570 merger and acquisition deals in the last 5 years" and "Every year our systems process 300 million airline ticket reservations." Both of these home pages work because the site personality works with the company personality. Whatever your personality, the way to achieve consistency is to make certain that all the written material and other content on the site conform to a defined tone that you've established from the start. A strong focus on site personality and character pays off. As visitors come to rely on the content they find on your site, they will develop an emotional and personal relationship with your organization. A website can evoke a familiar

---

[3] google.com/webhp?hl=xx-elmer

[4] accenture.com

and trusted voice, just like that of a friend on the other end of an email exchange.

For an example of a site with a very distinct personality that appeals to buyer personas, check out HOTforSecurity[5] from BitDefender. BitDefender is a particularly interesting example because the market that BitDefender serves is very competitive, and product differentiation is not easy to accomplish. A cornerstone of the company's marketing approach, HOTforSecurity was launched as a stand-alone site focused on key influencers within the IT security community. The new site was not a redesign of the existing company site but, rather, an informational supplement to the main BitDefender product site.[6]

HOTforSecurity is for people who are interested in the latest information on Internet threats. The BitDefender team clearly understands that the best online initiatives are those that deliver specific information tailored to a particular buyer persona. The HOTforSecurity site was developed to appeal to three different buyer personas:

1. Information technology security press (both mainstream press and social media).
2. BitDefender users.
3. A group of "Internet security geeks"—the most important buyer persona for HOTforSecurity.

The HOTforSecurity site appeals directly to the Internet security geek buyer persona with informational posts such as: "Windows 8 Stores Logon Passwords in Plain Text." The design is clearly that of an informational site that might be a media property—in stark contrast to the slew of boring sites in the technology industry. It delivers valuable information to everyone interested in Internet security issues (not just BitDefender users) but is not a sales site, so people trust it. While there are identifiers that the site is an online property of BitDefender, it is a subtle tie. They don't brag about it but don't hide the association. With a growing audience of approximately 15,000 RSS subscribers, 35,000 Twitter followers, and 300,000 Facebook fans, HOTforSecurity is a great example of effectively reaching buyers.

---

[5] hotforsecurity.com
[6] bitdefender.com

Photos and Images Tell Your Story

Content is not limited to words; smart marketers make use of nontext content—including photos, audio feeds, video clips, cartoons, charts, and graphs—to inform and entertain site visitors. Photographs in particular play an important role for many sites. Photos are powerful content when page visitors see that the images are an integrated component of the website. However, generic stock photographs (happy and good-looking multicultural models in a fake company meeting room) may actually have a negative effect. People will know instantly that the photo is not of real people in your organization. Neither you nor your users are generic. On a technical note, while photos, charts, graphs, and other nontext content make great additions to any site, be wary of very large image sizes and of distracting multimedia content like Flash Video. Visitors want to access content quickly, they want sites that load fast, and they don't want to be distracted. See Chapter 18 for much more on photos and images.

Include Interactive Content Tools

Anything that gets people involved with the content of a site provides a great way to engage visitors, build their interest, and move them through your sales cycle. Examples of interactive tools include such things as the stock quoting and charting applications found on financial sites and "email your congressman" tools on political advocacy sites. Interactive content provides visitors with a chance to immerse themselves in site content, which makes them more likely to progress through the sales consideration cycle to the point where they are ready to spend money.

Make Feedback Loops Available

Providing a way for users to interact with your organization is a hallmark of a great site. Easy to find "contact us" information is a must, and direct feedback mechanisms like "rate this" buttons, online forums, viewer reviews, and opportunities to post comments provide valuable information by and for site visitors.

Provide Ways for Your Customers to Interact with Each Other

A forum or wiki where customers can share with one another and help each other works well for many organizations as a way to show potential customers that there is a vibrant community of people using their products or services. In other words, an existing set of customers interacting with each other on your site is great marketing!

Make Sure Your Site Is Current

Many people are so busy creating new content for their sites that they forget to ensure that existing content is still current. Websites tend to become outdated quickly because of product changes, staff turnover, and other factors. You should make a point of auditing your site regularly, perhaps once per quarter, and revising as appropriate. At a minimum, you must change the copyright date, if you have one, each January 1. I've seen hundreds of pages with copyright dates many years old.

Include Social Media Share Buttons

A great way to extend the potential reach of your content—to people you do not even know yet—is to make it easy for readers to share your content with their networks. The best way to do this is to include share buttons on each important page of your site. Your videos, white paper download pages, blog posts, and similar content should definitely have them. Share buttons makes it easy for people to point to your content on social networking sites like Facebook, Pinterest, Google+, and Twitter. An example of a share button is the little thumbs-up Like button on Facebook. When your fans push that button on your website, the news that they like it is then reported to their Facebook friends. It sounds like such a simple thing, but these buttons are one of the most effective ways to share content on the web.

Create Content with Pass-Along Value That Could Go Viral

Web content provides terrific fodder for viral marketing—the phenomenon where people pass on information about your site to their friends and colleagues or link to your content in their blogs (more on viral marketing is in Chapter 8). When content proves interesting or useful, visitors tend to tell friends, usually by sending them a link. Creating buzz around a site to encourage people to talk it up isn't easy. Creating content that has a pass-along value is never a certain process, because it happens more organically. There are a few things you can do to help the process, though. When creating site content, think carefully about what content users might want to pass along and then make that content easy to find and link to. Make the actual URLs permanent so that no one finds dead links when visiting months (or years) later. To be successful with viral marketing is to say something interesting and valuable and to make it easy to find and share.

Using RSS to Deliver Your Web Content to Targeted Niches

It is so easy for those of us in the media and analyst community to get information via RSS (Really Simple Syndication) that I can't stress its importance enough as a component of a web marketing strategy; it's my preferred method in my work tracking markets, companies, and ideas. Once information is in RSS format, an RSS-aware browser such as Firefox or a separate application like NewsFire checks the feed for changes and displays them on a web page. Having the information come to me is just so much easier than in the days when I had to go looking for it myself. The RSS and news aggregation software is easy to use and usually free, and it provides a way to get information from any device. I particularly like that RSS provides a powerful information-management tool that bypasses the increasingly crowded and annoying email channel. Having my favorite websites, media outlets, and blogs feeding RSS is my own custom compilation of exactly what I want to see.

Surprisingly, only a small percentage of organizations deploy RSS for syndicating news and content to the outside world. Even fewer understand how RSS feeds are a preferred way to market to niche customers who have very specific needs. Learn from the way that most major news sites such as the BBC, the *New York Times*, the *Washington Post*, and thousands more deploy RSS. Almost any content that can be broken down into discrete items (such as news releases, blog postings, product updates, or SEC filings) can be syndicated via RSS.

Netflix offers RSS feeds[7] for which video fans sign up to receive updates based on their interests. Available feeds include Netflix Top 100, New Releases, Documentary Top 25, Comedy Top 25, and Classics Top 25, and they all target specific customers who select only the content that interests

---

[7] netflix.com/RSSFeeds

them. So if I'm a fan of independent films, I subscribe to the RSS feed, and anytime independent film–related content changes on the Netflix site, I'm alerted to it via my RSS reader.

What sets this apart from the standard one-size-fits-all marketing model is that it is highly targeted and delivered directly to microaudiences of interested consumers. Contrast this with the typical way that companies market to their customers on the web. Often when you become a customer, the organization signs you up for its special offers email. After you get two or three of these emails, it becomes painfully obvious that they are just untargeted messages to the entire customer list and have little value for you. No wonder that house email lists suffer from significant opt-out numbers. Note how different the Netflix approach is of offering information that has been selected and is welcome, when compared with the old world of blasting generic email ads to the masses.

Link Content Directly into the Sales Cycle

Marketers with the most successful sites specifically design content to draw buyers into the sales cycle. People considering a purchase always go through a certain thought process. In the case of something simple and low-cost, say, deciding to download a song from iTunes, the process is likely to be very straightforward and may only take seconds. But for a major decision such as buying a new car, sending your child to college, or accepting a job offer, the process may take weeks or months. For many business-to-business sales, the cycle may involve many steps and multiple buyer personas (a business buyer and an IT buyer, perhaps) and may take months or even years to complete.

Effective web marketers take website visitors' buying cycle into account when writing content and organizing it on the site. People in the early stages of the sales cycle need basic information about their problems and the ways that your organization solves them. Those further along in the process want to compare products and services, so they need detailed information about the benefits of your offerings. And when buyers are ready to whip out their credit cards, they need easy-to-use mechanisms linked directly from the content so they can quickly finish the purchase (or donation, subscription, and so on).

For an example of a very long sales cycle, consider our college example from earlier chapters. High school students in the United States apply to colleges in the fall of their senior year and typically make a decision about which school to attend in the spring. Having gone through the process with my daughter who is now in university, I know the sales cycle starts much earlier. When students visit colleges in person, they tend to be juniors in high school, but when students first visit college websites, they are probably freshmen or sophomores. The college website is often the first place that a student comes into contact with the college, and the site must cater to an audience of young teenagers (and their parents) who won't be ready to apply for admission for two or three years. Creating appropriate content to develop a lasting relationship over a long sales cycle is possible only when an organization knows the buyer personas well and understands the sales process in detail. The college must provide high school students with appropriate content so they get a sense of what college life would be like if they were to attend and what the admission process entails.

A focus on understanding buyers and the sales cycle and developing appropriate content that links visitors through the cycle to the point of purchase is essential for a great site. Based on my years of research, the vast majority of sites are little more than online brochures or vast one-way advertising vehicles. These sites are almost wholly ineffective. The web offers significant opportunities to those marketers who understand that content is at the forefront of the best sites.

A Friendly Nudge

After you've demonstrated expertise in the market category and knowledge about solving potential customers' problems, you can introduce your product or service. When creating content about your offerings, remain focused on the buyer and the problems, rather than elaborating distinctions between products. As people interact with your content at this middle stage in the buying process, it is appropriate to suggest subscriptions to related content—perhaps an email newsletter, webinar (web-based seminar), or podcast. But remember, if you're asking for someone's email address (or other contact details), you must provide something equally valuable in return.

Prospects want to poke, prod, and test your company to learn what sort of organization you are. They also have questions. That's why well-designed sites include a mechanism for people to inquire about products or services. Be flexible but also consistent; offer them a variety of ways to interact with your company, and make contact information readily available from any page on the site (one click away is best). Also keep in mind that, particularly with expensive products, buyers will test you to see how responsive you are, so you must make responding to these inquiries a priority. Do you respond to email requests in real time? At this stage, you want people to think: "This is an organization I can do business with. They have happy customers, and they are responsive to me and my needs."

Close the Sale and Continue the Conversation

As the customer approaches the end of the buying process, you must provide tools that facilitate the sale. Buyers may be unsure which of your products is appropriate for them, so you may need to provide online demonstrations or a tool that allows them to enter specific details about their requirements and then suggests the appropriate product.

Once the deal is closed, there's one more step. You must continue the online dialogue with your new customer. Add her to your customer email newsletter or customer-only community site where she can interact with experts in your organization and other like-minded customers. You should also provide ample opportunities for customers to give you feedback on how to make the products (and sales process) better.

An Open-Source Marketing Model

Franz Maruna, CEO of concrete5,[8] started an interactive media firm in 2002. His business was building custom websites and communities for businesses, including some major sites like Indie911.com, Lemonade.com, and School pulse.com. To create and deploy the sites, concrete5 built their own content management system (CMS), software that is used to build and manage web pages and other online content. Maruna's firm created a new system because he couldn't find the right tools in a commercially available package. As the concrete5 team built more complex sites, they constantly updated their own CMS system to fit their requirements and their clients' needs.

Maruna eventually became disenchanted with the process of constantly selling new web-development work, so he decided to focus on what he really

---

[8] concrete5.org

liked: the content management system. "We spent eight months building a release version of the concrete5 CMS," he says. "My partners and I knew that we had a better mousetrap, but we had a chance to decide what to do with it. So we made the CMS software available to anyone for free and as open source [i.e., the programming code is available to anyone, without registration; computer-savvy users may make changes to it and build new versions of the software as they see fit]. We decided that bigger and better things would happen for our firm if we let others get onto the bus with us."

Providing a free, open-source software application is a remarkably bold move, but Maruna believes it is a smart one. "We make money on the marketplace (modules and tools that we sell) and on web hosting," he says. "It's like I give you free beer (the software), but if you want pretzels and peanuts (tools and hosting), you have to pay. To have a party, you don't need to have a huge bar. All you need is a keg and people will show up. It doesn't take a lot."

Maruna then built a community[9] to spread the word about what the company was doing. "Bloggers started talking about it, and people started to tweet. We built our own forums where people can come together. The community is great with real-world bug testing, a superpowerful way to test ideas and concepts. The community has translated the product into a dozen languages."

The concrete5 community includes very active forums. While people from the company participate, they comprise a primarily community-contributed knowledge base. What makes this form of web content interesting as a marketing and PR tool is that it is totally open for customers and noncustomers alike. Many companies have interactive communities but lock them away in password-protected nooks. At concrete5, it is all out in the open—showing other interested potential users what's really going on.

Through web content, concrete5 first introduces people to the concepts of an open-source CMS system and then offers free working products. Next, the company encourages users to participate in the online forum and then finally makes money by selling enhancements and tools for the software and interactive web-hosting services. All of the resulting web content serves as the company's marketing engine. As I write this, the CMS application has been downloaded more than a million times. The company has an active forum of 150,000 developers and designers who are eagerly helping each other out.

---

[9] concrete5.org/community

"It is an exciting opportunity when people say both good things and bad things about you," Maruna says. "The focus group is all around you every day, and it's free. As a company, when you start engaging in an open-source way, you then have a community that becomes a passionate support base for you. Do this, and your customers will become your fans, and they will go to the end of the world to evangelize your product for you. Beyond the amazing work our open-source community puts in around translating our product, bug-testing it, and creating extensions, they've also sent us copious amounts of beer (thanks!) and flown halfway around the world to meet us. A digital community is awesome if you use it correctly. You don't own it; you participate in it. You can't buy it; you have to work at it. Be a good person, treat the world like you'd treat your family, and they'll do the same."

For every organization, the key to a great website is to understand buyers and build valuable content especially for them.

But there is one final step. Effective marketers constantly measure and improve. Because it is so easy to modify web content at any time, you should be measuring what people are doing on the site. Benchmarking elements such as the self-select links and testing different landing page content can help. If you have two offers on a landing page (a free white paper and a free demonstration, say), you might measure which one works to get more clicks but also measure how many people who respond to the offer actually buy something. This way you will know not just numbers of clicks, but revenue by offer type, and you can use that in future landing pages. Armed with real data, you make valuable modifications. You might want to just see what happens if you change the order of the links on the home page. Sometimes people just click the thing on the top of a list. What happens if something else is on top?

Let's close this chapter by meeting someone who has put all the ideas of this chapter to work: built an online content strategy, measured the results, and achieved impressive business growth.

How a Content Strategy Grew Business by 50 Percent in One Year

Sales Benchmark Index[10] is a professional services firm focused exclusively on B2B sales force effectiveness. Before making the switch to a content

---

[10] salesbenchmarkindex.com

marketing strategy, the company used classic old-rules marketing to try to reach customers. "We hired telemarketing firms to cold call," says CEO Greg Alexander. "We did batch and blast email. We did interruption-based marketing tactics of all kinds, and for a period of time from 2006 to 2010, that approach met our needs. And our needs are really well defined: We know how many inquiries we need to generate all the way through to paying customers. Then early in 2010, the effectiveness of the outbound channels just stopped. It was like somebody slammed the doors shut."

Alexander thinks that his interruption-based strategies stopped working because his target audience was incredibly busy. "I wasn't competing against other companies," he says. "I was competing for buyers' attention." Alexander did a great deal of research on how his buyer personas solve problems, and that was the starting point for his efforts to reach buyers with online content.

"When our target customer (the head of sales or the head of marketing in a B2B organization) has a problem or need in their business, the very first thing they do—and we've done a lot of research to support this—is start searching the web and reading and educating themselves," Alexander says. "They typically don't want to engage with a service provider, us or anybody else for that matter, for a long time. Through education on the Web, they develop a crisp, well-articulated problem statement. Then they reach out to a small number of people to ask for their assistance in how they might approach solving that problem. It's similar to the way somebody would hire a law firm or a strategy consulting firm or an advertising agency."

Once Alexander and his team understood how buyers solved problems, the next step was to develop buyer persona profiles. "We wanted to understand the key business objectives of each target audience," Alexander says. "What was standing in the way of them accomplishing those objectives? What were the things that were important to them when they made a decision to hire a service provider? How were they measured? What would the definition of success be? Once we understood that, we mapped the buying process for each persona. We identified when information requests were happening in the buying process, for example, and what those information requests were."

Alexander quickly realized that he had to develop a large number of new content channels, but outside firms couldn't provide writers, editors, and designers who understood well enough what his firm actually does. So he chose to create what he calls an "internal content marketing agency" using his company's smart subject experts. To do so, they needed to create an infrastructure to channel their expertise into the creation of blog posts, videos, and longer-form content like e-books.

Alexander's "internal agency" includes three staff members: a full-time editor, who manages an editorial calendar, production schedule, and set of media channels; an SEO expert, who increases the likelihood of the content getting found in search; and a copywriter, who works with subject matter experts inside the firm.

"But the actual writers, the contributors of all the content, are the subject matter experts in our company who are working with our clients," Alexander says.

Interestingly, the subject matter experts at Sales Benchmark Index are organized by buyer persona. I always recommend this buyer-centric approach, yet most companies focus on the product lines they offer rather than the personas they sell to. "It was a difficult transition for us," Alexander admits. "We used to be service-offering-focused. I had to break that. It was a painful transition, and it took us some time to get there."

Another of Alexander's smart strategies that is straight out of this book is that he named his buyer personas. At Sales Benchmark Index there are nine of them, and there are two people from the firm assigned to work with each persona and to create content for them. "For example, we have a persona called 'Big Company Mark,'" Alexander says. "Big Company Mark is the chief marketing officer or the VP of marketing. We have two individuals in our firm who have been serving the chief marketing officer in the B2B environment for many years, even prior to joining our company. They were the ones who actually constructed the buyer persona, so they understand what their needs and challenges are."

When it came time to start writing, the team started with a blog. They worked with HubSpot to deploy the HubSpot marketing platform[11] for hosting the content. "It started slowly," Alexander says. "Our early blog posts probably weren't our proudest moments. But then we started to build interest and get subscribers. Soon everybody in the company saw the success and wanted to participate, so we began posting to our blog every day."

In fact, the company blog is actually the homepage. This is a terrific way to showcase company expertise and also to surface content for SEO purposes. "Our best asset is our blog," he says. "So we thought, why not put that on

---

[11] hubspot.com

the homepage? That really helped." In a world where so many organizations treat their home page like the cover of a brochure, having a blog there that updates daily is excellent real-time marketing.

One thing I particularly love about the Sales Benchmark Index home page is how the blog posts are indexed both by buyer persona and by market problem. Brilliant! This means potential customers can find exactly the posts that were created for them.

The team at Sales Benchmark Index also creates long-form content, including a recent e-book targeted to newly promoted VPs of sales. "It was a heavy lift for us to put it together. But it has created over 4,000 leads for us so far this year.

Alexander and the company are also active on Twitter and LinkedIn.

Alexander knows from his buyer persona research that 75 percent of his potential U.S. clients are on a calendar-based planning cycle. "July through October is when they go through their annual operating plan," he says. This is the time when buyers are most receptive to Sales Benchmark Index services and when the majority of sales take place. "They are trying to figure out things like 'How many sales people do I need?' 'How should I place the territories?' 'What should the quotas be?' 'How should I pay them?' A lot of their research is centered around those issues, and we can help them with that."

Because most of Alexander's sales happen July through October, he has a calendar-based approach to content creation. "From November through June, the approach is to give away lots and lots of intellectual property to build up the subscriber base," Alexander says. "We believe that permission to have a conversation with buyers is a valuable asset. Within the blog, we will write about a problem. We'll offer up a tool that we used with one of our clients to solve that specific problem. All we ask is that they click on the link. We put it behind a form, and then they get the tool for free. During this quiet period, we don't bombard them with follow-up marketing activity."

Alexander's team shifts focus during the selling season, when buyers have a greater need for information because they are planning next year's budgets. "During that time period, we shift the focus of the blog to having subscribers participate in our annual research tour, which we call 'Make the Number: How Your Peers Plan on Allocating People, Money and Time for the Upcoming Year.'"[12]

---

[12] salesbenchmarkindex.com/bid/86763/Make-the-Number-How-Your-Peers-Are-Allocating-People-Money-Time-in-2013

"Make the Number" gives potential clients access to a personal review of benchmarking data and research. "This is an onsite seminar," Alexander says. "If you want access to all these tools, and you've been a subscriber of ours for months and sometimes years, one of our experts will come and give you a presentation for 90 minutes on a set of best practices heading into the New Year."

Alexander has had tremendous success with the calendar-based approach to content creation. "In prior years, we might do between 50 and 100 visits during the July to October period," he says. "But this year, we'll have done over 220 of them. We know that about half of those sites eventually, inside of six quarters, become clients of ours. When people prepare to buy a professional service like ours, the product is intangible. So we use the 'Make the Number' meetings to turn what we do into a tangible. It makes it easier for the buyer to buy."

Alexander's team measures every aspect of his content efforts. After all, this is a company that helps sales and marketing executives be more effective through measurement! In fact, they measure down to the blog-post level. "We grade posts based on things like how closely each are related to the problems of our buyer personas," he says. "We count the number of words in sentences, targeting between 6 and 14 words per sentence. And we grade the effectiveness of the title. Then there are the hard metrics like the number of comments, social shares, links generated, and view counts."

Alexander also analyzes what he calls "branded versus non-branded keywords" to understand how many people come to the blog on a monthly basis for each. He tallies a branded keyword hit when somebody arrives at the blog via a term like "sales benchmark index" (which means that person entered the company name into a search engine). A non-branded word is subject-specific but not company-specific, like "sales territory design."

HubSpot's analytics tools are important in Alexander's efforts. "We're looking at the number of incoming links, and we use the HubSpot Link Grader Search Engine Optimization Tool. This year we've generated 579 new domains linking to us, with 27,780 individual links coming from those domains. The thing that I'm probably the happiest about is that the quality of the links has gone up. HubSpot graded the links earlier in the year at 47 on a scale of 0 to 100. Now the average link rating is 82."

The ultimate measure of success for a business is revenue growth, and the strategies Alexander has implemented have contributed greatly to his company's success. "We're up a little over 50 percent this year," he told me. "That's our revenue number and our head [employee] count, which in professional services is a key metric. I can directly attribute much of that gain to content marketing. This is a mental shift to realize that you're really in the publishing business. If you embrace publishing, then the transformation will happen."

Yes, product superiority, advertising, the media, and branding remain important to the marketing mix. But on the web, smart marketers like Greg Alexander understand that an effective content strategy, tightly integrated to the buying process, is critical to success.

Yes, product superiority, advertising, the media, and branding remain important to the marketing mix. But on the web, smart marketers like Greg Alexander understand that an effective content strategy, tightly integrated to the buying process, is critical to success.

15 Mobile Marketing: Reaching Buyers Wherever They Are

As I write this, it's late afternoon in a hotel lobby. I'm getting hungry but also a little tired. A few years ago, that meant a mediocre meal at the hotel restaurant. Or perhaps I'd ask the hotel concierge for a nearby recommendation, if I wanted some fresh air and a short walk. If I was feeling adventurous, I'd probably search online sites like Zagat's or Yelp and then use Google Maps to find something nearby. But I don't do any of these things anymore. Now I pull out my iPhone, fire up the Foursquare or Layar application, and gaze on a listing of nearby restaurants, complete with information about how far away each one is from me. I can see tips that people have left about the different choices. I can even see if any of my friends are there right now.

The incredible growth of browser-equipped mobile devices like Black-Berrys, Androids, iPhones, and iPads means that people like me can now look for products and services while we are on the road. Indeed, in mobile-centric markets like Africa and Asia, mobile Internet connections are more widely used than standard computer connections to the web, since mobiles are what people can afford and since wireless infrastructure is more reliable than landlines. Even in Japan, a land connected by a last-mile optical fiber network that puts the United States to shame, mobile rules because online prime time is the two or more hours daily people spend riding trains.

According to the International Telecommunications Union,[1] there were 5.9 billion mobile phone subscriptions worldwide in 2011, and mobile

---

[1] itu.int/ITU-D/ict/statistics/at_glance/KeyTelecom.html

networks are available to more than 90 percent of the world's population. It's not just creaky old technology either; some 150 countries offer high-speed 3G service. These Internet access patterns have massive implications for all kinds of businesses worldwide. The ability to contact consumers at the precise moment they're near you and ready to buy exactly what you sell will transform how you market to them. And the use of mobile reaches all levels of society, not just those who choose mobile because phones are cheaper than computers. A *Forbes*-Google study called "The Untethered Executive: Business Information in the Age of Mobility"[2] reports that more than half of senior executives say that their mobile device is now their primary communications tool. Executives are making purchases on their mobile devices, too. Nearly two-thirds indicated they're comfortable making a business purchase on their mobile, and more than half would rather make a business purchase on the mobile web than by phone.

All sorts of people purchase products while going about their day. Rather than having to make a trip across town, a busy mom might use her iPhone to shop while waiting to pick up the kids at soccer practice. "It is clear that we've come to a point of no return in the impact and uptake of mobile devices, and yet still most businesses struggle with the mobile-social decisions," says Kern Wyman. Wyman is co-founder of Min-i-Mags 4 Mini People (mm4mp), an iPhone application boutique children's retailers use for global advertising. "Real-time decisions, instant mobile commercial transactions, and anywhere-everywhere collaboration is happening all around us now."

Make Your Site Mobile Friendly

As people use mobile web browsers on their iPhones, Androids, or other devices, it is important that your site be mobile friendly—displaying content quickly and optimizing it for viewing on smaller screens. Many sites still don't have a mobile-friendly architecture, so those organizations miss out on opportunities to sell to the many people now accessing their sites from wireless devices. Your site should have different sets of HTML code that recognize what kind of device visitors are using (computer or mobile) and display the site in the best format.

---

[2] forbes.com/forbesinsights/untethered_executive/index.html

"It is important to make sure the mobile content loads quickly," says Jim Stewart, CEO of Stew Art Media, a Melbourne-based web development and search engine optimization firm. "People accessing your site with mobile devices are doing so wirelessly, and it's costing them money in their data plans. You want the site to load quickly for them. And they've got a much smaller screen. We're almost back to the days of the early web, when smaller, 'lightweight' pages were better."

Stewart says that designing pages for mobile display requires rethinking the sort of content you offer. "You should display the most crucial information that you would think someone coming in through a mobile device would want," he says. "It might be the menu if you're a restaurant, or it might be the booking number. In Australia over 25 percent of PayPal users have made a purchase using a smartphone. If you use Google AdWords you can now target mobile users directly and place a clickable phone number in the ad so they simply call through to your business, bypassing your website entirely. We had a car dealership client that used this method and had an amazing result."

As you're developing content for mobile devices, remember that search engines have a separate ranking system for mobile. That means there are implications for the search engine optimization strategies that will get your site ranked highly. "Google has Mobile Google, which is a different version from the normal or classic Google," Stewart says. "It's designed and marked up differently, and Google gives preference to sites that are mobile friendly. For example, make sure that Google understands where your mobile content is by setting up what they call a site map for mobile users. This map will be different from the site map for normal users. And if the site is about a local business, you need to use geographic descriptors. For instance, many buyers just type 'flowers' into Mobile Google, and quite often they will get Google Places information in the results. That's because Google has made an assessment that people want that information locally or close to them, or they want a business that services their particular area."

Here are a few things you can do right now:

1. Make sure your site is mobile compliant. You need the pages to load properly in mobile devices.
2. Create a mobile sitemap so the search engines can index your pages for mobile browsers.
3. Use few words and small graphics. People don't read much on mobiles and they want the data to come quickly.

The challenge is to understand this new landscape so you can get your business into the mix at that precise moment of decision. I chose to work with experts and it was the right decision for me. Don't miss out on opportunities to sell to the many people now accessing sites and searching for products and services like yours from wireless devices.

Build Your Audience via Mobile

Because buyers use their mobiles to search for products and services in the time of need (like I do when I'm hungry on the road), you've got an opportunity to move them from being a one-time looker to a long-term fan. The challenge is to create a compelling reason for somebody to want further contact with your company into the future—beyond the initial moment they find you on their mobile.

"You want to use mobile to capture and build your audience as quickly as possible, because people have the ability to do data input on the fly and the ability to act," says Christopher S. Penn, vice president of marketing technology at SHIFT Communications, a digital PR agency. "The faster you can get someone to act on their initial curiosity by using a mobile application that's related to your marketing, the more likely it is that you're going to be able to kick off a relationship with a customer."

One way that companies can engage consumers quickly is by deploying SMS (short message service) codes. In the United States, SMS was first popularized by television shows like *American Idol*, which let viewers vote for their favorite singing contestant during live broadcasts by sending a text message. This same strategy is used by marketers to develop point-of-sale sign-up systems. "If you go to any retail store, there's a good chance that some of the major brands offer a way for shoppers to text their email addresses to a short code [special telephone numbers that are significantly shorter than full telephone numbers for use on mobiles] and get exclusive coupons or subscribe to the insider's newsletter," Penn says. "You want to capture people when they're in the moment, especially if it's a retail or service experience, where you can help satisfy a customer. You want to take advantage of that warm feeling right then and there to capture them. Many outlets have the person at the register say something like 'Hey, text your email address to us and you'll get 20 percent off your next purchase.' Well, you're in the moment, you've got your purchase, and you say 'Okay, I'm going to do it, because I want 20 percent off next time.'"

Penn says that companies are beginning to experiment with capturing sign-ups using mobile applications in addition to SMS. Marketers like this approach because it can be free, whereas SMS services require them to pay a fee to the telecom provider. "Imagine being at a restaurant, and there's a tent card on the table," Penn says. "It says, 'Get 5 percent off your check if you visit our Facebook fan page and become a fan.' Well, right there on the fan page is a button to enroll in the restaurant's mailing list, and all it requires is one click to sign up. You tap your mobile phone once, and it says 'Congratulations, you're on the mailing list.' There's no data entered and nothing to miskey, which is especially important when dealing with tiny mobile keyboards. Within two taps, you're on the company's mailing list, and it's all done using the social data you've already entered into Facebook. The restaurant can get extremely rapid intake of data and build a customer list just by using the features that are already present in many of the platforms."

Geolocation: When Your Buyer Is Nearby

Adding GPS (global positioning system) capability to a mobile transforms the device into a targeted lens focused on its proximate surroundings. With onboard GPS capability, a mobile gains awareness of nearby people, companies, and locations, even in unfamiliar territory (like when I'm in an unfamiliar city and looking for a restaurant). Mobile applications that make use of GPS technology include Facebook Places, Foursquare, Layar, Gowalla, and many others, but the concept is the same for all. When someone is using their mobile with geolocation capability, the location of that person is pinpointed for marketers to use.

Applications like Foursquare, a way for people to share with friends their location at any given time, open up all sorts of interesting marketing opportunities. Many bars and restaurants now offer specials for those people who check in to those locations via Foursquare. For instance, you might earn free dessert for your table if you alert your friends about where you're dining. This works best for location-based businesses such as schools, churches, restaurants, hotels, theaters, hair salons, and the like. Some companies that hold events use Foursquare techniques to increase engagement at conference or meeting sessions.

Since geolocation marketing with applications like Foursquare is so new, many companies are experimenting. For example, Netherlands-based airline

KLM surprises certain lucky Foursquare users with a "random act of kindness."[3] Passengers who have checked in on Foursquare have been met at the gate with a glass of champagne and a warm personal welcome. Others have gotten free upgrades to first class or gifts like books, wristwatches, or luggage tags. The key to this promotion is that when someone checks in, say, at a certain gate in Amsterdam's Schiphol airport, KLM staff know exactly where that person is at that precise moment and can orchestrate the surprise. And when people are delighted by the surprise, they tell their friends and rave about it on social networks, delivering positive awareness for KLM.

People and organizations of all kinds are getting active on Foursquare and the similar location-based services. The U.S. National Archives, including the Presidential Libraries and Museums, joined Foursquare to encourage visitors at locations across America to share tips and other information.

Part of the fun of checking in on Foursquare is that you can earn a badge for certain check-ins. For example, I've earned the JetSetter badge seven times, you get one for five airport check-ins. I also earned Campus Explorer for visiting a bunch of universities with my daughter while she was shopping for the right school. I checked in at each. And don't forget: People are checking in from all over the world and beyond. Commander Douglas H. Wheelock (@astro_wheels on Twitter) became the first human to use a location-based service from space. Wheelock checked into Foursquare from the International Space Station and unlocked the new NASA Explorer Badge.

QR Codes to Drive People to Your Content

In many countries, people now use mobile-phone cameras as bar code scanners to link from a QR code ("Quick Response" code) to a website. It is a great way to get people to link to it from your offline marketing. For example, many display ads on Tokyo subway trains (where most of the riders seem to be using mobile Internet) feature QR codes. As passengers scan images of these codes, they're taken to mobile websites that provide more information—and sometimes even discount coupons.

The real-time aspect of QR codes is important. At precisely the moment a buyer is interested, you can give them more information. I adapted this

---

[3] surprise.klm.com

QR Code for downloading *World Wide Rave* for free

technique myself for my live presentations. When I want to share the free download link for my book *World Wide Rave: Creating Triggers that Get Millions of People to Spread Your Ideas and Share Your Stories* (the full-length book is free as a PDF as well as on the iPad, Kindle, Nook, and Kobo readers), I just bring up the QR code image on the screen. Then people in the audience who want to download *World Wide Rave* simply use their mobile's code reader to scan the image and get the book.

QR codes are a great way for anybody to send people from offline marketing (advertisements, Yellow Page telephone listings, tradeshow booth graphics, etc.) to a site where they can learn more. When I was touring Space Center Houston, I noticed many of the exhibits had QR codes to help visitors learn more about the artifacts that interested them. A QR code can be a great way to deliver information to people via mobile wherever they are and at the exact moment of their interest—on the beach, at a sporting event, or in a theater.

To use QR codes, you need two applications: a QR code generator and a QR code reader. While there are many available, here are two free services that I use. To generate my codes, I use the Kaywa QR Code Generator.[4] This web application allows you to simply paste a URL that points to the content you want to generate a code for. The application then provides the code image for publication.

The other application you'll need (or, more accurately, that your customers will need) is a QR reader for your mobile phone. I have an iPhone, and the reader I use is by TapMedia.[5] The app uses the phone's camera to scan the code and then links to the associated content. Many readers will store a history of the codes you've scanned, so you can use the reader as a reminder of information you want to review in the future. There are readers available for Android, BlackBerry, and other types of mobile phones.

While not every buyer will scan QR codes, these days enough people will to make it worthwhile for you to consider adding them to your offline marketing. The average person might not know what a QR code is (my mother certainly doesn't). But I recall that in 1995, when website URLs started to appear in offline advertising, and again in 2008, when Twitter IDs

---

[4] qrcode.kaywa.com

[5] itunes.apple.com/us/app/qr-reader-for-iphone/id368494609

started popping up, that people didn't know what they were either. Now, I'm not saying QR codes will have the same uptake as websites or Twitter. But I do think that, to reach the geeky among your buyers, it is probably worth adding a QR code to your materials when possible.

To get you thinking about how you might make use of QR codes, here are a few ideas:

- B2B companies can hand out postcards at the tradeshow with their logo on one side and a QR code on the other, along with some minimal text such as contact information and a short company description. The QR code is for follow-up content delivery and replaces the expensive printed information packs that so many companies lovingly hand out only to be discarded by booth visitors at the next trash can.
- Speakers at conferences can pop up a QR code on a slide to point audience members to supplemental information to be downloaded, like I do with my free book download. This makes dissemination of the slide deck or handouts very simple.
- Consumer marketers can add a QR code to offline advertising in magazines, newspapers, subway and bus placards, and the like.
- Restaurants can use a QR code to take people from their yellow page telephone listing to a menu.
- Doctors, dentists, and vets can hand out a QR code on cards corresponding to commonly diagnosed conditions, so patients can learn independently about their illnesses.
- Physical therapists, personal trainers, and chiropractors can create QR-code-distributed videos on how to properly do exercises at home.
- Museums and art galleries can include QR codes to point to additional information about artifacts.
- Rock bands can offer free music downloads to fans at gigs. Mickey Hart, former drummer for the Grateful Dead, does exactly this. At a Rhythm Devils show I attended, he passed out music download cards (a bit larger than a business card) with a QR code for free tunes.
- Businesspeople can have a QR code on their business card that links to their blog.
- If you're a single who wants to meet geeky people at bars, you could wear a QR code t-shirt that sends prospective dates to some interesting web-based information about you. I know I'm pushing it here, but I want to get you thinking!

One of the most interesting uses of QR codes I've found is for a fishy business! My hometown newspaper, the *Boston Globe*, ran a fantastic series of investigative articles titled: "From sea to sushi bar, a system open to abuse." It turns out that DNA testing organized by the *Globe* revealed that nearly half of 183 fish samples collected at restaurants and supermarkets in the Boston area were not the species ordered. Fish misidentification is especially common at sushi restaurants, the *Globe* found, partly because they use various names for the same fish. Testing showed that 32 area sushi restaurants sold misnamed fish. In some cases, it was probably an honest mistake. But clearly many restaurants sell inferior species of fish at the high prices commanded by the delicious but expensive varieties.

But there is hope in the form of QR codes! A network of fishermen, distributors, processors, and restaurants called Trace and Trust,[6] has organized a system that uses QR codes to track individual fish from the ocean to your plate. Trace and Trust tells customers exactly who caught their seafood, as well as when, where, and how it was caught. Trace and Trust believes this level of transparency results in the highest quality and freshest possible seafood you have ever seen. I agree.

The system delivers complete transparency and is fun too. Do you know who caught your seafood? If you were sitting at the 606 Congress restaurant in Boston, you'd be able to scan the code on your Summer Flounder and learn the exact date that Chris Brown landed it, and where. You'd learn that Captain Brown's vessel, the F/V Proud Mary, is currently docked in the harbor in Point Judith, Rhode Island. And you'd see exactly when your fish was delivered by Wild Rhody Seafood wholesalers to the restaurant you're seated in. Heck, there's even a photo of Chris with the fish that you're about to take a nice bite out of. How lovely! This use of QR codes proves that your fish is what it is supposed to be and serves as excellent marketing for the restaurant and its suppliers.

The Mobile Media Room

Because the iPhone and other mobile devices use public software platforms, anybody can create an application to use for marketing and public relations purposes. I've got my own free David Meerman Scott iPhone and iPad

---

[6] traceandtrust.com

applications,[7] that were developed for me by Newstex, a real-time content technology company. My application includes my blog posts, Twitter feed, and videos, and they link to my online bookstore on Amazon.

Because more and more reporters are active on mobiles, I'm convinced that the public relations, analyst relations, and investor relations departments of companies need to create applications like mine to reach their editorial, analyst, investor, and other constituents. What we're seeing is the natural evolution of the online newsroom, which I discuss in Chapter 21. Companies need a content-rich online media room filled with blog posts, videos, podcasts, e-books, press releases, and background information, and I think those same companies need to think about mobile content delivery to journalists.

In my travels around the world, I've noticed more and more reporters and analysts using mobile devices, especially iPads, to take notes during meetings. I've also seen them with iPhones, BlackBerrys, and the like in constant use while on the go. When a reporter or analyst has an application for the company, or music artist, or nonprofit she covers on her mobile, then she can easily check what's going on, as well as generate alerts for things like press releases—all on her device of choice. An added benefit is that these applications can double as tools to reach employees and partners, as well as existing and potential customers.

An App for Anything

There really is an application for anything. For example, the SitOrSquat bathroom finder application for iPhone and other devices indexes, as of this writing, nearly 100,000 public restrooms, all geolocated and rated for cleanliness. Clean bathrooms receive a Sit rating, dirty ones, a Squat. While the application supports adding locations anywhere in the world, at this point most of the potties are located in the United States. If you've got to pee and you are in New York City, you're in luck! However, if you're feeling the urge to tinkle in Helsinki, well, you've got to hold it a bit longer; there are only four loos listed in that city.

The SitOrSquat bathroom finder is sponsored by Charmin, America's most popular toilet paper for more than 25 years. Gotta love that sponsorship! The press release announcing the sponsorship must have been a blast

---

[7] itunes.apple.com/us/app/david-meerman-scott/id399226943?mt=8

to write: "For nearly a decade, Charmin has been dedicated to giving consumers a great public bathroom experience. This commitment started in 2000 with 'Charminizing' public restrooms at State Fairs, then the mobile unit 'Potty Palooza' from 2003–2005 and finally, with the next evolution, The Charmin Restrooms in Times Square."

Another interesting application is the Live Scoring iPhone and Android applications from the Association of Tennis Professionals (men's professional tennis) and Women's Tennis Association (women's professional tennis). The ATP Live Scoring app delivers real-time point-by-point updates from matches being played on the WTA and ATP World Tour. The official Live Scoring mobile applications are free and allow fans to follow in real time their favorite professional tennis players, such as Rafael Nadal, Roger Federer, Caroline Wozniacki, and Serena Williams, as they compete around the globe across 115 events in 43 countries.

"There is a demand for real-time tournament scoring from our hard-core tennis fans," says Philippe Dore, senior director of digital marketing for the ATP World Tour. "If you are not lucky enough to see a match being played in Zagreb or Beijing on TV, this will be the best way to follow it, whether it is on your computer or your iPhone or your Android or on our mobile website. Journalists are using it too, when they are getting ready to write and are on deadline."

I found it interesting that mobile devices are used to gather the data that power the application. "The point-by-point scoring data comes directly from the umpire's chair," Dore says. "So it is the exact official data from the umpire. As the umpire taps a score on his PDA, we get the live scoring to our website and mobile applications. It's being used by both the Men's ATP Tour and the women's tour . . . and now we are rolling it out to the lower tournaments, called the challenger circuits." Just three months after launch, the ATP Live Scoring iPhone application has an impressive 80,000 downloads and averages nearly 1,000 new downloads per day. And these dedicated fans are also those who buy tickets to see events in person, so the app is driving revenue to the players and tournament sponsors.

Cyber Graffiti with WiFi Network Names as Advertising

I'd like to finish this chapter on mobile marketing with an idea that is admittedly rather far outside the mainstream.

You're on the road, perhaps at a coffee emporium, and you want to find a free WiFi network. You look at the network names, and there's the usual assortment: people who default to use a WiFi name associated with their technology provider like linksys, some who use their family name like Jones_Network, some random nonsense like FJ8673UHNN4, and the credit-card-required paid networks like Boingo_Hotspot.

But then you see a network called Hipster Doofus. Ha, ha, ha, ha! What fun! Someone has a sense of humor!

But wait.

Imagine how many people are seeing that network name. If it's in a crowded city, it could be thousands a day.

How about using the 32-character SSID space to broadcast a marketing message? Here are some ideas:

* An auto dealer: Free test drives
* A pub: Try Joes Martini
* A bookstore: Stop hacking and read a book

The idea of WiFi names as a marketing tool came to me courtesy of Alexandra Janelli. When Janelli was at a bar on the Lower East Side of Manhattan when she noticed that the network her iPhone brought up was called Alcoholics Shut In. The experience prompted the creation of a blog-turned-website at WTFwifi.com to chronicle interesting WiFi names. "Wireless router names are breaking through the walls of homes carrying with them virtual messages, airwave graffiti, or warnings only to be decrypted by our smart phones and computers," she says. "They are monocles into the cryptic world around us."

During Janelli's *warwalking* (searching for WiFi wireless networks by walking around), she learned that people use their WiFi names to send messages. "In many cases, the messages relate to staying off their connections," she says. "However, you do get the users who will send very direct messages such as 'We Won Too,' which plays off another WiFi network's name, 'We Won,' or even 'Hipster Doofus' and 'Son of Hipster Doofus.' While this is not a conventional form of social media, it's certainly an easily changeable medium where people are becoming more and more aware of its uses." Some of Janelli's favorite WiFi names are Stuck in the City, Squirrel Power, I Eat Children, Cheese Has Protein, Cupcake Bomb Squad, and Dirty Diapers for Lunch.

My guess is that it's just a matter of time before businesses use WiFi names as a marketing tool. The point in all this silliness is that mobile marketing is still in its infancy. There are no hard-and-fast right ways to reach people via the mobile devices they carry all day, every day. The new rules apply here: You don't want to spam people's mobiles with unwanted messages, so be kind to people whose contact information you've been given. The best content wins. But we're all making up best practices as we go because this is all so new—so try something! Create an application, or get clever with the GPS geolocation capabilities on mobiles. You'll reach buyers directly, no matter where they are.

16

Social Networking Sites and Marketing

The popularity of social networking sites such as Facebook, Twitter, and LinkedIn is phenomenal. Social networking sites make it easy for people to create a profile about themselves and use it to form a virtual network combining their off-line friends and new online friends. According to Twitter, there are more than 500 million Twitter accounts with about 200 million of those described as active, and people generate an average of a half a billion tweets a day. Facebook now reports more than a billion monthly active users and LinkedIn has more than 200 million. And it's not just the United States; social networking is extremely popular all over the world. For instance, about 80 percent of Facebook users are outside the United States. While not all visitors to these sites create their own profiles, but there are millions and millions of people who do—to share their photos, journals, videos, music, and interests with a network of friends.

While these huge numbers are impressive, we can easily lose track of what this means to us as marketers. When we consider the reach of influential people on social networking sites, we should rethink our notions about who can best spread our ideas and tell our stories. Many people tell me that they want to get quoted in important publications like the *Wall Street Journal* or have their products mentioned on television news networks like the BBC or on shows like *The Today Show*. These media hits are seen as the holy grail of marketers. But while mainstream media are certainly important (and who wouldn't want to be on BBC news), is that really the best thing for your business?

At the South-by-Southwest Interactive Festival in the past few years,[1] I've hung out for a while in the blogger lounge, a place where people who are active in social networking could get Internet connectivity, AC power, and a cold drink while they met their virtual friends in the flesh. As I looked around the room and saw the hundred or so influential people, I realized something important: The collective voices of the bloggers who were in the South-by-Southwest blogger lounge that day are likely more powerful and have more influence than the *Wall Street Journal*. As you think about reaching your audience using social networking, consider who really has the power. Is it mainstream media? Or someone else? And how can you reach them?

Television's Eugene Mirman Is Very Nice and Likes Seafood

"There is no middleman between me and an audience," says comedian Eugene Mirman,[2] known for his work in *Flight of the Conchords*, his book of satire, *The Will to Whatevs: A Guide to Modern Life*, and appearances on Comedy Central and late-night television shows. Mirman currently plays Yvgeny Mirminsky on *Delocated* and voices Gene Belcher for the animated comedy *Bob's Burgers*. He writes a blog, has a Facebook page,[3] and is on Twitter.[4] "I want to be entertaining on the web," he says. "That's what's fun for me. While there is a store on my website, the push is to provide things to entertain people, not to sell." And entertain he does. As I write this, Mirman's Twitter bio reads: "I am television's Eugene Mirman. I am very nice and like seafood." Sample tweet: "When it turns out the Black Eyed Peas are hostile aliens spying on earth, humanity will feel silly, since it'll be obvious in hindsight."

Mirman uses Facebook and Twitter as ways to get his information out to multiple audiences very quickly. For example, immediately after he delivered the commencement address at Lexington High School in Massachusetts, he posted the video on YouTube[5] and then pointed to it from his blog,

---

[1] sxsw.com

[2] eugenemirman.com

[3] facebook.com/pages/Eugene-Mirman/17472821218

[4] twitter.com/eugeneMirman

[5] youtube.com/watch?v=KZlQd2Eg-9w

as well as from his Twitter and Facebook profiles. The video got 100,000 views in just one week.

Mirman says that he writes what's interesting to him at the time and doesn't worry about productivity. "I want to do things that are funny and I want a lot of people to see it, but I do what I think is good and funny and then hope that others pass it on," he says. "It's easier for me to do what I like, and if it attracts fans, then that's great. And I'm lucky that it has been effective over the years to do it this way. With social media, you can tell a story. If you have a special interest, like cooking, then you can get an audience."

Think back to my metaphor of the web as a city and social media as a cocktail party, which I discussed in Chapter 4. Cocktail parties are fun. You go because you want to be there. And while the chance of meeting someone who could become a customer is a distinct possibility, that's a by-product of good conversation. Take a tip from Mirman and make sure you bring the right attitude to social media. With that in mind, let's look in detail at several of the most important social networking sites.

Facebook: Not Just for Students

In the time since I wrote the first edition of this book, Facebook has taken off as an online tool for businesspeople to connect to communities and to customers directly. The spark for this remarkable explosion was the September 2006 opening of Facebook to nonstudents. Prior to that time, you needed an email address ending in .edu to qualify for an account. According to comScore, in the months prior to allowing open registration, Facebook .com traffic hovered at approximately 14 million unique visitors per month. The number of visitors nearly doubled in the next nine months, reaching 26.6 million in May 2007. As of this writing, Facebook has reached a billion users worldwide and the site reports[6] that 580 million people log onto Facebook at least once each day.

The site connects members via a friend request process. Until you approve someone as your Facebook friend, your extended profile remains private. I've found Facebook to be a great way to maintain contact with school friends and work colleagues.

The most important thing to remember about marketing on Facebook (and other social networking sites) is that it is not about generating hype.

---

[6] http://newsroom.fb.com

The best approaches to Facebook marketing involve four useful ways to deliver information and ideas to a network of people who are interested in you and your products and services: (1) a personal profile for friend-to-friend communication, (2) company pages, (3) groups, and (4) applications. The first, your personal profile, is generally the easiest and really just requires that you describe yourself and add relevant data and a photo. For example, when I publish a new blog post, I'll typically post a message on my Facebook profile so my friends will know what I'm up to. I also post links to my upcoming speaking engagements and photos after the gig. Similarly, back when I set up my profile, I included a short video to give my Facebook friends an idea of what one of my speeches was like. My Facebook friends see my updates via their Facebook feed, basically an ongoing delivery of information from their circle of friends.

How to Use Facebook to Market Your Product or Service

A Facebook page is a great first step for getting your organization engaged. Think of a Facebook page as a personal profile, but for a company. For instance, you're likely to use a logo instead of a photo for the image in the upper-left corner (the profile picture). Once your page is complete, you should post interesting information there, like links to blog posts and videos as you create them.

One of the most useful aspects of Facebook is the ability for people to Like and Tag the things you do on the site. When users Like your page or something you posted on it (they do this by pushing the little thumbs-up Like button), the fact that they like it will likely appear on their Facebook profiles for their friends to see. The same thing is true when you Tag something. Tagging is when you identify people within a post or a photo on Facebook, such as all of the people appearing in a photo. When you tag people, they get notifications that point them to the tagged content. Isn't that great? When you create something interesting, your friends can spread it for you! But remember what we've discussed previously in these pages: As with other forms of web content, don't use Facebook to overtly sell. Rather, create information that people will want to share.

Steve Broadbelt, managing director at Ocean Frontiers Ltd. in the Cayman Islands, does exactly that. He and his team are constantly posting tagged photos and videos on their Ocean Frontiers Facebook page, photos and videos that people are eager to share. Ocean Frontiers specializes in small-group scuba diving off Grand Cayman's East End. Broadbelt runs a modern scuba-diving operation and dive shop with old-style Caymanian hospitality. Many clients return again and again. He's been active on the web since he first built his Ocean Frontiers site (in 1997), an email newsletter soon after, and more recently a presence in social media including Facebook, Foursquare, and Twitter.

It was the realization that people like to come back year after year that prompted him to create "The Green Short Challenge," where scuba divers who visit each of the 55 dive sites within the East End dive zone in Grand Cayman are given special recognition. The prizes include a pair of coveted, limited-edition green shorts (just like the Ocean Frontiers staff wear), a party to celebrate the achievement, a gold medal, a plaque embedded into the dock that leads to the boats, and special recognition on the Ocean Frontiers Facebook page—with photos documenting the achievement. Participants record their visits to each of the 55 dive sites in a custom-designed dive logbook with hand drawn illustrations. Anybody can download the book for free, with no registration required.[7]

Broadbelt recalls his creation of the award: "I had a customer at a dive show expo in New York who couldn't remember the name of our business, but he remembered that all of our staff wear these green shorts," Broadbelt says. "At the same time, I was frustrated that some of my longest-standing customers, people that have been diving with me for more than 10 years and come back every year, hadn't seen certain dive sites. So that got me on a mission to try to get all my customers to see all of my dive sites, because there's so much variety and diversity to see. So now we get them on this trail where they check off all the sites, and I found out it's quite addictive. So we made The Green Short Challenge and that's how we built our tribe of loyal followers. I never thought it was going to be such a marketing powerhouse and get the reaction that it has. Everybody who touches The Green Short Challenge seems to stick to it."

As I said, Broadbelt uses the Ocean Frontiers Facebook page to recognize the achievement. As I write this, several days after a customer hit the 55-dive milestone, the Facebook post reads: "Mike Lewis - 1st Green Shorts of 2013. Congrats to Mike and welcome to the club!" There are seven photos of Lewis on the Facebook post, including the staff toasting him with champagne and cutting a cake. Plus there's a beaming Lewis holding up his new shorts. "It ties

---

[7] oceanfrontiers.com/green-short-challenge.html

into social media because every time somebody completes the challenge, we have a celebration and they share with their friends on Facebook," Broadbelt says. "It is the scuba diving hall of fame for our customers; as they've reached the ultimate celebrity status with the dive community here. We use Facebook to make everybody aware of the achievement and then people share that with all their friends, and alumni that have already completed the Green Short Challenge comment. There's a lot of warm and fuzzy, feel-good vibes as they're welcomed to the club—and that cements them as a customer for life."

When customers see their achievements recognized on Facebook, they frequently "like" the posts and use tags to identify people in the photos, spreading the love to their own Facebook friends. This is one of the reasons that Ocean Frontiers has more than 12,000 "likes" on Facebook. "You couldn't ask for a more loyal and dedicated customer base than what we're building," Broadbelt says. "From whatever social media platform they communicate, if someone wants to go diving in the Caribbean, our customers are going to recommend us. There's a human element that can be brought in with Facebook. You humanize what your business does."

Speaking of humanizing a business, I found out about Ocean Frontiers from Mark Rovner, a communications consultant at Sea Change Strategies who told me about how he dove all 55 sites and now has his very own Green Short. "Steve Broadbelt is a really creative guy and developed a dive logbook with sketches of the dive sites, and little stickers you can put on each dive site," Rovner says. "He gamified it. The Green Short Challenge works in so many different ways. The ceremony gets put on their Facebook page, and then each of us who becomes a Green Short alumni puts that on our Facebook page. It gives us a story to tell to every diver friend we know. And the one thing that is true of divers, like any other sort of hyperpassionate hobby, is that there's little else that divers want to talk about more than diving."

Increase Engagements with Facebook Groups and Apps

A Facebook page is a great first step for your organization to engage with people. Think of a Facebook page as a personal profile, but for a company. For instance, you're likely to use a logo instead of a photo for the image in the upper-left corner. Once your page is complete, you should post interesting information there, like links to blog posts and videos as you create them.

One of the most useful aspects of Facebook is the ability for people to Like and Tag the things that you do on the social networking site. When users Like your page or something you posted on it (they do this by pushing the little thumbs-up Like button), the fact that they like it appears on their Facebook profiles for their friends to see. The same thing is true when you Tag something. Tagging is when you identify people within a post or a photo on Facebook, such as all of the people appearing in a photo. When you tag people, those people get notifications that link them to the tagged content. Isn't that great? When you create something interesting, your friends can spread it for you!

A great way for organizations of all kinds to keep interested people informed is to gather them into a Facebook group. All users can create groups, and their membership can be closed (invitation only) or open (anyone may join). There's also a similar place where people can meet called a Facebook page, which is a page of information that anybody can see (compared with groups, where you must register first). Facebook Groups are typically for more in-depth communications around a subject (such as a product launch), while Facebook fan pages are typically for a loose but longer-term presence. I know this sounds complicated, but it should be further incentive to join some groups and become a fan of a few companies to see what people are doing.

For example, Philip Robertson, director of marketing communications for ooVoo,[8] an application for conducting face-to-face video conversation with friends, family, and colleagues, wanted to establish social media connections soon after ooVoo was launched. "Facebook was quickly becoming a place for people to connect and catch up online," he says. "At the same time, we began to look at different ways to market." Robertson started a Facebook group as a way to communicate with existing ooVoo users and to help build a larger population of users as people discussed the service and shared it with their Facebook friends. "We've used the group to promote campaigns such as 'my ooVoo day' where top-tier bloggers used ooVoo to interact with people. We also use it as a way to post new software. People who are fans of the brand can use new software first."

Starting a Facebook group is very straightforward. It takes just a few minutes to set one up, and the process includes a built-in tool for sending invitations to your Facebook friends (and, as appropriate, the friends of your

[8] oovoo.com

colleagues). You should also mention the group on your organization's regular website or blog. "We got 250 members to the Facebook group really quickly," Robertson says. "We invited the initial members through our own fan base, and we also invited influential people who can give us feedback on the brand." There is also an ooVoo Facebook app with more than a million users and a Facebook page that more than 2 million people like.

People join Facebook groups because they want to stay informed, and they want to do it on their own time. Just as with blogs, the best way to maintain a Facebook group is simply to make valuable information available. Unlike intrusive email updates, which arrive only when the sender chooses, Facebook groups can be visited at the member's convenience. "You are not spamming people with information that they are forced to read," Robertson says.

The informal, two-way nature of Facebook's group dynamics is an important aspect for marketers. "Pass-along value is very important," says Robertson. "You can recommend Facebook groups and applications to friends in a much easier and more casual way than you can with email. And people can post information to the group themselves, to actively take part in the brand."

I've had some remarkable experiences with Facebook groups, experiences that never would have happened in the absence of social networking tools. One of the most interesting was with Stephen Quigley's New Media and PR class at Boston University.[9] The class uses this book as one of its texts, and for several terms, the students have invited me to join their invitation-only Facebook groups. One term's group was called New Media Rocks My PR World (love the name), and another set of students went with Media Socialites (love this one even more). Here is the Media Socialites' description of their group: "Professor Quigley's new batch of student social media sponges, eager to soak up as much information about New Media and PR in a semester as is humanly possible . . . and, in proper social networking fashion, making important connections along the way."

Social networking has given birth to new models for learning. I graduated from Kenyon College in 1983, and in four years, I don't recall ever giving textbook authors any thought whatsoever. I certainly never met any of them. But with social media tools like Facebook, smart professors (and students) are now involving textbook authors and other guests, effectively creating virtual classrooms to supplement the physical ones. The students and

---

[9] bu.edu/com/about-com/faculty/stephen-quigley

professors tell me it's transforming their learning process. How about your business? How is social media changing what you do? Take a lesson from these forward-thinking educators and become a part of the discussion.

The final feature I mention is the ability to make applications, which are a great way to build your brand on Facebook. As an open platform, Facebook allows anybody to create applications that allow friends to share information on the service in different ways. There are many thousands of applications available on Facebook, and the more popular ones are used regularly by hundreds of thousands of people each day—not bad for a marketing tool that costs nothing to launch and is easy to create. One of my personal favorites is the Cities I've Visited application from TripAdvisor.[10] It displays a map on my Facebook page where I can stick a virtual thumbtack in the cities I've visited. Since I am on the road a lot, this is a great way for me to keep track of my world travel.

TripAdvisor's business is providing unbiased hotel reviews, photos, and travel advice, so the Cities I've Visited Facebook application is a perfect marketing tool for the company. Facebook applications are a terrific way for marketers to be creative and try something new, and there is always the possibility for an application to catch fire and go viral like Cities I've Visited. Which, by the way, now has an amazing 3 million active users.

In short, Facebook is emerging as a primary means for folks to keep in touch with the people and the organizations that are important to them, and it follows that it has become an important marketing tool for many companies. As with other social networking media, success on Facebook comes from being a thought leader and developing information that people *want* to absorb.

Why Google Plus Is Important For Your Business

Since the third edition of this book was published, Google launched a new social network called Google Plus[11] (also referred to as Google+ or simply G+). As it launched, I blogged: "I really want to hate Google Plus, because the last thing I need is a new social network." But Google+ is just too important to ignore. As a service of Google, it has direct ties to how you and your company appears on Google search results.

---

[10] tripadvisor.com
[11] plus.google.com

Google+ is a Facebook-like application and is the fastest-growing social network in history. Upon launch, the network reached 10 million users in just two weeks and is now up to more than 400 million. While there are similarities to Facebook (you can use Google+ to connect with friends, post photos and videos, and do other Facebook-like activities), it's not an either/or choice for most people who want to market their business. Let me repeat: The connection to Google and the power of its search engine makes it too important.

For most people, Google+ is an essential component of personal branding. Why? Because when someone enters your name into the Google search engine, your Google+ profile will be among the top results. So if you haven't done so already, get yourself a profile and take some time to upload a photo and a bio. Make a few posts.

The first thing you notice about Google+ after you register is a feature called Circles. Circles allow you to create groups of people to follow. Unlike with Facebook, the other person need not reciprocate your follow in order to make the connection. You can maintain multiple Circles, so your contacts are segmented. For example, I've got one Circle for close business associates—people whom I have met in person.

Hangouts, a place for up to 10 people to communicate via free video-conference, is another important aspect of Google+, because you can record the conversation and post the resulting video to YouTube to serve as marketing content. Imagine a conversation between you and customers being made available to buyers as they evaluate your offerings: That's the power of this tool.

Interestingly, some Google+ posts are also appearing in the Google News real-time search engine. You'll see this when you go to Google News and click the "See realtime coverage" button. Frequently, Google+ updates will appear to the right of mainstream media stories. This means that many more people might see your blog posts if you also post them to your Google+ page.

After you've got your personal profile set up, you can create a business profile on Google+.[12] This helps with your search engine ranking, especially with local search. When buyers search on Google, the results may include relevant posts, photos, and videos from your Google+ page, so having one helps you get found across Google at the moment buyers are most receptive.

---

[12] google.com/+/business

All you need to do to get found in the local search results is update your Google+ business page with relevant content. This can be as simple as a few sentences about your latest blog post with a link to the post. You can also embed YouTube videos and photos that might also appear in other places on the web. If for no other reason, you need a Google+ account for search engine marketing. But perhaps you'll be like millions of people who find that Google+ is an enjoyable place to meet new people and connect with those you already know.

Check Out My LinkedIn Profile

Marketing on social networking sites can be tricky, because online communities disdain overt commercial messages. Acceptable marketing and promotion on these sites frequently involves brands or personalities creating pages to build and expand an online following, rather than directly advertising products.

For example, many business-to-business marketing and sales professionals rely on LinkedIn, the world's largest professional social network (over 200 million users in over 200 countries and territories), to meet business partners. Unlike social networks that people use to keep up friendships, LinkedIn's mission is to connect the world's professionals and make them more productive and successful. LinkedIn is a great way to network with others in your industry and to meet buyers of your products and services.

LinkedIn is used for identifying buyers and potential partners, understanding the competitors, conducting market research, sharing information, and promoting events. Like other social networks, your personal profile is your public face. Given LinkedIn's focus on business, your profile should emphasize the skills you bring to your market niche and the value you add to your community. With your profile up and running, you request to join other people's networks or invite them to join yours—both people must approve the connection. Once you're connected with someone, you can see contacts you share in common and how you might reach someone you want to meet through your connections. One of the fastest-growing aspects of LinkedIn are its company profiles, which deliver an overview of what a company does and for whom; the products and services they offer; and any positions available at the company. When you view a company profile, you can see how many company employees are on LinkedIn and if any are in your network.

"A profile on LinkedIn is not a 'presence' on LinkedIn," says Mark Amtower, director of the government market master's program at Capitol College in Laurel, MD, and an active LinkedIn user. "A presence occurs when people start to take serious notice. After you have set up your profile, your outreach begins. Determine who the key players are in your niche and develop a plan to connect with them. Keep in mind, your profile has to be interesting and informative enough to make them want to connect. Short, informative paragraphs and bullet points are more readable than long paragraphs. A great profile can open doors, help you get a job, get you consulting and speaking gigs, and more. A poor profile reverses these actions."

Amtower's goal with LinkedIn is to be among the most connected and most visible people in government contracting. He does this by regularly posting relevant information and starting discussions in groups to raise his visibility and demonstrate value to the community. He has a personal network of over 5,000 first-degree connections (people he is connected to directly) and manages contractor groups with another 6,000 members.

"For me, it has reinforced my position as a leading consultant in the government contracting market," he says. "Through my LinkedIn profile alone, I have landed over 20 consulting gigs with large, medium, and small government contractors, as well as several speaking gigs. At this point, I would suggest that those without a robust social networking presence will lose market share in direct proportion to their social networking inactivity."

A tactic that some smart nonprofit organizations use is to encourage employees to establish a personal page on Facebook or LinkedIn, with details of the cause they support, as a way to spread the word. Supporters of political candidates (as well as some candidates themselves) create pages on social networking sites, too. As with all good marketing, it is important to create content that is right for the people you want to reach and that starts with the choice of which social networking site (or sites) to post your profile.

As you consider a strategy to get yourself out there and onto a social networking site for marketing and PR purposes, just remember that authenticity and transparency are critical. Don't try to fool the community into thinking that the page is something that it is not. (You might want to skip to the discussion of ethics in Chapter 17.) Frequent eruptions within these communities happen when members uncover a fraud of some kind, such as an advertising agency creating fake profiles of people applauding products. Yes, you can use social networking sites such as LinkedIn to build a following, but avoid sleazy fake profiles of people who supposedly use your products.

An interesting use of Facebook and LinkedIn for business comes from KLM (Royal Dutch Airlines). The KLM Meet and Seat application[13] lets those booked on certain KLM long-haul flights find out who else will be on the flight too. With Meet & Seat, you can view other passengers' Facebook or LinkedIn profile details and see where they'll be sitting—long before the flight leaves the ground. So you might search for people who are going to the same conference as you or work in the same industry.

The KLM Meet and Seat service requires opting in; you can still be anonymous if you want. But plenty of people do choose to share their profiles. Once you share yours, you can see the profile details of other passengers who have opted in, as well as their seat assignment. You can even try to sit next to someone interesting.

In a market where offerings are similar and buyers typically choose based on price, getting them to think about something else (like who else will be on the plane) is a good thing. Imagine being seated next to your next customer, new business partner, or even future spouse as a result of this social matchmaking.

Indeed, KLM is a social media pioneer. As we saw in Chapter 15, they also created a surprise program for those who checked into their flight on Foursquare, just as that service was taking off. Both of these KLM initiatives are designed to get people talking about the airline on their social networks.

Tweet Your Thoughts to the World

Twitter, sometimes called a "microblogging" service, has become a very popular social network. And popularity is important because of the social nature of Twitter, a service for friends, family, and coworkers to communicate through the exchange of quick, short messages (with a maximum of 140 characters).

People use Twitter to keep their followers (people who subscribe to their Twitter feed) updated on their lives. For instance, you might tweet about the conference you're attending or the project you're engrossed in, or you might ask your network a question. Twitter is an excellent way to

---

[13] klm.com/travel/nl_en/prepare_for_travel/on_board/Your_seat_on_board/meet_and_seat.htm#richmedia

share links to videos, blog posts, and other content you find interesting. Users can choose to follow the Twitter updates of anyone they want to hear from: family members, colleagues, or perhaps the author of the last book they read. Because of the severe constraint on the length of tweets, people use Twitter to post information that is important to update their network about but is much more concise than a blog post and more casual than an email. You can update your Twitter feed from a web browser, a mobile phone, or an instant messaging service, so Twitter is always on. I update my feed a few times a day, tweeting about my travels around the world, who I'm meeting, and what's going on at the events where I speak. I also frequently send out links to examples of great marketing that people send me, things like e-books, YouTube videos, and blog posts. In this way, Twitter is a way of pointing people to things that I find interesting. As with other forms of social networking, it takes time to build a following. In particular, the best way to get people to pay attention to you is to participate by following others and responding to them, just like you should do in the blogosphere.

Every marketing and PR person should be aware of Twitter and understand how people use it. As a first step, you should immediately hightail it over to the Twitter search engine[14] to see what people are saying about you, your organization, your products and services, and perhaps your competitors and the category of product you sell. If you've never done this, please do it right now, because it can be an eye-opening experience to see what (if anything) people are saying. A great way to use Twitter to monitor what people are saying is to use a Twitter client application such as TweetDeck or HootSuite. These free applications allow you to monitor multiple keywords and phrases in real time so you know instantly when something important (such as the name of your CEO or a product your company sells) is mentioned.

When you're ready to set up your own Twitter profile and begin to tweet, the most important aspect from the marketing and PR perspective is—as I say time and again—don't use this service as an advertising channel to talk up your products and services. If that's your intention, you need to be very careful.

"If you want to use Twitter as a marketing channel, you have to put yourself out there as an interested member of the community," says

---

[14] search.twitter.com

Scott Monty,[15] head of social media at Ford Motor Company.[16] "I'm constantly amazed at what a powerful personal and professional network it is for me. Recently, I went online to find a hotel room in New York City, which is usually not a problem, especially with the last-minute travel sites. Only this time, no rooms in midtown were to be had. So I sent a tweet (@ScottMonty) to my network and immediately heard from a number of people with suggestions, including Tim Peter (@tcpeter), who works with a group that does luxury reservations. Within a few minutes, I had a reservation at the Mansfield, a boutique hotel in midtown Manhattan. Perfect! Thanks to a well-connected and attentive community, I was able to keep myself off a Central Park bench for the night. It just goes to show that if you take the time to invest in relationships and being a valued member of a community, it can work in your favor when you need it."

Some companies use Twitter to alert customers to special deals. Because of the broadcast-like nature of microblogging, thousands of potential buyers can receive this information instantaneously. "Woot has used Twitter as a way to alert people to new merchandise that is available, and JetBlue lets people know when they are running airfare specials," Monty says. But as with all new media, it is important to learn the unwritten etiquette of Twitter before using it. "*The Today Show* gives updates of feature stories and highlights of shows," Monty says. "When they started on Twitter, they bulk-followed a bunch of people and basically spammed them. It annoyed me and my colleagues, because they were trying to build up numbers rather than being a part of the conversation."

With all this online conversation going on, some people think that Facebook, Twitter, and other social networking tools can replace a face-to-face approach to business. I actually think strong social networking ties lead to *stronger* personal relationships because it is easy to facilitate face-to-face meetings that never would have occurred otherwise. For example, before a conference, I might send a tweet saying, "I'll be in San Francisco next Tuesday." I'll frequently get a message right back from someone who is planning to be at the same conference, or someone who lives there, and we end up meeting in person. I'll also create an impromptu meeting of my followers—called a TweetUp—that occurs when people who are connected on Twitter have a face-to-face meeting. I've had between 10 and 50 people

---

[15] scottmonty.com

[16] ford.com

show up in cities like Wellington, New Zealand; Mumbai, India; Atlanta; New York City; Amsterdam; and Phoenix, Arizona, to connect.

Social Networking and Personal Branding

I've had many conversations with people who are new to social networking sites such as Twitter, and often they are puzzled at first about what to do. Hey, I've been there, too. We all make mistakes. I recall when I was first getting going with Facebook and my teenage daughter was looking over my shoulder. She rolled her eyes and called me a big dork when I wrote a message on my own Facebook Wall (a place for your visitors to write). I found that with my own learning and the experiences with people I've helped over the past few years, getting a few things right at the start makes the experience more fun (and productive). While I'll be writing about Twitter here, the basic ideas apply to all social networking sites.

An important thing to consider is how your online actions are a reflection of your personal branding (the image that you project to the world). As you already know, *people* use Twitter to keep others updated on what they find interesting at that moment. Frequently when I am asked about Twitter and its use in personal branding and marketing, people immediately dive into stuff like "how often should I tweet," "what should I tweet about," "is it cool to DM [direct message] people," and other tweet-related details. Well, that's all fine, but the vast majority of people miss the most basic (and important) personal branding aspect of all.

> What does your Twitter page look like?

Most Twitter pages don't say enough and most have crappy design. While that's fine if you're just communicating with friends, if you care about your personal brand, you need to do better. Much better. And it is so easy! When you first set up your Twitter account, you have choices. And after you've set up the account, you can make these changes to any aspect of your profile at any time (except your Twitter ID) under the Settings tab in Twitter.

Twitter ID: (Mine is @dmscott.) Choose an appropriate ID. Something like @MrSillyGuy is probably not a good idea for most people. However, a silly ID might fit your personal brand, say, if you're a comedian. (Incidentally, the ID @MrSillyGuy has been taken by niki @ikiniki from Belgium after he read an early edition of this book.)

Name: (Mine is David Meerman Scott.) Use your real name. Don't just default to your user ID, which so many people seem to do. And don't just use a nickname like Pookie. You can put your nickname in quotes inside your real name if you want to. If you really care about your personal brand, you'll want people to know who you really are.

Location: (Mine is Boston, MA.) Use the town or nearest city that makes sense for you. Saying something cute like Earth or somewhere in Canada turns people off who don't know you. Besides, the location is a good way to make local contacts.

Web: (Mine is www.davidmeermanscott.com.) If you have a blog or site, put the URL here. Or maybe your profile on a company website makes sense for you. This should be somewhere people can go to learn more about *you*. If you don't have a blog or site, I recommend that you create a Google profile and link to that. Go back to Chapter 5 to learn about Google profiles. You can also leave the web link blank if you want, but that says to people that you don't want to be contacted or have people learn more about you.

Bio: As I write this, mine is "Marketing strategist, keynote speaker, and bestselling author of 8 books including *The New Rules of Marketing & PR* and *Newsjacking*." This is where you say something about yourself. You get only 160 characters. As a component of personal branding, this is a critical section. Don't leave it blank. And don't make a mini-resume from a laundry list of attributes like this: "father, husband, surfer, economics major, world traveler, marketer, and rockstar wannabe." (I confess, that would be my list.) I see this sort of thing all the time, and it is not good for personal branding because you don't really focus on your particular expertise. Try to be descriptive. And try to be specific.

Photo: Your photo is very important! Don't default to the placeholder that Twitter provides for those with no photo. And don't use something clever as a stand-in (like your cat). If you care about your personal brand, you should use a photo of you and not a pet or an image of your car. Photos appear very tiny on Twitter—like a postage stamp—so use a close-up shot. If you use a full view of yourself, then you will appear like a stick figure. Remember that your photo conveys a very important first impression when people see your profile for the first time. Are you wearing a hat? Is it a casual shot of you taken on a vacation with a beer in your hand? Or have you chosen a formal head-and-shoulders shot with business attire taken by a professional photographer? Is your son or daughter in the photo with you? There is no absolute right or wrong, but do keep in mind that each of these choices says a great deal about you.

Background image: The background image of your Twitter page is a place where you can really show off. The default background is like when you first open PowerPoint—it's a default. Twitter has some choices, but many people use them, so you will not be unique. Shoot a custom photo to really shine. I use a close-up photo of a nifty old typewriter keyboard. It's my personal brand on Twitter.

Banner image: Twitter also provides an opportunity to add a header photo to your profile, which serves as a background for your bio. A header photo is a great way to show your personal brand but don't try to sell. Many sales & marketing people add an advertising message to this real estate but I think that's a mistake and recommend resisting this tendency. Adding your messages or heavy-handed branding to the header detracts. Sure, I could have used an image of, say, all my book covers for my banner. Instead I chose an image I really like of me on stage at a speaking gig. Your header photo will show up on your Twitter web page as well as on mobile devices.

These choices are really easy to set up, but they're very important for your personal brand. If you are on Twitter, take the time to make some changes today. Again, the same ideas apply on other social networking sites like Facebook and LinkedIn, so don't forget to carefully consider your personal branding on those sites as well.

The Horse Twitterer

When I talk about Twitter and business, people often say, "That sounds good for some people, but I don't think it makes sense in my business." Or they tell me they are reluctant to try Twitter because they don't know how to measure the results. But those reactions are based on fear. People are reluctant to try Twitter because it is new and different. I like sharing with these people the story of how Mike Pownall, DVM (Twitter ID @McKeePownall), uses Twitter.

Pownall is co-founder of McKee Pownall Equine Services,[17] a veterinary practice with five locations in the Toronto area. Pownall and other vets in his practice reach horse owners in Toronto through their Twitter feeds, and this effort has led directly to business growth. This in a down market where other vets have told me they are struggling because of the current economy.

"Five of our vets are on Twitter," Pownall says. "We brought in Twitter mainly because the equine practice is based on relationships. If this is a way that people can start to follow veterinarians, get to know their personality, get to know what they're all about, then it's going to be a lot easier to develop a relationship. A couple of our vets have pretty good senses of humor that don't necessarily get translated during examination; often we're very serious through that. This is a way for people to read the other side of it and just to exchange good information."

Pownall's wife and business partner, Melissa McKee, DVM, is also on Twitter. "She works in a racetrack practice, so a lot of the stuff that she tweets about relates to the racing industry," he says. "She wants to be a resource for other people interested in the racing industry. But then we'll also talk about just interesting things that happen to horses, whether it's horse welfare or just amusing or entertaining stories. We're just trying to have fun with anything that's interesting. I get a lot of hits when I talk about stuff that's not even related to horses. There were a few things with SPCA [Society for the Prevention of Cruelty to Animals] issues going on in Toronto last year that I was tweeting about and I got a lot of responses on. That's a side that I want people to know. We're not just horses, but we love all animals, and again, just trying to show a more complete picture of who we are as people."

Their efforts on Twitter and on other social networks like Facebook and YouTube help drive new business to McKee Pownall Equine Services when competitors are struggling. "More and more people are finding us through online means," Pownall says. "We get people that will come to us the first time as clients and say, 'I heard about you on the Web, or I saw this on the Web.' Our business, in these tough economic times, has done well, and we've had growth over the last two years. I think some of it has to be related to social media. I hear people all the time saying, 'Every time I go on the Web, you guys are there.'"

---

[17] mpequine.com

Connecting with Fans

"Being a touring musician means meeting fans," says Amanda Palmer, an American performer who first rose to prominence as the lead singer, pianist, and lyricist/composer of the duo The Dresden Dolls and currently with her own act Amanda Palmer and The Grand Theft Orchestra. "I go out and meet fans after every gig. It's important to make contact in real life and not just online in social media like Twitter. If you don't meet fans in real life, too, then you're a fraud. If you're not comfortable getting into the sweat with them and talking with people at shows, then how can you do it successfully online? I love connecting with fans. Speaking to people at the merchandise table after the show is great. I can stay there forever."

This committed attitude has helped make Palmer a personal branding force of nature, using her infectious personality to connect with fans in person and on the web. She has amassed a large online following on her blog, her Facebook fan page[18] (more than 165,000 fans), and her Twitter feed (@Amanda Palmer, more than 800,000 followers). Note that Palmer's former band, the Dresden Dolls, also has nearly a quarter of a million friends on MySpace.

When the Dresden Dolls formed in 2000, Palmer created an email list from day one. Soon after, the personal connections she established at the band's concerts, which continued in email messages with fans, started to bleed onto her personal forum, The Shadowbox.[19] A collection of all things Amanda Palmer, The Shadowbox has accumulated a remarkable quarter of a million fan posts since its launch. "It's like I've built a house and people are hanging around in it," Palmer says.

Palmer is very active on Twitter and uses it as a tool for instant communication with her fans. She frequently answers fans' tweeted questions and comments. Because she truly enjoys her connection with her followers, Twitter comes naturally to her. "It's important to have the makeup that I do," she says. "I love to answer fans' questions, and I love to make people happy. You can't fake being authentic with your fans. It's so easy to see through when other musicians are faking it, such as when some employee of their record labels tweets on behalf of their artists. Fans can see through fake tweets like 'I'm about to play at a rad club. Get tix here.' Fake artists' blogs are the same. Who cares?"

---

[18] facebook.com/amandapalmer
[19] theshadowbox.net

Palmer frequently uses Twitter to bring together groups of fans quickly and spontaneously when she is on the road. She tweeted a secret gig in Los Angeles one morning, and about 350 people showed up five hours later at a warehouse space where she played the piano. It works great for her because, although she's able to get a large number of people to show up, she is not so popular that she would create a dangerously huge mob. "I'm in the sweet spot of popularity," she says. "I can send out a tweet and get 300 people to show up in a couple of days and do a free gig on the beach. I'll play the ukulele, sing, sign, hug, take pictures, eat cake, and generally hang out and connect. And I'll stay as long as it takes to talk with everyone personally. Trent Reznor of Nine Inch Nails can't do that because he's just too popular."

Palmer does struggle with the amount of time she spends connecting with fans both in person and through the tools of social media like Twitter. "I feel guilty sometimes that I'd often prefer to answer questions from fans and do interviews and meet people than work on new music," she says. Interestingly, she has fans who feel the same way; her prolific online *content* has earned a following of its own. "One person at a record store gig and signing came up to me and said, 'I don't really like your music, but I love your blog.'"

How Amanda Palmer Raised a Million Dollars via Social Networking

After a two-year fight with Roadrunner Records, musician Amanda Palmer freed herself from her record deal. For the seven years prior to her label divorce, anything she wrote and recorded (either solo or with her band, The Dresden Dolls) was technically owned and under the ultimate control of the label.

Palmer knew she could do better on her own, because she enjoys such a terrific relationship with her fans via social networks.

So after much planning, Palmer chose a 30-day Kickstarter to fund her new album: *Amanda Palmer & The Grand Theft Orchestra*. Kickstarter is a crowdsourced funding platform for creative projects such as films, games, art, and music. She wrote the following in her Kickstarter pitch[20]: "Since I'm now without a giant label to front the gazillions of dollars that it always takes to manufacture and promote a record this big, I'm coming to you to gather funds so that I have the capital to put it out with a huge bang. I think

---

[20] kickstarter.com/projects/amandapalmer/amanda-palmer-the-new-record-art-book-and-tour

Kickstarter and other crowdfunding platforms like this are the BEST way to put out music right now - no label, no rules, no fuss, no muss. Just us, the music, and the art. I'm also making sure EVERY PRODUCT sold through this Kickstarter is unique to this campaign, to reward all of you who KNEW ME WHEN and were willing to support me from Day One."

There were funding packages starting at just $1 (entitling the donor to a digital download of the album once it's released) and ending at $10,000 (good for dinner with Palmer plus all sorts of extras). The package I chose was a pledge of $300; it includes tickets to a VIP party and intimate show with Palmer and the band in Boston (there were similar options in other cities).

Through social networking, in just a few days, Palmer has raised more money from her fans than she would have gotten from her label. In the one month that the Kickstarter appeal was live, she raised nearly $1.2 million, the largest amount any musician has ever raised on the site. And she retains complete control of the production and the rights to the music.

To succeed at this technique, a musician must build a fan base, one person at a time. Social media is a great way to connect before and after the live gig, but the personal connection is essential.

The point is that social networking is an increasingly important way for people to connect and communicate. Organizations are using it cleverly to benefit their businesses, their followers, and themselves. So should you.

While your work may be completely different from that of a rock star, Palmer has something to teach you. Your product comes first and must be created with passion. And you've got to engage with your customers on a human level. Social networking can help you build this fan base. If you do it well, you can build a great company and a fantastic career.

Which Social Networking Site Is Right for You?

While some people might be tempted to create pages on lots of different social networking sites, this may not be necessary (or even useful), since each one appeals to different users. "While the top social networking sites are typically viewed as directly competing with one another, our analysis demonstrates that each site occupies a slightly different niche," says Jack Flanagan, executive vice president of comScore. "There is a misconception that social networking is the exclusive domain of teenagers, but [our] analysis confirms that the appeal of social networking sites is far broader." In fact, Facebook says that more than two-thirds of its users are out of college and that the fastest growing demographic is those 35 years old and older.

So think about the right social networking sites for you and your business. Besides Facebook, LinkedIn, and Twitter, here are a few other popular ones to check out.

Tumblr: People use Tumblr to post multimedia content (photos, video, images) to a sort of mini-blog. Very popular with young people, Tumblr hosts more than 70 million blogs. Within the Tumblr application, you can follow other users' blogs and "reblog" their posts to your own. Unlike the more traditional blogs that we discuss in Chapters 5 and 17, Tumblr is based on a template approach that makes it very easy to upload a photo, video, or some text—all it takes is a minute or two. If your buyers include teenagers and people in their twenties, you need to understand Tumblr. Just remember to keep it short.

Vine: Vine is the newest and hottest social media application available for the iPhone. It was launched in early 2013 to deliver six-second videos. I tell people that it's sort of like Twitter for video. And since it was released by Twitter, the integration with Twitter is seamless. It's really simple to use (download it now if you can and follow along): Just tap and hold on the iPhone screen to record and lift up to stop. Then you can alter the scene and do it again. This means you can easily do short segments of any length as long as they add up to six seconds total. At the end of the video, it repeats into an endless loop and you add a caption and release it to your Twitter feed and to your followers on Vine (that's where the social aspect kicks in). It's in its early days, but people seem to be using Vine for demonstrations or to capture the feeling of a location. With just six seconds, the challenge for marketing and PR use is to tell a story. In a weird way, I found the six-second constraint to be very liberating, much like with the 140-character limit of a tweet.

Myspace: As a social network strong in the entertainment businesses, Myspace is a popular place for musicians and other artists to showcase their work to their fans. Rock bands use Myspace to stream their music, show videos, blog from the road, post photos, and provide information on upcoming tours and album releases. While Facebook is a much more popular social network, Myspace is optimized for music. So if you're a fan (like me) or a musician, you need to be on top of it.

Squidoo: Unlike other social networking sites that are based on personal profiles of individuals, Squidoo[21] is based on people's expertise in a niche subject. Squidoo is another way for marketers to build an online presence easily and for free. Headed up by "original squid" Seth Godin,[22] creator of Permission Marketing and best-selling business author of *Purple Cow*, Squidoo is built around online lenses, which are a way to filter a person's expertise on a subject onto a single page. Interested people check out a lens on a topic and quickly get pointed to useful websites. A person who makes a lens is a lensmaster, and he or she uses a lens to provide context. "What's your story? Create a collection of the things you know and love," the Squidoo site says, and Squidoo helps everyone share that expertise with the world. Example lenses: Photographs of Roses, Best Valentine Gifts to Make, Top 10 Things You Must Do in Bali, and Top 5 High Paying Jobs in Pakistan.

Second Life: An online world entirely built and owned by its residents, Second Life[23] is a place where people interact in three virtual dimensions. But this is not a game (there is no goal, and nobody is keeping score); rather, it is a world with millions of residents and an economy built on the Linden dollar in which millions of U.S. dollars (at the current exchange rate) change hands each month. The Second Life world is teeming with people who use a self-created, in-world avatar to interact with others by buying, selling, and trading things with other residents (and just milling about and chatting). You can purchase land, build a store or business, and make money. Not surprisingly, there is even a sleazy underworld as well. But you don't have to be into commerce; you can just walk around and hang out. Quite a few of the companies that have jumped into Second Life seem to have done so just to be part of a new phenomenon, and many have since closed down their presence there. As with all social networking sites, it is important to consider if your buyer personas are active before jumping in. I hear that many software developers frequent Second Life, so it's no surprise that companies like IBM and HP set up shop there early on.

Local language sites: Keep in mind that many countries have local language social networking sites that may be much more popular than the global sites like Facebook. For example, the Japanese site Mixi is very

---

[21] squidoo.com

[22] sethgodin.typepad.com

[23] secondlife.com

popular, as is Orkut in both India and Brazil. And in the Netherlands, Hyves is the king of the world, with one in three Dutch on the social networking site. It is the second most visited site in the Netherlands after Google, but in terms of time spent, it is certainly tops. Hyves has more users in the Netherlands than Facebook, LinkedIn, and Twitter combined. I'm always amazed at how marketing in different parts of the world requires adaptation. I lived in Asia for nearly 10 years, most of that time as Asia marketing director for Knight-Ridder. When working in Indonesia, Japan, Singapore, Thailand, Hong Kong, Australia, and the other countries in the Asia-Pacific region, I always had to go local in some way. If you're in the global market, localization is important. Yet many marketers assume that one size fits all.

Shopping sites: Okay, I know this is an outlier. Most people don't consider shopping sites to be social networking, and they're nothing like the other sites I've mentioned in this chapter. But don't overlook the incredible communities that thrive on sites like Amazon, where customer reviews, profiles of those customer reviewers, and user conversations take place every day. For example, if a new book comes out in your marketplace, why not be the first to review it on Amazon? If you're a real estate agent and you write a thoughtful review on a new book about real estate investing, it may be seen by tens of thousands of people (as well as the author and members of the media). People who then visit your Amazon profile learn about you and your business, and some may contact you. Other review-based sites to check out include TripAdvisor (travel reviews), Rotten Tomatoes (movie reviews), Zagat (restaurant reviews), and Yelp (reviews of local businesses). There are many more such sites. Don't forget to create a useful profile for yourself with contact information.

You Can't Go to Every Party, So Why Even Try?

Think back to our social-media-as-cocktail-party metaphor for a moment. You can't go to every party thrown in your city. There are literally thousands of social networking sites out there, and it is simply impossible to be active in all of them. And once you choose a few parties to attend, you can't meet and have a conversation with each and every person there. You know there are tons of great conversations going on all around you, and you know that you can't be a part of them all.

What do you do at a party? Some people constantly look over the shoulder of the person they are talking to, always on the lookout for a better conversation. Some flit from one person to another every few minutes all night, having many short, superficial conversations. What I like to do at parties is have a few great conversations and be happy that I'm at a wonderful event. I know I can't be with everyone, so I have fun with the people I'm with. What more could I want?

If you're following my analogy here, you should apply the same thing to your participation in social media. For most people and organizations, it's better to be active in a few social networking sites instead of creating profiles on dozens of them and being too busy to spend much time in any one. In my own case, I have my own blog, I am on LinkedIn and Twitter, and I'm active on a few forums and chat rooms, but that's about it. I'm not on MySpace or Second Life. There are thousands of other social media and social networking sites that I choose not to participate in, such as Nexopia, Bebo, Hi5, Tagged, Xing, Skyrock, Orkut, Friendster, Xiaonei, Cyworld, and many, many more. Since you can't go to every party, you need to pick and choose. Where do you want to be? Where you can be most helpful? Where are the members of your buyer personas?

Optimizing Social Networking Pages

If you're creating pages on Facebook, LinkedIn, Twitter, and the other social networking sites, and if you've been following the planning process outlined in Chapter 11, then you're creating content that reaches your buyers and helps you achieve your goals. Although social networking sites aren't advertising, you can still use the sites to lead people into your buying process. For example, Amanda Palmer links to her blog from her Twitter profile.

Here are some ideas to get the most out of using social networking sites for marketing:

- *Target a specific audience.* Create a page that reaches an audience important to your organization. It is usually better to target a small niche market (e.g., people who want to do their own car repairs but don't know how to diagnose what's wrong).
- *Be a thought leader.* Provide valuable and interesting information that people want to check out. As you will remember from Chapter 12, it is

better to show your expertise in a market or at solving a buyer's problems than to blather on about your product.

- *Be authentic and transparent.* Don't try to impersonate someone else. It's a sleazy practice, and if you get caught, you can do irreparable harm to your company's reputation. If your mother would say it's wrong, it probably is.
- *Create lots of links.* Link to your own sites and blog and to those of others in your industry and network. Everybody loves links—they make the web what it is. You should certainly link to your own stuff from a social networking site, but it's important to expand your horizons a bit.
- *Encourage people to contact you.* Make it easy for others to reach you online, and be sure to follow up personally on your fan mail.
- *Participate.* Create groups and participate in online discussions. Become an online leader and organizer.
- *Make it easy to find you.* Tag your page and add it to subject directories.
- *Experiment.* These sites are great because you can try new things. If it isn't working, tweak it. Or abandon the effort and try something new. There is no such thing as an expert in social networking—we're all learning as we go!

Integrate Social Media into an Offline Conference or Event

As you participate in social networking, keep in mind the relationship between the online world of virtual networks and the physical world of in-person networks. There will be many times that one will complement the other.

Consider conferences and other events. Today, the best live events are the ones that integrate social media into the festivities. At conferences all over the world, audience members connect with one another while speakers are up at the podium. These back channels are truly revolutionary, since they allow listeners to discuss content as it is being delivered. What's more, it brings a new virtual audience into the room—sometimes from the opposite end of the Earth.

Alan Belniak, director of social media marketing at PTC, a software company producing product lifecycle management tools, integrated social media into the PTC/USER World Event. Belniak notes one of the benefits of the conference is integrating the physical event with social networking. "Participants are better off because they can absorb more of the event without being in every session," he says. "They may attend one session, but they can catch a blog of another session or skim the tweet stream of a third. By offering multiple forms of media, it lets people experience more of the event."

Here are some of the ways Belniak used social media at PTC/USER World Event:

- Developed a single page where all the social media feeds could be found.
- Gave out about a dozen video cameras and had the recipients create videos to upload onto a special YouTube video channel.
- Created a Flickr feed of photos shot at the event.
- Established a common hashtag and later archived its Twitter feed.
- Aggregated 35 different bloggers' posts.

The real-time social networking gave those who could not be present in person a taste of the action. "They can see what they're missing and possibly use these forms of real-time multimedia as justification that they should attend next year," Belniak says. In fact, at least one person didn't wait until the next year. "A local PTC customer wasn't registered for the event but had been following some of the chatter on the website. He was a short drive away, so he told his boss that he should go. And he did."

Start a Movement

For marketers, one of the most interesting aspects of social media is that people talk about you, your company, and its products and services. Most of the time, these discussions happen away from your influence. However, it is certainly possible to guide the discussion if you're a bit creative. For example, Ford Motor Company is helping to lead discussions with its Fiesta Movement, a social networking platform built around the new global vehicle of the same name. Ford provided 100 social media agents with personalized Fiestas that they could drive for six months and then relate their experiences through a variety of social media sites.

"This is a Euro-spec vehicle that was not yet available in the United States," says Ford's Scott Monty. "We're using this as a combination of test marketing and buzz generation. The agents are creating content all over the web, and people are talking about the Ford Fiesta on Facebook, Twitter, their blogs, and posting videos and photos on sites like YouTube and Flickr. Ford came on with an approach to social media that showed that we are different. We came at social media from a different perspective, a more personal one, and I think that has made all the difference for us."

Ford's strategy is betting on the continued rise in social media's popularity, and its online numbers reflect the buzz. Agent postings have garnered significant numbers on social media sites—including more than 1.8 million YouTube views, more than 270,000 Flickr views, and more than 1.8 million Twitter impressions, resulting in more than 13.2 million interactions.

Social Networking and Crisis Communications

The real-time aspects of social networking, and the way it creates opportunities for two-way communication, makes the tools of this chapter excellent ways to connect with constituents during a crisis. You can be certain that people are talking about you anyway, so getting your voice out during what can be a very tough time for your organization can help you get through the crisis.

Jerry Sandusky, a former Pennsylvania State University assistant football coach, was found guilty on 45 charges of sexual abuse and was sentenced to 60 years in prison. The story was at the forefront of the news cycle, from its breaking in November 2011, during the investigation and trial, and through the sentencing in October 2012.

Imagine you are responsible for social media within an organization faced with a major crisis like what happened at Penn State. How would you handle it? How would the senior executives handle it?

The right approach is to be honest and forthright. Communicate the facts quickly and don't hide. Assign a visible spokesperson. Silence and "no comment" are the enemy.

The Penn State story is certainly a tragedy. But the way communication about it was handled by the university administration is worth a look and some reflection. I spoke with Kelly Burns, a Penn State MBA graduate, about that experience. While a student, Burns interned with Penn State Football

Marketing & Promotions from May 2009 through April 2012, and for three summers (2009 to 2011) she ran the Penn State Football Facebook[24] and Twitter (@PennStateFball) accounts. "I was very lucky to have the opportunity to assist in developing the Penn State Football Facebook page back when it first launched in summer 2009," Burns says. She posted content (information, photos, videos, and the like) that fans enjoyed. "Having the opportunity to interact with Penn State Football fans was incredible, because Penn State Football has a history rich in tradition and 'Success with Honor,' and its fans literally wear their pride on their sleeves."

The Penn State Football Facebook page, currently with more than 450,000 Likes, targeted students, recruits to the football program, alumni, and Penn State football fans in the community. Burns also read each tweet and Facebook comment and responded personally to many. In this role, she frequently put in 40-hour weeks on a voluntary basis (!!).

Then the Sandusky story broke. The grand jury investigation was initiated in the spring of 2008 but had been kept quiet. In the summer of 2011, Burns was told to remove photos of Sandusky from the Facebook page. On November 4, 2011, Sandusky was indicted, and the next day he was arrested and charged and the story went worldwide instantly. "Our Facebook and Twitter lit up, but that was difficult because initially we were not allowed to post," Burns says. "We were not permitted to post anything about the scandal, nor were any other people working for the University. We were told to wait until Old Main [Penn State's administrative center on campus, which includes the university president's office] made a statement before we could say anything. So we went completely dark."

On November 11, the social media team was permitted to post about The Blue Ribbon Campaign against child abuse, and then on November 16 they were allowed to post some simple messages about football. But, still, they weren't allowed to say anything about the crisis.

"Penn State Football fans were never permitted to post directly onto the Facebook wall, but during this period fans were engaged on Facebook by commenting on posts that were already there, including the Blue Ribbon post. There were as many as 500 comments on some posts that I moderated. Many people aired their opinions, whether positive or negative."

While the majority of people were thoughtful, some were not. "We patrolled for foul language, rude jokes, and other disturbing comments

---

[24] facebook.com/PSUFball

and removed them," Burns says. Negativity was fine, but with such a sensitive issue, inappropriate language was not allowed. "In several cases we needed to block individuals who insisted on continuing to make fun of Penn State in very inappropriate ways," she says.

A full crisis management discussion is beyond the scope of this book. However, the response typically includes such steps as gathering facts, reporting facts quickly (even if the fact is that nothing is known), give the name of a spokesperson, acknowledge people's deep emotions, and communicate regularly. Social networks are a great way to communicate in real time during a time of crisis and in the case of Penn State, they had a tremendously active Facebook page ready to be used to communicate. However, Penn State Football elected not to take these crisis management steps. Burns says it took days before the Board of Trustees issued responses and put a face to leadership.

"We should have done a better job providing a way to communicate with the fans," Burns says. "That's not something critical about Penn State Football, because it goes up to Old Main, who decided what was allowed to be said. I think in our day and age of social media, that silence was not the right response. Keeping information private is not the way to go when people are talking 24/7 on social media and need reassurance."

Burns told me how fans of Penn State competitors also used social media and the Penn State Football Facebook page to show their support and understanding for the victims, the PSU Football players, PSU students, alumni, and fans. She shared one of the best examples of a positive fan post from what is usually considered the enemy, the Ohio State University. "In this situation, the fan laid aside the on-field rivalry to support a much greater cause (to say the least)," Burns says. Robert Benson, a Buckeye fan, posted in the Nov. 11 comment thread:

When people are so quick to make sick references to Penn St. I am disgusted. How can anyone label an entire group of people in a negative way and feel good about it? Taking advantage of people who are down, weakened and heartbroken for your own sick pleasure. Does that remind you of someone?

What I see is a community shell-shocked and hurt, trying to find their way through all of this. A horrible situation for them. Surely, among them are kids attending Penn St. who themselves have been victims.

Your negative comments about Penn St. must hurt them more than anyone would ever know. They want their university to stand for something better than this.

The whole world is watching Penn St. You will find your way and will come out on the other side to represent something good, and maybe something much bigger and important than before.

Keep your chin up Penn St. When we meet you next week, win or lose, we want you at your best.

A Buckeye fan

When people offer support like this on your social networks, it goes a long way to help mitigate the negative reactions.

If you don't have one already, your organization needs a crisis communications plan in place. As part of the plan, you should secure agreement from executives, public relations professionals, and your legal staff about how you can use social networks like Facebook and Twitter to communicate during a crisis. Don't wait until the bad news comes because there is too much happening to make quick decisions.

Why Participating in Social Media Is Like Exercise

One of the most common questions I get at my talks is this: "How do you find the time to do all this social media stuff?" People want the secret to regular participation on Facebook, Twitter, and the other sites that help them create valuable information for their buyers.

I've found that finding the time to participate in social media is just like finding the time for exercise. You have to choose to exercise regularly to stay fit. As far as I know, the only effective way is to make exercise part of your routine. Some people like fitness clubs. Others enjoy running outdoors or dancing or kickboxing. But in all cases, success comes from engaging in the activity regularly.

I enjoy an hour of exercise every morning. I have an elliptical trainer at home, so sometimes I use that. Other days, I go to a nearby health club and swim laps. If I'm near a beach, I enjoy running on sand and I do yoga and calisthenics when I'm in a hotel room. I get up early, around 4 A.M. most days, and I've been at it for more than a decade. I feel great. I don't even think about finding the time to exercise, because it is a very important part of my life.

It's the same with participating in social networks and creating online content—it becomes part of your life. In my case, I write about 100 blog posts per year and shoot maybe 30 videos. I comment on thousands of blogs. Most years, I write a free e-book. And I'm on forums, chat rooms, Twitter, and other social sites.

Many people are surprised when I say that I probably spend about six hours per week on social media, about the same amount of time I spend exercising. I don't even think about it. It's important, so I do it. And I can't really say how I fit it in. Unlike with my exercise routine, I do my social media work mainly in microbursts of a couple minutes each throughout the day.

I recommend that you don't even try to find the time to create content and participate in social media. You'll fail, just like many of us have in our attempts to find the time to exercise, leading to failure and no small waste of money.

Instead, make social media (and exercise) an important part of your life. A good way to start, in my experience, is to make television a less important part of your life or maybe even eliminate it completely. You will be amazed at how much time you free up.

Make social media both a part of your life and a part of your business, such as the way clever business use Twitter to reach out to buyers. I was once in Sofia, Bulgaria, to deliver a New Marketing Masterclass. When I'm in a city for the first time, I always want to poke around a bit. So when the people at Free Sofia Tour (@FreeSofiaTour) tweeted to invite me along (they had heard about my Masterclass), I knew I had to go. Free Sofia Tour relies on volunteer guides and donations from their guests to support the organization.

I love how Free Sofia Tour embraces social media, while the other city tour operators use traditional marketing. I saw the other guys' brochures in the hotel lobby. They have ads at the airport and in the tourist magazines, too. But Free Sofia Tour uses social media, including Facebook, Twitter, and good old-fashioned word of mouth. If you're social, it's easy to find them. They make you feel welcome beforehand, and they follow up via Twitter after the tour.

But you don't have to take my word for it. Free Sofia Tour is ranked the number one activity in Sofia on TripAdvisor, with 188 "excellent" ratings out of 200. In a world of commercial approaches (like the big bus tours that operate in many cities), sometimes the personal touch works best. If you ever find yourself in Sofia, now you know who should show you the sights. Just send them a tweet.

This story leads me to one last point about the connecting power of social networks. With all this online conversation going on, social media take the pervasiveness of the Internet one step further. And while we don't know where they're heading, what is certain is that marketing and PR on the web will continue to evolve—quickly. Success comes from experimentation. With a service like Twitter or a site like Vine (or whatever the next new thing is), nobody knows the rules at first. Smart marketers succeed just by trying. Reuters, for example, generated a ton of stories in the mainstream media and on blogs when it opened the first virtual news bureau in Second Life. They got a huge amount of buzz simply by trying something. Similarly, JetBlue and Dell have created huge followings on Twitter because they were early adopters. The trick to benefiting from any new medium is this: Participate in it; don't just try to take advantage of it. Be a *genuine* part of the action! Whatever your social networking site of choice, don't hesitate to jump in and see what you can do.

17 Blogging to Reach Your Buyers

Blogs are now a mainstream vehicle for organizations to get their ideas into the marketplace. The readers of blogs view the information shared by smart bloggers as one of the few forms of real, authentic communication. Audiences consume advertising with skepticism and consider pronouncements by CEOs to be out of touch with reality. But a good blog written by someone within a large or small company, a nonprofit, a church, or a political campaign commands attention.

At the same time, the term "blog" carries a negative connotation with some people who believe the content contained inside is frivolous. The best marketing and PR strategies must include creating your own content. If you are creating valuable information to market your business, don't let someone's anxiety with the term "blog" hold you back. Or maybe its best to not use the "B-word" at all—rather than a link on your home page to "Our Blog," you could link to the name of the blog or to "Our Industry Commentary." For more on this discussion about the term "blog," please refer back to the section in Chapter 5 called "A Blog (or Not a Blog)."

This chapter sets out the basics of how to establish your own blog. But I recommend that before you begin to write, you first monitor blogs in your market space and that you step into the blogosphere by commenting on a few blogs before you write your own. You might want to reread Chapter 5, where I introduced blogs and provided some case studies of successful bloggers. As you begin to comment on other people's blogs, you'll develop your own blogging voice and get a sense of what you like to discuss online.

That's great! You're experimenting on someone else's blog real estate. If you're like many people, soon you'll be itching to write your own blog. But if commenting is a painful chore for you, maybe you're not cut out to be a blogger. That's okay—there are many more blog readers than blog writers. This forum isn't for everybody.

It's impossible to tell you everything you need to know about blogging in this one chapter. While the case studies and basic information will certainly get you started, the best thing is to experiment to find your voice. Read other blogs and be aware of what you like and dislike about other bloggers' styles.

What Should You Blog About?

People often struggle to decide what to blog about. This is particularly true for marketing and PR professionals because we have been taught to be slaves to the notion of flogging our products and services with on-message advertising and press releases; for most organizations, that's exactly the wrong way to blog. The first thing to ask yourself is "Whom do I want to reach?" For many people, the answer is a combination of buyers, existing customers, and influencers such as analysts and the media. You need to find a topic that you are passionate about. If you aren't excited about the topic or if it feels painful to write, you're unlikely to sustain the effort, and if you do manage to keep going, the writing is likely to be forced.

Most first-time bloggers try to cover too much. It is better to start with a narrow subject and leave room to expand. Be authentic. People read blogs because they want to find an honest voice speaking passionately about a subject. You do not have to be harsh or controversial if that is not your style. If you are interesting and provide valuable information, your readership will grow.

Lawrence McGlynn is president of McGlynn, Clinton & Hall Insurance Agencies and maintains the *Massachusetts Family Insurance Blog*. His posts are inspired by his customers' questions. Several weeks prior to the big game, he wrote "Super Bowl, Super Party, Super Liability,"[1] in which he talked about the legal issues surrounding hosting a party. "What could go wrong?"

---

[1] www.massfamilyinsurance.com/2013/01/super-bowl-super-party-super-liability.html

he wrote. "I can quickly think of at least three incidents that could happen both on and off your premises. Also, keep in mind that friends can sue friends." Posts like these generate high search engine rankings and brand McGlynn as an expert.

"Most of my posts come from listening to people's questions," he says. "Whether it is in our office or in their office, my clients give me the best ideas." For many people, insurance is an unfamiliar and intimidating topic. When the time comes to learn about auto, home, or life insurance, they don't know where to turn. McGlynn realizes this and creates posts to help. "People use the Internet to search for answers to their insurance questions," McGlynn says. "If I can provide those answers, then people will see me as an expert, and it may lead to them contacting me for both advice and service."

Another blog that delivers interesting information rather than a sales pitch is published by GrabCAD,[2] a community where mechanical engineers share and find project designs and ideas. The multimedia blog features projects that members of the GrabCAD community are working on. One video post, "Volocopter Reinvents Flight," shows how a group of German engineers created a battery-operated machine that lifts off with help from 16 electric-powered rotors. The mechanical engineers in the GrabCAD community love posts like this, and they share the content on their networks.

In its "State of the Blogosphere" report,[3] blog search engine Technorati claimed that it tracked more than 112 million blogs in 81 languages and that about 100,000 new blogs are created every day, which means that, on average, a new blog is created every second of every day. That's a heck of a lot of competition, and you might ask yourself if it is worth the effort. But remember back to the *long-tail* theory we discussed in Chapter 2. If you write a niche blog (e.g., a blog about Massachusetts family insurance), then you're not competing with 112 million other blogs. You're writing in a space where there are few (if any) other blogs, and you will no doubt find readers who are interested in what you're saying. If you have a small niche, you may interest only a few hundred readers. But you'll reach the right readers—those people who are interested in what you and your organization have to say.

---

[2] blog.grabcad.com
[3] technorati.com/state-of-the-blogosphere

Blogging Ethics and Employee Blogging Guidelines

Some organizations such as IBM[4] and the U.S. Air Force[5] have created formal guidelines for employee bloggers and published them online for anyone to access. Your organization should decide for itself whether to create such guidelines, and the decision should be determined based on input from marketing, HR, and other departments. I think it is much better for organizations to establish policies about all communications (including verbal communication, email, participation in chat rooms, and the like) rather than focus on a new medium (blogs). I feel strongly that a company can and should set policy about sexual harassment, disparaging the competition, and revealing company secrets, but there's no reason to have different policies for different media. Once the policy is set, employees should be permitted to blog away as long as they follow it. No matter what decisions you make about who should blog and what the rules are, it is always better for the blogger to avoid passing individual posts through a PR department or legal team. However, if your blog posts *must* be reviewed by others in your organization before going live, then have your colleagues focus only on the content, not your actual words. Do not let others in your organization turn your authentic and passionate writing into another form of marketing gobbledygook.

Let's talk about ethics for a moment. All sorts of unethical practices go on in the blogosphere, and you must be certain to hold yourself and your organization accountable for your actions as a blogger. Some organizations have gotten caught using unethical practices on their blogs and have done great harm to their corporate reputations. I've included some of the issues you need to pay attention to, as well as an example of each unethical practice. This is not intended to be a comprehensive list, but rather a starting point for you to think about ethics.

- *Transparency:* You should never pretend to be someone you are not. For example, don't use another name to submit a comment on any blog (your own or somebody else's), and don't create a blog that talks about your company without disclosing that someone from your company is behind it.

[4] ibm.com/blogs/zz/en/guidelines.html
[5] www.af.mil/shared/media/document/AFD-090406-036.pdf

- *Privacy:* Unless you've been given permission, don't blog about something that was disclosed to you. For example, don't post material from an email someone sent you unless you have permission.
- *Disclosure:* It is important to disclose anything that people might consider a conflict of interest in a blog post. For example, if I write in my blog about a product from a company that is one of my masterclass clients or one that I am on the advisory board of, I put a sentence at the end disclosing my relationship with the company.
- *Truthfulness:* Don't lie. For example, never make up a customer story just because it makes good blog content.
- *Credit:* You should give credit to bloggers (and other sources) whose material you have used in your blog. For example, don't read a great post on someone else's blog, take the idea, change a few words, and make it your own. Besides being good ethical practice, links to other bloggers whose ideas you have used helps to introduce them to your blog, and they may link to you.

Again, this is not a complete list. The Word of Mouth Marketing Association has created an ethics code.[6] I recommend that you read and follow the guidelines. But you should also follow your gut. If a post feels funny to you for some reason or makes you uncomfortable, it may be unethical. What would your mother say about that post? If she would tell you it is wrong, it probably is, so don't send it. Please do the right thing.

Blogging Basics: What You Need to Know to Get Started

Unlike websites, which require design and HTML skills to produce, blogs are quick and easy to set up using off-the-shelf software with easy-to-use features. With just a little basic know-how, you can quickly and easily establish and promote your blog. Here are some specific tips to keep in mind:

- Before you begin, think carefully about the name of your blog which will be indexed by the search engines. It is very difficult to go back and change this information once you have established it.

---

[6] womma.org/ethics

- Easy-to-use blogging software is available from TypePad,[7] WordPress,[8] and others. Some of the services are free, and others require a small subscription fee. Research the services, and choose wisely based on your needs, because it is difficult to switch to a different service without losing all the content you have already created. And once your blog has been indexed by search engines, and people have subscribed to your RSS feed or bookmarked your URL, a change to different software is really tough.

- You will need to choose a URL for your blog. The blogging services all offer customizable URLs (such as yourblog.typepad.com). You can also map your blog to your company's domain (www.yourcompany.com/yourblog) or to a custom domain (www.yourblog.com).

- Blogging software makes it easy to choose color, design, and font and to create a simple text-based masthead. You might consider using a custom graphical image as your masthead—these are easy to design and will make your blog more attractive to readers.

- As you begin your blog, tweak your design, and tentatively try a few posts. I recommend you use password protection for the first few weeks or so. That way you can share your blog with a few friends and colleagues first and make changes before opening it up to the world.

- The look and feel of the blog could be complementary to your corporate design guidelines, but it should not be identical. For many blogs, it is better to be a bit different from the corporate look to signal to readers that the blog is an independent voice, not corporate-speak.

- Blogging software usually allows you to turn on a comments feature so your visitors can respond to your posts. There are several options for you to consider. Some people prefer their blogs to have no comments from readers at all, and that might be the right choice for you. However, one of the most exciting things about blogging is when your readers comment on what you've written. Depending on your blogging software, you may opt for open comments (where people can write comments that are not subject to your approval) or for a system where you need to approve each comment before it appears on your blog. Many bloggers use the approval feature to watch for inappropriate comments. But I encourage you to allow any comments from people

---

[7] typepad.com

[8] wordpress.org

who disagree with you—debate is one of the best indications of a well-read blog. Unfortunately, the blogosphere is plagued by the problem of comment spam, so to prevent automated comment robots from vandalizing your blog, some comment systems require people to answer a simple question called a *captcha*[9] before their comments go live. (I use this approach, and it works very well.) This will not eliminate comment spam but will greatly reduce it because it requires a human to enter the comment. You will want to review every comment as it comes in and either comment back to your readers or manually delete any obvious comment spam right away.

- Pay close attention to the categories you choose for your blog, and add social media tags for services like Technorati, Digg, StumbleUpon, and Delicious to each post.
- Add social networking sharing tools such as a Facebook "Like" button. The Pinterest "Pin It" button, and a Twitter "Tweet this" button to each post. Most blog software packages have these tools as a simple application that makes it easy to implement.
- RSS (Really Simple Syndication) is a standard delivery format for many of your readers. Make certain that your new blog has RSS capability. Most blogging software services have RSS feeds as a standard feature.
- Include an About page that includes your photo, biography, affiliations, and information about your blog. Often when people visit a blog for the first time, they want to know about the blogger, so it is important to provide background.
- Encourage people to contact you, make it easy for them to reach you online, and be sure to follow up personally on your fan mail. You'll get a bunch of inquiries, questions, praise, and an occasional detractor if you make it easy for people to contact you. Because of the huge problem with spam, many people don't want to publish email addresses. But the biggest problem is with automated robots that harvest email addresses, so to thwart them, write your email address so humans can read it but the machines cannot. On my website, for example, I list my email address as david (at) DavidMeermanScott (dot) com.
- Don't write excessively about your company and its products and services. You must resist this urge to blog about what your company offers. Instead, blog about a subject of interest to the people you are

---

[9] captcha.net

trying to reach. What problems do your buyers have that you can write about? How can you create content that informs and educates and entertains?

- Involve other blogs and bloggers by becoming a true participant in the online community. Link to and leave comments on other blogs. Let someone else's post serve as the starting point for a conversation that you continue on your own blog. You'll generate much more interest in what you're doing if you are inclusive.

Pimp Out Your Blog

Before my daughter started eighth grade, she spent the entire week pimping out her school binder. All the cool girls do it, transforming standard plastic three-ring binders with photos, stickers, song lyrics, and other bits and bobs on the outside. She even had a spot for a quote of the day that she updated each morning. Inside, the binder had page dividers she customized and pocket folders with pens and protractors and whatnot.

I got to thinking that the same is true of good blogs. A pimped-out blog shows the blogger's personality. I've pimped out my own blog with lots of cool stuff. On the top is a masthead that I had a friend who's a designer create. In TypePad (which I use for my Web Ink Now blog), if your blog is 800 pixels wide in total, you just have someone design an image that's 770 pixels wide by 100 or 150 pixels high and drop it in—TypePad automatically adds a border and replaces the rather plain-looking text masthead with the new design. Other blog software tools also support graphical mastheads, although the specific requirements and implementation methods will be different.

On the right column of my blog, I have links to Amazon from the cover images of my books. Because these links are part of my Amazon Associates program account, I'm even paid a small commission for every book sold. (Hey, it's not much money, but every few months I can take my family out for a decent dinner on the proceeds.) I've also got links to pages on my site and to my other web content, such as my blog about my collection of Apollo space artifacts,[10] my Twitter page, and my online video channels. I have easy sign-up links for people who want to view my

---

[10] www.apolloartifacts.com

blog as an RSS subscription via FeedBurner[11] and an email subscription option with FeedBlitz[12] so people can get each of my blog posts sent to their email inbox.

One of the downsides of a blog is that the reverse-chronological aspect (most recent post at the top) means that much of your best stuff, which may have been written last month or last year, is hidden away. Thus, I've also included easy navigation links on my blog so people can quickly find the good stuff. For example, I include "The Best of Web Ink Now" with links to a handful of my most popular posts, a scrolling list of recent comments on the blog, and navigation by category of post.

Pimping out your blog is easy. If you devote a few hours to it, you can make a very cool-looking blog that even my daughter would approve of. Sure, the standard templates offered by the blog software providers are great to get started, but once you are fully committed to blogging, it is important to make your blog personality shine through with links, images, a masthead, photos, and other add-ons.

Building an Audience for Your New Blog

When you send your first few blog posts, you are likely to hear a deafening silence. You'll be waiting for comments, but none will come. You'll check your site statistics and be disappointed by the tiny number of visitors. Don't get discouraged—that's normal! It takes time to build an audience for your blog. When you're just getting started, make sure people know it is there and can find it! Create links to your blog from your home page, product pages, or online media room. Mention your blog in your email or off-line newsletters, and create links to your blog as part of your email signature and those of other people in your organization.

The good news is that blogs that are regularly updated generate high search engine rankings because the algorithms that are used by Google and the other search engines reward sites (and blogs) that update frequently. It is likely that you will get significant search engine traffic once you've been consistently blogging for a while. I typically post two or three times a week to my blog, and most days my blog generates several hundred visitors via search engines,

---

[11] feedburner.google.com

[12] feedblitz.com

which is good because these are people who do not know me (yet). To ensure that your new blog is found by your buyers as they search for what you have to offer, be certain to post on topics of interest and to use the important phrases that people are searching on. (See Chapter 11 if you want to review how to identify the words and phrases that your buyers use.) Smart bloggers understand search engines and use their blogs to reach audiences directly.

Commenting on other people's blogs (and including a link to your blog) is a good way to build an audience. If you comment on blogs in the same market category as yours, you might be surprised at how quickly you will get visitors to your new blog. A curious thing about blogging etiquette is that bloggers who are competitive for business offline are usually very cooperative online, with links back and forth from their blogs. It's a bit like all the auto dealers in town congregating on the same street—proximity is good for everyone, so people work together.

Your customers, potential customers, investors, employees, and the media are all reading blogs, and there is no doubt that blogs are a terrific way for marketers to tell authentic stories to their buyers. But building an audience for a blog takes time. Most blog services provide tools for measuring traffic. Use these data to learn which posts are attracting the most attention. You can also learn what sites people are coming from when they visit your blog and what search terms they used to find you. Use this information to continually improve your blog. Once again, think like a publisher.

Tag, and Your Buyer Is It

With the total number of existing blogs now in the tens of millions and with the availability of niche blogs on virtually any topic, it is easy to get lost in the blogosphere. The simple truth is that it isn't always easy for people to find a blog post on subjects of interest. Recently, a colleague of mine needed new tires for his car. Instead of just heading to the local retailer to be at the mercy of a salesperson or poking around tire manufacturer websites, he went to one of the blog search engines to see what people were writing about tires. He entered the keyword *tires*, and sure enough, within a few clicks he reached several blogs that had useful information about purchasing tires. But he also faced a heck of a lot of useless noise with the word *tires* in the results—things like analysis of tires used in a recent NASCAR race, rants about the garbage on the sides of freeways (which includes discarded tires), and even posts about "spare tires" on middle-aged men.

It is precisely this problem—the false hits in word and phrase searches, not middle-aged men's lack of exercise—that led blog search engine Technorati to develop a tagging feature that lets bloggers categorize what their posts are about. To use this feature, a blogger simply creates a set of metatags for each blog post. So if someone is looking for a blog post about tires, he can go to Technorati and search on the tag for tires rather than on the keyword. This gets readers much closer to what they are looking for than a simple word search.

From the blogger's perspective, the benefits of adding tags to create increased precision about the post's content, whereby each post reaches more people, are worth the extra effort. For example, I assign each post that I write to multiple appropriate categories, such as marketing, public relations, and advertising. New visitors reach my blog every day as a result of searching on the tags that I had added to blog posts.

Fun with Sharpies (and Sharpie Fans)

I love Sharpie permanent markers. I carry one in my travel bag at all times because you never know when you might need one. For instance, there was the time that I accidentally gouged the wooden desk leg in a hotel room. I applied a bit of black Sharpie and it was as good as new! Other people dig Sharpies, too, such as the guy who decorated his basement with a Sharpie, teenagers who personalize their sneakers with multicolor Sharpies, celebrities like the Olsen twins who use them to sign stuff, or people like Mike Peyton, a snake artist who uses Sharpies in his work creating wooden snakes decorated with fantastic colors.

Thus, it was fun to come across the Sharpie Blog,[13] "a dedicated space where we can showcase some of the really fun, cool, creative stuff that gets made using Sharpie markers." The blog is written by Susan Wassel, better known as Sharpie Susan. I connected on Twitter with Bert DuMars, vice president of e-business and interactive marketing at Newell Rubbermaid (the makers of Sharpies), to learn more about the blog and others developed by the company.

"Customer surveys showed that Sharpies were fun and creative, but the site, because it is just a product site, was not so much fun," DuMars says.

---

[13] blog.sharpie.com

"So that led to the idea of a blog about creativity and art. The blog is about showing additional use for the pens."

I like that the Sharpie blog is not a hard sell. A lot of the blog is focused on art, and Sharpie Susan does a great job showing off the work of the artists. "Sharpie King," for example, creates works that can sell for thousands of dollars. Sharpies already had dedicated fan sites, Facebook groups, and video tributes, so the team needed to work with what was already happening. "We didn't want to invade and ruin much of the social media stuff going on around Sharpie," DuMars says. "We wanted to help push it along a bit."

If your brand is fun and useful, consider the approach taken by Sharpie. Showcase your fans' creativity, and let them market for you. And remember that sometimes a minimalist approach is best. As DuMars wisely realized, a heavy-handed campaign might have gotten in the way of the good thing that was already happening. By just joining the party and adding to the fun, the folks at Sharpie showed that they enjoy—and appreciate—their fans' efforts.

Cities That Blog

While many U.S. cities and towns have dabbled in social media, typically setting up a basic Facebook, YouTube, or Twitter presence, most local government employees and elected officials are averse to blogging. They assume that it's too risky, that it could create legal liability or become a source of primarily negative comments. Contrary to the vast majority of cities, College Station, Texas, has had a blog for years. Jay G. Socol, director of public communications, for the City of College Station maintains the blog, which has been working out very well for his community. According to a message on the homepage,[14] the purpose of the blog is "to be a two-way conversation between College Station residents and their government officials. We hope it allows us to get to know one another a little better in the process, while having genuine and transparent exchanges of ideas."

Socol sometimes tackles difficult topics through the blog. For example, he wrote about how the shooting death of a city law enforcement officer (which generated worldwide attention) brought the community closer together. But he also shows the lighter side of the city, with posts like "Treasure found in a drainage ditch." This story told how city maintenance crews through the

---

[14] cstx.gov/index.aspx?page=3609

years have found objects of value in muddy trenches: jewelry, wallets, purses, car keys, credit cards, and even wads of cash.

"I firmly believe strong, relevant content has helped shift community sentiment toward College Station," Socol says. "It's reduced rumors running rampant and mitigated media grabbing false stories and angles from anonymous chat forums. Blogging also has driven positive news content and given more texture to some of our biggest public announcements. We don't receive a ton of comments (because we require real names to be used), but the results tell me it's working in the ways we need it to. Sentiment and trust have increased, and those are the main wins for us."

Here's another example of a city using blog content to educate and inform (it also proves that cops can have a sense of humor): On Election Day, 2012, the people of Washington State passed Initiative 502, making it legal for adults over 21 years old to possess up to an ounce of marijuana for personal use (or 16 ounces of solid marijuana-infused product, like cookies, or 72 ounces of infused liquid, like oil). So, Washington residents wondered, what does that actually mean for me? To answer that question, the Seattle Police published on their *SPD Blotter* blog: "Marijwhatnow? A Guide to Legal Marijuana Use In Seattle." The post provides a practical guide for what the Seattle Police Department believes Initiative 502 means.

The "Marijwhatnow?" post uses a Q&A format. Here's one example: "Q: Can I legally carry around an ounce of marijuana? A: According to the recently passed initiative, beginning December 6th, adults over the age of 21 will be able to carry up to an ounce of marijuana for personal use. Please note that the initiative says it 'is unlawful to open a package containing marijuana . . . in view of the general public,' so there's that. Also, you probably shouldn't bring pot with you to the federal courthouse (or any other federal property)."

Many of the Q&A interchanges are quite funny: "Q: What happens if I get pulled over and I'm sober, but an officer or his K9 buddy smells the ounce of Super Skunk I've got in my trunk? A: Under state law, officers have to develop probable cause to search a closed or locked container. Each case stands on its own, but the smell of pot alone will not be reason to search a vehicle. If officers have information that you're trafficking, producing, or delivering marijuana in violation of state law, they can get a warrant to search your vehicle."

I love the use of humor in the blog. It provides valuable information about the new law, but in a fun and approachable way.

The SPD Blotter began in 2008 and is maintained by the staff of Seattle Police Department's Public Affairs Office. The "Marijwhatnow?" post was written by Jonah Spangenthal-Lee, a journalist who, as he says in his bio, covered "the always-exciting cops and crime beat at Seattlecrime.com, PubliCola.com, KIRO Television, and *The Stranger.*" Spangenthal-Lee joined SPD in March 2012 to tell those same stories on the department's SPD Blotter blog and publish real-time information on breaking news through SPD's @SeattlePD Twitter feed.

If College Station, Texas, and the Seattle Police Department can blog, so can you.

Blogging Outside of North America

People often ask me about blogging in other countries. They want to know if the marketing approaches I outline work elsewhere. Specifically, many people ask if blogs are a good way to do marketing and PR in Europe and Asia. While I cannot comment on every single country, I can say that blogging is a global phenomenon in countries with widespread web access and that many bloggers from other countries are active in the global blogging community. I've received links to my blog from bloggers in something like 50 different countries. It's so cool when a comment or a link comes into my blog from someone in, say, Bulgaria or Finland or Thailand.

There is other clear evidence that blogging is alive and well outside of North America. TypePad offers services in the United Kingdom, Japan, France, Germany, the Netherlands, Spain, Italy, Finland, and Belgium, in addition to the United States. My wife, Yukari Watanabe Scott,[15] a commentator on the Japanese book business, maintains a blog to reach her readers in Japan. This technique is especially important because her readers there are halfway around the world from where we live, near Boston.

For a true international blogging success story, consider the example of Linas Simonis, a marketing consultant from Lithuania who established in April 2005 one of the first business blogs[16] in that country. The reaction from the Lithuanian business community was almost immediate. "People didn't know what RSS was in Lithuania at that time, so I created an email subscription to my blog," Simonis says. "By the end of the first year, I had

---

[15] watanabeyukari.weblogs.jp/youshonews
[16] pozicionavimas.lt

400 subscribers, and you must remember that less than three-and-a-half million people live in Lithuania, so the equivalent would be something like 40,000 subscribers in the United States."

But what's really remarkable about Simonis's story is the new business that he generated via his blog. "Three months after I started the blog, my company stopped needing to make cold calls to solicit new business," he says. "The blog and the company website generated so many requests that we didn't need to actively seek new clients—they come to us. Soon after I started blogging, I was even hired by conference organizers to deliver speeches and seminars, and I had calls from universities to speak to students." Simonis now consults for corporate clients in Lithuania that wish to establish blogs, and he publishes an English-language blog[17] as a forum to write about positioning strategy in a Web 2.0 world.

What Are You Waiting For?

Everybody I've spoken with about starting a blog has said the same thing (but in slightly different ways). They were all a bit uncomfortable when they started a blog. They felt a little dorky because they didn't know all the unwritten rules. They were even a little scared to push the button on that first post. We've all been there. To get comfortable before you take the plunge, remember back to Chapter 5: You should follow a bunch of blogs in your industry first. What things do you like about those blogs? What's annoying? What would you do differently? Then before you jump into the water by creating your own blog, you can stick your toe in by leaving comments on other people's blogs. Test out your blog voice. Finally, when it feels right, start your own blog. And when you do get going, please send me your URL so I can check it out.

---

[17] linassimonis.com/category/posts

18

An Image Is Worth a Thousand Words

In the past several years, images have become increasingly popular marketing and public relations assets. The change is so significant that I'm including this new chapter in the fourth edition of the book to highlight some of the ways that you can use them. In particular, we'll look at storytelling through photographs, image-sharing applications (Instagram and Pinterest in particular), and delivering complex data clearly with infographics. As with other forms of content, success in this area comes from considering your buyers and creating the images that will be valuable to them as they consider doing business with your organization.

Photographs as Compelling Content Marketing

With all the talk about image-sharing *services* like Pinterest and Instagram, sometimes a basic premise of communication practice is lost. Images are important in all your marketing content. Don't get so excited about the latest tool that you forget about the value of the image itself.

> An original photo is great as a way to communicate with your buyers.

For example, consider Zürsun Idaho Heirloom Beans. The company was the first to offer authentic heirloom beans and unusual legumes to customers worldwide via specialty stores. Dozens of bean, lentil, and pea varieties are available, with colorful names like Dapple Grey, Scarlet Runner, White Emergo, and Tongues of Fire. "The glorious true-to-size pictures, carefully taken in natural light, have done more to promote the beans than any words possibly could," says Allison Boomer, the founder of Eco-Conscious Food Marketing. Boomer worked with Zürsun on site design and content.

It seems so simple, doesn't it? Photos help to tell a story, particularly for a product that comes in unusual shapes and colors. Yet so many marketers rely on boring stock photos that make their organization appear lazy and uncaring and that hide the uniqueness of their products.

You can read about the beans on the site: "Zürsun heirloom beans are grown on small-scale farms in the Snake River Canyon region of south central Idaho known as the Magic Valley Growing Area. The area's arid climate, rich, well-drained loamy soil, moderate temperatures and stable moisture level—internationally recognized as having ideal environmental conditions for bean growing—produce pure, distinctly flavorful beans, superior to common store-bought beans." Sounds yummy, right? Sure, the text Boomer wrote is compelling. But the beautiful photos seal the deal and get buyers to place an order.

"I was careful about writing the content," she says. "However, it turns out the photos resonated so much more with customers than the text. I didn't anticipate this going into designing the site, so I was lucky. Zürsun has reached an awesome tipping point, for which I give much credit to the website and those glorious bean photos. Sales in the last year have doubled. Responding to the many inbound queries through the website has become a daily task for me."

As you're creating the content for your site and blog, learn from the success of Zürsun Idaho Heirloom Beans: Shoot original photographs to tell your story to your buyers. Even organizations without photogenic product offerings can use images. As we will see next, even sellers of commodities and intangible services can still get into the photo game with Instagram and other new photo networking services.

Why I Love Instagram

It's rare that I get particularly excited about a new social network, but that's what happened to me when I first joined Instagram[1] in late 2011. Instagram is a photo-sharing application for iPhone and Android that makes it easy and fun to manipulate a photo; a variety of filters turn a snapshot into instant art. Then, with a few clicks, you can share your photo and caption to your Instagram followers and on other networks. While there are other photo-creation and photo-sharing applications (Hipstamatic is another), Instagram has quickly become the most popular, with more than 100 million users. This giant user base caught the attention of Facebook, which announced plans to acquire the company in 2012—less than two years after the Instagram application was launched.

I love that Instagram makes it so easy to create and share content. One of the first things people push back on in my conversations with marketers and entrepreneurs is how much time it takes to create content and publish it on the web. Many say they just can't manage to create daily content. But Instagram is so easy! It just takes a minute or two to shoot a photo, manipulate it with the filters, and share it with your network. Other critics tell me they're lousy writers and are therefore hopeless on social sites. But with Instagram, you do almost no writing, so even word-challenged people can create awesome content.

I've taken hundreds of photos as I've traveled the world, and my several thousand Instagram followers can see what I've been up to in just a few seconds.[2] If I want, I can also share the Instagram photo on other social networks like Facebook and Twitter. I love it.

There are tens of thousands of social networks out there. Many are copycats of existing networks or merely add incremental feature changes. These networks don't succeed. Truly original ideas for social networks are rare—I can count on one hand the number that made me say "wow." YouTube makes video sharing easy. Twitter is for sharing short messages. Facebook is for connecting with friends; Foursquare, for recording my whereabouts; and now Instagram, for beautiful photos. Instagram is cool because it combines content sharing (photos) with artistic expression. It's addictive, at least for me. When I have a few minutes of downtime, I like to

---

[1] instagram.com

[2] instagram.com/dmscott

pull out my iPhone and scroll through the photos of the people I follow on Instagram. It's like a stroll through an art gallery.

Okay, so Instagram is a fun way to share photos with your social network. But how can you use it to market your product or service?

How to Market an Expensive Product with Original Photographs

When Boston-based creative director Doug Eymer was ready to sell his home, he turned to photo-sharing services to get images of the home out to prospective buyers. "We have a unique house in a great spot on the water, and we know that water is prime real estate," Eymer says. "We also have an incredible view. We feel like that that adds a significant amount to the price of our house, although it's not something you can really measure. So I started documenting sunrise every morning, and putting them together into a collection. What's really cool is how the marsh grasses change colors and the leaves in the background change colors. It's an ever-changing view."

Eymer snaps the photo each morning and shares the series *Sunrises at 31 Bow Street* (now well over 100 photos) on a wide variety of social networks and photo-sharing sites, including Instagram,[3] Facebook, Twitter, Tumbler, Foursquare, Pinterest,[4] 500px,[5] and Flickr. "On 500px I have sets with all of my photographs, including a set for my sunrise photographs. 500px is great for followers; as soon as you post, you start getting feedback right away. Usually it's like one or two words: 'love it,' 'great.' And 500px also gives you a lot of information about the activity on your photos. You can see what people are responding to."

When Eymer listed his home with a realtor, the photo series became a valuable asset, which the realtor linked to. "The realtor that we used was pretty web-savvy," Eymer says. "He was posting information on his blog about the photos, and he mentioned them on Facebook and Pinterest."

Documenting the view from his home as the seasons change is a subtle but very effective form of marketing. "It has brought a lot of attention to our house, especially from people in town, and that's built positive word-of-mouth," Eymer says. "There are a few people who respond every morning,

---

[3] instagram.com/deymer

[4] pinterest.com/eymer/sunrises-31-bow-street-02025/

[5] 500px.com/Eymer/sets/sunrises_31_bow_street_cohasset_ma_02025

and I think they look forward to seeing what photograph I'm going to post. When I first started, we had a red canoe that was in the yard, and I always made the red canoe part of the photograph. One day we had some high water, and we moved the canoe so it wouldn't float away. People said, 'What happened to the canoe? Where did it go?' Then someone made the leap of, 'It looks like summer's over. The canoe has been put away.' That was pretty interesting. It was just one little thing, people letting me know that they were actually watching."

Eymer has also brought his photo series into the offline world to market his home when buyers are viewing it. In various rooms, he has laptop computers and iPads running a continuous slideshow of his photos of the ever-changing view toward the water from 31 Bow Street. "As buyers walk through the house, especially the rooms which overlook the view, we can show how it changes over time. There's summer, the beautiful changing leaves, and photos of wintertime with ice. It gives people another window on what's outside, and gives them an idea of what is there to look at."

Original photos, shared on Instagram and other photo-sharing social networking services, are a powerful way to showcase your offerings. And when you take your photos and integrate them into your online and off-line marketing, you set yourself apart from the pack.

Sharing with Pinterest

Many organizations create original photographs, like Eymer did to market his home. And like Eymer, many share those photos on Pinterest, a pin-board-style social network. Think of Pinterest as the virtual equivalent of a bulletin board where you can "pin" items of interest to come back to later. The marketing aspect is that other people can see and follow your "boards" to follow what you find interesting. In addition, if you create interesting visual content, people will pin it (from your website) or repin it (from Pinterest), driving traffic to your site. Pinterest boasts more than 10 million users as of this writing and is growing very quickly.

Whole Foods Market, which started with a small store in Austin, Texas, in 1980, is now the world's leader in natural and organic foods. They have more than 300 stores in North America and the UK. The company uses Pinterest[6] to showcase a wide variety of foods in interesting categories. Like Eymer,

---

[6] pinterest.com/wholefoods

Whole Foods uses original photography to showcase its product offerings. As I write this, Whole Foods has more than 1,500 pins on 45 boards, which include *Who Wants Dinner* (144 pins), *Eat Your Veggies* (217 pins), and *Cheese is the Bee's Knees* (56 pins).

Pinterest is also frequently used to share things you like that aren't your products or services but that get people interacting socially with you. For example, one Whole Foods board[7] showcases photographs of designer kitchens. Whole Foods isn't in the kitchen business, but the food they sell is, of course, prepared in home kitchens. Many of the kitchen photos have more than 100 repins, and many have multiple comments. One commenter wrote, "We live in Maryland now, however, plan to move to Florida by the New Year. I am getting some great ideas for our new/used home."

While creating and sharing content on your own board is a great way to showcase your organization, Pinterest is also extremely valuable as a source for inbound links to your web content, including your blog posts, videos, and images. Many people use Pinterest as a sort of virtual scrapbook, a way to catalog information that is important to them. Others use it as a reminder tool. These people might pin your stuff, which others will then be able to see.

For example, if I'm planning a vacation to a beach resort, I might catalog the locations I'm considering by making a board. It's simple to save the images or videos of the resorts as pins, which point to the web page or blog post where I found the image or video. It takes just seconds. Then I can share my "Dream Holiday" board with family members or friends, and they can help me decide where to stay. Then, after my holiday, I can make another board cataloging the places I visited, restaurants I ate at, and activities I enjoyed. These pins then become recommendations for others.

As I said, it's the social sharing of boards that creates the opportunity for marketing, because others can see my boards too. Maybe my friend or colleague wants to take a similar holiday. All I need to do is point them to my pinboard. Imagine how great that is for the owners of the restaurant I loved—people are sharing my content, introducing that restaurant to an audience of new customers.

To succeed with Pinterest, you need to—you guessed it—publish great content for people to pin. And that content needs to be visual. That means you need to have photographs, videos, and infographics on your blog and site. For example, that restaurant I enjoyed on holiday would be smart to have their

---

[7] pinterest.com/wholefoods/super-hot-kitchens

current menu available as an image ready to be pinned. They might also have photos of each dish and the labels of the wines they serve. Interior photos of the tables and exterior shots of the building might make sense too, particularly if the restaurant has unique design elements. The availability of these images makes it easy for happy diners to pin what they liked.

Whatever your business, you should have content available that people are eager to share. To make it really easy for them to pin your content, you should have a "Pin it" button on each piece of online content. Just like the Facebook "Like" button and the Twitter "Tweet" button, the Pinterest "Pin it" button helps get your content to others via their boards. I have a "Pin it" button at the bottom of each of my blog posts and get many pins of my posts. One recent post was pinned nearly 100 times. Thus, there are 100 new places on the web pointing to that post, and the followers of those 100 people's boards could choose to click through to read it. How great is that?! Pinterest is now an important source of many inbound links for my blog and for the content of all kinds of organizations. It's an exciting way to get your content seen.

Infographics

We finish this chapter on marketing using visual images with a discussion of information graphics (or simply "infographics"), which are graphical representations of complex data, information, or knowledge. Infographics take advantage of the human ability to visualize very complex data quickly. For most people, a visual representation is much easier to understand than columns of numbers or percentage representations. For example, a map of a train or metro system is an infographic, with train lines characteristically appearing as different colors. Frequently, the major stations where you can change trains figure prominently and sometimes the maps note the neighborhoods each line serves. Imagine using the London underground without the tube map? It would be nearly impossible!

Increasingly, marketers are delivering complex data to buyers in the form of infographics. Typically offered as an image file or PDF on a website or blog, an infographic that delivers information in a useful way is highly valuable to buyers. It may also be shared via social networks, including Pinterest.

For example, "The Sequel Map"[8] is published by BoxOfficeQuant, a blog about film statistics. It graphically compares whether movie sequels are

---

[8] boxofficequant.com/sequel-map

better or worse than their original, based on the consensus opinion of professional film critics from Rotten Tomatoes. In seconds, I can take in the relative sales ratios of movies and their sequels. The graphic is much easier to grasp than a table with star ratings.

As I was writing this section, I learned that LinkedIn just passed the 200-million-user milestone. To commemorate the achievement, LinkedIn marketers released an infographic called "200 Million Members"[9] on the LinkedIn blog. The infographic visually presents what countries have the most LinkedIn members, where the fastest subscriber growth comes from, what industries members work in, and much more. I learned that if LinkedIn were a country, it would have the fifth-largest population in the world, equal to France, the UK, and Italy combined. I thought the infographic was cool, so I tweeted it to my followers.

To learn about the ins and outs of creating infographics for marketing purposes, I spoke with Marta Kagan, director of brand and buzz for marketing software company HubSpot. "We're extremely dependent on data here: love it, live by it," she says. "Using infographics allows us to cherry-pick the juiciest pieces to draw your eye to what's most relevant in a very appealing way.

"The other way we use infographics a lot is to explain processes or to tell a story. We do that with our infographic 'The History of Marketing.'[10] With the short attention span people have as a result of all the devices they use and how much information everyone juggles at any given time, an infographic grabs your eye, it gives you a headline, and it includes color in a way that a text blog post can't. You can bookmark it and look at it later, share it, or subscribe. Whenever there's a thirst for information about how to do something, why I need to do it, what's the adoption rate, those types of things, we have a lot of success compiling that as an infographic, because it's a visual and highly shareable format."

Creating a good infographic is more like doing a video than writing a text blog post, because so many elements need to come together. "You're telling a story in a very visual media," Kagan says. "Buyers' brains are wired to work differently with images, and they notice different things than when they are just reading straight text. So we have to basically lead you down a path of

---

[9] blog.linkedin.com/2013/01/09/linkedin-200-million

[10] blog.hubspot.com/blog/tabid/6307/bid/31278/The-History-of-Marketing-An-Exhaustive-Timeline-INFOGRAPHIC.aspx

visual cues through how we create the hierarchy of the information. This is different from reading; you read from left to right, from top to bottom."

HubSpot brings employees with varying skills into the process of creating infographics. "Part of our marketing team will focus on brainstorming ideas around what's the topic we want to cover. Another group may be the ones that actually pull together the data, either from our own sources or research from external sources. Another few folks will actually then map out the story like you would for a video.

"Is it vertical? Is it horizontal? What's the art direction around it? Is there photography? Is this handwritten? What's the style? What's the tone we're trying to strike? All those questions need to be answered like they would for a video or for another creative piece of media."

HubSpot has a team of in-house graphic designers who create the final artwork. If you don't have your own team, there are a number of options. You can make a simple infographic in PowerPoint. Kagan's team at HubSpot has developed a free resource to make it easy, *The Marketer's Simple Guide to Creating Infographics in PowerPoint.*[11] Another option is to use the templates offered by Piktochart, a drag-and-drop infographic editing tool. Or you can outsource the work. A company called visual.ly has created a marketplace to tap the expertise of thousands of designers who can make an infographic for you.

Once the infographic is created, post it in appropriate places on your blog and website. You might consider sending links to your customers and the media who cover your industry. And don't forget to put a "Pin it" button on the download page!

Marketing with photos and images is a fast-growing way to tell a story for your buyers. In combination with text-based content and video, images are an important component of any organization's new marketing plan.

---

[11] blog.hubspot.com/blog/tabid/6307/bid/33499/The-Marketer-s-Simple-Guide-to-Creating-Infographics-in-PowerPoint-Template.aspx

19

Video and Podcasting Made, Well, as Easy as Possible

Creating audio and video content for marketing and PR purposes requires the same attention to appropriate topics as other techniques outlined in this book. It requires targeting individual buyer personas with thoughtful information that addresses some aspect of their lives or a problem they face. By doing so, you brand your organization as smart and worthy of doing business with. However, unlike text-based content such as blogs or news releases, audio and video require a modest investment in additional hardware such as microphones and video cameras, as well as software, and, depending on the level of quality you want to achieve, may also necessitate time-consuming editing of the files. Although the actual procedures for podcasting and video are a bit more convoluted than, say, starting a blog, they are still not all that difficult.

Video and Your Buyers

Organizations that deliver products or services that naturally lend themselves to video have been among the first to actively use the medium to market and deliver information about their offerings. For example, many churches routinely shoot video of weekly services and offer it online for anyone to watch, drawing more people into the congregation. Many amateur and professional sports teams, musicians, and theater groups also use video as a marketing and PR tool.

The idea of *companies* using video for web marketing is still relatively new. Video follows both blogs and podcasting on the adoption curve at organizations that don't have a service that naturally lends itself to video. Companies are certainly experimenting, typically by embedding video (hosted at YouTube or another video site) into their existing blogs and online media rooms. I'm also seeing video snippets of CEO speeches, customer interviews, and quick product demonstrations.

Business-Casual Video

In the United States, there has been a 15-year trend toward so-called business-casual clothing in the workplace. My first job, on Wall Street in the 1980s, required me to wear a suit and tie with polished shoes every day. At that time, casual (for men) meant that after 5 P.M. you could loosen your tie. When I lived in Japan in the late 1980s and early 1990s, things were even more formal; you could loosen your tie only while drinking beer late at night.

Casual Fridays started as a parallel to the dot-com boom on both American coasts in the mid-1990s and was partly led by Dockers, a clothing company. Casual Fridays very quickly became casual everyday and spread throughout the United States. These days, except for banking and a few other professions, business casual is the norm and the trend has spread around the world.

I've noticed in the past five years or so that business video has been going through a similar trend toward the casual. More and more content is created with much less formality. This is a good thing! Both professionals and citizen content creators now reach readers and viewers faster and with less interference from the stuffy conventions associated with content creation.

Perhaps the tremendous rise of social networking tools has helped fuel the desire to consume content that is less formal. At the same time, stiff and structured media like white papers aren't getting as many readers as they did a decade ago.

My friend Cliff Pollan, CEO of VisibleGains, is the one who first brought my attention to what he calls business-casual video. I love the description! I've been sharing the idea at my recent talks, and the idea really resonates with people. The concept, I say, is simple: In the beginning, corporate videos were highly produced, like an episode of *60 Minutes*. They tended to cost tens of thousands of dollars and take months to create.

Some classics of the formal online corporate video genre include slickly produced corporate overviews; in-studio, lights-and-makeup customer testimonials; and product managers explaining their amazing new offerings.

Because many executives' experience with video is of this genre, when the subject of online video is discussed at companies, most people immediately think expensive and difficult. It's because they're thinking *formal*.

But if you think about business-casual video, all of a sudden videos can be low- or even no-cost and can be completed in a few hours or even a few minutes. Some people say that quality is essential. While I agree that a video should be appealing, I'm convinced that a lack of studio, high-wattage lighting, and makeup artists isn't a big deal. If the subject is interesting, people are plenty tolerant of the conditions under which the video was filmed. Of course, you need to stay within reason. I don't advocate poorly shot video, terrible lighting, or bad editing.

I'm convinced that the trend toward casual content means consumers want to get closer to the organizations they do business with. When a company, hospital, educational institution, government agency, or other outfit comes across as friendly and engaging because of the way it communicates with people online, the content will be better received. It's okay if the person in your video doesn't speak like someone with an Ivy League MBA—in fact, it's probably preferable.

Like that transition from wearing formal clothes to putting on a polo shirt, it might feel unprofessional at first. But the increasingly informal nature of business—a willingness to tell it like it is—will make us more efficient and successful. Like the business-casual video that is the result, the equipment you use to create videos for your organization need not be fancy.

Stop Obsessing over Video Release Forms

Part of the trend toward business-casual video is the rise of interviews quickly recorded and used for marketing purposes. However, many people tell me that their companies' legal departments obsess over getting signed release forms from interview participants prior to posting the video online.

In my experience, the mere act of thrusting a legal document in front of potential participants and demanding that they sign causes many of them to rethink the whole thing; some end up choosing not to participate. When this happens, you miss opportunities.

I want to emphasize that I am not a lawyer, and I am not offering legal advice. As always, you should check with an expert before proceeding with an action that may have legal consequences. However, I do want to offer a practical alternative to the formal, signed release. It's a simple strategy that I use myself. When I first press Record on my video camera, I simply ask the person I am about to interview if it's okay to post the video on YouTube. I also ask about name spellings and company affiliation and title. I then know how to refer to my interview subjects throughout the video, and I have a record of them giving me permission to record! During the video-editing process, I save the video permissions and post the interview. It works great.

I've interviewed and posted video of rock stars, Fortune 500 CEOs, and top government officials using this method. And it turns out I'm not the only one. I was recently interviewed for a special segment to be aired on MSNBC's *Your Business* program. The first thing the producer did was have me spell my name on camera. There you have it—a technique even the pros use.

Your Smartphone Is All You Need

One development that is helping change the relative formality of corporate marketing video is the ease of use and high quality that you can achieve with today's smartphones. I currently use an Apple iPhone 4s and the videos it produces are stunning. I love mine and have it with me at all times when I am on the go. You never know where a great video interview might present itself, like the one I did with Frederick "Fritz" Henderson, then CEO of General Motors. Other times, an idea pops up that is best told in video, like the idea in *Social media drove the Egyptian revolution but can it bring back the tourists??*,[1] which I filmed at the Pyramids and at Tahrir Square in Egypt on 2013.

Your smartphone's camera allows you to always be ready to interview customers, employees, and industry analysts and to quickly post the video on your site or blog. It can also help you shoot short clips showing how your products are made or used. No professionals required.

The thing couldn't be easier to use. Even a technology-challenged person like me can use it. Once you're done, you use the USB drive adapter to simply upload videos to your computer for easy editing and then upload. I use Apple's iMovie to edit (it comes free with most Macs). I do simple edits like shortening clips, adding graphics, or including B-roll footage (video to show the location that the video is about), such as images of the area around Tahrir Square in my Egypt video mentioned above. Or you can upload directly to

---

[1] youtube.com/watch?v=6satH7GF73c

YouTube, Vimeo, or other video-sharing sites. Really, it's that easy. In fact, when people push back on the idea of creating a corporate blog or writing an e-book, I always suggest making some simple and short video interviews as an easy way to create valuable content that helps get the word out right away. Hey, did I mention that this is easy?

Video to Showcase Your Expertise

When Mary McNeight couldn't find anyone in the Seattle area who would help her train her own dog Jasper for service work (dogs who help people manage diseases like diabetes), it fell to her to teach her pet to be her service dog. Later, she enrolled in puppy classes to train Liame, her new Labrador retriever puppy. In the process, she became addicted to dog training—so she made it her business. McNeight spent countless hours learning all aspects of the business, got her accreditation from the Certification Council for Professional Dog Trainers, and is now owner and director of training and behavior at Service Dog Academy.[2] This business offers private training sessions and small-group adult-and-puppy training classes for both service and pet dog training. They even offer a groundbreaking "train your own Diabetic Alert Dog" program.

But credentials, skills, and even passion alone don't bring in customers. Her excellent website (featuring dozens of videos that she shot and edited herself) educates buyers and generates high search-engine rankings, driving business her way. "I've gone from barely having any students to getting anywhere from 20 to 40 emails per day requesting my services and advice and verbally praising my work," McNeight says. "If that isn't a story of success, I don't know what is. I have the power to create an audience for any product or service I put my mind to. But I think I will stick with what makes me happiest: helping dogs and the disabled live more productive lives."

In 2010, McNeight started making YouTube videos with an inexpensive video camera and the software that came installed on her Mac notebook computer. "Seeing a need for my students to understand how to make a Kongsicle, I produced my first instructional video," McNeight says. Kongs are natural rubber-food puzzle toys for dogs, and a Kongsicle is a Kong with frozen food inside. The video is titled Best Dog Food Puzzle: The Kongsicle.

---

[2] servicedogacademy.com

"A couple of months later, I went to the Association of Pet Dog Trainers conference, and I was startled by a young trainer who said, 'You're Mary McNeight right? You made that video on Kongsicles! I use it as a reference video for my students.' Here was this dog trainer in Florida using my materials for her classes. That was the day I understood the power of YouTube." Since then, McNeight has made many instructional videos, with titles that include "Diabetic Alert Dog Scams," "Puppy Doggie Ants in the Pants," and a multipart series on diabetic alert dog training.

The content on the Service Dog Academy site, including the video series, is created for three buyer personas: pet dog owners, service dog owners, and people who want to train their own diabetic alert dog. After her initial success, McNeight purchased a $400 HD video camera, a $20 microphone, Final Cut Pro software, and, as she describes it, "some funky alien-adjustable-arm-looking lights at Home Depot, since I couldn't afford to light my videos with professional lights. The really cool thing about my content is that it proves that it doesn't have to be shiny, flashy, spiffy or cost thousands of dollars to produce. People will watch anything as long as its packed full of useful information."

McNeight's notoriety and search engine results are aided by her willingness to post content that others in the dog training business are fearful to post because they don't want to give away information for free. "A great success was a video on how to travel with your service dog, something nobody on the entire Internet was teaching people how to do," she says. "I also hosted a webinar that gave an overview of how to train a diabetic alert dog. I placed the webinar capture video on YouTube and was afraid of being banned in the dog-training community. This information was not available on the web because nobody wanted to share how they trained dogs for tens of thousands of dollars. I started getting emails and phone calls from people all over the world asking me for advice on training their dog or just outright purchasing my online diabetic alert dog training program. I've had dog trainers who want me to fly out to their location and teach a class on diabetic alert dog training for them.

"How cool is it that this now three-person service dog training organization is getting worldwide attention? I never would have gotten that type of exposure printing brochures or running expensive ads on local television. A couple of months ago, I even had a woman tell me the video I made saved her life! It allowed her to get enough information to help her train her own medical alert dog by herself."

You could hardly ask for a more dramatic example of how low-cost videos can expand reach and drive business. And it all started because McNeight identified a problem that no one online was helping people solve.

Getting Started with Video

Whether they're new to the game or have been offering web video for years, organizations get their video content onto the computer screens (and video iPods) of buyers in several different ways:

- *Posting to video-sharing sites:* YouTube[3] is the most popular video-sharing site on the web, although there are others, such as Vimeo[4] and blip.tv. Organizations post video content on YouTube and send people a link to the content (or hope that it goes viral). You can also embed a YouTube video into your site, your blog, or even your news release. Creating a simple video is easy—all you need is a YouTube account and a digital video camera (note that your mobile phone may have video capability). There are all sorts of enhancements and editing techniques you can use to make the video more professional. An example of compelling video from a major consumer brand and available on YouTube is the Smirnoff "Tea Partay" video[5] which features old-money New Englanders rapping. It reminds me of people I went to college with, so I've watched it a bunch of times. IBM has experimented with mockumentaries, including a hysterical six-part series called "The Art of the Sale," which is like a cross between *The Office* and a sales training video. And the viral components of these corporate videos clearly work, because here I am sharing them with you.[6]
- *Developing an online video channel:* Companies that take online video programming seriously develop their own channel, often with a unique URL. Examples include Weber Grills' Weber Nation website,[7] which features videos of grilling classes.

---

[3] youtube.com

[4] vimeo.com

[5] youtube.com/watch?v=4y4-5Zouvjs

[6] youtube.com/watch?v=MSqXKp-00hM

[7] webernation.com

- *Attempting stealth insertions to YouTube:* Some companies try to sneak corporate-sponsored video onto YouTube in a way that makes it seem like it was consumer generated. The YouTube community is remarkably skilled at ratting out inauthentic video, so this approach is fraught with danger.
- *Vlogging:* Short for "video blogging," this term refers to video content embedded in a blog. The text part of the blog adds context to each video and aids with search engine marketing.
- *Vodcasting:* A vodcast is like a podcast but with video—a video series tied to a syndication component with iTunes and RSS feeds. For example, BMW[8] offers a weekly vodcast series of two- to three-minute videos about what's going on at BMW. The company uses the vodcasts to publicize the cool things it's doing around the world.
- *Inviting your customer communities to submit video:* This technique is how some companies, including Mentos and Tourism Queensland (which we learned about in Chapter 6) try to generate viral marketing interest. These companies sponsor contests where customers submit short videos. The best are usually showcased on the company site, and the winners often get prizes. In some cases, the winning videos are also played on TV as real commercials.
- For much more detailed information about video, check out *Get Seen: Online Video Secrets to Building Your Business* by Steve Garfield and *Beyond Viral: How to Promote and Sustain Your Brand with Online Video* by Kevin Nalty.

Owen Mack,[9] co-founder and head of strategy and development for coBRANDiT, a company that does social media video production, is a pioneer in using video for marketing and PR purposes. From the early days of online video, Mack has helped companies like Puma and Pabst Brewing create video strategies. "Video is an extension of the blogging ethos," Mack says. "Do you have an interesting story to tell? If you don't, can you develop something? You need to see what people are saying about you already and know how you can mesh with that. Transparency and openness are required. Done properly, video is very compelling."

---

[8] bmw.tv/web/com/video.do
[9] cobrandit.com

Video Created for Buyers Generates Sales Leads

As I've mentioned throughout this book, tailoring content to buyer personas is essential to good marketing. Guess what—it's true for video as well. Rather than creating gobbledygook-laden drivel about products and services, shooting video especially for your buyers makes it important for them.

Attivio, an enterprise software company, uses a buyer-persona-based approach on the company's website. While the different personas might actually all purchase the same product, each one has different problems that can be solved by the company. For instance, marketers at Attivio target what they refer to internally as tech-savvy business champions, people who care about new revenue sources, better customer relationships, regulatory compliance, competitive advantage, and controlling costs. Another buyer persona, information technology professionals, describes the people responsible for getting and keeping the company's systems up and running, so they want to hear about reliability, security, performance, scale, and ease of integration. A third buyer persona is those who work within government and the intelligence agencies. These buyers don't want to hear about improving profitability; instead, they care about sharing information among agencies, which improves their ability to connect the dots and detect threats. Each set of buyer persona pages has video made especially for that buyer, and the goal of the video is to drive buyers to want to learn more by connecting with an Attivio salesperson.

"Video has been a particularly valuable tool in helping us convey the appropriate [information] to each customer segment," says MaryAnne Sinville, senior vice president of marketing at Attivio. "When we do a video shoot, we often ask the same question two or three times, guiding the speaker to frame their answer with a specific audience in mind so we get relevant content to parse out to multiple persona pages."

One of the benefits of this approach is that salespeople know what a buyer is interested in and what persona that buyer represents based on what page the buyer was on when he or she asked to learn more. "When a visitor comes to the site, self-selects a persona path, and then converts to a lead, it's much easier for us to respond with additional information they're likely to find compelling," Sinville says.

Now let's take a look at how to create a podcast. While the general approach of creating valuable information especially for your buyer personas is the same, you do have technology choices to make.

Podcasting 101

A podcast is a piece of audio content tied to a subscription component so people can receive regular updates. The simplest way to think of podcasting is that it's like a radio show except that you listen to each episode at your convenience by downloading or streaming it either to your computer or to a mobile device like an Android phone or iPhone. The equipment you need to start podcasting will range in cost from a few hundred dollars at the low end to a bit over a thousand dollars for professional-level sound. Plus, you'll probably want to host your audio files on an external server requiring a monthly fee.

How do you get started? "I've found that the most important thing is show preparation," says John J. Wall, producer and cohost of Marketing over Coffee,[10] a 20-minute show covering both new and classic marketing. "Unless you are real comfortable talking extemporaneously, you will want to have a script laid out ahead of time. It just sounds more polished when you do." I don't have my own podcast, but as a frequent guest on radio shows and podcasts, I agree with Wall—the best shows I participate in are those where the interviewer knows the material and keeps things focused.

Beginning with developing a script, following are the steps and technical issues involved with producing a podcast.

- *Show preparation* includes gathering ideas for the show and creating a script. Think about your buyer personas and what you can discuss that interests them. If you plan to interview guests, make sure you know how to pronounce their names (don't laugh, this is a frequent mistake) and you have their titles, affiliations, and other information correct. It's common practice to plug a guest's business, so know ahead of time what URL or product you will mention.
- *Recording when you are near your computer* is done with a microphone (many options to choose from) that delivers the audio into your computer. You'll need podcasting software such as GarageBand, Audacity, or Goldwave as an interface to create and publish your podcast.
- *Mobile recording gear* is required if you are going to do the roving-reporter thing and interview people at events or perhaps your

---

[10] marketingovercoffee.com

employees around the world. Mobile recording gear is made by several companies including Marantz.

- *Phone interviews* require a way to record both sides of a conversation. A good way to go is to use Skype[11] or Google Hangouts on your computer and then record on a digital recorder (again, try Marantz).
- *Editing your audio files* is optional; you can always just upload the files as you recorded them. If you choose to clean them up, you can edit at the microscale (removing *um*, *uh*, and other audible pauses) or at the macroscale (e.g., removing the last five minutes of an interview). Many podcasters edit segments that they recorded at different times, putting them together to create a show. Audacity[12] and Apple's GarageBand[13] are two software packages that include many of the audio capabilities of a professional radio station and make editing simple.
- *Postproduction editing* sometimes includes running a noise-reduction program (to get rid of that annoying air-conditioner noise in the background) and sound compression (to even out the volume of sections that have been recorded at different times and places). The Levelator[14] is an excellent free tool that does compression and other dynamic adjustments.
- *Tagging the audio* is an important step that some people overlook or perform without taking due care. This step involves adding text-based information about the audio to make it easier for people to find. This information is what appears in the search engines and audio distribution sites such as iTunes. Your tags also display on listeners' iPod displays, so don't ignore or gloss over this step. If you are hosting your podcast on a blog, look for a plugin that allows you to automate this tagging when you post the file.
- *Hosting and distribution* are necessary to ensure that people can easily obtain your podcasts. Services such as Liberated Syndication[15] host the (sometimes very large) audio files and syndicate them to the distribution networks such as iTunes.

---

[11] skype.com

[12] audacity.sourceforge.net

[13] apple.com/ilife/garageband

[14] conversationsnetwork.org/levelator

[15] libsyn.com

- *Promotion* is essential to make sure that people find out about your podcasts. If you do interview shows (which are an easy way to get started and provide excellent content), make sure that you provide links to the show to all of the guests. Many people will help you promote a show that featured them. You will also want to network with other podcasters in your space, because very short on-air plugs cross-promoting other podcasts are common and a good way for people to build audiences. Don't forget to put links to your podcast on your website, in your email signature, and on your off-line materials including business cards and brochures. Also, you should tweet about every show and add a link to your Facebook page, as well as send out a news release alerting people to important shows.

- A *companion blog* is a key component used by nearly all podcasters to discuss the content of each show. An important reason for having a companion blog is that its text will be indexed by the search engines, driving more people to sign up for the podcast feed. A blog also allows the show's host to write a few paragraphs about the content of that particular show and to provide links to the blogs and websites of guests (so people can get a sense of a show's content prior to listening). Most organizations that use podcasting as a marketing tool also use the podcast blog as a place to move people into the sales process by providing links to the company site or to demonstrations or trial offers.

"You can be up and running with your new podcast in less than a month," says Wall. "The principles are all quite simple, but it takes a bit of time to figure out the various hardware and software elements. But the community is very helpful. Be sure to write up accurate show notes, including time codes. Listeners can find the content they want and you get some extra search engine juice."

Audio and video content on the web is still new for many marketers and communicators. But the potential to deliver information to buyers in fresh and unique ways is greater when you use a new medium. And while your competition is still trying to figure out that blogging thing, you can leverage your existing blog into the new worlds of audio and video and leave the competition way behind.

20

How to Use News Releases to Reach Buyers Directly

As the fascinating case studies from Chapter 7 show, the web has changed the rules for news releases. Buyers now read your news releases on Google, Yahoo!, and other search engines, on vertical market portals, and with RSS readers. Thus, smart marketing and PR professionals craft news releases to reach buyers directly, propelling books to number-one spots on best-seller lists, driving more web traffic, securing more donations, and selling more products. Again, this is not to suggest that mainstream media and media relations programs are no longer important. In most markets, mainstream media and the trade press remain vital. But your primary audience is no longer just a handful of journalists. Your audience is millions of people with Internet connections and access to search engines and RSS readers. So how do you get started with a direct-to-buyer news release program? Let's start by recalling the new rules of news releases from Chapter 7:

- Don't just send news releases when big news is happening; find good reasons to send them all the time.
- Instead of just targeting a handful of journalists, create news releases that appeal directly to your buyers.
- Write releases that are replete with keyword-rich copy.
- Include offers that compel consumers to respond to your release in some way.

- Place links in releases to deliver potential customers to landing pages on your website or to other valuable information published by your organization, such as online video.
- Optimize news release delivery for searching and browsing.
- Add social media tags for Technorati, Digg, StumbleUpon, and Delicious so your release will be found.
- Drive people into the sales process with news releases.

In this chapter, we'll use these rules to develop a news release strategy.

Developing Your News Release Strategy

The most important thing to think about as you begin a news release program is, once again, the need to write for your buyers. You should consider what you learned through the buyer persona research part of your marketing and PR plan (described in Chapter 11) and develop an editorial calendar for news releases based on what buyers need to know. Implementing a news release strategy to reach buyers directly is like publishing an online news service—you are providing your buyers with information they need to find your organization online and then learn more about you.

Part of thinking like a publisher is remembering the critical importance of content. "Everything is content-driven in public relations," says Brian Hennigan, marketing communications manager for dbaDIRECT, a data infrastructure management company. "I like using news releases to reach the market and my potential customers. With news releases, for a hundred bucks you can talk to the world." Hennigan supplements his news releases with longer and more detailed white papers to get dbaDIRECT ideas into the market. "I write the news releases like news stories," he says. "We look at the needs of the market and entrepreneurial trends as interesting, and we write to these trends."

As you make this fundamental change in how you do news releases, you will probably find yourself wondering, at first, what to write about. The rule of thumb is: Big news is great, but don't wait. Write about pretty much anything that your organization is doing.

- Have a new take on an old problem? Write a release.
- Serve a unique marketplace? Write a release.
- Have interesting information to share? Write a release.

- CEO speaking at a conference? Write a release.
- Win an award? Write a release.
- Add a product feature? Write a release.
- Win a new customer? Write a release.
- Publish a white paper? Write a release.
- Get out of bed this morning? Okay, maybe not—but now you're thinking the right way!

Publishing News Releases through a Distribution Service

The best way to publish news releases so they are seen by your buyers is to simultaneously post a release to your own website and send it to one of the news release wires. The benefit of using a news release distribution service is that your release will be sent to the online news services, including Yahoo!, Google, Bing, and many others. Many news release distribution services reach trade and industry websites as well. In fact, you can often reach hundreds of websites with a single news release. The significant benefit of this approach is that your release will be indexed by the news search engines and vertical market sites, and then when somebody does a search for a word or phrase contained in your release, *presto*, that potential customer finds you. As an added bonus, people who have requested alerts about your industry from sites that index news releases will get an alert that something important—your news release—is available.

There are a number of options for wire distribution of news releases. I've included some of the U.S. news release distribution services here. Similar services exist in other countries, such as CanadaNewsWire[1] serving the Canadian market News2U in Japan. Take a look at the various services and compare them yourself.

A Selection of the Larger U.S. News Release Distribution Services

- Business Wire: businesswire.com
- GlobeNewswire: globenewswire.com
- Marketwire: marketwire.com
- PR Newswire: prnewswire.com
- PRWeb: prweb.com

---

[1] newswire.ca

To get your news releases to appear on the online news services, including Google News, you just have to purchase a basic news release coverage area offered by a news release distribution service. Coverage is based on geographical distribution of your release to reporters. Because I am located in the Boston area, the cheapest distribution with some services for me is the Boston region. The services also have many value-added options for you to consider, such as national distribution. But what is important to know is that most news release distribution services include distribution to online media such as Google News in *any geographical distribution*. So as you make your choice, remember that when your purpose for sending news releases is to reach buyers via search engines and vertical sites, maximizing the newsroom and geographical reach offered by a service is less important than ensuring that your releases are included on major online news sites.

Reaching Even More Interested Buyers with RSS Feeds

Many news release distribution services also offer RSS (Really Simple Syndication) feeds of their news releases, which they make available to other sites, blogs, journalists, and individuals. This means that each time you publish a news release with the service, the news release is seen by potentially thousands of people who have subscribed to the RSS content feeds in your market category (as offered by the distribution service). So if you tag your release as being important for the automotive industry, your news release will be delivered to anyone (or any site) that has subscribed to the news release distribution service's automotive RSS feed. And online news services such as Google News have RSS feed capability, too, allowing people to receive feeds based on keywords and phrases. Each time your release includes a word or phrase of importance to someone who has saved it as part of their alerts, a link to your news releases will appear via email or RSS feed in near real time in the future.

Simultaneously Publishing Your News Releases to Your Website

Post your news releases to an appropriate and readily findable section of your website. Many organizations have a media room or press section of their website, which is ideal (see Chapter 21 for details on how to create your online newsroom). You should keep the news release live for as long as the content is appropriate, perhaps for years. This is very important because most of the online news sites do not maintain archives of news for more than a few months. If potential customers look for the content of your news release the week after it is distributed via a service, they will certainly find it on Google News and the others. But they won't find it if they do the search next year unless the release is on your own site as a permanent link so that it is indexed by Google.

The Importance of Links in Your News Releases

Particularly because your releases may be delivered by feeds or on news services and various sites other than your own, creating links from your news releases to content on your website is very important. These links, which might point to a specific offer or to a landing page with more information, allow your buyers to move from the news release to specific content on your website that will then drive them into the sales process, as we saw in the previous chapter.

However, there is another enormous benefit to including links in news releases. Each time your news release is posted on another site, such as an online news site, the inbound link from the online news site to your website helps to increase the search engine ranking of your site, because the search engines use inbound links as one of the important criteria for their page-ranking algorithms. So when your news release has a link to your site and it is indexed somewhere on the web, you actually increase the ranking of the pages on your site! Said another way, when your news release appears on a website somewhere and there is a link in your news release that points to a URL on your site, the search engines will increase the rankings of the page where the URL is pointing. Sending a news release that includes links increases your own website's search engine rankings.

Focus on the Keywords and Phrases Your Buyers Use

As I've suggested before, one thing successful publishers do that web marketers should emulate is to understand the audience first and then set about to satisfy their informational needs. A great way to start thinking like a publisher and to create news releases that drive action is to focus on your customers' problems and then create and deliver news releases accordingly. Use the words and phrases that your buyers use. Think about how the people you want to reach are searching, and develop news release content that includes those words and phrases. You can get the information you need to do so by thinking back to your buyer personas. Don't be egotistical and write only about your organization. What are your buyers' problems? What do they want to know? What words and phrases do they use to describe these problems? I know, I've said this already several times—that's because it is very important.

CruiseCompete.com,[2] cited by *Kiplinger* as one of the 25 best travel sites, helps people secure quotes for cruises from multiple travel agencies, based on the dates and ports specified. CruiseCompete.com is a great example of a company that uses news releases to reach people based on the phrases that their buyers are searching with. For example, during the lead-up to the holiday season, the company issued a news release via Market Wire with the headline "Cruise Lines Set Sail with Hot Holiday Vacation Prices." Importantly, part of an early sentence in the release, "some seven-night vacations can be booked for well under $1,000 per person, including Thanksgiving cruises, Christmas cruises, and New Year's cruises," included three critical phrases. Not only did this release's mention of "Thanksgiving cruises," "Christmas cruises," and "New Year's cruises" generate traffic from users searching on these common phrases but also it helped guide searchers into the sales cycle; each of the three phrases in the news release was hyperlinked to a purpose-built landing page on the CruiseCompete.com site that displayed the holiday cruise deals. Anyone who clicked on the "Christmas cruises" link was taken directly to deals for Christmas cruises.[3]

What makes this case so exciting is that at the time I was writing this, the CruiseCompete.com holiday cruise news release was at the top of the Google News search results for the phrases "Thanksgiving cruises," "Christmas cruises," and "New Year's cruises." More important, the bump that the links in the news release gave to the three landing pages helped those pages reach the top of the Google web search results lists. For example, the

---

[2] cruisecompete.com

[3] cruisecompete.com/specials/holiday/christmas_cruises/1

CruiseCompete.com landing page for the phrase "Christmas cruise" was ranked in the fourth position among 5,830,000 other hits on Google.

"We know that people have thought about traveling for the holidays," says Heidi M. Allison-Shane, a consultant working with CruiseCompete .com. "We use the news releases to communicate with consumers that now is the time to book, because there are dynamite prices and they will sell out." Allison-Shane makes sure that CruiseCompete includes the ideal phrases in each news release and that each release has appropriate links to the site. This strategy makes reaching potential customers a matter of "simply understanding what people are likely to be searching on and then linking them to the correct page on the site where we have the content that's relevant," she says. "We try to be useful with the right content and to be focused on what's relevant for our consumers and to provide the links that they need. This stuff is not difficult."

The CruiseCompete.com news release program produces results by increasing the Google rankings for the site. But the news releases also reach buyers directly as those buyers search on relevant phrases. "Each time we send a targeted news release, we see a spike in the web traffic on the site," Allison-Shane says.

As you craft your own phrases to use in your news releases, don't get trapped by your own jargon; think, speak, and write like your customers do. Though you may have a well-developed lexicon for your products and services, these words don't necessarily mean much to your potential customers. As you write news releases (or any other form of web content), focus on the words and phrases that your buyers use. As a search engine marketing tool, news releases are only as valuable as the keywords and phrases that are contained in them.

Include Appropriate Social Media Tags

Many (but not all) news release distribution services provide a way to include social media tags to make the news releases easy to find on services like Twitter, Facebook, Google+, Pinterest, Technorati, StumbleUpon, Digg, and Delicious. Use them! Social media tags make your releases much easier to find. For example, the Technorati search engine, which many people turn to for the latest blog posts from around the world in categories that interest them, also includes news release content. So if I check out the Marketing category on Technorati, I will see not only the latest blog posts that are tagged "Marketing" by the blogger but also any news releases that are tagged "Marketing" by the organization that issued the release. The key is that in an online world, you must do everything you can to ensure that your news releases are displayed and retrievable in as many relevant places as possible.

To make it easy to remember all the various tags and other features (such as associated photos and audio feeds) of a well-executed news release, Todd Defren, principal at SHIFT Communications, created a social media news release template.[4] "All news release content will ultimately wind up on the web," he says. "So why not put it out in such a way that makes it accessible to anybody who can use that content? Both traditional and new media journalists are used to working in a hyperlinked environment and are used to people providing context through social bookmarking sites such as Delicious and buttons to add to StumbleUpon and Digg. The template makes it easy to remember to do all of those things." Defren's template is an excellent tool to use as you develop your news releases because it helps you get the most out of all the available features that can make the release more useful and easier to find.

If It's Important Enough to Tell the Media, Tell Your Clients and Prospects, Too!

Many companies devote extensive resources to their PR and media relations programs. Often, the results of these efforts are buried in a difficult-to-find news section of the company website. Consider rewriting your news releases in an easy-to-read paragraph or two and making it a section of your email newsletter for clients and prospects. Or establish RSS feeds to deliver your news to anyone who's interested. And don't forget your employees—if they know about your news, they can be your greatest evangelists.

One of the most cost-effective ways to reach buyers is to look for ways to leverage the work you're already doing by repurposing content for other audiences. Too often, organizations spend tons of money on, say, a PR program that targets a handful of journalists but fails to communicate the same information to other constituents. Or a company's advertising program

---

[4] pr-squared.com/index.php/resources

designed to generate new sales may drive people to a website that doesn't match the message of the ads, resulting in lost interest. Sadly, failure to integrate sales, marketing, and communications—both online and off-line—will always result in lost opportunities. Happily, the web makes it a relatively simple task to integrate your news release program into your larger online strategy.

Here's one more thing that you may never have considered: Having a regular editorial calendar that includes a series of news releases also means your company is busy. When people go to your online media room and find a lack of news releases, they often assume that you are not moving forward or that you have nothing to contribute to the industry. In the new world of marketing, consistent, high-quality news release content brands a company or a nonprofit as a busy market player, an active expert in the industry, and a trusted resource to turn to.

21 Your Newsroom: A Front Door for Much More Than the Media

The online newsroom (sometimes called a press room, media room, or press page) is the part of your organization's website that you create specifically for the media. In some organizations, this section is simply a list of news releases with contact information for the organization's PR person. But many companies and nonprofits have elaborate newsrooms with a great deal of information available in many different formats: audio, video, photos, news releases, background information, financial data, and much more. A close cousin to the newsroom is the online investor relations room that many public companies maintain; however, I don't cover IR sites in this book.

Before I give you ideas on how to create a valuable newsroom of your own, I want you to consider something that is vitally important: All kinds of people visit your newsroom, not just journalists. Stop and really let that soak in for a moment. Your buyers are snooping around your organization by visiting the media pages on your website. Your current customers, partners, investors, suppliers, and employees all visit those pages. Why is that? Based on casual research I've done (I often speak about visitor statistics with employees who are responsible for their organizations' newsrooms), I'm convinced that when people want to know what's *current* about an organization, they go to a newsroom.

> Your newsroom is for your buyers, not just the media.

Visitors expect that the main pages of a website are basically static (i.e., they are not updated often), but they also expect that the news releases and media-targeted pages on a site will reveal the very latest about a company. For many companies, the news release section is one of the most frequently visited parts of the website. Check out your own website statistics; you may be amazed at how many visitors are already reading your news releases and other media pages online.

So I want you to do something that many traditional PR people think is nuts. I want you to design your newsroom for your *buyers*. By building a media room that targets buyers, you will not only enhance those pages as a powerful marketing tool but also *make a better media site for journalists*. I've reviewed hundreds of newsrooms, and the best ones are built with buyers in mind. This approach may sound a bit radical, but believe me, it works.

Your Newsroom as (Free) Search Engine Optimization

When news releases are posted on your site, search engine crawlers will find the content, index it, and rank it based on words, phrases, and other factors. Because news release pages update more often than any other part of a typical organization's website, search engine algorithms (tuned to pay attention to pages that update frequently) tend to rank news release pages among the highest on your site, driving traffic there first.

"There's no question that a well-organized media room often has higher search results and drives more traffic because of the way the search engines work," says Dee Rambeau, vice president of customer engagement at PR Newswire. "A news release dynamically builds out a new set of content in your newsroom, with each news release generating its own indexable page, which the search engines all capture. Google and the other search engines love fresh content that relates back to similar content on the other pages of the site. Aggressive companies take advantage of this by sending news releases frequently to get high rankings from the search engines. Frequency has a great deal to do with search engine rankings—if you do 10 news releases, that's great; 20 is better, and 100 is better still."

Best Practices for Newsrooms

The Kellogg Company—the the world's leading producer of cereal and second-largest producer of cookies, crackers, and savory snacks—uses their newsroom[1] for SEO purposes and as a tool to reach various audiences, including reporters and editors who cover the company.

"What we found through our research is that, more and more, our newsroom is extending beyond just media to other stakeholders," says Stephanie Slingerland, senior manager of corporate communications at Kellogg Company. "Anyone coming to the site, be it an investor, an NGO or other partner agency, or even a consumer—the newsroom is inviting for them to get the information which may be relevant."

Slingerland has strong partnerships with people who work in other departments at the company and who also provide information to the public. "Our investor relations team are having conversations and engagements with analysts and investors. So, from our partnership with that team, we know what those stakeholders might be looking for. Or, for example, our government-relations team are regularly engaging with government and non-governmental officials. Again, we have a strong partnership with them. We know what they're looking for and can make sure that they have what they might be looking for on our site. The same with our corporate social responsibility team, who engage with agencies and others as part of our philanthropic activities."

Based on what she learns about the needs of the news media and other stakeholders, Slingerland creates the right content, including news releases, fact sheets, news alerts, and more. "Since we are the folks that regularly engage with the media, we know what we're getting asked for over and over, like the fact sheet section," she says. "And we also know that many people want to know the latest news about the company, but they don't necessarily come to our newsroom every day. So that's why we created our news alerts section, so they opt in to be alerted whenever a new press release hits."

Kellogg Company has an interesting approach to feeding news to consumers through a consumer-facing site at Kelloggs.com (a different domain than the corporate site at KelloggCompany.com, which houses the newsroom). They use the MediaRoom service from PR Newswire to feed content to both sites. "We post everything for the media on KelloggCompany.com, knowing that consumers may land on this page but typically go to our Kelloggs.com branded site," Slingerland says. "We have the ability to choose when we issue a press release: If we feel that it would be relevant for our consumer audience, we feed it to our Kelloggs.com site as well." And when all that content hits both

---

[1] newsroom.kelloggcompany.com

sites in real-time, it is indexed by the search engines and will rise to the top positions.

A newsroom is an important part of any organization's website and a critical aspect of an effective media relations strategy. When done well, a newsroom will turn journalists who are just browsing into interested writers who will highlight your organization positively in their stories. And more important, a newsroom can move your buyers into and through the sales process, resulting in more business for your organization and contributing to meeting your organization's *real goals* of revenue and customer retention. I've noticed as I've checked out hundreds of newsrooms that most fail to deliver compelling content. Sure, they may look pretty, but often the design and graphics, not the content that journalists (and your buyers) require, are in the forefront. The following sections give you useful tips that will help your newsroom work as effectively as some of the best ones I've seen.

You Control the Content

One important consideration that many marketing and PR people overlook when considering the benefits of a newsroom is that *you control the content*, not your IT department, webmaster, or anyone else. The best practice idea here is for *you* to design your newsroom as a tool to reach buyers and journalists, and you don't need to take into consideration the rules for posting content that the rest of the organization's site may require. If you build this part of your site using a specialized newsroom content-management application, such as the MediaRoom[2] product from PR Newswire, you will control a corner of your organization's website that you can update whenever you like using simple tools, and you won't need to request help from anyone in other departments or locations. So start with your needs and the needs of your buyers and journalists, not the needs of those who own the other parts of your organization's website.

Start with a Needs Analysis

When designing a new newsroom (or planning an extensive redesign), start with a needs analysis. Before you just jump right into site aesthetics and the organization of news releases, take time to analyze how the site fits into your

---

[2] mediaroom.com

larger marketing, PR, and media relations strategy. Consider the buyer persona profiles you built as part of your marketing and PR plan. Talk with friendly journalists so you can understand what they need. Who are the potential users of the newsroom and what content will be valuable to them? When you have collected some information, build buyers' and journalists' needs into your newsroom. As you work toward starting your design, try to think a bit more like a publisher and less like a marketing and PR person. A publisher carefully identifies and defines target audiences and then develops the content required to meet the needs of each distinct demographic. Graphical elements, colors, fonts, and other visual manifestations of the site are also important but should take a back seat during the content-needs analysis process.

Optimize Your News Releases for Searching and for Browsing

The best newsrooms are built with the understanding that some people need to search for content and others are browsing. Many people already know what they are looking for—the latest release, perhaps, or the name of the CEO. They need answers to specific questions, and organizations must therefore optimize content so that it can be found, perhaps by including a search engine. The second way that people use content is to be told something that they do not already know and therefore couldn't think to ask. This is why browsability is also important; it allows users to discover useful information they didn't even know they were looking for. While many web-savvy marketers understand the importance of search engine optimization, they often forget that sites must be designed for browsing, too. Failing to do so is particularly unfortunate because the high traffic on news release pages comes partly from the many people who browse these pages as they conduct research.

You should deploy a navigational design in a way that provides valuable information visitors might not have thought to ask for. Consider including multiple browsing techniques. For instance, you can create different links to targeted releases for different buyer personas (maybe by vertical market or some other demographic factor appropriate to your organization). You might also organize the same releases by product (because some members of the media may be covering just one of your products in a review or story), by geography, or by market served. Most organizations simply list news releases in reverse-chronological order (the newest release is at the top of the page, and ones from last year are hidden away somewhere). While this is fine for the main news release page, you need to have additional navigation links so people can browse the releases. Don't forget that people may also need to print out news releases, so consider providing printer-friendly formats (e.g., PDF format as well as HTML).

Include Links to Your Social Networking Feeds

If you maintain social networks for use with the media, you need to make sure the feeds are easy to access from your newsroom. You'll want your Twitter ID prominently displayed on each page along with other feeds such as your YouTube or Vimeo channel for images, Flickr or Instagram for photos, Pinterest and so on. If you're creating a newsroom for a smaller organization, it's likely you'll be linking to the corporate social networking feeds. However, in larger organizations you might have a separate Twitter feed for the media relations team like the Kellogg Company does with their @KelloggCompany Twitter feed.

Create Background Information That Helps Journalists Write Stories

You should publish a set of background materials about your organization, sometimes called an online media kit or press kit, in an easy-to-find place in your newsroom. This kit should contain a lot of information, basically anything you think journalists might need to write about you and your products or services. Company history and timeline, executive biographies, investor profiles, board of advisors' or board of directors' bios, product and service information, information about analysts who cover your company, and links to recent media coverage will help your media kit save journalists time and tedious effort. Make this content easy to find and to browse with appropriate navigational links. A set of information organized around customers and how they use products and services offered by the company is another key component of a newsroom, and I rarely see it. Case studies in the customers' own words are particularly useful, not only for journalists but also for buyers. Remember, the easier you make a journalist's job, the more likely she is to write about your organization, particularly when she is on a tight deadline. I recall researching a feature story I was writing for *EContent* magazine called "On Message: The Market for Marketing-Specific Content Management." In the article, I was looking at companies and products that help marketers to organize information, and I knew the top players in the field and interviewed company executives for the article. But to round out the piece, I needed to include some newer niche companies. How did I choose the companies that made it in? You guessed it—the ones that made my job easiest by having an effective newsroom that helped me to instantly understand the company and its products.

Include Multimedia Content

Smart communicators make use of nontext content, such as photos, charts, graphs, audio feeds, and video clips, to inform site visitors and the media. Include executive photos, logo images, product photos, and other content that is ready (and preapproved) to be published or linked to by journalists. You should offer audio and video clips (such as parts of executive speeches or product demonstrations), photos, and logos in such a way that journalists can use them in their written stories, as well as on TV and radio shows. Again, you will find that many people besides journalists will access this, so include appropriate content for your buyer personas as well as for the media.

For an excellent example of the use of video, check out how INgage Networks[3] integrated video into the company's newsroom.

Include Detailed Product Specs and Other Valuable Data

Communicators who use newsrooms to offer valuable content are more likely to score the positive story. However, organizations often shy away from posting much of their best content because they deem it proprietary. On many sites, even information like detailed product specifications and price lists are available only through a direct connection with a PR contact or a lengthy registration form with approval mechanisms. Yet this is exactly the sort of content that, if freely available, would help convince journalists to write a story. All communicators and marketing professionals working at corporations, government agencies, or nonprofits struggle to decide what content is appropriate to post on their organizations' sites. However, with well-meaning executives who worry about

---

[3] ingagenetworks.com/newsroom.aspx

corporate image, legal departments with a reflexive tendency to say no, and salespeople who think it is easier to sell when they're the sole source of knowledge, it might be difficult to gain the necessary approvals to post proprietary content. But there is no doubt that the more valuable your media room's content looks to reporters and buyers, the more attractive your company will look to them as well.

If Appropriate, Go Global

The web has made reaching the world far easier, so when it is appropriate, the effort to create and offer local content to customers worldwide can help an organization better serve both local and global journalists. Many organizations, particularly those headquartered in the United States, make the mistake of including site content that reflects (and therefore has value for) only the home market. Basic approaches to get your site up to global standards might include offering case studies from customers in various countries or spec sheets describing products with local country standards (such as metric measurements or local regulatory compliance). Sometimes the little things make a difference. For example, don't forget that the rest of the world uses standard A4 paper instead of the U.S. letter size, so having fact sheets and other materials that print properly on both formats is useful to users outside the United States. Providing content in local languages can also help show the global aspect of your business, though this need not mean a wholesale translation of your entire newsroom. A simple web landing page with basic information in the local language, a few news releases, a case study or two, and appropriate local contact information will often suffice.

Provide Content for All Levels of Media Understanding

To be effective, communicators at many organizations specifically design media room content that supports journalists' level of knowledge of your organization. Some journalists may never have written about your company before; they need the basics spelled out in easy-to-understand language. In other cases, a reporter or analyst may have been covering the company for years, enjoy personal relationships with the executives, and know a great deal about what's going on with you, your competitors, and your market. You need content for this person, too; he may want to compare your offerings, and he therefore needs detailed company information, lists of features and benefits, and stories about your customers. Of course, all reporters need easy navigation directly to content so they get what they need quickly. In my experience, the vast majority of newsrooms are little more than online brochures with a bunch of news releases. Don't let the opportunities that the web offers pass your newsroom by. Help journalists along the path to their keyboards by offering content directly linked to their various levels of understanding.

List Executive Appearances, Conferences, and Tradeshow Participation

One of the best ways to positively influence journalists is to visit with them in person. Many journalists attend tradeshows, conferences, and other events on a regular basis and use that time to meet with representatives of companies that they may consider writing about. The best way to get your organization on journalists' calendars is to make certain that they know where your executives will be appearing. List all appropriate public speaking appearances, tradeshow and conference participation, and other events in a separate calendar section in your newsroom. Make certain to list all appropriate future events, and remember to include any international events. Keep the older listings up for at least a few months after the events to show that you are in demand as experts in your field, but be sure to keep the list up to date. Don't forget that even this information is not just for the media. Even if they do not attend industry events, your buyers will see that your company is active and that your executives are in demand as speakers and presenters; this adds to your corporate credibility and your image as an industry leader.

Include Calls to Action for Journalists

It is a great idea to include special offers for the media. Perhaps the simplest thing to offer is an executive interview. But why not include a trial or demonstration offer of some kind, where journalists get to test your offerings, attend your events, or in some way experience what your organization does? You can even create a landing page specifically for journalists with a registration form and special offers. Include this link within news releases and other pages in the newsroom to drive interested journalists to the landing page.

Embrace Bloggers as You Do Traditional Journalists

Bloggers who cover your company visit your newsroom. Encourage them by responding to inquiries quickly, by including bloggers in your news release distribution email list, and by granting them interviews with executives upon request. The fact is that bloggers are influential, and they want to be treated with the same respect as traditional journalists. It's to your advantage to do so.

Avoid Jargon, Acronyms, and Industry-Speak

I scan a bunch of news releases in an average week. Some releases are sent directly to me from companies that want me to write about them in a magazine article, an upcoming book, or my blog, and others I find by checking out newsrooms. I visit many newsrooms in an average month and read the other content available as well as news releases. Unfortunately, most newsrooms are chock-full of jargon, three-letter acronyms that I don't understand, and other egocentric nonsense. I'm interested in what companies are up to, but I'm just too busy to decipher gobbledygook. I normally give a news release 10 seconds to catch my attention, but the surest way to get me to delete a release in frustration is to write in a way that I just can't understand. If your mother doesn't understand your news, a journalist probably won't, either.

A Newsroom to Reach Journalists, Customers, and Bloggers

One of the finest examples I've seen of an online newsroom comes from Tourism Whistler, the member-based marketing and sales organization representing Canadian leisure and meeting destination Whistler. The Tourism Whistler newsroom[4] incorporates each and every best practice outlined in this chapter. What struck me about the Tourism Whistler media room is how much it resembles a media site like CNN, the BBC, or the *New York Times*, with text-based content, video, images, and social network links. It turns out that that's no coincidence. Both the organization's manager of corporate communications and CEO come from a media background.

---

[4] media.whistler.com

The content on the site is simple to browse, and using their Media Marmot Search Tool,[5] also easy to search based on keywords and phrases. (The Media Marmot was named in honor of the hoary marmot, from which Whistler earned its name, due to the whistling sound made by these furry residents.) There's an extensive multimedia library accessible with no registration, including real-time photos and videos. For example, media can access photos of the recent Whistler snowfall. There's also a B-roll video gallery that allows media outlets to preview highlights of Tourism Whistler's significant collection of B-roll footage, which they can then request to use.

One aspect of the newsroom I particularly like are the Whistler Story Starters, which provide journalists with story ideas about Whistler's role in Canadian history, in the 2010 Winter Olympic Games (some events were held in Whistler), and in the area's role as one of the world's top resort destinations.

The Tourism Whistler newsroom is used extensively by the media, including writers, broadcasters, and bloggers. As the Tourism Whistler example shows, providing a great newsroom with lots of content proves useful to journalists. For most organizations, the amount of money spent to create a newsroom will be far less than the quantifiable benefit derived from it.

Really Simple Marketing: The Importance of RSS Feeds in Your Newsroom

To provide alternative content routes, many organizations use digital delivery methods, including email newsletters for journalists and bloggers and RSS feeds, as part of their newsrooms; this pushes content directly to the media and other interested people. Smart organizations are using RSS (Really Simple Syndication) to easily update prospects, customers, investors, and the media, but too few organizations are using this simple marketing technique for sharing valuable information.

The RSS feeds can (and should) be added to most parts of your website. But because they are essentially subscription mechanisms to regularly updated content, many organizations have the RSS subscription page as part of the newsroom and use it as a primary way to deliver news release content. Companies such as Microsoft, IBM, and Intel syndicate information

---

[5] media.whistler.com/search

via RSS feeds to reach specific external audiences such as the media, Wall Street analysts, customers, partners, distributors, and resellers. For example, Intel[6] offers a suite of feeds that includes Intel Products, Intel Press Room, Intel Investor Relations, Software at Intel, Networking and Communications, Intel Reseller Center, and IT@Intel. It also offers country-specific RSS feeds from Brazil, China, France, Germany, Italy, Japan, Russia, and others. How cool is it that interested people subscribe to just-right corporate information from Intel in the same way that they subscribe to media feeds from major newspaper and magazine sites and those of independent bloggers? This is just another example of how the main currency of online marketing is excellent content delivered in the way that people demand.

The newsroom is a place where many people congregate, not just journalists. It is one place on your organization's website that *you can control*, without interference, approval processes, and IT support, so it presents a terrific opportunity for marketing and PR people to get content out into the marketplace. On the web, success equals content. And one of the easiest ways to get content into the market is via a newsroom with RSS feeds.

---

[6] intel.com/intel/rss.htm

The New Rules for Reaching the Media

A s the web has made communicating with reporters and editors extremely easy, breaking through using the online methods everyone else uses has become increasingly difficult. These days, you can find the email addresses of reporters in seconds, either through commercial services that sell subscriptions to their databases of thousands of journalists or simply by using a search engine. Unfortunately, way too many PR people are spamming journalists with unsolicited and unrelenting commercial messages in the form of news releases and untargeted broadcast pitches. I hate to say it, but among the many journalists I speak with, the PR profession has become synonymous with spammers. For years, PR people have been shotgun-blasting news releases and blind pitches to hundreds (or even thousands) of journalists at a time—without giving any thought to what each reporter actually covers—just because the media databases the PR people subscribe to make it so darn simple to do.

> Barraging large groups of journalists with indiscriminate PR materials is not a good strategy to get reporters and editors to pay attention to you.

Nontargeted, Broadcast Pitches Are Spam

As I've said, I get dozens of news releases, pitches, and announcements from PR agency staffers and corporate communications people every week. Like all journalists, my email address is available in many places: in the articles I write, on my blog, in my books, and in the column I write for the *Huffington Post*. That easy availability means that my address has also been added to various databases and lists of journalists. Unfortunately, my email address also gets added (without my permission) to many press lists that PR agencies and companies compile and maintain; whenever they have a new announcement, no matter what the subject, I'm part of the broadcast message. *Ugh*. The PR spam approach simply doesn't work. Worse, it brands your organization as one of the bad guys.

Okay, that's the depressing news. The good news is that there are effective new rules that work very well to get your messages into the hands (and onto the screens) of reporters so they will be more likely to write about you. Don't forget that reporters are always looking for interesting companies, products, and ideas to write about. They want to find you. If you have great content on your website and your online media room, *reporters will find you* via search engines.

Try to think about reaching journalists with ways that aren't just one-way spam. Pay attention to what individual reporters write about by reading their stories (and, better yet, their blogs) and write specific and targeted pitches crafted especially for them. Or start a real relationship with reporters by commenting on their blogs, interacting with them on Twitter, or sending them information that is not just a blatant pitch for your company. Become part of their network of sources, rather than simply a shill for one company's message. If you or someone in your organization writes a blog in the market category that a reporter covers, let him know about it, because what you blog about may become prime fodder for the reporter's future stories. Don't forget to pitch bloggers. Not only does a mention in a widely read blog reach your buyers but also reporters and editors read these blogs for story ideas and to understand early market trends.

The New Rules of Media Relations

The web has changed the rules. If you're still following the traditional PR techniques, I'm sure you're finding that they are much less effective. To be much more successful, consider and use the new rules of media relations:

- Nontargeted, broadcast pitches are spam.
- News releases sent to reporters in subject areas they do not cover are spam.
- Reporters who don't know you yet are looking for organizations like yours and products like yours—make sure they will find you on sites such as Google and Technorati.
- If you blog, reporters who cover the space will find you.
- Pitch bloggers, because being covered in important blogs will get you noticed by mainstream media.
- When was the last news release you sent? Make sure your organization is busy.
- Journalists want a great online media room.
- Include video and photos in your online media room.
- Some (but not all) reporters love RSS feeds.
- Personal relationships with reporters are important.
- Don't tell journalists what your product does. Tell them how you solve customer problems.
- Follow journalists on Twitter to learn what interests them.
- Does the reporter have a blog? Read it. Comment on it. Before you pitch, read (or listen to or watch) the publication (or radio program or TV show) you'll be pitching to.
- Once you know what a reporter is interested in, send her an individualized pitch crafted especially for her needs.

Blogs and Media Relations

Getting your organization visible on blogs is an increasingly important way not only to reach your buyers but also to reach the mainstream media that cover your industry, because reporters and editors read blogs for story ideas. Treat influential bloggers exactly as you treat influential reporters: Read their stuff, and send them specifically targeted information that might be useful to them. Offer them interviews with your executives and demonstrations or samples of your products. Offer to take them to lunch.

"For a company or product that sells into a niche, you'll never get noticed by editors at major publications like the *Wall Street Journal*, but you will get niche bloggers to be interested in you," says Larry Schwartz, president of Newstex,[1] a company that syndicates blogs for distribution to millions of

---

[1] newstex.com

people in corporations, financial institutions, and government agencies. "For example, if you are in the consumer technology business, getting your product mentioned in Gizmodo[2] and getting a link back to your site from Gizmodo are probably more important than even a mention in the *Wall Street Journal*. Increasingly, the way for people to find out about products is through blogs, and you often get a link to your website, too. It used to be that the moment of truth was when somebody went to the store to find your product. Now the moment of truth is a link to your site from a blog."

Pitching influential bloggers as you would pitch mainstream media is an important way to get noticed in the crowded marketplace of ideas. But even more effective is having your own blog so that bloggers and reporters find you. "Blogging gives me a place in the media community to stand out," says John Blossom, president of Shore Communications Inc.,[3] a research and analysis company. Blossom has been blogging since 2003 and writes about enterprise publishing and media markets. "In ways that I didn't expect, my blog has allowed me to become a bit of a media personality. I've been picked up by some big bloggers, and that makes me aware that blogging is a terrific way to get exposure, because the rate of pickup and amplification is remarkable. The press reads my blog and reaches out to me for quotes. Sometimes I'm quoted in the media by a reporter who doesn't even speak with me. For example, a reporter from the *Financial Times* recently picked up a quote and used it in a story—based on my blog alone."

How Blog Mentions Drive Mainstream Media Stories

Promoting a valuable, one-of-a-kind object for sale at the best price requires a seller to be clever and utilize both traditional public relations and new media.

This study in extreme cleverness begins with Richard Jurek. Jurek is a marketing and communication professional, as well as a space enthusiast and collector. When he decided to part with a few unique and treasured items from his collection, Jurek put his 20 years of professional experience to work. He knew that one of his items needed special attention.

That item was the unofficial fourth crewmate of *Apollo 12*.

---

[2] gizmodo.com

[3] shore.com

In a prank of lunar proportions, a vintage November 1969 color calendar photo of *Playboy* Playmate Miss August 1967, DeDe Lind, was stowed away in the *Apollo 12* command module Yankee Clipper during its November 1969 voyage to the moon.

The photo was affixed to a cardboard cue card and, unbeknownst to the crew, secreted onboard their spacecraft. The iconic piece of 1960s pop culture made the 475,000-mile round-trip to the moon and back and still retains the Velcro strips used to affix it to inside the spacecraft for easy viewing.

Jurek acquired the item directly from *Apollo 12* astronaut Richard Gordon. "This is an absolutely singular item, unique in the space-collecting world," Jurek says. "But it also has tremendous crossover appeal. I figured that DeDe would appeal not only to space collectors but collectors of 1970s pop culture, because *Playboy* was at its peak in 1970s America. There are also collectors of erotica and collectors of *Playboy* items. So it appeals to a lot of audiences."

Jurek knew that he wanted to sell DeDe through a recognized auction house, and he had narrowed the choice down to a handful. "I selected RRAuction for the sale because the auction house has a phenomenal Internet and social media platform, and they leverage it in their marketing," he says.

Working in the auction business is an incredibly old profession, having been around, well, almost as long as the so-called oldest profession. The idea that you can apply new forms of marketing to an ancient business is fascinating to me, and I wanted to learn more.

I spoke with Bobby Livingston, an auctioneer with a traditional PR background. Livingston is vice president of sales and marketing at RRAuction. He worked with Jurek to write the catalog description for the item and promote the auction itself.

"The Apollo 12 calendar has a great story," Livingston says. "It has a bunch of things going for it: It's Apollo, it's flown, and it's cheesecake, so it's easy to understand and easily translates around the world. It brings back the 1969 time frame. It's just a remarkable piece."

Livingston worked with Mike Graff of the Investor Relations Group in New York City to craft a press release and get it directly to bloggers who write about current events and technology. Graff also made follow-up phone calls. Very quickly, sites like Gawker, Nerdist, and io9 picked up on the story.

"When Gizmodo talked about the auction, suddenly we got 20,000 visitors," Livingston says. "We got 40 new auction registrations. On the best day, we [typically] do 7 to 10 registrations. Then we got 30 the next day. Well, this is all coming from viral and new media."

Soon, the international media got news of DeDe from the blogs. Stories appeared in Australia, Brazil, France, China, Japan, and a dozen other countries. Large outlets like BBC, CNN, the Discovery Channel, the *Sun, Daily Mail,* UPI, *Toronto Star,* and *Time* wrote about the Apollo Playmate stowaway. Even the Playboy Satellite Radio Channel and website got in on the fun.

As Livingston was working the media, Jurek was helping things along by contacting appropriate bloggers via social networking. "Every time I would see an article, I would push it out using appropriate hashtags and try for cross-over appeal," Jurek says. The strategy was to target related audiences, so Jurek tagged his tweets with things like #playboy, #photography, #space, #NASA, #auction, #apollo, #moon, #porn, and more. "I wanted to reach not only space collectors but also *Playboy* folks or, hell, even pornography people!"

Jurek says many tweets came from women who run their own webcam businesses and have thousands of followers. "Others were tweeting about space porn and moon porn and so on," he says. "It's hilarious, but I viewed DeDe as perfect for social media and the Internet. Because porn is a huge business on the Internet, and so are collectibles, and so is history. It was right in the center of all of that, and people were picking up on it."

The story even made "Weekend Update with Seth Myers" on *Saturday Night Live.* I gotta say, I've worked in and around PR for 20 years, and this is the first time I've known anyone who's made "Weekend Update"!

Jurek says he's learned some valuable lessons from this marketing effort. "Content drives marketing," he says. "DeDe, from a content perspective, is perfect. She has appeal not just as a moon-flown artifact for space geeks like me but for collectors of Americana, collectors of erotica, and collectors of unique niche pop culture items. Once you have the content, it is connecting it with the right audience, making sure the pitch is real and right on."

All of these efforts have driven large volumes of traffic to the RRAuction site. Visitors were up 350 percent over the previous month, according to data from Alexa. The DeDe Lind item received 30 bids and sold to a high bidder at $17,511.

"DeDe realized phenomenal results," Jurek says. "From a marketing perspective, she also achieved the goal because she drove lots of traffic to the auction. So much so that DeDe, while beating the estimate on where she would sell, also helped many, many other lots realize record results. The knock-off effect of the DeDe media coverage expanded the pool of global bidders and collectors of this material by a dramatic amount, and bidding was healthy across all lots."

Launching Ideas with the U.S. Air Force

The websites of the U.S. Air Force are chock-full of photos, video, and articles written by Air Force Public Affairs officers, all serving to provide the media with information they need to craft a story. These officers don't sit around all day writing press releases and pitching the media with story ideas. Rather, they publish information themselves, information that generates interest from reporters.

"Instead of pushing things out, people are finding us and our information," says Captain Nathan Broshear, director of public affairs at 12th Air Force (Air Forces Southern), the Air Force component to U.S. Southern Command and based at Davis-Monthan Air Force Base in Tucson, Arizona. Broshear is no stranger to working with mainstream media representatives, having previously managed hundreds of Iraq- and Afghanistan-based reporters in that high-pressure war zone environment.

"People are finding our websites to be valuable. For example, many reporters are currently interested in the Predator, Global Hawk, and Reaper systems, our unmanned aerial vehicles. And when they see the pages on our site about Predator and Reaper, then they know whom to contact."

For example, Technical Sergeant Eric Petosky, who works with Broshear in public affairs, wrote a story called "Global Hawk Flying Environmental Mapping Missions in Latin America, Caribbean,"[4] which he posted on the site with photos.[5] When a reporter becomes interested in a system like the Global Hawk, he or she can find the information on the site. "The Air Force is a big organization, and if a reporter goes to the Pentagon, it is hard to find the right person. We write stories so reporters can envision what their angle might look like." And together with the stories, photos, and videos is the necessary contact information for getting in touch with the appropriate Air Force Public Affairs staff member.

---

[4] www.12af.acc.af.mil/news/story.asp?id=123147613
[5] www.12af.acc.af.mil/photos/index.asp

The published information about unmanned aerial systems proved valuable when *60 Minutes*, the weekly CBS television magazine, became interested in the story. Broshear teamed with Captain Brooke Brander, chief of public affairs at Creech Air Force Base in Nevada (where the pilots of the unmanned systems are based), to help lay the groundwork for the story. They worked with *60 Minutes* producers for more than five months. "Drones: America's New Air Force" aired on *60 Minutes*, with Lara Logan reporting on the increasing use of drones in the battlefield.

Another success story from Broshear's use of online content to help reporters involves Operation New Horizons in Guyana. Operation New Horizons is part of an Air Force program to build infrastructure, partnerships, and relationships in other countries. "The Air Force is building a school and a clinic while providing free medical care for about 100,000 people," Broshear says. "We partner with nongovernmental organizations to make certain the local school, clinics, and doctors have what they need to continue providing services even after U.S. military members depart."

To get the story out to both the local community in Guyana and people back in the United States, Broshear works with those on the ground to create content reporters can draw from to craft their stories—without the need for constant contact from public affairs staff. "We post photos onto Flickr[6] and have a Facebook page[7] and a blog[8] written by people on the ground. And what's interesting is that the blogs get three times more traffic than our main pages. The newspapers in the local communities are pulling photographs from the sites. After we introduce the projects and key military personalities to the local media the first time through a press release or visit to the construction sites, we don't need to do anything, because the media are pulling information from the blog that we created."

As you know if you've read this far, the importance of creating valuable content (photos, video, news stories) and posting it on your site is the theme of this book. When you create that content, you reach people who are looking for what you have to offer. Broshear reminds us how sometimes those people are members of the mainstream media, and great content can serve as the catalyst to getting the coverage your organization desires. "Here in U.S. Air Force Public Affairs, we're not launching missiles," he says.

---

[6] flickr.com/photos/newhorizonsguyana
[7] facebook.com/pages/New-Horizons-Guyana/47224824949
[8] newhorizonsguyana.blogspot.com

"We're launching ideas." And those ideas lead to major stories in top-tier media.

How to Pitch the Media

As marketers know, having your company, product, or executive appear in an appropriate publication is great marketing. That's why billions of dollars are spent on PR each year (though much of it's wasted, I'm afraid). When your organization appears in a story, not only do you reach the publication's audience directly but also you can point your prospects to the piece later, using reprints or web links. Media coverage means legitimacy. As I've said, broadcast spamming of the media doesn't work so well and can actually be harmful to your brand. But sometimes you really want to target a specific publication (your hometown paper, perhaps). So what should you do?

- *Target one reporter at a time:* Taking the time to read a publication and then crafting a unique pitch to a particular journalist can work wonders. Mention a specific article he wrote, and then explain why your company or product would be interesting for the journalist to look at. Make certain to target the subject line of the email to help ensure that it gets opened. For example, I recall getting a perfectly positioned pitch crafted especially for me from a company that provides a web-based sales-lead qualification and management system. The PR person had read my blog and knew what I was interested in, so I emailed back within minutes to set up an interview with the company's CEO.
- *Help the journalist to understand the big picture:* Often it's difficult to understand how some product or service or organization actually fits into a wider trend. You make a journalist's job much easier if you describe the big picture of why your particular product or service is interesting. Often this helps you get mentioned in the reporter's future articles or columns about trends in your space.
- *Explain how customers use your product or work with your organization:* Reporters hear hundreds of pitches from company spokespeople about how products work. But it's much more useful to hear about a product in action from someone who actually uses it. If you can set up interviews with customers or provide written case studies of your products or services, it will be much easier for journalists to write about your company.

- *Don't send email attachments unless asked:* These days, it is a rare journalist indeed who opens an unexpected email attachment, even from a recognized company. Yet many PR people still distribute news releases as email attachments. Don't do it. Send plain-text emails instead. If you're asked for other information, you can follow up with attachments, but be sure to clearly reference in the email what you're sending and why, so the journalist will remember asking for it.

- *Follow up promptly with potential contacts:* Recently I agreed to interview a senior executive at a large company. An eager PR person set it up, and we agreed on date and time. But I never got the promised follow-up information via email, which was supposed to include the telephone number to reach the executive. Needless to say, the interview didn't happen. Make certain you follow up as promised.

- *Don't forget, it's a two-way street—journalists need you to pitch them!* The bottom line is that reporters want to know what you have to say. It is unfortunate that the spam problem in PR is as big as it is, because it makes journalists' jobs more difficult.

As an illustration of this last point, a company executive I met at a conference made a comment on a new trend that gave me a brilliant idea for a magazine article I was working on. I was delighted because it made my life easier. Thinking of subjects is hard work, and I need all the help I can get. The executive's company fit in perfectly with the column idea, and I used his product as the example of the trend he told me about. Without the conversation, the story would never have been written—but a straight product pitch wouldn't have worked. We reporters need smart ideas to do our job. Please.

"The single most effective thing PR people do is read what I write and send me personalized, smart pitches for stories that I am actually likely to write," says Peter J. Howe, a business reporter for the *Boston Globe*. Howe has been at the *Globe* for 20 years and has covered telecommunications, the Internet, energy, and, most recently, airline companies. Howe prefers to be pitched by email, with a subject line that helps him know it's not spam. "'PR pitch for *Boston Globe* Reporter Peter Howe' is actually a very effective way to get my attention. If you're getting literally four or five hundred emails a day like I am, cute subject lines aren't going to work and in fact will likely appear to be spam."

Howe's biggest beef with how PR people operate is that so many have no idea what he writes about before they send him a pitch. "If you simply put 'Boston Globe Peter Howe' into a Google.com/news search and read the first 10 things that pop up, you would have done more work than 98 percent of the PR people who pitch me," he says. "It's maddening how many people in PR have absolutely no sense of the difference between what the *Boston Globe* covers and what, say, *Network World* or *RCR Wireless News* or the *Nitwitville Weekly News* covers. And I don't mean to sound like a whining diva; the bigger issue is that if you're not figuring out what I cover and how before you pitch me, you are really wasting your own time."

Howe also encourages people to try to think big. "If you have a small thing to pitch, pitch it. But try to also think of the bigger story that it can fit into, a page-one or a Sunday section front story," he says. "That could even wind up meaning your company is mentioned alongside three or four of your competitors, but wouldn't you rather be mentioned in a page-one story than in a 120-word news brief?"

There is no doubt that mainstream media are still vital as a channel for your buyers to learn about your products. Besides all the people who will see your company, product, or executive's name, a mention in a major publication lends you legitimacy. Reporters have a job to do, and they need the help that PR people can provide to them. But the rules have changed. To get noticed, you need to be smart about how you tell your story on the web—and about how you tell your story to journalists.

23 Newsjacking Your Way into the Media

S hortly after halftime during Super Bowl XLVII on February 3, 2013, the Mercedes-Benz Superdome in New Orleans suffered a power outage causing half of the lights to go dark and play to be suspended for some 35 minutes. It took just seconds for people to start talking about #BlackoutBowl on Twitter and other social networks. Within a few minutes, Oreo, a popular sandwich cookie, tweeted from @Oreo, "Power out? No problem," with a photo of an Oreo cookie on a table in a dark room with the caption "You can still dunk in the dark." Some 14,000 people re-tweeted in real-time and over the next few hours, hundreds of mainstream news outlets and bloggers including CNN, NBC, CNET, and *Forbes* talked up the tweet.

Newsjacking.

As hundreds of millions of people pondered the power disruption, Oreo seized the moment in real-time and injected their brand into the most talked about news story at that time. As a result of a single tweet that took only several minutes to create, millions of people were exposed to the Oreo brand. Compare this to the traditional approach of paying a reported $3.7 million for 30 seconds of television airtime plus the creative and production costs to make a 30 second spot, which was how most brands chose to get noticed.

As we'll see in this chapter, this newsjacking from Oreo succeeded because it was very fast to market, it was witty and fun, it was non-controversial, and it tied back to the brand and its messages.

It's not just consumer brands that newsjack. On January 3, 2012, President Obama joined the social photo-sharing service Instagram, using the ID @BarackObama.

The timing of Obama joining Instagram is fascinating; the sign-up came on the exact same day as the Republican presidential candidates' Iowa Caucus.

President Obama newsjacked the Republican candidates for president!

The Republican candidates had campaigned in Iowa for months, spending tons of money and loads of time (the Iowa Caucus gives the first indication of who might emerge as the challenger to the incumbent in the general election that November). The media, eager to spot a Republican front-runner in the 2012 race, turned out in force.

Obama joining Instagram became big news that day. By attracting the attention of the world's media to the new presidential Instagram feed, the Obama campaign stole a bit of light away from the Republicans and onto their own reelection efforts.

The Obama campaign proved to be newsjacking masters, employing this technique several times during the campaign. For example, "Super Tuesday" (March 7, 2012) was the biggest day of the Republican primary season. But it was also the day President Obama chose to hold his first solo news conference from the White House since October 6, 2011.[1]

President Obama and his advisors' choice to answer journalists' questions on Super Tuesday, when voters in 10 U.S. states were casting their ballots in the Republican primaries, is a classic example of political newsjacking. The entire Republican primary season was a referendum on the President, so when he conducted a news conference from the White House, with all its symbolic trappings of power, the media covered his comments in conjunction with the stories of the Republican challengers. And, when the most delegates were awarded to determine Obama's challenger, the Super Tuesday winners had to share the top story position with the President in online news stories, the evening's television and radio broadcasts, and the next day's newspaper articles.

But newsjacking isn't just for U.S. presidential candidates. This technique is an ideal way for you to generate attention for your business too.

---

[1] whitehouse.gov/photos-and-video/video/2012/03/06/president-obama-holds-news-conference

Journalists Are Looking for What You Know

The real-time web has opened a tremendous opportunity for anyone to inject ideas into a breaking news story and generate tons of media coverage. I've been a marketer for two decades, and I have never seen a technique as powerful. But newsjacking requires speed-to-market that most organizations reserve only for crisis communications. We'll be covering the basics of newsjacking in this chapter, but if you want to learn even more, you can check out my book, *Newsjacking: How to Inject your Ideas into a Breaking News Story and Generate Tons of Media Coverage.*[2]

As journalists scramble to cover breaking news, the basic facts of the story are often easy to find. That's what goes in the first paragraph of any news story. The challenge for reporters is to get background information that rounds out the basic facts, or the details that appear in subsequent paragraphs. If they're lucky, journalists also find unique story angles that competitive media are not yet reporting.

That's what makes newsjacking possible. Reporters are actually looking for additional information for their stories, and they're doing it by searching Google and the other search engines, as well as Twitter and other social networks.

If you have a legitimate tie to a breaking news story and you react in real-time—by providing additional content in a blog post, tweet, video, or media alert—journalists may find you while they are researching material for their story.

Newsjacking opportunities can turn up in unlikely places. But you've got to be quick when the opportunity arises.

Remember the tabloid item about a naked Prince Harry in Vegas, first published by TMZ?[3] It was one of the most searched and discussed cell phone photos of all time. Lots of marketers tried to newsjack the stories of the Vegas romp. While most attempts went unnoticed, several were highly successful.

For example, soon after the photos appeared, Unilever-owned Lynx Men's Deodorant responded with a parody of the World War II UK Government "Keep Calm and Carry On" posters. Their version used the line, "Sorry Harry

---

[2] newsjacking.com

[3] tmz.com/2012/08/21/prince-harry-naked-photos-nude-vegas-hotel-party

if it had anything to do with us." Many people talked about the ads in social networks, and the UK media wrote stories—all generating positive buzz for Lynx Men's Deodorant.

Likewise, the scene of the Prince Harry photo incident was the luxurious Encore Wynn Hotel. In what was another very clever newsjack of the story, owner Steve Wynn publicly waived the hotel bill (we're talking tens of thousands of dollars), which got the Encore Wynn into a stunning 3,657 stories by my Google News count. Stories like the one appearing in the UK's *Daily Mail*, "Living like a king: Prince Harry's £30,000 hotel bill 'waived' by Vegas billionaire,"[4] were essentially huge, free advertisements for the hotel. Such stories often came with descriptions and photos of the Encore Wynn and its royal suite.

This is a perfect example of newsjacking success. For the price of waiving a few hotel nights, the Wynn gets mentioned in thousands of stories. How cool is that?

This isn't the first time that representatives from the Wynn Hotel have successfully newsjacked a story. They also scored thousands of press mentions when they banned infamous party girl Paris Hilton from their properties after she was arrested for cocaine possession. So as the media reported on Hilton's arrest, many also mentioned that she had been banned from the Wynn.

Get Your Take on the News into the Marketplace of Ideas

Your goal with newsjacking is to get your take on a breaking news story in front of journalists at the moment they are looking for additional information to put in their stories. There are a number of ways to do that, with the techniques falling into two categories. The first category relies on journalists searching online for interesting story angles. Here, your job is to create the content they will find. The other category is to quickly push your message to the media directly.

Let's look first at the search-based techniques. Here are some of the ways you can make your message stand out.

---

[4] dailymail.co.uk/travel/article-2192974/Prince-Harrys-Las-Vegas-hotel-waived-billionaire-resort-owner.html

Blog It and Post It to Your Online Media Room

Google, Bing, and other search engines now index in real-time, which means that your blog post or update to your online media room will instantly appear in search results. This capability allows journalists working on a fast-moving story to find your post. The beauty of this technique is that reporters are looking for you by searching for keywords and phrases of the moment as they write their stories. Many journalists also use Google Alerts, which email them whenever certain keywords and phrases appear in blogs or on websites. To get found in this way, as reporters are looking for experts, you've got to post your take on a story right now. Not tomorrow. Not this afternoon. Now. Make sure to feature appropriate keywords and phrases that journalists are likely to enter, and write your headline so it clearly shows reporters that you have a fresh and compelling take on the story.

Send a Real-Time Media Alert

A media alert is similar to a news release, but designed to provide reporters with specific information as they write about breaking news (see Chapter 20 for more information about creating and publishing news releases). To ensure it gets wide exposure, you'll want to publish your media alert quickly both in your online media room as well as through a press-release distribution service. Services like PR Newswire, Business Wire, and PRWeb are available in many countries and languages.

Harness the Power of the Podium

If you or the executives in your organization have an opportunity to deliver a speech at a well-timed live event, this can be the perfect opportunity to add your take to breaking news. Politicians who have reporters hanging on their every word do this all the time. By dropping a reference in a speech or mentioning details to reporters afterward, the pols are able to elbow their way into stories that would not otherwise mention them.

Live-Stream It

If your company is in the thick of a story, another great way to get your information out there is to hold a live news conference with reporters and bloggers. News conferences are a time-honored tool for politicians and corporations covered by beat reporters. When a story breaks in real-time, you can announce an online news conference at a time a few hours in the future and then live-stream the Q&A session. It's a good idea to archive the feed so people can watch it later. Live-streaming news feeds are still rare, which surprises me given the increasing ease of this technique on the technology side and the tremendous value of reaching reporters and bloggers in real time.

Post It on Google Plus

Google News results now prominently show results from Google Plus (aka Google+ or just G+). This presents an exciting opportunity for real-time marketers who use this service (and if you aren't, you should be). In many countries and languages, if you go to Google News, you'll see a drop-down arrow button if you "mouse over" to the right of a headline. Clicking the arrows reveals more stories, and those frequently include G+ listing. What's cool about this technique is that if you publish interesting and timely content via G+, it just might get indexed in Google News as well.

These are some of the many techniques you can use to stand out online to reporters searching for news. Now let's look at techniques that allow you to target individual reporters or media outlets.

Comment on Breaking News Stories at Online Publications

Many reporters now blog, and most online publications give readers space to comment on stories. You can comment on breaking stories, pointing out facets of the story they may have overlooked—along with a link to your own blog or website. If your contribution offers real value, the reporter will sometimes follow up.

Use Media Tip Lines

Many media outlets have created simple ways for anybody to contribute to news stories. Sometimes called "tip lines," these entry points can be used when you have important contributions to offer. For example, TechCrunch has the following tip-line callout on the homepage: "So you've got the inside scoop on a story or topic that we've covered? We respect your anonymity. Feel free to directly email us at mailto:tips@techcrunch.com." Another powerful direct route is CNN iReport, which allows anyone to pitch a story to the global news network.

Tweet to Appropriate Reporters

Twitter is an excellent way to reach journalists directly. If a reporter is on Twitter—and by now most of them are—you can usually find his or her Twitter ID at the beginning or end of a story. If not, use a search engine to find it. Then you can offer a one-sentence take on their recently filed stories. Better yet, point them to your blog post. That way the reporter can see that you've got something to add to the story. You may get lucky and receive a message back to schedule an interview.

How to Find News to Jack

The most important aspect to successfully inject your ideas into a breaking news story is to follow the new rules of speed. You've got to build that real-time mind-set that I wrote about in Chapter 10. The traditional marketing and PR model—creating "campaigns" with long lead times—just doesn't work when a story breaks quickly. Now doesn't mean tomorrow. It means *now*. Newsjacking is amazingly powerful, but only when executed in real time.

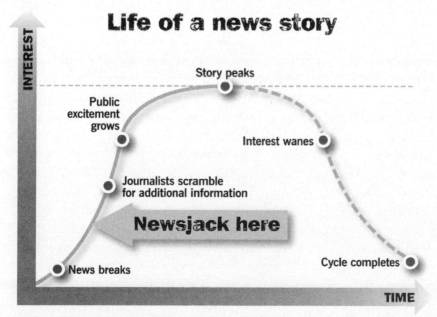

Life of a news story

INTEREST

Story peaks

Public excitement grows

Interest wanes

Journalists scramble for additional information

Newsjack here

Cycle completes

News breaks

TIME

There are three broad areas in which to find stories for newsjacking opportunities:

1. Things you already know—the news that's happening in your marketplace, geographical location, or areas of personal interest.
2. Things you didn't think to ask in the wider sphere of breaking national or global news.
3. Widely known current events in the immediate future to which you can tie a news hook. The trick is to devise news-monitoring strategies that keep you instantly informed on each of these levels.

To cover the news that's happening right now within your immediate sphere, you will want to monitor media and journalists you may already know, including influential bloggers and the trade publications that cover your marketplace. If you run a local business—a home renovation company, perhaps—then your hometown paper is a perfect place to start. We'll take a look at how to monitor this news first. Then we'll turn our attention to news you don't see coming from outlets you may not yet know, followed by a look at current events such as holidays, elections, and other types of activities that you do know will be occurring.

Tracking People You Know

To find news that you might have something to say about, follow bloggers, analysts, journalists, and others who cover your business and its wider industry. As we discussed in Chapter 5 when we looked at monitoring blogs, start by identifying as many voices as you can. Check the search engines (Google, Yahoo!, Bing, etc.) to help you list relevant keywords and phrases: your company, customers, competitors, prospects, product categories, buzzwords, and whatever else you can think of. Then list all the bloggers and reporters who have discussed issues relating to these keywords.

The next step is to begin monitoring what these people say in real-time. You could keep a list of these bloggers and journalists and make a point of checking on their posts and articles a few times a day. Or, to automate the task, you might use RSS feeds, a tool that allows you to harvest content from hundreds of blogs and news feeds without having to visit each one. When you use an RSS reader, you're alerted each time a site changes. I use NewsFire[5] for this task, but there are many others to choose from.

The goal here is to know immediately what people who talk about your industry or marketplace are saying, so you can comment in real time as appropriate.

Monitoring Keywords and Phrases

Besides tracking the journalists and bloggers who write about the subjects you are qualified to comment on, you should also set alerts to notify you instantly when something is said about your industry or marketplace, outside the realm of the known bloggers and journalists. Monitoring Twitter and the web for items that mention your important keywords and phrases ensures you are instantly aware of stories you might be able to contribute to.

You can use Google Alerts[6] or another platform for this purpose. Google Alerts allows you to enter many different search terms, so you can create a comprehensive list relevant to your business. Include anything you might want to comment on in an interview or email that could become the second paragraph of a story: industry terms, competitors, customers, prospects, products, and any relevant buzzwords or phrases—every term you can think of. Google Alerts will send you an email each time your search term is used.

Once you start monitoring, you will likely need to modify your search terms, usually because of a flood of "false hits" (notifications from when your search term is used in stories unrelated to your business). Some services offer advanced features that allow you to refine your searches. For instance, you can make your searches more specific by using the Boolean operators *and*, *or*, and *not*. If you work for an organization that follows many important search terms, you might consider retaining a consultant with a background in information science to help you with search strategies.

Tying Your News to Current Events

While the best newsjacking opportunities come at you as a surprise, sometimes a holiday, sporting contest, entertainment release, or other

---

[5] newsfirerss.com

[6] google.com/alerts

event is a perfect hook on which to hang your news. It's more difficult to get news coverage around these events (many more people will try to newsjack stories they see coming), but you never know what might work.

How to Newsjack

News breaks second by second, 24 hours a day

1 Find news to jack

Real-Time To-Do List

- Be open to serendipity (happy accidents)
- Monitor keywords, phrases & trending word clouds
- Track journalists & media outlets
- Follow Twitter hashtags

SPEED

Quickness is essential

2 Formulate a strategy in real-time

Strategy Questions

- Does your organization have the mind-set to act in real time?
- How are you related to the breaking news?
- Why should the media care?

SPAM

Always use good judgment

3 Instantly get your ideas into the market

Possible Actions

- Blog your take on the news
- Tweet using an established hashtag
- Send a real-time media alert
- Give a speech
- Hold a physical or virtual news conference
- Contact directly a journalist who might be interested

For example, to newsjack the Academy Awards, marketers at Urgent Genius created a terrific little YouTube application called The Artistifier.[7] Released during the Oscar broadcast, the app allows you to turn any YouTube video into an "award-winning" silent movie in the style of the 2012 Oscar winner, *The Artist*. You can even add your own captions before sharing your finished black-and-white masterpiece via Facebook and Twitter. I transformed one of my speaker videos and thought it looked really cool. Many others must have liked the app as well, because about 14,000 such films were created around the time of the Oscars, and thousands of people tweeted the link or "Liked" the application on Facebook. Dozens of bloggers and journalists wrote about the application, generating interest in the work of Urgent Genius.

This is a terrific example of newsjacking a current event. The team knew that the film would be talked about in the news (*The Artist* had been nominated for 10 Academy Awards). And, they released the application right when the broadcast announced *The Artist's* Best Picture win (its fifth of the night).

The Artistifier is a collaboration between Jon Burkhart, social content creative consultant and innovation director at UrgentGenius.com, and two other Johns: John O'Sullivan and Jon Plackett.

"This was our chance to create something that would provide an interactive platform for fans to easily create content in real time around the Oscars," Burkhart said. "We tested it out in front of [a] live audience, asking them to name the worst film they've ever seen. We then found clips of these films including *Titanic* and *Star Wars: Phantom Menace* and a team of comedy writers wrote loads of captions for the films and in minutes the YouTube clips were transformed into black-and-white films with funny full-screen captions."

The goal of newsjacking is to get noticed and let the buzz you create in both social media and traditional outlets drive business. That's exactly what happened to Burkhart and the Urgent Genius team. "The Artistifier has benefited my business in numerous ways," he said. "It has led to consultancy gigs in the entertainment sector and helped me develop a real-time content workshop where I help clients build interactive platforms. It's important to look at newsjacking not just as a PR tool but as a cultural trigger that gives

---

[7] theartistifier.com

you a chance to launch interactive platforms that you have pre-created and are waiting to launch at the right moment."

This approach doesn't just work for major televised events like the Academy Awards. Sometimes you can predict other newsworthy events ahead of time and become a part of the story before it breaks. That's what Toyota did to newsjack the story of the newly retired Space Shuttle Endeavor as it made its way from the Los Angeles airport to its permanent home at the California Science Center. The Shuttle had to be towed through the streets of Los Angeles, and at one point on the route, a bridge had a weight limit too low for the machines doing the towing. To avoid any issues for that short part of the journey over the bridge, a Toyota Tundra pickup pulled the Endeavor instead.

Because marketers at Toyota were able to plan ahead, they built a website for the stunt.[8] To get people to talk up the effort, they offered to donate $50 to the California Science Center for every tweet mentioning the #TundraEndeavor event. The total came to just over $200,000 (and yes, I tweeted).[9] That price tag might be a little steep by newsjacking standards, but it did get a lot of people talking about the Tundra.

When the Story Is Already (Sort of) about You

Sometimes, a story falls right into your lap. That's what happened to Ohio Arts, the maker of Etch A Sketch. If you recall, during the 2012 U.S. presidential campaign, an aide to Republican candidate Mitt Romney said in an interview that the candidate could reset his post-primary campaign "like an Etch a Sketch."

The reference to the classic toy played into the narrative that Romney changed positions frequently to appeal to whoever he was talking to at the moment. It was a perfect story, and journalists ran with it, resulting in thousands of stories mentioning the toy.

Sometimes, the newsjacking gods shine on you and present an opportunity that is so perfect you can't help but jump in. But how do you do it to the greatest effect?

---

[8] tundra.toyota.com/#videos/the-challenge
[9] twitter.com/dmscott/status/257430078378614785

For starters, Ohio Arts did an excellent job with media relations. At least three Ohio Arts executives were dispatched to do media interviews. They used humor, which got some wonderful quotes into stories. I especially love this line by marketing director Martin Killgallon in "Ohio Art's Etch A Sketch Shakes Up Political Debate" from the *Wall Street Journal*: "One thing the Etch A Sketch won't do is pick sides in the campaign. We have a left knob and a right knob, so we neutrally speak to both parties."

The company also sent boxes of Etch A Sketches to the campaigns, because Rick Santorum, Newt Gingrich, and other candidates had been holding up the toy. This generated tons of free image appearances in the media for Ohio Arts.

When yours is the product of the moment, you can generate ink just by having people hold it in front of cameras. But you've got to seize the moment in real time. Tomorrow is too late.

Twitter Is Your Newsjacking Tool

For dedicated newsjackers, there is no tool more essential than Twitter. It is both a primary source of newsjacking ideas and a powerful channel to get your message out to the media in real time.

Twitter is used by both journalists and media outlets to share links to stories being published. If you follow the Twitter feeds of the reporters and media outlets covering your market, industry, or company, then you'll know about fresh content as it appears. So as you identify key sources, be sure to follow them on Twitter. You can also use a Twitter application like TweetDeck or HootSuite to monitor your key phrases.

Many journalists rely heavily on Twitter to research the stories they're working on. Especially when news breaks, reporters immediately turn to Twitter in search of eyewitness reports or direct comments from people in the know. A vital link between newsjackers and journalists is the Twitter hashtag—a keyword or phrase preceded by the hash mark (#). Hashtags serve as unique identifiers to make it easy to instantly locate references to a particular subject.

For example, Peter Knox's commute was affected by flooding in the New York City area in the aftermath of Hurricane Sandy, which devastated the U.S. East Coast in October 2012. Knox works in Hoboken, New Jersey, but the PATH rail stop he uses had been closed. Knox (@PeterKnox) tweeted,[10] "I can't afford

---

[10] twitter.com/peterknox/status/269435304375619585

the $60 a week ferry anymore. Now attempting the PATH walk from Newport to Hoboken today. pic.twitter.com/8RI9jChu." The attached image was a map of his route. Soon Matt Flegenheimer (@mattfleg) from the *New York Times* tweeted back about a story he was working on. The two used Twitter to agree on a time to speak that day. The resulting story,[11] "In a Hobbled Hoboken, Overbooked Buses, Unfamiliar Ferries and Long Lines," quoted Knox.

When news breaks and you have something to say about it, post your comment as a tweet with the appropriate hashtag. Your idea just might be seen by a journalist eager to fill out a story with additional quotations. Sometimes they'll even quote your tweet directly.

Beware: Newsjacking Can Damage Your Brand

To successfully newsjack a story, it is best if you have a legitimate tie to it. Especially in the case of negative news such as Hurricane Sandy, the connection is essential. After all, preliminary estimates of losses (including business interruption) surpassed $50 billion, which would make Sandy the second-costliest Atlantic hurricane, behind Hurricane Katrina. At least 209 people were killed along the path of the storm.

This was not the sort of story to use to promote cosmetics and fashion. For example, *InStyle* magazine offered a special package of cosmetics on a page titled *Hurricane Sandy Have You Stuck Inside? 5 Beauty Treatments to Help Ride Out the Storm.*

"The weather outside is frightful—which is all the more reason to stay indoors and pamper yourself," wrote Marianne Mychaskiw. "So we rounded up 5 beauty treatments that will help keep you occupied (and gorgeous) as you safely wait out the storm."

Similarly, American Apparel promoted a "Hurricane Sandy Sale" to its email list. The retailer offered customers located in the states affected by the storm 20 percent off everything ("in case you're bored during the storm," they wrote). For a 36-hour sale period, customers could enter the code SANDYSALE at online checkout.

These sorts of frivolous newsjacking attempts give the concept of news-jacking (and also marketers in general) a bad name. They are blatant

---

[11] nytimes.com/2012/11/19/nyregion/hoboken-commuters-find-new-routines-as-restoration-of-path-service-lags.html

attempts to exploit a tragedy. Worse, they run the risk that their customers and the media will call the perpetrators out for their insensitivity to the suffering of others.

Newsjacking is a powerful tool, but you risk unleashing the power in a negative manner that can seriously harm your brand if you try something that's in poor taste.

To be successful, attempts at newsjacking must have a legitimate tie to the story, especially when the story is about a disaster, death, or any other negative event.

There were product categories outside of fashion and cosmetics that could *legitimately* newsjack Hurricane Sandy, and some did. For example, in the days immediately following, battery manufacturer Duracell set up mobile phone charging centers in communities that were without power. The locations were updated frequently on the Duracell Facebook page, and many people "Liked" the effort and left positive comments. The media noticed and wrote positive stories about Duracell.

Newsjacking for Fun and Profit

You can newsjack too. All it takes is some creativity and the ability to respond very quickly.

Remember when Jeremy Lin's success was the hottest story in sports? In February 2012, the previously unremarkable basketball player unexpectedly led the New York Knicks on a winning streak and was promoted to the starting lineup. The story generated a global following known as Linsanity, partly because he was the first American of Chinese or Taiwanese descent to play in the National Basketball Association. Less than two weeks after the Lin story took off, Alan Goldsher published an e-book about it, *Linsanity: The Improbable Rise of Jeremy Lin*.[12]

Welcome to a new era of newsjacking via Kindle. Sometimes, a blog post isn't enough and the best type of content is a long-form e-book, given away or sold at a profit.

According to a *Fast Company* interview with Goldsher,[13] it took 72 hours to write the 15,000-word manuscript, 36 hours using Amazon's Vook

---

[12] amazon.com/exec/obidos/ASIN/B007BG5OBQ/freshspotpubl-20
[13] fastcompany.com/1818498/lindles-jeremy-lin-amazon-kindle-and-rise-insta-authors

technology to build the e-book, and then another 24 hours to arrange distribution. The result? The media were not only talking about Lin the basketball player; they were also talking about *Lin* the book, and about its author.

Whenever there is a hot story in the news, there is an opportunity to create and publish original content that the media will find and cover. You can newsjack a story by writing a blog post, shooting a YouTube video, creating an infographic, or even publishing an e-book.

Newsjacking is cool. It's fun. And it gets you ink!

24 Search Engine Marketing

Search engine marketing is remarkable because, unlike almost every other form of marketing, it does not rely on the interruption technique. Think again for a moment about what I've called old-rules marketing and its interruption-based advertising techniques. As I've discussed in previous chapters, the old rules required you to interrupt TV viewers and hope they weren't already flipping to another channel, interrupt people as they sorted through the mail and hope your message wouldn't go into the junk mail pile, or interrupt magazine readers and hope they would pause at your stinky pull-out perfume sample. These days, ads are everywhere—on signs along the highway, on the sides of supermarket carts, in elevators. These interruptions are not only annoying for consumers (and harmful to a brand if overdone) but also increasingly ineffective.

Now think about how you use search engines. Unlike nontargeted, interruption-based advertising, the information that appears in search engines after you've typed in a phrase is content you actually want to see. You're actually *looking* for it. This should be a marketer's dream come true.

For example, when Shaquille O'Neal was on David Letterman's talk show a few years ago discussing how he had enjoyed his life in Boston since he joined the Boston Celtics, Shaq said he found his multimillion-dollar house on Google! "I live in a small town called Sudbury," he told Letterman. "I signed kind of late, so I really didn't have a chance to find a house. So I went on Google and put [in] 'big house outside of Boston,' and I found this big 10-acre farmhouse." A smart real estate mind with just the right information on the web scored big time with that one.

Here's something very important to consider: *This entire book is about search engine marketing.* Please pause to reflect on that. If you followed the new rules of marketing and PR as outlined in these pages, you will have built a fantastic search engine marketing program! You started with your buyer personas, then you built content especially for these buyers—content that talks about the problems they face in the words and phrases they actually use. Then you delivered the content in the online forms they prefer (podcasts, blogs, e-books, websites, and so on). This terrific content designed especially for your buyers will be indexed by the search engines, and that's it. You already have a terrific search engine marketing program!

But even a great program can benefit from focused enhancements, so in this chapter we'll talk about how to further develop and improve your search engine marketing strategies. Let's start with a few basic definitions:

- *Search engine marketing* means using search engines to reach your buyers directly. Search engines include general search engines such as Google, Bing, and Yahoo!, as well as vertical market search engines that are specific to your industry or to the people you are trying to reach.
- *Search engine optimization (SEO)* is the art and science of ensuring that the words and phrases on your site, blog, and other online content are found by the search engines and that, once found, your site is given the highest ranking possible in the *natural search results* (i.e., what the search engine algorithm deems important for the phrase entered).
- *Search engine advertising* is when a marketer *pays* to have advertising appear in search engines when a user types in a particular phrase that the marketer has purchased. Usually this advertising comes in the form of small text ads appearing next to the natural search results for a particular search term. Google AdWords,[1] Bing Ads,[2] and Yahoo! Search Marketing[3] are the three large search engine advertising programs. Marketers bid to have their ads appear based on keywords and phrases, competing against others who want the same phrases. Your ad will appear somewhere in the list of ads for that phrase based on a

---

[1] adwords.google.com

[2] advertise.bingads.microsoft.com

[3] advertising.yahoo.com/article/search-advertising.html

formula used by the search engine that takes into account two main factors: how much you are willing to bid (in dollars and cents) for each person who clicks the ad, plus your click-through rate (the number of people who click your ad divided by the number of people who see it in the search results).

Making the First Page on Google

Colin Warwick, signal integrity product manager in the Design & Simulation Software Division of Agilent Technologies, is responsible for marketing software to help engineers overcome limitations in high-speed digital connections. As he was working on marketing plans, he came to the realization that traditional business-to-business marketing techniques like trade shows are expensive and increasingly ineffective. He also came to understand the importance of search engines for his business. "Everyone understands Google," he says. "Everybody can instantly see when you enter a phrase into Google if your competitors come up and you don't or vice versa."

The most important search term for Warwick's products is "signal integrity," and Agilent product information was coming up on the fifth page of results—clearly not ideal. So Warwick set out to make Agilent appear at the top of the search results by creating a blog focused on signal integrity.[4] Everything, from the name and URL of the blog to the excellent content, was designed to appeal to the buyer personas interested in this topic and to drive solid search engine rankings. "There are only 50,000 signal integrity engineers in the entire world, and our average sale is about $10,000 with a six-month sales cycle," Warwick says. "While the competitors show their brochures, we have a valuable blog. It helps a great deal to have such valuable information, both for search engine results and in the selling process."

Warwick says that executives at Agilent were very supportive of his starting the blog, but there were some guidelines that he had to work within. "The company said I could blog but that the IT department would not support it," he says. "So I needed to create the blog outside of the company domain. I was required to follow some very commonsense rules: Don't mention the competition, link to the Agilent terms of service and privacy policy, and include a copyright notice. It has been a very good experience. Companies need to trust that employees will do the right thing and let people blog."

---

[4] signal-integrity-tips.com

The results have been very encouraging. "Many customers say that they like the blog, and our salespeople tell prospects about it," Warwick says. "Having a blog allows me to be spontaneous. For example, I can put diagrams up very quickly and let people know valuable information. If we needed to put content on the corporate site, it would take three days. With the blog I can get into a conversation in just five minutes."

So what about the search results? On Google, Warwick's blog is now on the first page of results for the phrase "signal integrity" (at the number four position when I checked). "Prior to starting the blog, the company products page was ranked number 44 on Google," Warwick says. "That's a huge improvement."

But there are many added benefits to blogging that took Warwick by surprise. "Trade magazine journalists read the blog, and they include links to it in their blogrolls," he says. "And I am making great web connections. For example, I asked Paul Rako, an important journalist at *EDN* [a news and information source for electronics design engineers], to moderate a panel for me, and he did because he knows me from the blog."

Search Engine Optimization

In my experience, people often misunderstand search engine marketing because there are a slew of SEO firms that make it all seem so darned complicated. To add to the problem, many (but certainly not all) SEO firms are a bit on the shady side, promising stellar results from simply manipulating keywords on your site. Perhaps you've seen the spam email messages of some of these snake oil salesmen (I've received hundreds of unsolicited email messages with headlines like: "Top Search Engine Rankings Guaranteed!"). While many search engine marketing firms are completely reputable and add tremendous value to marketing programs, I am convinced that the single best thing you can do to improve your search engine marketing is to focus on building great content for your buyers. Search engine marketing should not be mysterious and is certainly not trickery.

However, the many intricacies and nuances that can make good search engine marketing great are beyond the scope of this small chapter. Many excellent resources can help you learn even more about the complexities of search engine marketing and especially search engine algorithm factors such as the URL you use, placement of certain words within your content, tags, metadata, inbound links, and other details. These resources also add to our discussion in Chapter 11 of how to identify appropriate keywords and phrases. A great place to start understanding search engine optimization is Search Engine Watch,[5] where you will find resources and active forums to explore. To learn more about search engine advertising, start with the tutorials and frequently asked questions pages of the Google AdWords, Bing Ads, and Yahoo! Search Marketing sites.

The Long Tail of Search

Perhaps you've already tried search engine marketing. Many marketers have. In my experience working with many organizations, I've learned that search engine marketing programs often fail because the marketers optimize on general keywords and phrases that do not produce sufficiently targeted results. For example, someone in the travel business might be tempted to optimize on words like *travel* and *vacation*. I just entered "travel" into Google and got over a billion hits (!). It is virtually impossible to get to the top of the heap with a generic word or phrase like *travel*, and even if you did, that's not usually how people search. *It is ineffective to try to reach buyers with broad, general search terms.*

You have a choice when you create search engine marketing programs. One method is to optimize on and advertise with a small number of words and phrases that are widely targeted to try to generate huge numbers of clicks. Think of this approach as an oceangoing drag fishing boat with huge nets used to harvest one species of fish. Sure, you capture thousands of fish at a time, but you throw away all that are not the species you're after, and it is a very expensive undertaking.

True success comes from driving buyers directly to the actual content they are looking for. Several years ago, I wanted to take my family on vacation to Costa Rica, so I went to Google and typed in "Costa Rica Adventure Travel." I checked out a bunch of sites at the top of the search results (both the natural search results and the advertisements) and chose one that appealed to me. After exchanging several emails to design an itinerary, I booked a trip for several thousand dollars, and a few months later I was checking out howler monkeys in the rainforest. This is how people *really* search (for what they are looking for on the web, not for howler monkeys). If you're in the Costa Rican adventure travel business, don't waste

---

[5] searchenginewatch.com

resources optimizing for the generic term *travel*. Instead, run search engine marketing programs for phrases like "Costa Rica ecotourism," "Costa Rica rainforest tour," and so on.

The best approach is to create separate search engine marketing programs for dozens, hundreds, or even tens of thousands of *specific* search terms that people might actually search on. Think of this approach as rigging thousands of individual baited hooks on a long line and exposing them at precisely the right time to catch the species of fish you want. You won't catch a fish on each and every hook. But with so many properly baited hooks, you will certainly catch lots of the fish you are fishing for.

Carve Out Your Own Search Engine Real Estate

One rarely discussed but very important aspect of search engine marketing is choosing product and company names so that they will be easy to find on the web via search engines. When you consider the name of a new company, product, book, rock band, or other entity that people want to find on the web, you typically go through a process of thinking up ideas, getting a sense of whether these names sound right, and then perhaps seeing if you can copyright or trademark the ideas. I would suggest adding one more vital step: You should run a web search to see if anything comes up for your proposed name. I urge you to drop the name idea if there are lots of similarly named competitors—even if the competition for the name is in a different industry. Your marketing goal should be that when someone enters the name of your book or band or product, the searcher immediately reaches information about it. For example, before I agree to book titles, I make certain those names are not being used in any other way on the web. It was important for me to own my titles on the search engines; searching on *Eyeball Wars*, *Cashing in with Content*, *The New Rules of Marketing and PR*, *World Wide Rave*, and other titles brings up only my books plus reviews, articles, or discussions about them.

Many people ask me why I use my middle name in my professional endeavors, and I've had people accuse me of being pretentious. Maybe I am a *bit* pretentious, but that's not why I use my middle name—Meerman. The reason is simple: There are so many other David Scotts out there. One David Scott walked on the moon as commander of *Apollo 15*. Another is a six-time

Iron Man Triathlon champion. Yet another is a U.S. Congressman from Georgia's 13th district. Good company, all, but for clarity and search engine optimization purposes, I chose to be unique among my fellow David Scotts by becoming David Meerman Scott.

A side note on creating your own search engine real estate: You should avoid using special characters in your company or product names. Characters such as @, #, %, and so on are not easily indexed by the search engines. While there are exceptions (the popular C++ software program comes to mind), it is just too difficult to make product names using special characters index properly in search engines.

The lesson here is that if you want to be found on the web, you need a unique identity for yourself, your product, and your company to stand out from the crowd and rise to prominence on search engines. As you are thinking of names to use for marketing, test them out on the search engines first and try to carve out something that you alone can own.

Web Landing Pages to Drive Action

Although I won't try to cover all the details of search engine marketing, I definitely want to touch on one of the most common mistakes made by search engine marketers. Most people focus a great deal of time on keyword and phrase selection (that's a good thing!), and they also do a good job of ensuring that their organization ranks highly for those phrases by optimizing the site and/or purchasing search engine advertising. But most organizations are terrible at building a landing page—the place people go after they click on a search hit.

Think back to our last example. As I was planning my Costa Rican vacation, many of the sites that were ranked highly for the phrase I entered were a kind of bait and switch. I thought I would be getting targeted information about Costa Rican travel and was instead taken to a generic landing page from a big travel agency, an airline, or a hotel chain. No, thanks, I'm not interested. I wanted information on Costa Rica, not an airline or hotel chain, and so I clicked away in a second. Because I wanted information about Costa Rican adventure travel, I chose the landing page that had the best information, one from an outfit called Costa Rica Expeditions.[6] This means that you're likely to need dozens or hundreds of landing pages to implement a great search engine marketing program.

---

[6] costaricaexpeditions.com

> You need to build landing pages that have specific content to enlighten and inform the people who just clicked over to your site from the search engine.

Marketing with web landing pages is one of the easiest and most cost-effective ways to get your information read by a target market, and it's a terrific tool for moving buyers through the sales cycle. A landing page is simply a place to publish targeted content for a particular buyer persona that you're trying to market to, and they are used not only in search engine marketing but also in other web marketing programs. For example, landing pages are ideal for describing special offers mentioned on your website or calls to action referenced in another content page (such as a blog or e-book). Landing pages also work well for telling an organization's story to a particular target market, promoting a new product offering, or providing more information to people who link from your news releases. Marketing programs such as search engine optimization are—to borrow an idea from the classic sales cycle definition—designed to attract the prospect's attention. The landing page is where you take the next step; once you've got your audience's attention, you must generate and develop customer interest and conviction, so that your sales team gets a warm lead ready to be worked to a closed sale, or so you can point people to an e-commerce page where they can buy your product right away.

Effective landing page content is written from, you guessed it, the buyers' perspective, not yours. Landing pages should provide additional information to searchers, information based on the offer or keyword they just clicked on. Many successful organizations have hundreds of landing pages, each optimized for a particular set of related search engine marketing terms.

Don't make the mistake so many organizations do by investing tons of money into a search engine advertising program (buying keywords) and then sending all the traffic to their home page. Because the home page needs to serve many audiences, there can never be enough information there for each search term. Instead, keep the following landing page guidelines in mind:

- *Make the landing page content short and the graphics simple:* The landing page is a place to deliver simple information and drive your prospect to respond to your offer. Don't try to do too much.

- *Create the page with your company's look, feel, and tone:* A landing page is an extension of your company's branding, so it must adopt the same voice, tone, and style as the rest of your site.
- *Write from the buyer's point of view:* Think carefully of who will be visiting the landing page, and write for that demographic. You want visitors to feel that the page speaks to their problems and that you have a solution for them.
- *A landing page is communications, not advertising:* Landing pages are where you communicate valuable information. Advertising gets people to click to your landing page, but once a prospect is there, the landing page should focus on communicating the value of your offering to the buyer.
- *Provide a quote from a happy customer:* A simple testimonial on a landing page works brilliantly to show people that others are happy with your product. A sentence or two with the customer's name (and affiliation if appropriate) is all you need.
- *Make the landing page a self-contained unit:* The goal of a landing page is to get buyers to respond to your offer so you can sell to them. If you lose traffic from your landing page, you may never get that response. Thus, it is sometimes better to make your landing page a unique place on the web and *not* provide links to your main website.
- *Make the call to action clear and easy to respond to:* Make certain you provide a clear response mechanism for those people who want to go further. Make it easy to sign up, express interest, or buy something.
- *Use multiple calls to action:* You never know what offer will appeal to a specific person, so consider using more than one. In the business-to-business world, you might offer a white paper, a free trial, an ROI calculator, and a price quote all on the same landing page.
- *Ask only for necessary information:* Don't use a sign-up form that requires your buyers to enter lots of data—people will abandon the form. Ask for the absolute minimum you can get away with—name and email address only, if you can, or perhaps even just email. Requiring any additional information will reduce your response rates.
- *Don't forget to follow up!* Okay, you've got a great landing page with an effective call to action, and the leads are coming in. That's great! Don't drop the ball now. Make certain to follow up each response as quickly as possible.

Search Engine Marketing in a Fragmented Business

The market that Scala, Inc.[7] serves is so fragmented, people can't even agree on what the product category is called: digital signage, digital in-store merchandising, electronic display networks, electronic billboards, and any of a dozen other names are used. And to make the marketing challenge even more difficult, potential customers in this market don't congregate at any one tradeshow, magazine, or web portal. And that's just the way Gerard Bucas, president and CEO of Scala, Inc., likes it because he uses search engine marketing to his advantage to reach buyers. "We pioneered the digital signage industry," he says. "Our services are used for retail, corporate communications, factory floor, and many other diverse business applications." Because Scala serves so many buyers in diverse market segments, there is no clear decision maker. In retail, it's the marketing department. In corporate communications for internal purposes, it is often the CEO or the HR department. And the company serves many verticals such as cruise lines, casinos, and more. "Since we can't possibly advertise in so many different places to reach these people, we rely on a great website with a strong focus on search engine marketing."

Bucas says it is critical to use the same terminology as his target market and to include industry terms that lead to an appropriate Scala page. "We continuously monitor the top 30 to 40 search terms that people look for when they search for us on the Net," he says. "When we find new terms, we write content that incorporates those terms, and as the term becomes more important, we expand on the content."

For Bucas, effective search engine marketing means understanding his buyers and creating compelling content using important keywords and phrases and then getting each one indexed by the search engines. "For example, *digital signage* is one of our search terms," he says. "We want to be at the top of the results. But we also care about similar phrases such as *digital sign* and *digital signs*. Each of the terms gives different results. It's amazing to me."

The Scala site includes detailed product content, client case studies, and information on how digital signage is used in different industries. "Regular news releases and case studies are all intended to bring search engines to us,"

---

[7] scala.com

he says. "With case studies and news releases, we're getting some phrases into the market that we don't often use, which cause some long-tail results with the search engines."

Scala has a lead-generation system using search engines to drive buyers to landing pages where traffic converts into leads that are funneled into the company's reseller channel. In this system, the company gathers names through offers (such as a free demo DVD) on each landing page. "Our resellers love us because we're constantly pumping them with new leads," Bucas says. "We effectively help to generate business for them, so they become very loyal to us. Our partners see the value of the lead generation." According to Bucas, the lead system, which manages more than 4,000 open sales leads at any one time, automates communication at particular points in the sales process by sending email to buyers.

The success Scala enjoys shows how a well-executed content strategy on the web will deliver buyers to landing pages who are actually looking for a product. "We are growing very rapidly," Bucas says. "And a large percentage of the business comes from web leads—certainly more than 50 percent of our business comes from the web."

If you're planning on implementing the ideas in this book, you will, by definition, be doing search engine marketing. You will understand your buyers and create great, indexable web content especially for them. The best search engine marketing comes from paying attention to and understanding your buyers, not from manipulating or tricking them. Still, once you've executed a great content strategy, adding effective landing pages and focusing on the long tail of search terms will give you an even more powerful marketing asset that will generate results for months and years to come.

Make It Happen

Thanks for hanging in there with me and for reading this far! When I speak to audiences and run seminars on the new rules of marketing and PR, this is the point at which many people are stimulated to get out there and make it happen. They want to start a blog right away, shoot a video for YouTube, generate some news releases, or begin buyer persona research in preparation for writing a marketing and PR plan that will guide them to create a content-rich website. If that describes you, great!

But in the audiences of my seminars and speeches, there is always another group of people who tend to feel a bit overwhelmed. There is just too much information, they say, or too many new and unfamiliar ideas. If you are in this category, you might be thinking that the people profiled in the book were able to figure out things that are just too complex and time-consuming for you to tackle, especially given your already hectic schedule. Hey, we all have stuff on our plates, and for most of us, implementing the ideas in the book will represent an addition to our workload. But here's one of the greatest things about the new rules of marketing and PR: You can implement these ideas in bits and pieces! In fact, I don't expect anybody to implement *all* the ideas here. I don't do *that* many of them myself (okay, I admitted it—don't tell). Yes, I have a blog, and it is very important to me. I'm on Twitter, and I create some original videos. But I don't have a podcast, and I'm not on MySpace. I just do what I can and what works for me. And so should you.

Unlike a linear, offline marketing campaign where you must take a methodical, step-by-step approach leading up to a big release day, the web is, well, it's a *web*. You can add to the web at any time because it is iterative, not linear. Think about the last print advertisement you or others in your organization did. Everything had to be perfect, requiring thorough proof-reading, tons of approvals from your colleagues (or your spouse), lengthy consultation with a bunch of third parties such as advertising agencies and printers, and—above all—lots of money. Your neck was on the line if there was a screw-up, so you obsessed over the details. Contrast that with a web content initiative that you can implement quickly, get people to check out live, and make changes to on the fly. It really is much less stressful to create an online program. If you create a web page that doesn't work for you, you can just delete it. You can't do that with a print ad or direct-mail campaign. So I would urge you to think about how you might *selectively* experiment with the ideas in these pages rather than fret about coordinating them all and trying to get everything right on the first go.

Many organizations I've worked with have found that an excellent approach is first to do some buyer persona research. By reading the publications that your buyers read, perhaps attending a webinar that they attend, reading a few of the blogs in the space, and maybe interviewing a few buyers, you can narrow down the book's large list of techniques to determine the most appropriate web-based marketing and PR initiatives for you and work on them first.

Others have found that the best way to get started is to add a few pages of targeted thought leadership content for an important buyer persona to an existing website (perhaps with links from the home page). What's great about this approach is that you don't have to redesign your site; all you are doing is *adding* some valuable content to what you already have. That's easy, right?

Still another first step might be to read the blogs in your market and begin to comment on them in order to coax your blogging voice out of its shell. Once you feel comfortable, you can take the plunge by creating your own blog and Twitter feed. But the good news is that you don't need to show the world right away—you can password-protect your fledgling blog and share it with only a few colleagues at first. Then, with some feedback, you can tweak your approach and finally remove the password protection, and you're off. The important thing is to just get out there. Remember, on the web, you are what you publish.

Your Mind-Set

To make the new rules of marketing and PR part of your personal world, you're going to have to change your mind-set. You'll need to understand your buyers, rather than just talking about your products and services. You'll need to be aware of what's going on in the real-time news and on social networks. You'll need to create content and publish it on the web, and sometimes you'll need to do it urgently to be successful. On social networks, two-way communications is required, not just the typical broadcast approach that most marketers are used to. These habits and techniques do not come naturally to entrepreneurs, business owners, or marketing and PR professionals steeped in more traditional ways.

I've talked with people all over the world who are struggling to adapt to these new rules. The process often starts with your coming to understand just how severely conventional methods can handicap your business and your career. But since you've read this far in the book, you know that already. So let me share a few general ideas for making the mind-set shift I'm describing. It will take some time, but I've seen thousands of people thrive in the always-on world of instant communication—and you will too.

Manage Your Fear

Every day, I encounter fear in the people I work with. Many company executives and public relations people trace their worries about the new rules of marketing and PR to their belief that "people will say bad things about our company" via social media.

This fear leads them to ignore blogs and online forums and to prohibit employees from participating in social media. And, yet, in every discussion that I've had with employees who freely participate in social media, I've confirmed that this fear is significantly overblown. Let me repeat: Everyone who has experience tells me this fear is overblown.

Sure, an occasional outlier might vent frustrations online, and now and then a dissatisfied customer will complain (unless you're in the airline industry, and then it might be more than a few).

But the benefit of this kind of communication is that you can monitor in real time what's being said and then respond appropriately. Employees, customers, and other stakeholders are talking about your organization offline anyway, so unless you are participating online, you'll never know what's being said at all.

The beauty of the web is that you benefit from instant access to conversations you could never participate in before. And frequently you can turn around impressions by commenting on a "negative" post. So not only is this fear overblown—it's often dead wrong. Participating in social media gives you the chance to make sure *fewer* bad things are being said about your company.

Getting the Help You Need (and Rejecting What You Don't)

As you develop a strategy to get started implementing the new rules of marketing and PR, you may find occasions to call on others for help. Many people tell me that they occasionally need the services of an agency to provide them with some extra people to help execute a big project. But I constantly hear that they have difficulty finding people skilled in using the ideas that we've been discussing in this book. Still others report that well-meaning colleagues and meddlesome bosses have an annoying tendency to look over shoulders and second-guess them as they start a blog, get going on Twitter, or begin filming YouTube videos. Add to that mix the fact that, in many larger organizations, the legal department tends to muck things up with nitpicky rules about what can and cannot be said. If these sound like some of the problems that you're encountering, fear not! Here are some things you can do to get the help you need, while rejecting what you don't.

The One Question to Ask a Prospective Agency

An increasingly large cadre of self-proclaimed new marketing gurus claim to be really good at generating attention using the new rules of marketing and PR. In addition, I've noticed that in the past several years, established agencies of all kinds are adding departments devoted to social media. Traditional advertising agencies that have focused on television commercials for decades all of a sudden claim to be experts on blogging. Public relations agencies skilled in relating to the media somehow become instant experts in Facebook and Twitter. So how do you navigate all these potential partners if you really do need some help implementing the ideas in this book?

Many people ask me if I can recommend an agency that understands social media or to help them evaluate agencies that claim to be good at this kind of work. My answer to the challenge of finding good people is simple: Ask the prospective agency to show you its social media presence. Ask about such things as blogs, Twitter feeds, YouTube videos, e-books, websites, Facebook profiles, and any other stuff they have. Make it an open-ended question. This is not to say that an agency needs to be active in every medium, but if they are worthy of taking your money to advise you on the use of these tools, then they should certainly be out there using them. My theory is that if an agency can't blog or tweet or create interesting content such as videos for themselves with any success, then they're going to come up short for clients as well. The answers can be fascinating! All of a sudden many of these self-styled experts clam up and don't say much. This vetting tool eliminates 95 percent of agencies that just plain stink at understanding social media.

When Lawyers Get in the Way

At many larger organizations, the legal department is heavily involved in all marketing and communications initiatives, frequently requiring every blog post and press release to be vetted by a lawyer. In some extremes, corporate legal eagles even forbid employees from starting a blog or participating on Twitter and Facebook at work. I've found that the restrictions come down to two factors: *ignorance of social media* and *a lack of trust in employees*.

Since legal people don't usually understand social media themselves (and don't use them for business in their jobs), they naturally respond by just slapping on controls. After all, their job is to reduce risks within a company, so it's temptingly simple to just say no. This is especially true in companies that mistrust their employees. However, if a company trusts its employees and understands that social media can be a powerful way to do business, then it is the lawyers' job to create an environment where you can do what you know is right.

My recommendation is to work with your managers and your organization's legal team (and perhaps the human resources department as well) to create guidelines that you can operate under. Your company's guidelines should include advice about how to communicate in any medium, including face-to-face conversations, presentations at events, email, social media, online forums and chat rooms, and other forms of communication. Rather than putting restrictions on social media (that is, the technology), it's better to focus on guiding the way people behave. The corporate guidelines should include statements that employees can't reveal company secrets, can't use inside information to trade stock or influence prices, and must be transparent and provide their real name and affiliation when communicating. You might take a look at how IBM, a company on the forefront of embracing employee use of social media, has handled this issue. IBM has developed a set of social computing guidelines[1] for employees' use of blogs, wikis, social networks, virtual worlds, and social media. You may have to take the lead on creating the guidelines at your organization, but the effort will be worth it.

Bring a Journalist onto Your Team

A remarkable convergence is upon us right now, creating a perfect opportunity for you to hire someone with the skills that you need. Sadly, many mainstream media outlets are reducing their pools of staff journalists. Newspapers, magazines, radio stations, and television outlets face tough economic challenges, and unfortunately, that means that many talented reporters and editors have been (or will be) laid off. I've had a chance to speak with several dozen journalists recently, and many are downcast about career prospects.

> Hire a journalist to help you create amazing content. Journalists know how to tell a story.

At the same time, people like you in many different organizations—corporations, nonprofits, government agencies, and educational institutions—understand the value of the ideas we've explored in this book. One of the best ways to create great web content is to actually hire a journalist, either full-time or part-time, to create it. Journalists, both print and broadcast, are great at understanding an audience and creating content that buyers want to consume—it's the bread and butter of their skill set. I'm not talking about PR and media relations here. This isn't about hiring a journalist to write press releases and try to get his or her former colleagues to

---

[1] ibm.com/blogs/zz/en/guidelines.html

write or broadcast about you. Instead, I'm talking about having journalists create stories just as they are doing now—but for a corporation, a government agency, a nonprofit, or an educational institution instead of a media outlet.

Editors are in demand by companies that create terrific online media rooms, like the one over at Cisco Systems.[2] What better background than journalism could there be for the person running your online media efforts? Is running the Cisco newsroom really that much different than running a newspaper site? For much smaller organizations, maybe it makes sense to hire a freelance print journalist to help you with that e-book. Again, what better way to create valuable information than to hire someone who has done it for years? Sure, web marketing represents a dramatically different job description from, say, beat reporter. Yet times (including the *New York Times*) are changing. And that gives smart marketers an amazing opportunity to hire people with the skills we need.

Managing Your Colleagues and Bosses

If I may be so bold as to boil down into one word thousands of conversations I've had over the past 10 years, as well as my 7 years' worth of blogging and the entire contents of this book, it would be this: *attention*. Entrepreneurs, CEOs, and business owners want people to pay attention to their company. Marketers, PR pros, advertisers, and salespeople are on the payroll to generate attention. Hopefully, this book opened your eyes to a new approach to this classic problem.

I've identified four main ways to generate attention in today's marketing landscape. We've discussed them throughout these pages, so this list is not really new, but seeing them all collected together will give us some fresh perspective for dealing with people who might be skeptical or meddlesome.

1. *You can buy attention with advertising* such as television commercials, magazine and newspaper ads, the Yellow Pages, billboards, trade show floor space, direct mail lists, and the like.
2. *You can get attention from the editorial gatekeepers* at radio and TV stations, magazines, newspapers, and trade journals.

---

[2] newsroom.cisco.com/home

3. *You can have a team of salespeople generate attention one person at a time* by knocking on doors, calling people on the telephone, sending personal emails, or waiting for individuals to walk into your showroom.
4. *You can earn attention online by using the ideas in this book*, creating something interesting, and publishing it online for free: a YouTube video, blog, research report, series of photos, Twitter stream, e-book, Facebook fan page, or other piece of web content.

To understand the motivations of your colleagues and bosses as they offer advice and give you unwanted criticism, I recommend that you know and understand these four means of generating attention. And you should understand the point of view of the person you are talking to about attention, especially when their inevitable pushback about earning it in new ways surfaces.

You see, most organizations have a corporate culture centered around one of these approaches. For examples, P&G primarily generates attention through advertising, Apple via PR, EMC via sales, and Zappos via the new rules of marketing and PR. Often the defining organizational culture springs from the founder or CEO's strong point of view. So if the CEO came up through the sales track, all attention problems are likely to become sales problems. Chances are that your colleagues and bosses did not come up via the social media track or read this book. The point is, you'll have to *convince* your boss to invest in social media, because it's likely he or she doesn't consider it the most important way of gaining attention. Most organizations overspend on advertising and sales and underinvest in social media, but nearly all organizations should be doing some combination of each. If you can help your bosses and colleagues understand this trend, they'll probably lighten up a little.

Great for Any Organization

There's no doubt that your organization will benefit from your getting out there and creating web content in whatever form you're most comfortable with. But I'm also convinced that no matter who you are or what you do, your professional and personal life will improve, too. If you are an innovator using the ideas in this book, it may lead to greater recognition in the office. And if you're like many bloggers and podcasters I know, you will derive a therapeutic benefit as well.

> It's fun to blog and tweet, and it makes you feel good to get your ideas out into the world.

If you're like me, you will prefer to write rather than create audio or video content. But I know plenty of people who hate to write and have created terrific photo, video, and audio content to reach buyers. And it works for all kinds of organizations: corporations, nonprofits, rock bands, and politicians. People often say to me: "But I'm just a _____ [fill in the blank with *pastor, painter, lawyer, consultant, sales representative, auto dealer, real estate agent*]; why should I blog or create a podcast?" My answer is that you'll not only reach your buyers directly with targeted content, you'll have fun, too—web content is for everyone, not just big companies.

In fact, one of my all-time favorite examples of success with the new rules of marketing and PR comes from an unlikely marketer: the pastor of a church in Washington, DC. But his isn't a typical church, because he doesn't actually have a church building. Instead he uses video technology, blogs, podcasts, and the web to tell stories and build a spiritual community both online and off.

"The church should be using technology to reach people; that's what Gutenberg did in the fifteenth century with the printing press," says Mark Batterson, lead pastor of National Community Church (also known as TheaterChurch.com), a multisite church in the Washington, DC, metropolitan area that conducts many services per week in six nontraditional locations. "Most churches have a church building, but we feel that a building can be an obstacle to some people, so we do church in theaters and have built the largest coffee house in the Washington, DC, area."

What distinguishes National Community Church is Batterson's approach of embracing technology and web marketing and applying it to church. The TheaterChurch.com site[3] includes a content-rich website, podcasts of the weekly services, a motivational webcast series, video, an email newsletter, Batterson's extremely popular Evotional blog[4] (tagline: "Spirit Fuel"), and Twitter feed (@MarkBatterson) with more than 60,000 followers. "The

---

[3] theaterchurch.com
[4] markbatterson.com

greatest message deserves the greatest marketing," Batterson says. "I am challenged that Madison Avenue and Hollywood are so smart at delivering messages. But I believe that we need to be just as smart about how we deliver our messages."

Attendance at National Community Church includes several thousand adults in an average weekend; 70 percent of them are single people in their 20s. "I think we attract 20-somethings because our personality as a church lends itself to 20-somethings," Batterson says. "Our two key values are authenticity and creativity. That plays itself out in the way we do church. I think that church should be the most creative place on the planet. The medieval church had stained glass to tell the gospel story to the churchgoers, who were mostly illiterate. We use the movie studio to tell the story to people. We use video to add color and to add flavor to what we do. If Jesus had video in his day, it wouldn't surprise me if he made short films."

Batterson's focus on the website, podcasts, and online video (as well as video at the services) means that National Community Church staff members have some unique job titles, including media pastor, digital pastor, and buzz coordinator. "We want to use technology for really good purposes," Batterson says. "Our website and my blog are our front door to National Community Church. The site is a virtual location in a sense. We have a lot more people who listen to the podcast and watch the webcast than who go to the services, so it is a great test drive for people. They can get a sense of the church before they arrive physically."

Batterson has gained online fame well beyond the Washington, DC, area—his blog is followed by tens of thousands of readers all over the world, and the podcast is one of the fastest growing church podcasts in America. He has also written several books including *In a Pit with a Lion on a Snowy Day: How to Survive and Thrive When Opportunity Roars*. "Blogging cuts six degrees of separation into three," he says. "I write knowing that my audience is another pastor in Australia, a housewife in Indiana, my friends, and people in Washington, DC. Marketing through my blog is powerful. For example, last week I did a blog post about my book and asked my blogging friends to also post about it. We went up to number 44 on the Amazon bestseller list, and Amazon sold out of the book that day. They just ordered another thousand copies."

Batterson's enthusiasm for how churches can use the web has caught the attention of thousands of other church leaders who follow his blog. "The two most powerful forms of marketing are word of mouth and what I call word of mouse. A guy named John Wesley, who founded the Methodist church, traveled 250,000 miles on horseback and preached something like 40,000 sermons. With one click of the mouse, I preach that many sermons with my podcast—that's word of mouse. It is about leveraging the unique vehicles on the web. The message has not changed, but the medium has changed. We need to continually find new vehicles to get the messages out."

Now It's Your Turn

Isn't the power of web content and the new rules of marketing and PR something? Here's a guy who's a church leader *without* a church building, and through innovative use of a blog, a podcast, and some video, he has become a leader in his field. He's got a best-selling book and tens of thousands of devoted online followers. Whether you're religious or not, you've got to be impressed with Batterson's business savvy and with the way the new rules have helped him reach his buyers.

You can do it, too. It doesn't matter what line of work you're in or what group of buyers you're trying to reach. You can harness the power of the web to reach your target audience directly.

If you're like many of my readers, those who see me speak at conferences, and the people who attend my masterclasses, you have colleagues who will argue with you about the new rules. They will say that the old rules still apply. They will tell you that you need to spend big bucks on advertising. They will tell you that the only way to do PR is to get the media to write about you. By now you know that they are wrong. If I haven't convinced you myself, surely the 50 or so successful people profiled in these pages must have. Go on. Be like the people you met in this book—get out there and make it happen!

Acknowledgments for the Fourth Edition

First, a disclosure: Because I do advisory work, run seminars, and do paid speaking gigs in the world that I write about, there are inevitable conflicts. I have friends in some of the organizations that I discuss in this book, as well as on my blog and on the speaking circuit, and I have run seminars for or advised several of the companies mentioned in the book.

I would like to offer my special thanks and gratitude to Robert Scoble, coauthor of *Naked Conversations*, for writing the terrific Foreword to this book.

At John Wiley & Sons, my publisher Matt Holt and my editor Shannon Vargo have steered me through the publishing business with wit and wisdom. We've now done six books together and more are on the way. Also at Wiley, thanks to Elana Schulman, Melissa Torra, Peter Knapp, Deborah Schindlar, and Lori Sayde-Mehrtens for their help and support.

Kyle Matthew Oliver read every word of each draft of this book, and his sound advice and practical suggestions made it much better.

I would also like to thank the thousands of bloggers who added to the conversations around the *New Rules of Marketing & PR* by writing on their blogs or by leaving intelligent and useful comments on my blog.

And especially, thank you to my wife, Yukari, and daughter, Allison, for supporting my work and understanding when I am under deadline or away from home speaking in some far-flung part of the world.

About the Author

Photo credit: Bruce Rogovin, rogovin.com

David Meerman Scott is a marketing strategist, best-selling author of eight books including three international best sellers, advisor to emerging companies, and a professional speaker on topics including marketing, leadership, and social media. The strategies he has developed have won numerous awards and are responsible for selling more than $1 billion in products and services worldwide.

For most of his career, Scott worked in the online news business. He was vice president of marketing at NewsEdge Corporation and held executive positions in an electronic information division of Knight-Ridder, at the time one of the world's largest newspaper companies. He's also held senior management positions at an e-commerce company, been a clerk on a Wall Street bond-trading desk, worked in sales at an economic consultancy, and acted in Japanese television commercials.

Today he spends his time evangelizing the new rules of marketing and PR by delivering keynote speeches to groups all over the world and teaching full-day masterclasses for companies, nonprofits, and government clients. His keynotes and masterclasses enlighten and inspire audiences through a combination of education, entertainment, and motivation. He has presented at hundreds of conferences and events in nearly 40 countries on six continents.

David writes for *Huffington Post* and his work has appeared in dozens of magazines and journals. He is a marketer in residence and on the board of advisors of HubSpot, and on the board of advisors of Eloqua, Speakerfile, Libboo, VisibleGains, GutCheck, and Newstex. He also advises nonprofits and is on the advisory board of the Grateful Dead Archive at UC Santa Cruz, and a member of the digital media advisory board of HeadCount.

A graduate of Kenyon College, Scott has lived in New York, Tokyo, Boston, and Hong Kong.

Check out his blog at www.WebInkNow.com, follow him on Twitter @dmscott, or download his free iPhone or iPad application.

Preview: *Real-Time Marketing & PR*

How to Instantly Engage Your Market, Connect with Customers, and Create Products That Grow Your Business Now, Revised and Updated

The following is an excerpt from the *Wall Street Journal* best-seller *Real-Time Marketing & PR* by David Meerman Scott, from John Wiley & Sons.

Prologue

Awareness of information as it happens, in real time, can give you an enormous competitive advantage—if you know how to use it. This was a key lesson I learned working on Wall Street in the go-go 1980s.

It's 1985, and I'm on the institutional trading floor of an investment bank in lower Manhattan. It's nearly noon, time for lunch, and nothing has happened all morning. But none of the bond traders leave. They're scared they might miss something. The bank doesn't want them leaving either, so everyone gets pizza delivered to their desks.

Inhabiting a world of split-second decisions, bond traders earn big money-making trades involving hundreds of millions of dollars. It's a daily battle that involves incredibly long periods of tedium punctuated by occasional short bursts of intense action.

Fortunes are made in seconds; reputations lost in a minute.

Nothing is happening now, though. All is quiet, and boredom reigns because no significant news has broken all morning.

Some traders desperately search their real-time news feeds from Dow Jones, Reuters, and the Associated Press for an angle, any angle, in the quiet market. What's Ronald Reagan up to today? What about Margaret Thatcher? Any news from Paul Volcker, the Federal Reserve chairman? Any economic data due to be released this afternoon? Any large companies announcing quarterly earnings today?

As they pore through data and news, the traders are poised, ready to commit huge sums of money when the moment is right. They peer intently at the Bloomberg screens displaying bond prices *the moment they change*. Data from futures markets and stock exchanges update *the instant a trade is made*.

Speed on the trading floor is so crucial that traders are linked one to one with their counterparts at other institutions by direct, dedicated lines—just like the Kremlin and the White House.

At a nearby desk, I see a phone panel light up (no ringing on the trading floor), and a trader answers by jabbing the button with his middle finger. But when he sits back relaxed, his body language tells me he's simply swapping the latest off-color joke or talking football.

Suddenly, one of the senior traders yells, loud as he can: "The Fed's in!"

For a split second, the room is completely silent as all listen.

When the senior trader then bellows "Buying Treasuries!" it's as if a bomb has hit. The entire room erupts in highly organized chaos. Pizza is tossed aside, and phones are grabbed in one fluid movement. It's time to earn those huge salaries.

In a heartbeat, everyone is on at least one phone, and many are on two or more, alerting customers in an instant: "The Fed is in!"

Within seconds, the screens light up in seas of green as bond prices rise steeply across the board. Before the same minute expires, financial news-wires like Dow Jones and Reuters write and issue newsflashes that appear instantly on trading room screens from Albuquerque to Zagreb. *Within just 60 seconds, everywhere knows and everyone is equal again*. The competitive advantage disappears.

But within that minute the traders who got their orders placed a split-second faster had earned their daily bread. *Being first* with the news is valuable currency that earns them lucrative deals from their clients. Hearing it first and acting on it fast equals money—*lots of money*—on Wall Street.

Since I first witnessed a Wall Street minute in 1985, trading technology has advanced light-years. But what I saw then was still new: Technology was transforming financial trading into a game where instant information informs split-second decisions worth millions of dollars.

It's impossible to overstate the impact of innovations in computing and telecommunications on the financial markets in the 1980s. Within a decade finance was transformed from a clubby, old-boys' network to a 24-hour global trading system. With that revolutionary shift a new currency of success emerged: the ability to gather, interpret, and react to new information in fractions of a second—real time.

It has taken a quarter century. But in fields like marketing and public relations the impact of the real-time revolution in finance is finally beginning to hit the so-called "real economy."

Who's leading the way? As you will read in these pages, it's not mega-corporations with billion-dollar information technology budgets. Far from it!

In today's real-time revolution the swift are out in front. As you discover in Chapter 1, one of the largest, most technically sophisticated marketers in the United States proved no match for one irate Canadian with a broken guitar and a video camera.

Revolution Time

Wake Up, It's Revolution Time!

Your accustomed methods and processes may be already fatally out of sync with the world around you. The narrative of your business now unfolds, minute by minute, in real time. And it's driven by your customers, talking among themselves—it's no longer guided by the mass media your ad budget can buy.

In a world where speed and agility are now essential to success, most organizations still operate slowly and deliberately, cementing each step months in advance, responding to new developments with careful but time-consuming processes.

This time lag can leave your business fatally exposed. But it doesn't have to! As you discover in Part I of *Real-Time Marketing & PR*, there are clear paths to follow in adapting your course and your culture to the new environment.

Allow me to introduce you to the rules of real-time marketing and public relations (PR).

Chapter 1

Grow Your Business Now

In the emerging real-time business environment, where public discourse is no longer dictated by the mass media, size is no longer a decisive advantage. Speed and agility win.

In this chapter we examine a Dave-versus-Goliath contest that shows how even one individual can outgun one of the largest, most scientific, marketing, PR, and customer-service organizations on the planet. We also discover how other agile players quickly harness the momentum of Dave's slingshot.

> Now, more than at any other time in history, speed and agility are decisive competitive advantages.

"My God, they're throwing guitars out there," said a woman in a window seat as passengers on a United Airlines flight waited to deplane in Chicago on March 31, 2008.

Singer-songwriter Dave Carroll and fellow members of Sons of Maxwell, a Canadian pop-folk band, knew instantly *whose* guitars. Flying from home in Halifax, Nova Scotia, for a one-week tour of Nebraska, their four guitars were in the airplane's hold. Sure enough, when the bass player looked out the window he witnessed United Airlines baggage handlers tossing his bass.

The band did not have to wait to retrieve their luggage in Omaha, their final destination, to start complaining, because they had actually observed this abuse of their equipment. As they made their way out of the plane, they told the flight attendants what they had seen. "Talk to the ground staff," they were told. But the O'Hare ground staff said, "Talk to the ground staff in Omaha."

Sure enough, when Dave opened his hard-shell case in Omaha he discovered his $3,500 Taylor guitar had been smashed. And United Airlines staff in Omaha refused to accept his claim.

So Dave spent months phoning and emailing United in pursuit of $1,200 to cover the cost of repairs. At each step, United staff refused to accept responsibility and shuffled him off: from telephone reps in India, to the central baggage office in New York, to the Chicago baggage office.

Finally, after nine futile months, Dave got a flat no. No, he was told, he would not receive any form of compensation from United.

"At that moment, it occurred to me I'd been fighting a losing battle all this time," Dave told me. "I got sucked into their cycle of insanity. I called and emailed and jumped through hoops, just as they told me to do. The system is designed to frustrate customers into giving up their claims, and United is very good at it. However, I realized that, as a musician, I wasn't without options. So when I finally got the 'no,' I said, 'I urge you to reconsider, because I'm a singer-songwriter and I'm going to write three songs about United Airlines and post them on YouTube.'"

Making good on this promise, on July 6, 2009, Dave posted on YouTube "United Breaks Guitars," a catchy tune with memorable lyrics that tells the saga of his broken guitar:

> *United, United, you broke my Taylor Guitar*
> *United, United, some big help you are*
> *You broke it, you should fix it*
> *You're liable, just admit it*
> *I should have flown with someone else*
> *Or gone by car*
> *'Cause United breaks guitars*
> *Yeah, United breaks guitars*

Within just four days, the video reached 1 million views on YouTube. And then another million. And another.

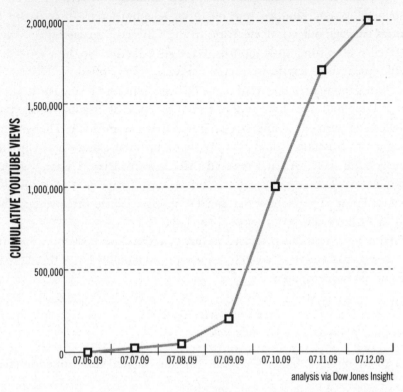

United Breaks Guitars: **YouTube Video Views**

analysis via Dow Jones Insight

Momentum built from July 8 to 11 as up to 100 bloggers a day alerted their readers to the video. Incidentally, notice how the number of blog posts per day follows a bell-shaped curve—starting slowly (because Dave Carroll wasn't well known), building to a peak, then trailing off. We come back to this in Chapter 3 when I discuss the importance of what I call the Real-Time Law of Normal Distribution.

This is a story about speed in media relations.

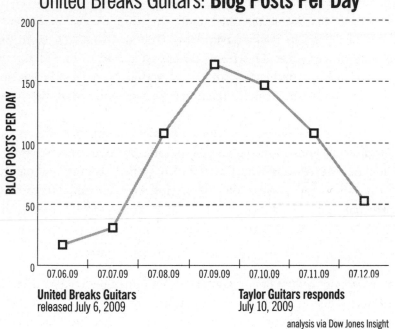

United Breaks Guitars: **Blog Posts Per Day**

United Breaks Guitars
released July 6, 2009

Taylor Guitars responds
July 10, 2009

analysis via Dow Jones Insight

"United Breaks Guitars" soon became a real-time phenomenon that propelled Dave into the spotlight. It continued to grow in the spotlight because Dave was ready and able to speak with the media in real time, conducting dozens of interviews in a few days while the story was hot.

This is also a story about real-time market engagement.

The maker of Dave's instrument, Taylor Guitars, seized the real-time opportunity to build goodwill among customers. Within days of Dave's initial YouTube post, Bob Taylor, the company's president, had his own video up on YouTube, advising traveling musicians how to pack equipment and use airline rules to best advantage.

There's more: This is a story of real-time product creation, too.

Calton Cases, a specialist maker of highly durable instrument cases for professional musicians, likewise seized the moment. Within mere days, Calton had a new product on the market: the Dave Carroll Traveler's Edition Guitar Case.

Finally, this is about a company that chose not to connect with customers.

As millions of potential customers saw a video that persuasively cast its brand in the worst possible light, negating the value of tens of millions of dollars in media advertising, United Airlines chose to make absolutely no response. This from the largest player in one of the most consumer-facing of industries, an industry that over decades has spent billions on advertising, public relations, and scientific customer-service methodology.

As a YouTube phenomenon "United Breaks Guitars" has drawn attention from thousands of media commentators. But two aspects have been overlooked: the reasons why Dave's video gained so much momentum, and the way agile players on the periphery were able to surf that momentum.

Dave's Slingshot Goes Viral on Goliath

I learned about "United Breaks Guitars" from one of my readers three days after Dave posted it on YouTube. At that time the video had about 200,000 views, and after watching for 30 seconds I said, "I need to blog this *right now*!" It was so fresh and exciting that I wanted my blog readers and Twitter followers to hear about it from me first.

So I quickly wrote a blog post, embedded the video, and pushed it live within half an hour of discovering it. I also tweeted the link to my tens of thousands of Twitter followers. I was just one of many triggers that helped spread the video to millions. But I was early—because I reacted *in real time*. I felt like a bond trader eager to make a deal.

The video's first viewing growth spike came on Day 2 (July 7). After *The Consumerist* website posted a link to it, the number of views jumped to 25,000. The *Los Angeles Times* called Dave that day. So did several local Canadian publications.

Next day, July 8, after CNN broadcast part of "United Breaks Guitars," Dave was suddenly the media celebrity of the moment.

Improvising with the snowball, Dave mounted a real-time PR effort that many agencies would be hard-pressed to match. Family members set up a communication room, fielding media requests that flooded in by phone and email, and triaging Dave's schedule in real time to ensure he made it onto the highest-profile outlets. His 15 minutes of fame were happening *right now*, and he needed to ride it as hard as he could.

"I knew I was reaching a big audience when I was about to tape an interview with CTV and the host said I was on *The Situation Room with Wolf Blitzer* on CNN at that moment," Dave says. "We raced from one interview to another. While someone drove me studio to studio, I did newspaper interviews on my cell phone."

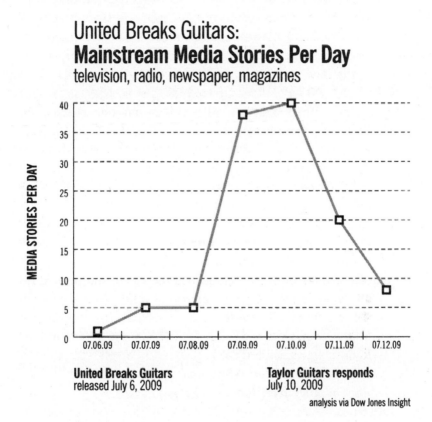

United Breaks Guitars:
Mainstream Media Stories Per Day
television, radio, newspaper, magazines

United Breaks Guitars
released July 6, 2009

Taylor Guitars responds
July 10, 2009

analysis via Dow Jones Insight

In this way, Dave managed to do dozens of interviews in a few days with print outlets like the *Wall Street Journal*, *USA Today*, and the *Los Angeles Times* and broadcasters like CBS, CNN, and FOX. With each media appearance the number of YouTube views spiked higher.

Evolution of a Real-Time Media Explosion

Monday, July 6, 2009: Dave Carroll posts "United Breaks Guitars" at midnight Atlantic Daylight Time. "There were six views by the time I went to bed," he says.

July 7, 8:00 A.M.: "There were 330 views when I woke up," Dave says. "I was excited, and called the videographer." That morning, Carroll is interviewed by his local newspaper, the *Halifax Herald*, and an online story appeared later in the day.

July 7, 12:00 P.M.: Video up to 5,000 views. *The Consumerist* website posts a link to the video that delivers 25,000 YouTube views in a few hours. Bob Taylor of Taylor Guitars and Jim Laffoley of Calton Cases also see the video. Laffoley contacts Carroll, asking how they might collaborate. *Got that? A mere 12 hours after posting the video, Carroll had an offer to collaborate with Calton Cases!*

July 7, 8:00 P.M.: While Dave Carroll is playing a gig, United Airlines calls and leaves a message: They want to speak with him. So does the *Los Angeles Times*.

July 8: "By Wednesday, things got busy," Carroll says. He is interviewed by the *LA Times* and several Canadian publications. Parts of the video air on CNN, as the video passes 50,000 views on YouTube. FOX News and CBS both call for interviews. United calls again, and Carroll sets a time to talk—two days later. *Why bother rushing to talk with United? After all, they blew him off for nine months.*

July 9: As the video passes 200,000 YouTube views one of my readers points me to it and I post it to my blog right away. Laffoley and Dave make plans for the Calton Cases Dave Carroll Traveler's Edition Guitar Case.

July 10: "United Breaks Guitars" reaches 1 million YouTube views. Taylor Guitars posts its YouTube response. Dave talks to United Airlines by phone—and even now they don't apologize. But with some weasel words about the regrettable incident, he is finally offered compensation. He rejects this as too late, suggesting the money be given to someone in a similar situation.

July 12: "United Breaks Guitars" reaches 2 million YouTube views.

July 19: Website for Calton Cases Dave Carroll Traveler's Edition Guitar Case goes live. *Note how quickly the new product is developed and launched.*

July 22: BBC television interviews Dave. "Minutes after the interview ran, competing stations called wanting to speak with me. I did nine phone interviews in one day," Carroll says. "United Breaks Guitars" is released on iTunes and becomes the number one Country and Western download in the United Kingdom.

July 23: "United Breaks Guitars" reaches 3 million YouTube views.

August 18: The second song in Dave's United trilogy is released.

September 14: In a meeting at O'Hare Airport (scene of the crime, so to speak) three senior United executives finally apologize to Dave. *Note the contrast between United Airlines' glacially slow and sluggish apology and communication efforts and the speed and agility of Dave Carroll, Taylor Guitars, and Calton Cases.*

September 22: Dave speaks at a U.S. Senate hearing on airline passenger rights.

The Stories Behind the Story: United Airlines, Taylor Guitars, and Calton Cases

The phenomenon that Dave Carroll created with "United Breaks Guitars" is a textbook example of what I call a World Wide Rave (see my 2009 book with that title), an online chain reaction that takes off when people spread your ideas by repeating your story. And there is much to learn from it if we dig a little deeper.

What Dave achieved is amazing in its own right. As of this writing, there are nearly 11 million views of "United Breaks Guitars"—song number 1 on YouTube. But as an observer of these phenomena, what fascinates me is the way Taylor Guitars and Calton Cases were able to react in real time to seize the marketing opportunity that Dave's momentum created. On the other hand, United Airlines exhibited a paralysis in the face of a snowballing crisis. In the spread between the small, speedy, and agile players and the slow, clumsy giant I see prima-facie evidence that a revolution has indeed been set in motion.

It's worth taking a closer look at how each of the players reacted.

Break a Taylor Guitar and You Break This Man's Heart

When "United Breaks Guitars" burst on the scene Dave Carroll was already on Taylor Guitar's radar. The El Cajon, California–based guitar maker had featured his band in its owners' magazine, *Wood & Steel*. And having played a Taylor for 10 years, Dave was a brand devotee—so the song's lyrics weren't about any old guitar getting broken. United broke his *Taylor*.

With lyrics that paid his product such respect, no surprise that Bob Taylor, the guitar-maker's founder and president, heard about it within 24 hours, via a tip from an ex-employee. "I was a fan a tenth of the way through . . . even before he talked about his Taylor guitar," Bob Taylor told me. But as soon as he heard that the damaged instrument was a Taylor, Bob contacted Dave and offered a free replacement. And he didn't stop there.

"I was discussing with our marketing people how we could send a gentle message supporting Dave and the hundreds of others who've had guitars broken on airplanes," Taylor says. "We know this sort of thing happens a lot, and I wanted to let others know 'it's not your fault . . . we feel your pain . . . we can advise you on how to travel safe in future.' We also wanted to let people know that we can fix their instruments."

That's what led Bob to shoot his own YouTube video, "Taylor Guitars Responds to 'United Breaks Guitars.'" Set in the company's service center, the video features no slick production values. "We wanted to convey that we're like family and you're inviting us into your living room," Taylor says. "The idea was to say, 'Hey, we're just people, too, and we have some resources that can help you.'"

Watching the video, I was struck by its deep sincerity, and when I spoke to Bob I learned why. Taylor Guitars is a personal enterprise. Bob started making guitars in high school and founded the company when he was 19. Thirty-five years later he's still in love with his high-school sweetheart—and that shines through in everything he says.

In his short video, Bob offers tips about how to pack and travel with musical instruments. He told me he's been using video for about 10 years, first for training new hires, more recently for marketing purposes on taylorguitars.com and a YouTube channel.

"If the subject is guitars, I'm comfortable in front of the camera," Bob says. "I did three takes of my 'United Breaks Guitars' video—and the whole thing took about 15 minutes' work for me, plus a few more hours for the people working on the rest: things like the logistics and posting."

While the Transportation Security Administration (TSA) and the American Federation of Musicians (AFM) came to an agreement to allow guitars to be considered as carry-on luggage in 2003, thousands of musicians can relate a personal tale of instrument mistreatment at the hands of any number of airlines.

Know the pertinent policies of the airline on which you are traveling. Print them out and take them with you. Many flight attendants do not know their own airline's policy regarding carry-on guitars, so if you can calmly explain that your instrument is within their mandated guidelines, and actually show them those guidelines, you will be way ahead of the game.

The Taylor Guitars' video response to "United Breaks Guitars" was quickly seen by hundreds of thousands of YouTube viewers, and more than 500 viewers left positive ratings and comments. Given the informational content of the video (guitar travel and repair), most viewers were likely professional musicians: Taylor's core market.

To me, that's an impressive return on investment: less than one day's work yields several minutes of detailed attention from, as of this writing, more than a half million core customers—all because Taylor was alert and agile enough to seize a real-time marketing opportunity: the fleeting moment when Dave Carroll's video was all the rage.

While working on this book, I was struck by how few marketers are prepared to move as fast as Taylor Guitars did. Even if they spotted the chance, most companies would still be discussing it when the window closed.

So why was Bob Taylor able to act so fast?

A Teachable Moment

Although Taylor Guitars had been talking about the proper care and handling of guitars for years, customers tend to ignore such advice—along with everything else found in the back of an owner's manual. So Bob Taylor immediately saw Dave Carroll's experience as an ideal platform on which to build a sense of urgency around a key topic.

Bob was among the first to see "United Breaks Guitars," which had then racked up only 5,000 YouTube views.

"I saw it as a teachable moment because so many people were talking about guitars on airplanes," Taylor says. "We already knew you have to jump on opportunities to communicate when something happens, because it is too late when it is over. And since Dave used video, we figured that was the way for us to tell our story, too."

Taylor's team had already shot many videos, so they were able to act fast once the decision was made. They already had a YouTube video channel in place.

"We don't wait for the stars to align, we just shoot it quickly. It's just a grassroots sort of thing. We just wanted to talk to our peeps while they are enjoying Dave's video."

He may not wait for the stars to align, but Taylor has learned to spot rare opportunities that arise when stars take his product on stage.

"There are very few times something happens that takes our brand forward a few steps," Taylor says. "Newscasters were saying Dave's guitar was a Taylor guitar. I've been doing this for 35 years, and only about a dozen times has something this big come our way . . . like when Taylor Swift began to play Taylor Guitars on stage. When luck turns your way, you can't squander it. Thanks to Dave, now many more people know Taylor guitars. This was a big branding leap for Taylor Guitars."

Case Study in Real-Time Product Development

Dave Carroll's predicament was hardly a case Jim Laffoley could fail to notice: Damage to guitars in transit is specifically what his product is designed to prevent. What's more, Dave's Halifax home is three hours down the road from Moncton, New Brunswick, where Laffoley is president of Calton Cases (North America) Inc.

Musicians around the world consider Calton's products among the most secure cases for stringed instruments, from violins to cellos to guitars. And guitar cases are the company's biggest seller. In fact, had Dave Carroll used a Calton Case when flying United he may not have had an issue with the airline.

"Our primary customer is a professional musician," Laffoley told me. "My goal is to get more professional artists as customers. I wanted to put an artist up on a pedestal because artists are the perfect spokespeople for our products."

"On the Tuesday morning, my lawyer called saying that he'd just seen the 'United Breaks Guitars' video," Laffoley says. At the time, the video had about 25,000 views. "So I called Dave and said, 'You are the perfect spokesman for my product,' and he was immediately receptive to working together."

For starters, Laffoley offered to provide Dave with cases for the band's upcoming tour. But the collaboration quickly moved further.

"It took about two days to go from offering a few cases to proposing a custom-branded line of products," Laffoley says. "And Dave saw the value right away."

As the video passed 200,000 YouTube views, the Dave Carroll Traveler's Edition Guitar Case was born. Every hard-shell case is handmade, and available in 16 exterior and 12 interior colors.

"We came up with an aggressive price point to attract people who wanted to get into a Calton case," Laffoley says. "$725, including shipping anywhere in North America."

Dave Carroll is happy because he gets a cut from each sale and his fellow artists are likewise happy because it's priced lower than a regular Calton case. But the only difference from a regular Calton is the custom badge Laffoley created almost overnight.

As a result, the Dave Carroll edition was offered for sale on Calton's website—and promoted on Dave's site—within days of the YouTube video release.

Sure, it was only a rebadging effort. But in today's corporate world where product-development efforts involve months or years of process, it is remarkable to see a product go from concept to sale in just days.

"My background is product management," Laffoley says. "So I was able to work quickly. But all I really did was get Dave to agree, change the label, change the price point, and work out distribution. Sales are going well so far. We're selling cases that we never would have sold without the Dave Carroll edition."

United Comes Untied

Although Dave Carroll's video was making United baggage handlers famous for the wrong reasons, everyone *but* United Airlines was working to seize the moment. Dave was all over the media worldwide. Bob Taylor was teaching musicians how to safeguard and fix their prized instruments. And Jim Laffoley was seizing the moment with a custom-branded guitar case.

Meanwhile, United said absolutely nothing in public. Its PR staff provided no explanation on the corporate website, offered no statement to the media, and posted no comments on the many blogs that (like mine) talked up the video. In other words, they did not react in real time.

By failing to do so, United missed a huge opportunity to dampen and deflect criticism before it snowballed—and a chance to present a sympathetic, humane face to its customers. Instead of doing something interesting and creative, United chose stony silence. This was just the first of countless opportunities the airline missed. How about this as a response—what if United had made a suitcase camera that recorded the journey a bag makes at O'Hare as it goes from one plane, through the bowels of the airport baggage system and onto another plane. The video could be sped up to about a minute and narrated by the chief baggage handler. Now that would have generated positive, real-time attention!

United did try to make amends behind the scenes by contacting Dave—but even this effort was ham-handed. "They did not say that they were sorry," Dave recalls. "They did say it was *regrettable*, and they offered some compensation—only because I'm a *good customer* and not because of the video. But I said from the outset that if I had to go the video route, I wouldn't accept compensation personally; that they could give the money to another customer with a damage issue."

It took a lot of punishment for the message to sink in, but Dave thinks United may have finally learned from this experience. He's been told that "United Breaks Guitars" is now used in customer-service training to illustrate how quickly things can turn ugly. And on September 14, 2009, he met with senior United Airlines executives in Chicago.

"They were friendly and engaging and actually said that they were sorry," Dave says. "They took responsibility. Although they did not make excuses, they did talk about some of the reasons for the issues. I told them that there should be some clarity about the United policy on guitars and allowing musicians to take guitars on board. While the policy was always there, they did not make it clear, so they have added a link."

Sadly, the nonreaction *in public*—the instinct to ignore a huge online uprising—is still way too common in the corporate world. I've identified many reasons for this behavior, including undue influence by legal departments who fear saying something that admits responsibility, sheer panic among frontline staff, bad advice from PR agencies, and executives steeped in a business culture of "no comment."

Although they may have learned something from this, United continues to miss opportunities. As part of my research for this book, on October 7, 2009, I emailed the airline's media relations staff to request an interview. In fairness, I wanted to offer you United's side of the story; to let them tell you what they had learned.

Although my initial email was returned promptly, the media relations staff declined to grant me an interview. And so the damage continues as you read. Does all this make you want to "Fly United"?

Has United Airlines really learned from this disaster? In a similar situation would they now realize the importance of engaging the online dialogue in real time? Would they create their own interesting YouTube video to deflect some of the criticism? Would they take the opportunity to humanize the company and show they care about their passengers?

Dave's Big Win

If United learned and gained nothing from this encounter, the opposite is true for Dave Carroll. His career blossomed under the YouTube spotlight. His band is constantly in demand for live gigs, and listeners buy songs from his website and iTunes.

"If my guitar had to be smashed due to extreme negligence, I'm glad it was United that did it," Dave says. After more than 12 million views of his videos, Dave jokes, "United broke my career!"

Dave may be famous now, but that was not what he set out to achieve. "My expectations were low," he says. "I was just hoping people at United would see the video and take it seriously."

What made Carroll's video turn into a World Wide Rave while so many others go unnoticed? People I've asked all point to the song itself—which is really good. "I've been working on the songwriting craft for a number of years," Dave says. "The story was laid out well and had hooks in all the right places. But for an independent musician it is tough to get things heard. I don't think the song would have spread without the United Airlines aspects. This song could only have been a success in this particular way."

The song itself was certainly essential, but I'm convinced that Dave's availability to do dozens of media interviews in the hectic first days of the song's release that pushed the video from a few hundred thousand views to several million views in just a few days. In other words, Dave's real-time media-relations effort was essential to the viral explosion of the video.

Sudden success has taken Dave's career through many unexpected turns. Having successfully reinvented his personal brand in real time, like it or not, he will be known forever as "that United Breaks Guitars guy." But it's a role he is eager to play.

"Everybody knows this song," he says. "It's the perfect door opener. And now I'm even getting asked to speak about customer service at corporate events."

Dave has also become an unlikely spokesperson for airline passenger rights, having testified at the September 2009 U.S. Senate hearings on the issue. "I'm recognized all the time now when I fly with my guitar," he says. "Many musicians contact me to thank me about drawing attention to the challenge of traveling with guitars. After all, we're talking about our livelihood."

Real-Time Engagement

Real-time marketing.
Real-time product development.
Real-time communication.
Real-time customer service.

What can we learn from a Dave-versus-Goliath contest in which one irate Canadian musician utterly and completely whips one of the largest marketing and customer-service operations in the United States? What gives when a single improvising amateur can defeat an outfit that should be one of the most sophisticated of its kind on the planet? And how was it that two other small players were able to ride the victor's momentum?

The answer is that the rules have changed. The balance of power has been irrevocably altered.

Scale and media buying power are no longer a decisive advantage. What counts today is speed and agility.

It takes speed and agility, plus the kind of creative imagination and craft skill that allowed Dave Carroll to write a song every bit as powerful as a Stinger missile.

It takes quick thinking and guts to put your organization out there, to react to events in real-time like Bob Taylor did. But the rewards can be huge. Taylor Guitars is working hard to keep up with market demand. The company is making a record number of guitars, nearly 25 percent more in 2010 than the highest production level in 2008. So a real-time mind-set can affect the bottom line.

If you run a huge business like United Airlines, this should scare the living corn flakes out of you. Perhaps this should cause you to reflect on whether combining two huge bureaucracies in search of greater scale solves your problem or magnifies it.

If you're big, this should scare you—but it need not cause you to lose heart. Whether you run a one-person start-up or a vast global enterprise, you have an equal opportunity to grow by engaging the world around you in real time.

In the chapters to follow we take a practical look at what it takes to win in this new environment. And yes, as you'll see in Chapter 5, large organizations also win . . . if they know what to do.

Preview: The New Rules of Social Media Book Series

David Meerman Scott is editing a series of social media books for John Wiley & Sons.

The New Rules of Social Media series features books that expand on the ideas of Scott's best seller, *The New Rules of Marketing & PR*, providing valuable insights and detail on the different aspects of social media marketing.

Each book in David Meerman Scott's The New Rules of Social Media series is written by social media experts addressing a topic within their realm of expertise. While some titles, like *Inbound Marketing: Get Found Using Google, Social Media, and Blogs*, cover broad topics, others are more specific, for example, *Get Seen: Online Video Secrets to Building Your Business*.

No matter what the business need relating to social media, The New Rules of Social Media series offers an unprecedented resource.

Inbound Marketing: Get Found Using Google, Social Media, and Blogs

Brian Halligan and Dharmesh Shah

Stop pushing your message *out* and start pulling your customers *in*.

Traditional "outbound marketing" methods like cold calling, email blasts, advertising, and direct mail are increasingly less effective. People are getting better at blocking these interruptions out using Caller ID, spam protection, TiVo, and so on. People are now increasingly turning to Google, social media, and blogs to find products and services. *Inbound Marketing* helps you take advantage of this change by showing you how to get found by customers online.

Inbound Marketing is a how-to guide to getting found via Google, the blogosphere, and social media sites.

- Improve your rankings in Google to get more traffic.
- Build and promote a blog for your business.
- Grow and nurture a community in Facebook, LinkedIn, Twitter, and so forth.
- Measure what matters and do more of what works online.

The rules of marketing have changed, and your business can benefit from this change. *Inbound Marketing* shows you how to get found by more prospects already looking for what you have to sell.

Content Rules: How to Create Killer Blogs, Podcasts, Videos, Ebooks, Webinars (and More) That Engage Customers and Ignite Your Business

Ann Handley and C. C. Chapman

Whether it's bite-sized tweets that allow you to forge relationships on Twitter, blog posts that give your readers must-have advice, ebooks or white papers that engage (and don't bore), videos that share the human side of your company, interactive webinars that deliver a valuable learning experience, or podcasts that can be downloaded and listened to on the fly (and more!) . . . now more than ever, content rules!

Today, you have an unprecedented opportunity to create a treasury of free, easy-to-use, almost infinitely customizable content that tells the story of your product and your business, and positions you as an expert people will want to do business with. They'll show you how to:

- Understand why you are generating content—getting to the meat of your message in practical, commonsense language, and defining the goals of your content strategy.
- Explore ways to integrate searchable words into your content without sounding forced (or sounding like "Frankenspeak").
- Write in a way that powerfully communicates your service, product, or message across various web mediums.
- Create a publishing schedule that allows you to create different kinds and types of content at once.

Offering examples of businesses using content effectively across a wide range of industries and fascinating explanations of how you might approach your own content strategy, *Content Rules* is the essential field guide to creating your story, finding the right balance of humor and humanity in your content, and building a portfolio of value that will keep delivering for the long haul.

Social Media Metrics: How to Measure and Optimize Your Marketing Investment

Jim Sterne

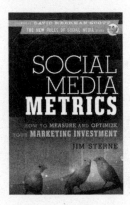

Whether you are selling online, through a direct sales force, or via distribution channels, what customers are saying about you online is now more important than your advertising. Social media is no longer a curiosity on the horizon but a significant part of your marketing mix.

A shift in philosophy, a modification in strategy, and brand-new metrics are the keys to marketing success in this interconnected world. While other books explain why social media is critical and how to go about participating, this book focuses on measuring the success of your social media marketing efforts.

Success metrics in business are based on business goals where fame does not always equate to fortune. Having more Twitter followers or Facebook friends than the competition might not result in value. Read this book to determine which social media efforts are working for you, where to allocate more social media resources, and how to convince those who are afraid of "new things" that social media is a valuable business tool and not just a toy for the overly wired.

Knowing what works and what doesn't is terrific, but only in a constant and unchanging world. *Social Media Metrics* is loaded with specific examples of specific metrics you can use to guide your social media marketing efforts as new means of communication.

Get Seen: Online Video Secrets to Building Your Business

Steve Garfield

The era of online video has arrived—make it work for your business.

In 2008, the world of online video exploded. Hollywood got into the game, professional actors and writers joined in, and independent producers looked to find their niche. Now, companies are wide awake to the opportunities for product and brand promotion as well as customer engagement. So how do you want to fit into the new online video universe?

The must-have guide, *Get Seen* by Steve Garfield, the "Paul Revere of video blogging, " offers a quick and complete toolkit to get you up to speed on the latest that online video and related media have to offer:

- Examines success stories of companies using online video.
- Presents a series of plans and tools businesses can follow as they expand onto the social web.
- Provides clear direction on how to record, edit, and export videos, where to post them, how to build a community around their content, and how to increase views by going viral.

If you're ready to take full advantage of online video's many benefits, *Get Seen* is the one resource you need.

Go Mobile: Location-Based Marketing, Apps, Mobile Optimized Ad Campaigns, 2D Codes, and Other Mobile Strategies to Grow Your Business

Jeanne Hopkins and Jamie Turner

Set up, run, and measure successful mobile media marketing campaigns.

Go Mobile is packed with tools, tips, and techniques that will help readers set up, launch, run, and measure mobile media campaigns. This book will help readers understand the different mobile media platforms, learn how to us SMS for business, incorporate 2D and QR Codes into their campaigns, develop mobile websites and mobile apps, see case studies, and much more.

Go Mobile offers practical, step-by-step guidance for implementing a mobile marketing campaign. Readers will learn how to:

- Use location-based marketing to get new customers and keep existing ones.
- Integrate social media with your mobile media campaign.
- Use mobile E-commerce to improve brand loyalty.
- Measure the ROI of a mobile media campaign.
- Develop mobile media business models you can use to grow revenues.

With these effective, efficient, and integrated mobile marketing campaigns, business owners and marketers will garner enviable response rates and watch their revenue grow more rapidly than ever before.

Beyond Viral: How to Attract Customers, Promote Your Brand, and Make Money with Online Video

Kevin Nalty

What would one of the most viewed YouTube comedians have to say about effective online videos? What would a highly respected marketing professional say? Kevin Nalty happens to be both—he's a sought-after marketer for major clients as well as "Nalts," whose mischievous videos have been seen by millions. Now, in *Beyond Viral*, Nalty reveals winning techniques for making and promoting videos that will build customer loyalty, increase brand awareness, and boost sales. Go behind the scenes of Nalty's online video success and find out:

- Why viral video is dead . . . and why that's a good thing for your business.
- How online "stars" are born and how they can help you.
- Measuring ROI and performance of online videos.
- If you can make money from online video (yes, you can!).

Index

Have David Meerman Scott Speak at Your Next Event!

David Meerman Scott is available for keynote presentations and full-day masterclasses. He is a frequent speaker at company meetings, trade shows, conferences, and events around the world and has presented in nearly 40 countries on six continents.

David knows that sitting through a boring or off-topic speech is utterly painful. So he keeps things a bit edgy and uses stories and humor to make his points. But whenever he is in front of a group, be it six or six hundred, he provides valuable and actionable information about the new rules of marketing and PR, online thought leadership, and reaching buyers directly with web content.

David speaks to all kinds of organizations: consumer goods companies, Business-to-Business, entrepreneurs, small business owners, nonprofits, and more. His audiences have included Cisco, HP, PwC, GenRe, Microsoft, Nestle Purina, Jackson Healthcare, Abbott, Ford Motor Company, Century 21, The New York Islanders, NASDAQ Stock Market, Dow Jones, the government of Ontario, McKesson, the U.S. Air Force, McCormick, SAP, Google, Digital River, Hill & Knowlton, Text100, Entrepreneurs Organization, Fortune Growth Summit, America Credit Union Conference, Realtors® Conference, and many, many more.

All of David's presentations are a combination of three things: education, entertainment, and motivation.

Visit www.davidmeermanscott.com for information on booking David to speak at your event.

To see David in action, visit www.dmscott.tv.